New Essays on the Nature of Propositions

These are exciting times for philosophical theorizing about propositions, with the last 15 years seeing the development of new approaches and the emergence of new theorists. Propositions have been invoked to explain thought and cognition, the nature and attribution of mental states, language and communication, and in the philosophical treatments of truth, necessity and possibility. According to Frege and Russell, and their followers, propositions are structured mind- and language-independent abstract objects which have essential and intrinsic truth-conditions.

Some recent theorizing doubts whether propositions really exist and, if they do, asks how we can grasp, entertain and know them? But most of the doubt concerns whether the abstract object approach to propositions can really explain them. Are propositions really structured, and if so where does their structure come from? How does this structure form a unity, and does it need to? Are the representational and structural properties of propositions really independent of those of thinking and language? What does it mean to say that an object occurs in or is a constituent of a proposition?

The volume takes up these and other questions, both as they apply to the abstract object approach and also to the more recently developed approaches. While the volume as a whole does not definitively and unequivocally reject the abstract object approach, for the most part, the chapters explore new critical and constructive directions.

This book was originally published as a special issue of the *Canadian Journal of Philosophy*.

David Hunter is Associate Professor at Ryerson University, Toronto, Canada. He works on issues at the intersection of belief and action, and is the Editorial Board Coordinator of the *Canadian Journal of Philosophy*.

Gurpreet Rattan is Associate Professor at the University of Toronto, Canada. His primary interests are in the philosophy of language, mind, and epistemology. His current project attempts to articulate unified accounts of truth, disagreement, and relativism, accounts organized around the semantics and epistemology of the meta-representation involved in critical reflective thinking and disagreement. His longer term project is on the comparative metaphysics and epistemology of propositions and numbers.

New Essays on the Nature of Propositions

Edited by
David Hunter and Gurpreet Rattan

LONDON AND NEW YORK

First published 2015
by Routledge

2 Park Square, Milton Park, Abingdon, Oxon OX14 4RN
711 Third Avenue, New York, NY 10017, USA

Routledge is an imprint of the Taylor & Francis Group, an informa business

First issued in paperback 2017

Copyright © 2015 Canadian Journal of Philosophy

All rights reserved. No part of this book may be reprinted or reproduced or utilised in any form or by any electronic, mechanical, or other means, now known or hereafter invented, including photocopying and recording, or in any information storage or retrieval system, without permission in writing from the publishers.

Notice:
Product or corporate names may be trademarks or registered trademarks, and are used only for identification and explanation without intent to infringe.

British Library Cataloguing in Publication Data
A catalogue record for this book is available from the British Library

ISBN 13: 978-1-138-85899-2 (hbk)
ISBN 13: 978-1-138-08296-0 (pbk)

Typeset in Times New Roman
by RefineCatch Limited, Bungay, Suffolk

Publisher's Note
The publisher accepts responsibility for any inconsistencies that may have arisen during the conversion of this book from journal articles to book chapters, namely the possible inclusion of journal terminology.

Disclaimer
Every effort has been made to contact copyright holders for their permission to reprint material in this book. The publishers would be grateful to hear from any copyright holder who is not here acknowledged and will undertake to rectify any errors or omissions in future editions of this book.

Contents

Citation Information   vii
Notes on Contributors   xi

1. Introduction   1
   David Hunter and Gurpreet Rattan

Part I: On Act- and Language-Based Conceptions of Propositions

2. Two aspects of propositional unity   4
   Gary Ostertag

3. An empirically-informed cognitive theory of propositions   20
   Berit Brogaard

4. What are the primary bearers of truth?   44
   Peter Hanks

5. Not the optimistic type   61
   Ben Caplan, Chris Tillman, Brian McLean and Adam Murray

6. Why it isn't syntax that unifies the proposition   76
   Logan Fletcher

7. Why we should not identify sentence structure with propositional structure   98
   Thomas Hodgson

Part II: Constituents and Constituency

8. Individuating Fregean sense   120
   Jeff Speaks

9. The metaphysics of propositional constituency   141
   Lorraine Keller

Part III: Theoretical Alternatives to Propositions

10. Propositions, attitudinal objects, and the distinction between actions and products 165
    Friederike Moltmann

11. What are Propositions? 188
    Mark Richard

12. Conversational implicature, communicative intentions, and content 206
    Ray Buchanan

13. Propositions and higher-order attitude attributions 227
    Kirk Ludwig

Part IV: Modal Metaphysics

14. Unnecessary existents 252
    Joshua Spencer

15. Contingently existing propositions 262
    Michael Nelson

Index 291

Citation Information

The chapters in this book were originally published in the *Canadian Journal of Philosophy*, volume 43, issues 5–6 (October–December 2013). When citing this material, please use the original page numbering for each article, as follows:

Chapter 1
Introduction
David Hunter and Gurpreet Rattan
Canadian Journal of Philosophy, volume 43, issues 5–6 (October–December 2013) pp. 515–517

Chapter 2
Two aspects of propositional unity
Gary Ostertag
Canadian Journal of Philosophy, volume 43, issues 5–6 (October–December 2013) pp. 518–533

Chapter 3
An empirically-informed cognitive theory of propositions
Berit Brogaard
Canadian Journal of Philosophy, volume 43, issues 5–6 (October–December 2013) pp. 534–557

Chapter 4
What are the primary bearers of truth?
Peter Hanks
Canadian Journal of Philosophy, volume 43, issues 5–6 (October–December 2013) pp. 558–574

Chapter 5
Not the optimistic type
Ben Caplan, Chris Tillman, Brian McLean and Adam Murray
Canadian Journal of Philosophy, volume 43, issues 5–6 (October–December 2013) pp. 575–589

Chapter 6
Why it isn't syntax that unifies the proposition
Logan Fletcher
Canadian Journal of Philosophy, volume 43, issues 5–6 (October–December 2013) pp. 590–611

Chapter 7
Why we should not identify sentence structure with propositional structure
Thomas Hodgson
Canadian Journal of Philosophy, volume 43, issues 5–6 (October–December 2013) pp. 612–633

Chapter 8
Individuating Fregean sense
Jeff Speaks
Canadian Journal of Philosophy, volume 43, issues 5–6 (October–December 2013) pp. 634–654

Chapter 9
The metaphysics of propositional constituency
Lorraine Keller
Canadian Journal of Philosophy, volume 43, issues 5–6 (October–December 2013) pp. 655–678

Chapter 10
Propositions, attitudinal objects, and the distinction between actions and products
Friederike Moltmann
Canadian Journal of Philosophy, volume 43, issues 5–6 (October–December 2013) pp. 679–701

Chapter 11
What are Propositions?
Mark Richard
Canadian Journal of Philosophy, volume 43, issues 5–6 (October–December 2013) pp. 702–719

Chapter 12
Conversational implicature, communicative intentions, and content
Ray Buchanan
Canadian Journal of Philosophy, volume 43, issues 5–6 (October–December 2013) pp. 720–740

CITATION INFORMATION

Chapter 13
Propositions and higher-order attitude attributions
Kirk Ludwig
Canadian Journal of Philosophy, volume 43, issues 5–6 (October–December 2013) pp. 741–765.

Chapter 14
Unnecessary existents
Joshua Spencer
Canadian Journal of Philosophy, volume 43, issues 5–6 (October–December 2013) pp. 766–775.

Chapter 15
Contingently existing propositions
Michael Nelson
Canadian Journal of Philosophy, volume 43, issues 5–6 (October–December 2013) pp. 776–803.

Please direct any queries you may have about the citations to clsuk.permissions@cengage.com

Notes on Contributors

Berit Brogaard is Professor of Philosophy in the Department of Philosophy and The Center for Neurodynamics, University of Missouri, St. Louis, MO, USA. Her publications have appeared in journals such as *Journal of Philosophy*, *Nous*, *Philosophy and Phenomenological Research* and *Philosophers' Imprint*. Her book *Transient Truths* was published in 2012. In her academic research she specializes in philosophy of language, philosophy of mind and the cognitive sciences.

Ray Buchanan is an Assistant Professor in the Department of Philosophy at the University of Texas, Austin, TX, USA. His work to date has primarily focused on the questions of how, and to what extent, we can express our thoughts by our actions – linguistic, or otherwise.

Ben Caplan is a Professor in the Department of Philosophy at Ohio State University, Columbus, OH, USA. His first publication was in the *Canadian Journal of Philosophy*.

Logan Fletcher is a doctoral candidate in Philosophy at the University of Maryland, College Park, MD, USA. His primary research interests are in philosophy of mind, philosophy of cognitive science, and aesthetics. His current research focuses on the epistemology of visual proofs in mathematics.

Peter Hanks is an Associate Professor in the Department of Philosophy at the University of Minnesota, St. Paul, MN, USA. His research is in philosophy of language and the history of analytic philosophy, with a focus on propositions, names, attitude reports, Russell, and early Wittgenstein. In his latest book, *Propositional Content* (forthcoming 2015), he defends the view that propositions are types of actions.

Thomas Hodgson recently completed a PhD at the University of St. Andrew's, UK. His dissertation was entitled 'Propositions Need Not be Intrinsically Representational'.

NOTES ON CONTRIBUTORS

David Hunter is Associate Professor at Ryerson University, Toronto, Canada. He works on issues at the intersection of belief and action, and is the Editorial Board Coordinator of the *Canadian Journal of Philosophy*.

Lorraine Keller is a recent PhD from the University of Notre Dame, South Bend, IN, USA, whose dissertation critically evaluates the theory of structured propositions. She currently teaches at Niagara University, NY, USA.

Kirk Ludwig is Professor of Philosophy at Indiana University Bloomington, IN, USA. He has published numerous papers on the philosophy of language, mind, action and epistemology. He is the editor of *Donald Davidson* (2003), co-author with Ernie Lepore of *Donald Davidson: Meaning, Truth, Language and Reality* (2005) and *Donald Davidson's Truth-theoretic Semantics* (2007), and co-editor with Ernie Lepore of the *Companion to Donald Davidson* (2013).

Brian McLean is a graduate student in the Department of Philosophy at Ohio State University, Columbus, OH, USA. His primary research interests are in meta-ethics and ethics. His first publication is in the *Canadian Journal of Philosophy*.

Friederike Moltmann is Research Director at the Centre national de la recherche scientifique (CNRS) in Paris, France. She previously taught both linguistics and philosophy at various universities in the US and the UK. She is author of *Parts and Wholes in Semantics* (1997) and *Abstract Objects and the Semantics of Natural Language* (2013).

Adam Murray is a graduate student in the Department of Philosophy at the University of Toronto, Canada. His primary research interests are in metaphysics and the philosophy of language. He has recently published papers in the *Canadian Journal of Philosophy* and *Oxford Studies in Metaphysics*.

Michael Nelson earned his PhD from Princeton University, NJ, USA in 2002. After teaching for 3 years at Yale University, New Haven, CT, USA, he moved to the University of California-Riverside, USA in 2005, where he is currently an Associate Professor of Philosophy.

Gary Ostertag is the Director of the Saul Kripke Center at The Graduate Center of the City University of New York, New York City, USA, where he is also Adjunct Associate Professor of Philosophy. He is also on the faculty of Nassau Community College, New York, USA. He is the editor of *Definite Descriptions: A Reader* (1998) and *Meanings and Other Things: Essays on Stephen Schiffer* (forthcoming).

Gurpreet Rattan is Associate Professor at the University of Toronto, Canada. His current project attempts to articulate unified accounts of truth, disagreement, and relativism, accounts organized around issues about the reference to propositions in critical reflective thinking and deep disagreement. His longer term project is on the comparative metaphysics and epistemology of propositions and numbers.

Mark Richard is a Professor of Philosophy at Harvard University, Cambridge, MA, USA. He is the author of *Propositional Attitudes*, *When Truth Gives Out*, *Meaning in Context: Context and the Attitudes*, and the forthcoming *Meaning in Context: Tense, Truth, and Tribulation*.

Jeff Speaks is an Associate Professor of Philosophy at the University of Notre Dame, South Bend, IN, USA. His areas of specialization are the philosophy of mind and the philosophy of language.

Joshua Spencer is an Assistant Professor in the Department of Philosophy at the University of Wisconsin-Milwaukee, USA. He is interested in the metaphysics of material objects, space, time, modality, fundamentality and meaning.

Chris Tillman is an Associate Professor in the Department of Philosophy at the University of Manitoba, Winnipeg, Canada.

Introduction

David Hunter and Gurpreet Rattan

These are exciting times for philosophical theorizing about propositions. The last 15 years have seen the development of significantly new approaches, and the papers in the volume represent the state of the art, with contributions from both established and emerging theorists. In this brief introduction, we sketch these recent developments, and describe the contributions of the present volume.

Propositions have figured prominently in a wide variety of theories. They have been invoked in accounts of thought and cognition, in theories of the nature and attribution of mental states, in accounts of language and communication, and in philosophical treatments of truth, necessity and possibility. Call these the *theoretical roles* of propositions. On a traditional view of propositions, one that derives from Frege and Russell, propositions are structured, mind- and language-independent abstract objects that represent and have truth-conditions essentially and intrinsically, that thinkers can stand in cognitive relations to, like grasping or entertaining, and which can be expressed in language. Call this the *abstract object approach* to propositions.

H.P. Grice once quipped (1975) that he didn't mind allowing propositions into his theoretical house, so long as they helped with the chores. Propositions understood according to the abstract object approach are supposed to help with various explanatory chores. For example:

- Propositions are supposed to explain how those who speak different languages can say and believe things in common. The explanation is that saying and believing are relations to propositions, not to sentences (not even to interpreted or mental sentences), and that since propositions are mind- and language-independent, they are potentially accessible even when the relevant sentences are not.
- Propositions are supposed to explain how thought, mental attitudes, and language can be representational and truth-apt. The explanation is that thought, mental attitudes and language involve grasping and expressing mind- and language-independent propositions that represent and have truth-conditions essentially and intrinsically.
- Propositions are supposed to explain, at least in outline, what makes for successful communication. The explanation is that a proposition is

expressed or somehow conveyed by a speaker, and this proposition is then passed, in successful communication, from speaker to hearer.
- Propositions are supposed to explain what it is for a speech act or mental state to be singular or object-directed – to be *about* an object in some immediate or direct sense. The explanation is that they are singular or object-directed when they are appropriately related to a *structured* proposition having the relevant object as a constituent, or, for Fregeans, when related to a sense that appropriately presents the relevant object.

A theory of propositions should explain how they can help with these explanatory chores.

Much theorizing in the last 15 years has been motivated by doubt that the abstract object approach to propositions can provide this explanation. Some of the doubt stems from general metaphysical and epistemological questions about abstract objects. Do propositions really exist? If they are abstracta, then how can we grasp, entertain and know them? But most of the doubt concerns whether the abstract approach to propositions can really help with the explanatory chores. For example: How are we to understand the idea of an object being intrinsically representational and possessed of truth conditions? Are propositions really structured, and if so where does their structure come from? How does the structure of a proposition together with its constituents form a unity? Does it need to? Are the representational and structural properties of propositions really independent of the structural and representational properties of thinking and language? What does it mean to say that an object occurs in or is a constituent of a proposition? Are the constituents of a proposition essential to it? How do we evaluate a singular proposition about contingent existents at a possible world where the individual the proposition is about does not exist? Do propositions even exist at worlds in which their constituents do not?

The volume takes up these and other questions, both as they apply to the abstract object approach and as they apply to the more recently developed approaches. While the volume as a whole does not definitively and unequivocally reject the abstract objection approach, for the most part, the papers head in new critical and constructive directions.

We plan to let the papers speak for themselves. Here we offer just a very brief description of how the volume is organized.

The papers in the first section of the volume, 'On Act- and Language-Based Conceptions of Propositions', evaluate two new approaches to propositions (one developed in different ways by Peter Hanks (2011) and Scott Soames (2010), and the other due to Jeffrey C. King (2007)) that have arisen in response to the problems faced by the abstract approach. The papers consider whether these new approaches explain how propositions can play their explanatory roles, and focus on issues about propositional unity, representation and truth conditions, communication, and the source of propositional structure. The papers clarify these new approaches while pinpointing some of their vulnerabilities.

The papers in the second section of the volume, 'Constituents and Constituency', concern the idea that propositions have constituents. The papers make a strong case that more work needs to be done to clarify the very idea of propositional constituency, both as a general theoretical concept and in the particular case where the constituents are Fregean senses.

The papers in the third section of the volume, 'Theoretical Alternatives', explore the idea that things other than propositions are better qualified to help with the household chores. The authors provide accounts in which propositions are replaced in at least some of their theoretical roles by attitudinal objects, states of affairs, proposition-types, and sentences. The existence of these theoretical alternatives forces us to confront the question whether we really need propositions at all.

The papers in the final section of the volume, 'Propositions and Contingent Existence' concern whether an account of singular propositions can accommodate the apparent contingent existence of objects. They consider whether everything exists necessarily, whether propositions are themselves contingent existents, and whether a proposition's constituents are essential to it.

We believe these papers make a significant contribution to our understanding of the nature of propositions, and we are confident that they will stimulate further research on these irresistible, but elusive, philosophical houseguests.

References

Grice, Paul. 1975. "Method in Philosophical Psychology (From the Banal to the Bizarre)." *Proceedings and Addresses of the American Philosophical Association* 48: 23–53.
Hanks, Peter. 2011. "Structured Propositions as Types." *Mind* 120 (1): 11–52.
King, Jeffrey. 2007. *The Nature and Structure of Content*. Oxford: Oxford University Press.
Soames, Scott. 2010. *What is Meaning?* Princeton, NJ: Princeton University Press.

ON ACT- AND LANGUAGE-BASED CONCEPTIONS OF PROPOSITIONS

Two aspects of propositional unity

Gary Ostertag

The Saul Kripke Center, The Graduate Center, CUNY, and Nassau Community College, New York, USA

The paper builds upon familiar arguments against identifying the proposition that *Brutus stabbed Caesar* with a given sequence containing Brutus, Caesar, and the *stabs* relation. It identifies a further problem, one that affects not only traditional Russellian accounts of propositions, but also the recent act-theoretic approach championed by Scott Soames and Peter Hanks. The problem is that there is no clear content to the idea that the pair <Brutus, Caesar> instantiates the *stabs* relation. It is argued that this further problem presents a decisive objection to the act-theoretic approach to propositions.

The contemporary Russellian identifies a singular proposition with an ordered pair of an *n*-ary sequence of entities and an *n*-ary relation.[1] But since such pairs correspond to propositions many–one, this raises the question, *which pair* is the proposition that (say) Brutus stabbed Caesar? The question points to a more general worry, what I shall call 'the representation problem': How can it be that a sequence – in effect, a mere *set* – represents the world, and, in particular, represents it as being thus-and-so? The Russellian has no answer, and would seem forced to acknowledge that, although propositions are *like* sequences in being structured, only in the case of sequences is it clear how the attribution of structure is to be understood; in the case of propositions, the attribution of structure must remain unanalyzed. Thus, although she recognizes on intuitive grounds that the proposition that Brutus stabbed Caesar differs from the proposition that Caesar stabbed Brutus, when pressed to explain *how* they differ, the Russellian is forced either to remain silent, or traffic in uncashed metaphors.[2]

Recently, certain theorists have advocated the view that a proposition is in fact a cognitive act – in the current case, the act (or act *type*) of predicating *stabbed* of Brutus and Caesar. What unifies these diverse elements, yielding a representational entity, is the act itself; considered independently of such an act, the elements, however configured, are void of representational power.

This view promises to fill a gap in our understanding of content, explaining how a collection of entities can be brought together to form a representational unity. I argue here, however, that the act-theoretic approach, as I shall call it, ultimately fails to account for the structure of predication for the same reason that the traditional Russellian approach fails to account for the structure of propositions. If this is correct, then the appeal to predication can hardly be said to constitute an advance over the traditional approach.

Recent discussions have tended to emphasize the representation problem – *How can a sequence represent the world as being thus-and-so?* – over the problem of unity – *How, in the proposition that Brutus stabbed Caesar, are Brutus, Caesar and stabbing synthesized into whole?*[3] Indeed, Scott Soames goes so far as to dismiss the latter as a 'metaphysical pseudo-problem... which... serves only to mask *the real problem* of explaining how propositions can be representational, and so have truth conditions' (2010, 106–107; emphasis added).[4] This, however, is incorrect – it is the representation problem that gets in the way of our understanding the problem of unity. To see this, consider that both act theorists and traditional Russellians take it for granted that a property has satisfaction conditions. That is, it is intrinsic to the property of being, say, blue, that it applies to all and only the blue things. The question, 'How does it do this?' rightly strikes us as a pseudo-question. The only answer that seems appropriate is: 'It is in the nature of properties to have the satisfaction conditions that they have.' But then the question is raised as to why a parallel response isn't available to the traditional Russellian.[5] Why can't she say that the representation problem is itself a pseudo-problem – that it is in the nature of propositions to represent the world in a particular way?

The question is pointed. Yet notice that even when it is acknowledged that no special problem of *propositional* representation exists – properties also represent, albeit in the particular sense that applies to properties – the problem of unity remains. We still have a question as to how the separate elements comprising the aforementioned proposition combine to form a whole. That is to say, the question of how things represent, in the most general sense of that term, is independent of the unity question. While blue is a simple property, it has, one might say, built-in satisfaction conditions – conditions that it has independently of any act that might predicate it of an object. If so, then it seems a perfectly reasonable policy on the one hand to dismiss the representation problem and yet still take the problem of unity seriously. The mere fact that *stabs* is satisfied by all and only the stabber-victim pairs doesn't help to answer, or somehow make irrelevant, the question how it can bind Caesar and Brutus to form the proposition under consideration.

Thus, I take the central question to involve unity and not representation, although with an important qualification: unity and representation are intimately related in the context of complex properties and propositions. *Why* the property of *stabbing Caesar* has the satisfaction conditions it has is intimately related to the question, how the elements *stabbing* and Caesar are united – the wrong unification would get us the set of those stabbed *by* Caesar. Similarly, why the proposition that Brutus stabbed Caesar has the truth conditions it has is intimately related to the question, *how* the constituent elements are united.

That being said, what follows does not depend on accepting my claim that the problem of unity has priority over the representation problem. The challenge I raise for the act-theoretic view does not presuppose any view about that theory's motivation.

The paper is organized as follows. I begin (Section 1) by reviewing King's argument for the view that propositions cannot be identified with sequences. I then (Section 2) relate King's worry to Russell's problem of the unity of the proposition, distinguishing two forms of the problem. In Section 3, I show how one generally unrecognized form of the problem – the problem of structurally-determined unity – applies to traditional Russellian theories; in Section 4, I show how it applies to the act-theoretic approach, recently espoused by Peter Hanks and Scott Soames. Section 5 considers and rejects a potential response to the problem. Finally, Section 6 develops a Benacerraf-style objection to the act-theoretic approach. One consequence of this objection is that that even the most straightforward application of that approach – i.e., to cases of monadic predication – fails to explain how a given state of affairs is represented by a predicative act.

1.

It is well known that, while both Zermelo and von Neumann analyzed the natural numbers in terms of sets, the analyses are not equivalent: a given number n corresponds to one set on the Zermelo reduction, to another on von Neumann's. This raises the question, which reduction is correct – is n to be identified with the corresponding element in the Zermelo progression, or von Neumann's? The problem is that both answers seem arbitrary. If each candidate is equally good, then no principled choice can be made. It looks, then, that n cannot be a set, since we have no answer to the question, '*Which* set?'

The above argument, due to Benacerraf (1965), extends to structured propositions (King 2007, 7). Consider the proposition asserted by (1):

1. Brutus stabbed Caesar.

A contemporary Russellian might analyze this as follows (to keep matters simple, I omit tense):

2. <<Brutus, Caesar>, *stabs*>

As we can see, (2) is the ordered sequence containing the *pair* <Brutus, Caesar> and the stabbing relation, in that order. According to the Russellian, the sequence is true just in case <Brutus, Caesar> is in the extension of this relation. The Russellian here implicitly appeals to the following convention:[6]

(C-1)   <s, R> is true just in case the sequence s is in the extension of R.

But now consider a different abstract entity:

3.   <*stabs*, <Brutus, Caesar >>

Had we adopted a different convention, namely (C-2), this would be true in precisely the same circumstances:

(C-2) <*R, s*> is true just in case the sequence *s* is in the extension of *R*.

Of course, there is no non-arbitrary answer to the question, 'Which is the correct convention, (C-1) or (C-2)?' But then there is no non-arbitrary answer to the question, which of (2) or (3) is the proposition asserted by (1), any more than there is an answer to the question, which of the two set-theoretic analyses counts as *n*.

Moreover, even if we stipulate that, e.g. (C-1) is correct, there is still the question, why (1) cannot be identified with (2′) and not (2):

2′.   <<Brutus, Caesar, Caesar>, *stabs*>

If we assume that a sequence counts as being 'in' the extension of an *n*-ary relation *R* just in case its first *n* elements are in the extension of *R*, then (2′) is true just when (2) is true. But then a choice between (2) and (2′) is arbitrary as well, even setting aside the question of interpretation.

2.

One upshot of the above argument is that, since there is no non-arbitrary answer to the question, which of (2) or (3) is the proposition asserted by (1), (1) can be identified with neither (2) nor (3). As King and Soames have pointed out, Russell (1903) presents a related argument and draws a similar moral. Let me turn to this discussion.[7]

There is, Russell noted, a difference between the contribution a verb makes to a proposition and the contribution a 'verbal noun' would make were it to replace the verb – between what is said by '*a* differs from *b*' and what, if anything, is conveyed by '*a* difference *b*.' As Russell put it, there is a difference between 'a relation in itself and a relation actually relating' (§54). The semantic contribution of the verb is not merely a relation 'in itself' – but a relation synthesizing the diverse elements into a unity.

Ironically, Russell's problem of unity seems to manifest itself in the contemporary approaches to Russellianism championed by David Kaplan, Nathan Salmon and, at one time, Scott Soames, wherein propositions are identified with ordered sequences such as (2) and (3). In these analyses, the relation occurs 'in itself' and not 'actually relating.'

To see the problem, note that *stabs* as it occurs in (2) and (3) fails to relate Caesar and Brutus, just as Caesar fails to relate *stabs* and Brutus and Brutus fails to relate Caesar and *stabs*. This can be seen to be the root of the problem that neither sequence, *qua* sequence, represents the world as being thus-and-so. If the stabbing relation were somehow capable of relating the diverse elements, then we would at least have an entity with truth conditions – one that did not require a supplementary convention for its interpretation. As it stands, in each case the relation is inert, with the result that neither (2) nor (3), *qua* sequence, represents any state of affairs.

What is often overlooked is that the problem of unity has two facets.[8] When Russell writes of 'a relation actually relating' he has two things in mind: (*i*) That the relation binds the separate elements into a unity, something possessing the capacity to represent the world. This is the phenomenon of *generic unity*. (*ii*) That the relation binds the separate elements into a *particular* unity – one that not only represents the world, but represents it in a way that is not solely a function of the constituent entities. This is the phenomenon of *structurally-determined unity*. We can imagine a process indiscriminately taking two elements and unifying them in a manner that produces a truth-evaluable entity – for example, *stabs* bringing together Brutus and Caesar in order to yield something that is true just in case one particular member of the pair stabs the other, but indifferent as to who stabs whom. The process here has two pre-assigned slots for the distinct roles of *stabber* and *victim* (or *agent* and *patient*), but being insensitive to the structure of the input, it yields a content that is not predictable on the basis of this structure.[9] But we can equally imagine a process's being sensitive not merely to the elements it unifies, but also to the structural descriptions accompanying them. In such a case we can predict the particular content generated by the process of applying the relation to these separate elements.[10]

This distinction will be important in what follows. I will argue that there can be no explanation as to how a structurally-determined unity can be generated, even assuming (merely for the sake of argument) that an arbitrarily generated unity can be. This poses a difficulty for act-theoretic approaches, which are motivated in part by problems concerning unity. As I will show, no theory of propositions is adequate unless it addresses and resolves the problem posed by the proposition's structurally-determined unity. That is to say, it is not enough to explain why a proposition is unified. What must also be explained is why it possesses the particular unity it does, and not another.

3.

Let me begin by posing a question that remains even if we arbitrarily adopt one of the above principles of interpretation, say (C-1), namely: what does it mean for $<a, b>$ to be in the extension of *stabs*? Or, more precisely:

Q-1. If *stabs* is true of $<a, b>$, which of $<a, b>$ and $<b, a>$ is in its extension?

Q-2. Let us mark the two 'positions' in the '*x* stabbed *y*' relation as 'stabber' and 'victim'. If we say that $<a, b>$ is in the extension of *stabs*, which element in the pair is assigned *stabber*, which *victim*?

To answer, we make two uncontroversial assumptions: (*i*) that the extension of *stabs* is a set of ordered pairs; (*ii*) that the occupant of a given position in the pair – say the first – always corresponds to a given role – say *stabber*.

The two questions are ultimately the same: let's imagine that we scan (*per impossible*) the list of pairs that constitute the extension of *stabs*. We will not know merely by looking, as it were, who stabbed whom – even if we know that a given pair is within the extension. That is, we will not know the answer to (Q-2). If we *did* know, however – if a given element in the pair was marked as 'stabber', the other as 'victim' – then we would also know the answer to (Q-1): we would know, when we were told that (say) <*a, b*> is in the extension of *stabs*, precisely who did the stabbing and who was stabbed. Similarly, if we did know the answer to (Q-1), we would know which role corresponds to which position in the sequence, *stabber* or *victim*, giving us the answer to (Q-2).

One initial thought is that *stabs* is true of <*a, b*> just in case <*a qua* stabber, *b qua* victim> instantiates *stabs*. There is some confusion here, however. First, roles are assigned positions in pairs only by convention: there is nothing about the *x* position in <*x, y*> requiring that it be reserved for stabbers.[11] Moreover, the information concerning roles can be specified without invoking sequences – indeed, the above thought is redundant on precisely this score. Cleaned up, the suggestion should look as follows:[12]

4. *stabs* is true of <*a, b*> just in case *a qua* stabber and *b qua* victim instantiate *stabs*.

But this only gets us part way to a solution. The truth condition is meaningless unless the '*x* stabbed *y*' relation actually *has* roles. Let's assume, at least provisionally, that it does.[13] We can then say that:

5. *stabs* is true of <*a, b*> just in case *a qua* stabber and *b qua* victim instantiate the *stabber* and *victim* positions, respectively, in *stabs*.

The truth condition contains a variant of <*a qua* stabber, *b qua* victim>, which should make us uncomfortable. We can purge the formulation of all sequential terminology as follows:

6. *stabs* is true of <*a, b*> just in case *a* instantiates *stabs*$_{STABBER}$ and *b* instantiates *stabs*$_{VICTIM}$.

But this is defective: it claims that *stabs* holds of <*a, b*> just when both *a* stabbed someone (not necessarily *b*) and someone (not necessarily *a*) stabbed *b*. That is, Brutus, *qua* stabber, can instantiate the *stabber* position in *stabs* while Caesar, *qua* victim, instantiates the *victim* position, without its being the case that the former stabs the latter.

We can, in desperation, add a condition *R* linking the occupants in the desired way:

7. *stabs* is true of <*a, b*> just in case *a* instantiates *stabs*$_{STABBER}$ and *b* instantiates *stabs*$_{VICTIM}$ and $R(stabs_{STABBER}, stabs_{VICTIM})$

R can be viewed as a relation between roles, requiring that the occupant of the first bear the stabs relation to the occupant of the second. But the condition works only because it presupposes precisely what is being analyzed – that *stabs* is true of $<a, b>$. Moreover, it would seem doubtful that any *other* condition providing a true completion of (7) would be immune to a similar charge of circularity.[14]

The result is surprising: even if we bracket the problem of unity by stipulating that a given principle for interpreting structured propositions holds – such as (C-1) or (C-2) – we cannot stipulate our way out of the sub-problem – of stating precisely what it means for a binary relation to hold of a given pair.

4.

The conclusion is relevant both to theories of structured propositions as well as to recent attempts to address the problems of unity and arbitrariness voiced by Russell and King – in particular, Soames (2010) and Hanks (2012). Soames responds to these problems as follows. In asserting (1), the speaker predicates *stabs* of Brutus and Caesar (see, e.g., Soames 2010, Chapters 6 and 7). The 'proposition' asserted is in fact not a structured entity, as the Russellian would have it, but an 'act type' (or 'event type' – the differences won't matter here), one in which the agent predicates a relation of Brutus and Caesar (or Brutus 'followed by' Caesar) (111).[15]

For present purposes, we can assume that the general suggestion – that propositions are in fact act types of a particular sort, namely acts of predication – is unproblematic when applied to monadic predicates: identifying the proposition that Coriolanus is proud with the act type of predicating pride of Coriolanus would seem to raise no immediate problems.[16] And it at least appears to provide a solution to the problem of unity. But the proposition that Brutus stabbed Caesar introduces problems – problems we are now in a position to appreciate. We cannot blithely identify *this* proposition with the act type of predicating *stabs* of Brutus and Caesar, in that order (or, more formally, of $<$Caesar, Brutus$>$).

To see this, consider:

8. The act type of predicating *stabs* of $<$Caesar, Brutus$>$ is true just in case $<$Caesar, Brutus$>$ is in the extension of *stabs*.

This won't do, of course, for act types any more than for propositions. Our questions (Q-1) and (Q-2) (slightly modified) still apply:

Q-3. Consider the act type of predicating *stabs* of $<a, b>$. Which of $<a, b>$ and $<b, a>$ is thereby said to be in the extension of this relation?

Q-4. Let us mark the two 'positions' in the *stabs* relation as 'stabber' and 'victim'. If we predicate this relation of $<a, b>$, which element in the pair is assigned which position?

It is not enough, then, to identify the proposition expressed by (1) with the act type of predicating *stabs* of $<$Caesar, Brutus$>$, since there are two distinct act types to which this description corresponds.

To answer these questions we need an acceptable completion of the following:

9. The act type of predicating *stabs* of <Brutus, Caesar> is true just in case...

But (9) appeals to an arbitrary convention of flagging the stabber by placing him in the first position and the victim by placing him in the second. This is easily made explicit:

10. The act type of predicating *stabs* of Brutus *qua* stabber and Caesar *qua* victim is true just in case Brutus and Caesar instantiate the *stabber* and *victim* positions, respectively, in *stabs*.

The problem here, as before, is to rid ourselves of 'respectively' as it occurs in the analysis; this is done as follows:

11. The act type of predicating *stabs* of Brutus *qua* stabber and Caesar *qua* victim is true just in case Brutus instantiates $stabs_{STABBER}$ and Caesar instantiates $stabs_{VICTIM}$.

As we have seen, this fails, since according to it the act type can be true whenever it is the case the Brutus stabs someone and someone stabs Caesar. Moreover, adding an extra condition (as in (12), below) amounts to adding an unanalyzed proposition to the mix – indeed the very proposition we were supposed to be avoiding!

12. The act type of predicating *stabs* of Brutus *qua* stabber and Caesar *qua* victim is true just in case Brutus instantiates $stabs_{STABBER}$ and Caesar instantiates $stabs_{VICTIM}$ and $R(stabs_{STABBER}, stabs_{VICTIM})$

Once again, the result is surprising. Previously, we sidestepped the problem of interpretation (and thus the general problem of unity) by appealing to an arbitrary principle of interpretation – (C-1). We are now considering the proposal that no such principle is required, allowing ourselves the full resources of the act-theoretic conception of propositions. We can thus help ourselves to the idea that the separate elements Brutus and Caesar are unified in an act of predication, creating a unity that is somehow truth-evaluable. But merely bringing together Brutus and Caesar by predicating *stabs* of them, in this or that order, is not yet to get us to *the proposition that Brutus stabbed Caesar*. For that is a particular unity, and the act theorist has not provided an explanation as to how *it* came about.

Hanks (2011) addresses the problem, albeit briefly. He has us consider the respective act types of predicating *kisses* of George and Ann and predicating *kisses* of Ann and George. He writes: 'The only difference between [these act types] is in the order in which the relation of kissing is predicated of George and Ann' (18). That is, the order of the referring expressions in a canonical description of these act types represents '*predicational order*, the order in which the relation of kissing is predicated of George and Ann' (18; emphasis added).

It is unclear what Hanks has in mind here. Perhaps it is that the canonical ordering indicates that we apply *kisses* to George and Ann by first applying it to George, yielding the monadic property, *being kissed by George*. This then is applied to Ann, yielding the desired unification. Reversing the order of the referential items would then reverse the order of predication, yielding an alternative unification.

But a variation on our previous worry applies here, and with the same force: what is it about the *kisses* relation that gives priority to the kisser? Why should applying *kisses* to George yield *being kissed by George* and not *kisses George*? Canonical ordering only tells us which item 'goes first' – it tells us nothing about which *slot* in *kisses* gets saturated first.

A theorist such as Hanks might view predicational order as *sui generis* – something not amenable to formal analysis or representation. But it is hard to see why this would be attractive to the proponent of the act-theoretic view. Such a theorist has already recognized that the sequential ordering of propositional constituents cannot uniquely determine a proposition and has rejected the idea that propositional structure is *sui generis*. Why then would he believe that a similar sequence uniquely determines an act of predication? There is no obvious explanatory gain achieved by taking predicational order as basic and unanalyzable. If not, there is no clear advantage that the act theoretic approach enjoys over the traditional Russellian account.

5.

'Isn't there is an easy solution to this?' someone might say. 'Let's list the argument positions in *stabs* in some canonical order, taking the first position to be the *stabber* position, the second, the *victim* position. Then we can apply this relation to sequences that follow the canonical ordering – first guy in the sequence, *agent*, second guy in the sequence, *patient*. (This latter ordering isn't necessary – we can reverse the order of course – but we need the respective orderings to be coordinated, so we'll stick with the obvious.) So (ignoring tense) we have:

    13.   The proposition that Brutus stabbed Caesar is the result of predicating *stabs(agent, patient)* of <Brutus, Caesar>.

How could (13) fail to give us the desired proposition? What could the proposition that Brutus stabbed Caesar *be* but the result of predicating *stabs (agent, patient)* of <Brutus, Caesar>?'

Note that, if (13) gives us the desired proposition, then an assignment of truth conditions is superfluous – we already know when it is true. But *do* we already know when predicating *stabs(agent, patient)* of <Brutus, Caesar> is true? Recall that the ordering merely indicates that Brutus is to go into the *agent* slot and *Caesar* is to go into the patient slot. But then (13) simply claims that (1) is the proposition that results from predicating *stabs(agent, patient)* of Brutus *qua* agent and Caesar *qua* patient. And this, we have seen, is inadequate. It can be true when (1) is false.

There is a parallel with standard model theory that might mislead here. It makes perfect sense, we are told, to speak of its being that case that the *open sentence* '*x* stabbed *y*' is true of $<a, b>$. (Or, less misleadingly, that '*x* stabbed *y*' is true relative to the assignment of *a* to *x* and *b* to *y*.) The truth condition is often stated as follows (here *I* is an interpretation function):

14. '*x* stabs *y*' is true, relative to an assignment of *a* to *x* and *b* to *y*, just in case $<a, b>$ is in the extension of *I*(stabs).

For example, a standard account, chosen more or less at random, has it that: 'If *R* represents "love", then *I(R)* is the set of pairs $<a, b>$ such that *a* and *b* are the members of the domain for which *a* loves *b*' (Schapiro 2009). The interpretation of 'stabs' is then just the relevant set of pairs. Accordingly, we can write that '*x* stabs *y*' is true, relative to an assignment of *a* to *x* and *b* to *y*, just in case $<a, b>$ is in 'stabs'. But it is unclear precisely what this means: 'stabs' is a set of ordered pairs, in which a given position in the pair is the stabber slot and a given position is the victim slot. But the truth conditions as stated in (14) fail to indicate who goes where.

The following gives us precisely what we need:

15. '*x* stabs *y*' is true, relative to an assignment of *a* to *x* and *b* to *y*, just in case $<a, b>$ is in $\{<x, y> \mid x \text{ stabs } y\}$.

Note that the right-hand side of (15) represents the *x* position in $<x, y>$ as occupied by the stabber and the *y* position as occupied by the victim. It does so, however, by presupposing that we know when '*x* stabs *y*' is true relative to an assignment of objects to *x* and *y*.[17]

Of course, this is not a problem for the model theorist. Since she does not claim to tell us what it is for the proposition that *a* stabbed *b* to be true, or even for *stabs* to hold of $<a, b>$, she is not guilty of any circularity.[18] But our theorist is concerned with precisely these questions and thus cannot get off so easily.

Perhaps, however, the proponent of the act-theoretic account can learn from the model-theoretic account. Just as the model theorist uses

'*x* stabbed *y*' is true of $<a, b>$

as shorthand for

'*x* stabbed *y*' is true relative to the assignment of *a* to *x* and *b* to *y*

so the proponent of the act-theoretic account uses

the act type of predicating *stabs* of $<a, b>$

as shorthand for

the act type of predicating *stabs* of $<a, b>$ relative to an assignment of *a* to stabs$_{STABBER}$ and *b* to stabs$_{VICTIM}$

13

Described in this way, she argues, the act type cannot fail to be equivalent to the proposition that a stabbed b.

The problem here is in making sense of the paraphrase. Assignments in model theory are literally just that – assignments. The entities that *receive* assignments are linguistic types – entities subject to convention and stipulation. Just as we arbitrarily assign an entity to a name, we arbitrarily assign a value to a variable. But it is hard to give sense to the idea of assigning an entity to a 'position' in a relation. Pending further clarification of the above, it seems that we have here a mere placeholder for where more work needs to be done, and not a genuine analysis.

One strategy of clarification would run as follows. We take '[' and ']' to function as meaning quotes. Just as 'Brutus stabbed Caesar' refers to the contained sentence, '[Brutus stabbed Caesar]' refers to the proposition that Brutus stabbed Caesar. Here, propositional structure directly mirrors syntactic structure. Now just as 'Brutus' as it occurs in 'Brutus stabbed Caesar' refers to a linguistic item, the same expression as it occurs in '[Brutus stabbed Caesar]' refers to the contribution that 'Brutus' makes to the relevant proposition. Proceeding in this vein, we can say that 'stabbed Caesar' refers to the contribution that the verb phrase makes to this proposition. And, finally 'Brutus stabbed' would refer to the contribution these combined expression make to the proposition.[19]

We can now say that the 'stabbed Caesar' component contains an unoccupied position, α, and that the 'Brutus stabbed' component contains an unoccupied position, β. It would follow that the contribution 'stabs' makes has two unoccupied positions, α and β, and is best represented as: [α stabbed β]. Now it is entirely arbitrary *where* we place the position indicators (i.e., to the left or the right of one another): the point is that α corresponds to the position that 'Brutus' occupies in the proposition and β corresponds to the position that 'Caesar' occupies.

Having isolated something akin to argument positions in *stabs*, it is now possible to line these positions up with propositional constituents. We get the proposition that a stabbed b when we predicate [α stabbed β] of $<a, b>$. This proceeds as follows: we take the first item in the input sequence to serve as argument to the α position in [α stabbed β], yielding as value [a stabbed β]. We then take the second item in the sequence to serve as argument for this function, yielding the proposition [a stabbed b].

This solution provides the traditional Russellian with an entity that can serve as a propositional constituent.[20] So long as we have a canonical ordering of objects and a canonical ordering of positions in a relation, we can frame a convention that allows us to generate truth conditions for structured propositions. Of course, the appeal to extra-propositional conventions remains problematic. But this just means that the traditional theorist doesn't face any *new* problems.

It is unclear, however, just how happy the act theorist should be with this suggestion. As I've shown, there is a method of arriving at propositional constituents by abstracting from complete propositions, and even of identifying roles or positions in the processes. But it is far from obvious that the process can coherently be applied to an *act* of predication. First, the act theorist cannot help herself to some of the propositional building blocks – properties and relations – if these are understood as derived from a process of abstraction from entities that are intrinsically representational, possessing their truth conditions essentially and absolutely. After all, the theorist denies that there are such entities. At best, the theorist can attempt to derive such an entity by abstracting from the act type of predicating a relation of a sequence of entities. But on reflection this is a non-starter: the very description of the act type of predicating *stabs* of Brutus and Caesar already involves three discrete entities: the *stabs* relation and Brutus and Caesar. That is to say, describing the act type already presupposes that the relevant propositional building blocks exist – including, crucially, the *stabs* relation.

6.

It remains to be shown that the monadic case is also problematic. To see this, recall that <<Brutus, Caesar, Caesar>, *stabs*> is a candidate for the proposition that Brutus stabbed Caesar. After all, there is, a convention according to which a sequence s satisfies an n-ary relation R just in case its first n elements are in the extension of R (see Section 1). Accordingly, in interpreting a Russellian proposition we look only to a particular segment of the initial sequence (for those sequences greater than n). In the case of a binary relation, we look only to the initial two elements. But an alternative account of satisfaction is also possible, one on which a sequence s satisfies an n-ary relation R just in case the right-shifted sequence s' – i.e., the sequence beginning at s_2 – is in the extension of R. Relative to such a convention, <<Brutus, Brutus, Caesar>, *stabs*> is a candidate for the proposition that Brutus stabbed Caesar. Here, the initial occurrence of Brutus is passed over, just as the second occurrence of Caesar is passed over in the previous sequence. (Note that, on such an interpretation, <<Brutus, Caesar>, *stabs*> cannot count as a proposition, as its initial sequence has too few elements.)

This allows me to make the following point: The essential worry put forward by King is that there are indefinitely many instantiation relations that we can define over Russellian propositions. But if this is correct, then there can be no fact of the matter as to whether a given sequence represents the world as being thus-and-so – it can only do so relative to a given convention regarding instantiation, and there are a variety of such conventions available. But then a parallel worry can be raised about predication. We can now ask: 'What, if anything, is represented when we *predicate R* of *s*?' If we accept King's Benacerraf-style objection to Russellian theories of propositions, then it becomes hard to see why we shouldn't also accept a parallel objection to act-theoretic accounts. Take, for example, the sequence <Brutus, Caesar, Brutus>. When we predicate *stabs* of this sequence, does the unity thereby created represent Brutus as stabbing Caesar, or the converse?

There seems to be no answer. The former is represented if we assume that the 'x predicates R of s' relation holds only if s is in the extension of R; the latter is represented if we assume that the relation holds only if s' (the right-shifted cousin of s) is in the extension of R. And this spells trouble even for the monadic case. If the proposition that results from predicating R of s is true just in case s' is in the extension of R, then predicating *pride* of <Coriolanus> would not yield anything truth-evaluable: the right-shifted sequence is empty.

It might be countered that predication is only defined for relation-sequence pairs of matching adicity. (Even if we assume this, there are problems, as I've shown above.) Notice, however, that 'predicates' is a technical term – as technical as 'instantiates'. Ordinary usage cannot be a guide as to how the relation-sequence interpretation is to be understood. One might argue that in the simplest case – one consistent with ordinary usage – it holds between a property and an individual. But this gives us no help when we face the question, how to make sense of the more generalized relation, holding between a relation and a sequence.

Conclusion

The act-theoretic approach can quite naturally account for something that eludes the Russellian. It seems entirely extrinsic to the sequence (2) that it has the truth conditions that it is said to have. But it cannot be an extrinsic feature of any proposition that it has the truth conditions it has. So (2) cannot be a proposition. The problem would seem to evaporate when we identify propositions with acts of predication. On this approach, the proposition simply *is* the result of applying *stabs* to <Brutus, Caesar> and there can be no further question of 'unity'. Still, a question remains – namely, what it means to apply *stabs* to <Brutus, Caesar> and achieve one unity and not another. This question, far from being a mere residual concern, is at the core of the very problem of unity that exercised Russell. And it remains a problem: nothing that the act theorist has said points the way to a solution.[21]

Notes

1. Contemporary Fregeans hold a similar view, and differ from Russellians only in the nature of the constituents. I will limit discussion here to the Russellian approach, but the conclusions apply with the same force to contemporary Fregean approaches. (I will, however, omit discussion of the traditional Fregean approach to the unity problem.)
2. Of course, most Russellians do not address the question raised here. But it would seem that, between (*i*) assuming arbitrarily that, say, <<Brutus, Caesar>, *stabs*> and not, for example <*stabs*, <Brutus, Caesar>> counts as the proposition that Brutus stabbed Caesar and (*ii*) acknowledging that propositional structure is resistant to analysis, she would choose (*ii*).

3. Brandom (1994, 6–7) expresses a more general worry, concerning how representations represent. But since his particular concern is with 'intentionality in the sense of the *propositional* contentfulness of attitudes' (7; emphasis added) it seems not too far removed from the representation problem.
4. See also Jubien (2001) and King (2007).
5. I owe this point to Robert Stalnaker, made during the question period after Peter Hanks' paper, 'Propositional Content, Semantic Content, and Types of Speech Acts,' Columbia University, 28 September 2013.
6. If Williamson (1985) is correct, then a relation like *stabs* is identical to its converse. In that case, not only is there no unique proposition corresponding to, say, (2), there is no unique interpretation of (2) even relative to (C-1).
7. One might have argued as follows: 'If something is to count as the proposition that Brutus stabbed Caesar it must be intrinsically representational: that is, have its truth conditions essentially and absolutely, without relativization to a language or set of conventions. Since neither (2) nor (3) has its truth conditions independently of (C-1) or (C-2), it immediately follows that neither (2) nor (3) can be identified with this proposition.'

    The general thrust of the argument is that since, say, (2) is not intrinsically representational, it cannot count as the proposition that Brutus stabbed Caesar. As I have already stated above, in my view the central problem concerns unity, and not representation. Accordingly, the reason that (2) is not a proposition is precisely that it lacks unity – it is a mere list of propositional building blocks (a phrase I've appropriated from Stephen Schiffer) rather than a content-bearing item. Moreover, as a mere list it is in competition with other lists that would seem to be equally good candidates for the relevant proposition. Thus, while the quoted argument is indeed a more expedient route to our conclusion, it obscures the real problem – namely Russell's problem of unity.
8. But see Candlish (1996, 111–112) and Sainsbury (1996, 141–142).
9. To get a feel for what I have in mind, imagine an indexical relation, R, such that aRb if either a is taller than b and it is an even-numbered day or b is taller than a and it is an odd-numbered day. R here unifies a and b but does so differently depending on the day. I am imagining a similar relation, but where the mode of unification is entirely random – not a 'function' of anything.
10. It may well be that there can be no process that unifies a and b without doing so in a structurally determined manner – i.e. such that the resulting unity is a function of a, b and their order of occurrence. This is just to say that the two problems are at root one. If so, then one cannot address the problem of generic unity without addressing the problem of structurally determined unity. This would suggest that, to the extent that the efforts of Soames and Hanks to solve the problem of unity fail to solve the subproblem, they really do not solve the problem at all: the 'sub-problem' just *is* the problem of unity in another manifestation. See Candlish *op. cit.* and Sainsbury *op. cit.*
11. In contrast, we are assuming for argument's sake that there is intuitive sense to be made of the definiendum. But there may be a problem here as well; see Section 5, below, for discussion.
12. I defer, for the moment, discussion of the '*qua*' idiom.
13. In Section 5 I try to make sense of what this might mean; for the moment I take the attribution of argument structure as a primitive.
14. I can rest with a weaker point here: Unless the proponent of (7) shows that the added requirement does not simply amount to the condition that the occupant of $stabs_{STABBER}$ stabs the occupant of $stabs_{VICTIM}$, we are not assured of a non-circular analysis. It is difficult to see how this could be done.

15. Soames appears generally insensitive to the worry about predetermined unity, but he clearly has in mind that an agent predicates a relation of a sequence, and not an undifferentiated multiplicity.
16. I assume this for the sake of argument. As I show (Section 6), the monadic case is also problematic.
17. This is clear from an equivalent formulation:

   15* 'x stabs y' is true of $<a, b>$ just in case $<a, b>$ is in $\{<z, w> \mid$ 'x stabs y' is true of $<z, w>\}$.

18. But it is crucial to see that merely being told that S is true just in case $<a, b>$ is in I (stabs) doesn't tell us *when* S is true. A convention is typically adopted according to which the ordering in $<a, b>$ mirrors the ordering in 'aRb' – that is, that $<a, b>$ is in $I(R)$ just in case 'aRb' is true. Once we know this, we can know precisely when 'aRb' is true. The problem is that, *without* the convention, the statement of the truth condition is incomplete – we don't know yet *when* the sentence is true – and *given* the convention, the statement of the truth condition is superfluous – we *already* know when it is true. Again, since the model theorist is providing a definition of truth, not revealing a mysterious property of sentences in the language, this is not a problem. Still, it is important to appreciate what she is *not* doing.
19. This and the following paragraph use techniques developed in Kaplan (1968).
20. Collins (2011, 33–34) argues (convincingly, to my mind) that we cannot genuinely explain unity if we begin, as here, with a unified whole. In particular, if we begin with a unity we cannot explain why there are certain unities or wholes and not others. I cannot do justice to Collins' arguments here. For further discussion, see Chapter 3 of Collins (2011).
21. Thanks to Ray Buchanan, David Hunter, Oliver Marshall, Frank Pupa, Gurpreet Rattan, Adriana Renero and Rosemary Twomey for helpful comments on a previous draft, and to Frank, Ray and Gurpreet for extended and fruitful discussions on the topic.

References

Benacerraf, Paul. 1965. "What Numbers Could Not Be." *The Philosophical Review* 74 (1): 47–73.

Brandom, Robert. 1994. *Making it Explicit*. Cambridge: Harvard University Press.

Candlish, Stewart. 1996. "The Unity of the Proposition and Russell's Theories of Judgement." In *Bertrand Russell and the Origins of Analytic Philosophy*, edited by Ray Monk, and Anthony Palmer, 103–135. Bristol: Thoemmes.

Collins, John. 2011. *The Unity of Linguistic Meaning*. Oxford: Oxford University Press.

Hanks, Peter. 2011. "Structured Propositions as Types." *Mind* 120 (1): 11–52. doi:10.1093/mind/fzr011.

Jubien, Michael. 2001. "Propositions and the Objects of Thought." *Philosophical Studies* 104 (1): 47–62. doi:10.1007/0-306-48134-0_10.

Kaplan, David. 1968. "Quantifying In." *Synthese* 19 (1/2): 178–214.
King, Jeffrey. 2007. *The Nature and Structure of Content*. Oxford: Oxford University Press.
Monk, Ray, and Anthony Palmer, eds. 1996. *Bertrand Russell and the Origins of Analytic Philosophy*. Bristol: Thoemmes.
Russell, Bertrand. 1903. *The Principles of Mathematics*. Cambridge: Cambridge University Press.
Schapiro, Stuart. 2009. Classical Logic. *The Stanford Encyclopedia of Philosophy*, edited by Edward N. Zalta. http://plato.stanford.edu/entries/logic-classical/. (Winter 2012 Edition).
Sainsbury, Mark. 1996. "How Can We Say Something?" In *Bertrand Russell and the Origins of Analytic Philosophy*, edited by Ray Monk, and Anthony Palmer, 137–153. Bristol: Thoemmes, Reprinted as How Can Some Thing Say Some Thing? Chapter 5 in Sainsbury, *Departing from Frege*. London: Routledge, 2002.
Soames, Scott. 2010. *What is Meaning?* Princeton: Princeton University Press.
Williamson, Timothy. 1985. "Converse Relations." *The Philosophical Review* 94 (2): 249–262.

ON ACT- AND LANGUAGE-BASED CONCEPTIONS OF PROPOSITIONS

An empirically-informed cognitive theory of propositions

Berit Brogaard

Department of Philosophy, University of Missouri-St. Louis, St. Louis, MO, USA

Scott Soames has recently argued that traditional accounts of propositions as n-tuples or sets of objects and properties or functions from worlds to extensions cannot adequately explain how these abstract entities come to represent the world. Soames' new cognitive theory solves this problem by taking propositions to be derived from agents representing the world to be a certain way. Agents represent the world to be a certain way, for example, when they engage in the cognitive act of predicating, or cognizing, an act that takes place during cognitive events, such as perceiving, believing, judging and asserting. On the cognitive theory, propositions just are act types involving the act of predicating and certain other mental operations. This theory, Soames argues, solves not only the problem of how propositions come to represent but also a number of other difficulties for traditional theories, including the problem of *de se* propositions and the problems of accounting for how agents are capable of grasping propositions and how they come to stand in the relation of expression to sentences. I argue here that Soames' particular version of the cognitive theory makes two problematic assumptions about cognitive operations and the contents of proper names. I then briefly examine what can count as evidence for the nature of the constituents of the cognitive operation types that produce propositions and argue that the common nature of cognitive operations and what they operate on ought to be determined empirically in cross-disciplinary work. I conclude by offering a semantics for cognitive act types that accommodates one type of empirical evidence.

1. The problem of intentionality

Scott Soames has recently argued that traditional accounts of propositions as n-tuples of objects and properties or functions from possible worlds to extensions cannot adequately explain how these abstract entities come to have intentional properties that enable them to represent the world as being a certain way (Soames

2010, 2012, 2013a, 2013b, 2013c, 2013d). Let's call this 'the problem of intentionality'. I shall here use the phrases 'representational' and 'intentional' (with a 't') synonymously.

Frege (1892a, 1892b, 1918) and Russell (1903) took propositions to be structured entities with a structure that mirrors the sentences that express them, at least in an ideal language. Moreover, they took propositions to be the primary bearers of truth. When we say of a sentence, utterance or belief that it is true, then this is to be understood derivatively. A sentence is true in virtue of expressing a proposition that bears a truth-value. Propositions have their truth-values in virtue of representing the world to be a certain way. If they represent correctly, they are true; otherwise, they are false. Other entities, such as beliefs and judgments, represent only in virtue of being related to propositions with inherent intentional properties.

According to Soames, the problem Russell and Frege faced was that of accounting for how in an abstract propositional entity, such as *o is red*, redness is predicated of o in a way that results in o being represented as red. If the proposition simply consists of the object o and redness, then how does it come about that it's redness that is predicated of o, and not vice versa? A simple answer would be to say that the proposition itself specifies what is predicated of what but if this were so, then the relation of predication would need to be a constituent of the proposition, which it is not. While the sentences 'o is red' and 'redness is predicated of o' may be taken to express the same proposition, the complexes *o is red* and *redness is predicated of o* are two different propositions with potentially different truth-values. The reason that these complexes are different propositions is that, on a Russellian or Fregean account, propositions are exhausted by their constituents and perhaps a structure that supervenes on properties inherent to the constituents of the proposition.

Frege (1892b) made an attempt to solve the problem of intentionality by proposing that different constituents inherently function as either a subject or a predicate. In *grass is green*, for example, *grass* can only function as a subject and *green* can only function as a predicate. So, it is inherent to the proposition that *green* is being predicated of grass and not vice versa. This means that *green* cannot occur as a constituent of which something is being predicated. This restriction on predicative constituents of propositions has independent motivation (see Brogaard 2006). Consider the sentences:

(1) Green is a concept
(2) *Green* is a concept

(1) appears to express a *false* proposition that (on, say, a physicalist theory of color) wrongly predicates *being a concept* of the color green, whereas (2) appears to express a *true* proposition that truly predicates *being a concept* of the sense associated with green. But a Fregean cannot straightforwardly accept propositions of this sort. For Frege, the constituents of propositions are not objects and properties but senses (or modes of presentation or concepts). (1) and (2) thus appear to contribute the same conceptual constituents to the propositions:

The sense corresponding to 'green' and the sense corresponding to 'a concept'. But if propositions are the primary bearers of truth, then two sentences with different truth-values cannot express one and the same proposition. If they did, then there would be no fact of the matter as to whether the proposition in question is a true proposition about the concept green or a false proposition about the color green.

There is some evidence that Russell took this type of problem to be a serious problem for his own theory of denoting concepts, which he defended in *Principles of Mathematics*. In paragraph 38 of "On Fundamentals" (p. 383 of Vol. 4. of Russell's *Collected Papers*), for example, in which Russell rejects the theory of denoting concepts, he seems to rely on the problem of indeterminate propositions to argue against the view that denoting concepts are capable of occurring in different kinds of ways (e.g., denotatively or non-denotatively) in different propositions. In reply to the above argument it may be suggested that the two occurrences of 'green' in (1) and (2) contribute different conceptual constituents to the propositions expressed. This suggestion, however, has a number of independent problems that appear to have motivated the Gray's Elegy argument, which Russell presents in 1905 in "On Denoting" as a final argument against his earlier theory of denoting concepts (Brogaard 2006).

Frege himself does not run into this problem, as he does not think sentences like (2) are intelligible. According to him, it is impossible for the sense of a predicate to be the same as the sense of a singular term. Frege's proposal, however, has numerous problems. To mention one, if different constituents of propositions inherently function as either a subject or a predicate, then we cannot intelligibly express the core of Frege's theory that what is expressed by a singular term is a mode of presentation.

Soames thinks that Russell and Frege were looking in the wrong place for a solution to the problem of the intentionality of propositions. They were looking for a relation that holds the constituents together to form a single entity, thinking that an answer to that question would also provide an answer to the question of the intentionality of propositions. However, Soames argues, if the problem of how propositions represent could be solved by finding a relation of this kind, then we would already have a solution to the problem. If the constituents of propositions form a set, for example, then they are unified by the relation of being members of that set. The real problem, though, is that of explaining how propositions can be non-derivatively representational. But this problem, Soames says, cannot be solved if the entities that are supposed to play the role of propositions are Russellian or Fregean structures, as there is nothing inherent in these structures that makes them representational. What makes something representational is the relation of predication. But a structure of the kind that is supposed to play the role of the proposition for Frege and Russell does not contain constituents that ensure that one thing is predicated of another, because predication is something only agents can do.

Because predication is something that only agents can do, it does not help to reject the Russell/Frege picture of propositions as n-tuples or sets of entities and turn to possible worlds or functions from worlds to extensions to solve the problem. Neither sets of worlds nor functions from worlds to extensions are intrinsically representational. If an account has already been offered of propositions as intentional entities, propositions can then (perhaps) be modelled as sets of worlds or their characteristic functions, but neither sets of worlds nor their characteristic functions can possess the properties it takes to make them represent anything non-derivatively.

2. A cognitive theory of propositions

Soames' response to the problem of what makes propositions inherently representational is to deny that they are *inherently* representational (Soames 2012, 2013b). According to Soames, the basis of all representation (intentionality) is the perceptual and cognitive activity of agents. The representational properties of propositions derive from the representational activities of agents. Agents represent the world as being a certain way when they predicate something of something else. For example, an agent represents an object o as being red when she predicates redness of o. All instances of event types, such as seeing o as red, imagining o as red, judging that o is red, and asserting that o is red, are instances of the event type *cognizing o as red*, which is identical to the event type *predicating redness of o*. All the event tokens involve a distinctive kind of cognizing, viz. that of predicating redness of o, in addition to other cognitive acts. To judge or assert that o is red is to predicate redness of o and to endorse that o is red, where predicating and endorsing are two distinct cognitive acts.

According to Soames, propositions are associated with act types of predicating. For example, all the acts of predicating redness of o correspond to the proposition that o is red. Soames actually takes propositions to be identical to act types. So, the proposition that o is red is identical to the act type of predicating redness of o. In my view, that conflates the act of doing something with the information that is produced during the act. When you retrieve a memory, perceive something or make a belief explicit, information is thereby being processed. This cognitive processing generates new information. So, cognitive acts are mental doings that produce information. A cognitive act type is a class of mental doings that consist in the same kind of doing and lead to the same kind of information. For example, the act type of predicating greenness of grass produces the information that grass is green. The act type of predicating greenness of grass is the class of all conceivable acts that predicate greenness of grass. So, I think that rather than saying that propositions are identical to certain act types (e.g., the act type of predicating), it would be more accurate to say that propositions are the information produced by these act types. But I don't think a lot hangs on whether we use this wording or Soames'. So, I will mostly use Soames' particular suggestion in what follows.

The act type of predicating a property of an object is representational, Soames says, because every conceivable instance of it is one in which an agent represents something as being a certain way. The representational properties of the type are essential to it. The act type could not be what it is without having the intentional properties it has. So, propositions inherit their representational properties, not from a particular cognitive act, but from all conceivable instances of a certain type of cognitive act. Propositions represent what is representationally common to all such instances.

According to Soames, the verb phrase 'predicating of' is to be understood as an intensional, transitive verb. This means that the object of the cognitive act of predicating doesn't need to exist in order for the act to produce an instance of a proposition. For example, the act of predicating maleness of the King of France does not require the King of France to exist. So, the existence of the proposition that the King of France is male does not require the King of France to exist either. The proposition just cannot be true without the existence of a King of France. Soames is not suggesting that acts of predicating involve predicating something of a Meinongion non-existing entity but only that 'predicating of' expresses a cognitive relation between an agent, a property, and a content.

Once we have a picture of propositions as inheriting their representational properties from the cognitive activities of agents, we can speak, derivatively, of propositions themselves representing the world as being thus and so, for example, we can speak of the proposition that o is red as representing o as red.

Complex propositions derive their representational properties from the cognitive acts of agents in the same way as atomic propositions. The cognitive acts resulting in complex propositions involve acts of predicating, acts of employing truth-functional operations and other related cognitive operations. For example, the proposition that it is not true that o is red results from an act of predicating redness of p, negating the property of being true, and predicating that property of the result of the initial act of predicating, and the proposition that o is red and round is generated by conjoining the properties of being red and round and predicating the result of o. Conjunctive and disjunctive propositions may come from the act of applying the operations of conjunction and disjunction to the results of predicative acts. For example, employing the disjunctive operation to *a is red* and *b is round* results in *a is red or b is round*. Complex propositions inherit their representational properties from both acts of predicating and other acts, such as conjoining, disjoining and negating properties or propositions.

The roles the constituents joined together play in the sequence of cognitive operations determine the structure of propositions. (Soames 2013b, 46). By 'roles' Soames means things like being predicated (of certain things), being targets (of certain predications), being applied (to certain arguments), being arguments (to which certain things are applied), etc.

According to Soames, the cognitive theory of propositions has several attractive features. First, it does away with the problem of intentionality. The answer to the question of how propositions come to have representational properties is that they derive from the cognitive activities of agents. It's agents who most fundamentally represent things as being a certain way. When agents represent, their acts of predicating (or cognizing) thereby become representational, and these acts result in instances of propositions with representational properties.

Second, the cognitive theory offers a naturalistic picture of what it is to bear epistemic relations to propositions, sometimes expressed using terminology such as 'grasping a proposition', 'being acquainted with a proposition', and so on. On the Russellian and Fregean accounts of propositions, it is somewhat mysterious how we can come to stand in these epistemic relations to abstract entities. On the cognitive theory, by contrast, we come to stand in these relations by performing cognitive acts of cognizing. When agents perform cognitive acts of cognizing, they thereby entertain a proposition. The notion of entertaining a proposition may seem to require a notion of a proposition that is independent of the cognitive act of entertaining. However, this is not how Soames' suggestion should be understood. Although we speak of 'entertaining a proposition', the act of entertaining is a cognitive act the performing of which gives rise to an instance of the proposition. As Soames puts it, 'To entertain p is not to have p in mind or to cognize it in any way; it is to perform a cognitive act resulting in an instance of p.' (Soames 2013c, 7)

Third, the cognitive theory makes the relation of expression between sentences and propositions less mysterious. The act types of predicating and other types of cognitive operation serve as the interpretation of sentences and utterances. Users of the language learn to associate certain sounds with certain mental representations and cognitive acts linking these mental representations together. Once this skill has been acquired a speaker will, in most circumstances, more or less automatically perform a cognitive act of predicating when uttering a sentence. As this cognitive act of predicating produces an instance of a proposition, the utterance of the sentence can then be said to express that proposition. In some cases the tokening of a sentence may overlap significantly with the tokening of the act of predicating; for example, if I have a thought explicitly in English, we might say that I am both tokening a sentence and an act of predicating. In those cases, the very act of tokening the sentence may simultaneously amount to an act of predicating. As Soames puts it,

> *When an event is an instance of both a sentential and a propositional type, there is no extra inner event of "grasping the proposition" over and above using the sentence meaningfully.* So, when S expresses p, one who understands S can entertain p by tokening S. For some propositions, this may be our only feasible way of entertaining them. In such cases what distinguishes p from S is the *possibility* that an event could be an instance of one but not the other. More generally, the heretofore mysterious *expressing* relation holding between a sentence and a proposition may be grounded in something like the *by* relation that holds between two things that are done when an agent can do one of those things (entertaining the proposition) by doing the other (uttering or inscribing the sentence). (2013b, 23)

Fourth, the cognitive theory of propositions can help us solve several puzzling semantic phenomena, including the problem of substitution into hyperintensional contexts and the problem of de se propositions. I will go over Soames' treatment of the latter two puzzles in some detail, as my critique in subsequent sections will have some bearing on what he says about these examples. As examples of substitution into hyperintensional contexts, Soames presents the following pair of examples:

(3)
(a) Russell defended logicism
(b) Russell defended the proposition that arithmetic is reducible to logic.
(4)
(a) Mary believes that Russell defended logicism
(b) Mary believes that Russell defended the proposition that arithmetic is reducible to logic.

As 'logicism' is a proper name for the proposition that arithmetic is reducible to logic, the two expressions are necessarily equivalent, so the latter can be substituted for the former in 3(a) without a change in truth-value. But this is not the case in 4(a), because 'believe' is a hyperintensional operator, an operator that does not allow for substitution of necessarily equivalent propositions within its scope.

A good theory of propositions should be able to explain this substitution failure. Soames explains the above case as follows. Entertaining the embedded proposition in 4(a), for example, by believing it, requires possessing the name 'logicism' but does not require knowing its precise referent. So, a cognitive agent may be able to entertain and believe the embedded proposition in 4(a) but be unable to entertain and believe the embedded proposition in 4(b). Event types from which propositions derive can thus impose different conditions on the cognitive operations it takes to entertain them, even when the propositions are necessarily equivalent and what Soames calls 'representationally identical'; they are representationally identical 'in the sense that their truth conditions are derived from predicating the very same properties of the very same things' (2013b, 25).

Soames exemplifies the problem of de se propositions, also known as the 'problem of the essential indexical', using Perry's well-known example of the messy shopper.

> I once followed a trail of sugar on a supermarket floor, pushing my cart down the aisle on one side of a tall counter and back the aisle on the other, seeking the shopper with a torn sack to tell him he was making a mess. With each trip around the counter, the trail became thicker. But I seemed unable to catch up. Finally it dawned on me. I was the shopper I was trying to catch. (Perry 1979)

The problem is to explain what about Perry's belief changed when 'it dawned on him' that he was the messy shopper. All de se cases involve believing or asserting in a special first-person or immediate present tense way, whereas de re and de dicto cases involve believing or asserting in a neutral way. Perry argues that though it may seem that he comes to believe something new when it dawned on him that he was the messy shopper, this is not really the case. Rather, he comes to believe the old proposition in a new way. One of the best known alternatives to Perry's solution to the puzzle is Lewis' (1979) self-ascription theory. Lewis proposes a revisionary solution that consists in taking belief to be a self-ascription of a property, for example, the property of being the one who is making a mess as opposed to the property of being such that someone is making a mess. On this view, Perry does indeed come to believe something new when he finally figures out who is making a mess. Both theories leave something to be desired. Perry's doesn't preserve the intuition that Perry learns something new when he realizes that he is the one who is leaving the trail behind, and Lewis solves the problem only by making radical revisions to how we understand belief.

Soames proposes a different take on the problem that seems to avoid both of these drawbacks. According to him, Perry is performing different cognitive acts before and after the discovery. Before the discovery he is predicating the property of making a mess of the person who left the trail behind. After the discovery he is predicating the property of making a mess of himself. These are different cognitive acts resulting in instances of different propositions. Acts that result in instances of de se propositions place further requirements on the agent compared to acts that result in instances of de re and de dicto propositions. De se propositions are propositions that can only be entertained by an agent who thinks about them in the special first-person way. De se propositions, however, are representationally identical to de re propositions. Soames explains: 'Since these special ways of cognizing a predication target do not, for the reasons indicated above, involve any new predications of that target, the new propositions are representationally identical to ordinary de re propositions' (2013b, 34).

3. Two hidden assumptions

On Soames' view, a proposition receives its intentional properties from the cognitive operations (predicating, disjoining, conjoining, etc.) performed on its constituents by all the conceivable agents who perform these operations. Because it's a type of event rather than a token that is, or corresponds to, the proposition, individual differences in how the act is performed leave no marks on the proposition, except when the proposition is de se and hence can only be entertained by a single agent.

Soames makes clear that he treats the most basic cognitive operation, viz. that of predicating, as having similar logical properties as the relation of looking for. Graeme Forbes (2013) argues that search verbs like 'look for' are intensional transitives that are anomalous in that 'substituting one expression for another that is coreferential with it in the complement of the verb can change the truth-value of the sentence in which the VP occurs'. Lois Lane may be looking for Superman. But, Forbes argues, it does not follow that she is looking for Clark Kent, even though Superman is Clark Kent. By definition, necessarily co-extensional terms are co-substitutional in merely intensional contexts but not in hyperintensional contexts. So, on Forbes' treatment, search verbs are hyperintensional (Forbes

2003). According to Forbes, search verbs furthermore admit of 'a special "unspecific" reading if it contains a quantifier'. For example, Lois may be looking for an extraterrestrial, but no particular one. Finally, Forbes argues, 'the normal existential commitments of names and existential quantifiers in the complement are suspended'. Lois might be looking for the exit even if there isn't one. According to Forbes, there may or may not be different mechanisms underlying these three features.

Unlike Forbes, Soames appears to treat 'look for' as an intensional transitive that is not also hyperintensional and hence need not suspend existential commitment. He offers the following example:

> At this point, a word must be said about how I am using the verb 'predicate'. I begin here with the account previously given in *What is Meaning?* According to that account, the verb 'predicate' needed by the conception of propositions as cognitive-event types is analogous to the intensional transitive 'look for'. *If Bill is looking for Maria, and Maria is Mary, who, in turn, is the chief of police, then Bill is looking for Mary*, but it doesn't follow (on one reading) that he is looking for the chief of police [italics added] (2013b, 16).

Whereas co-extensional terms fail to be co-substitutional in both intensional and hyperintensional contexts, necessarily co-extensional terms are co-substitutional in intensional but not in hyperintensional contexts. As Soames holds that proper names are co-substitutional in intensional transitive 'look for' contexts, it follows that he treats names as necessarily co-extensional and 'look for' as an intensional but not a hyperintensional verb phrase. Necessarily co-extensional terms function the same way in extensional and merely intensional contexts. So, if 'look for' is merely intensional, as is entailed by Soames' view, then the normal existential commitments of proper names in the complement are not suspended.[1] The reason for this turns on the difference in the semantic values different operators operate on. Whereas extensional operators operate on referents, merely intensional operators operate on content. However, names that are necessarily co-extensional have their referents as their content. So, the normal existential commitments of proper names are not suspended when the operator is intensional but not hyperintensional.

Soames doesn't explain why he is treating 'predicating of' on the model of 'look for'. It might be because he wishes to preserve a relatively traditional semantic view of propositions, which leaves open the possibility of *modeling* propositions in terms of objects and properties. For example, the proposition that o is red can be modeled as the pair $<$ o, redness $>$. Here I use the expression 'model propositions' in the standard sense, also used by Soames. To model a proposition is to use a formal construction to represent certain target properties of propositions. Models of propositions need not, and typically do not, tell us anything about properties not being modeled.

Soames further assumes a Millian notion of proper names, according to which the content of a proper name is its referent. It is this feature that makes proper names necessarily co-extensional and therefore co-substitutional in 'look for' contexts, when the latter are treated as intensional but not hyperintensional. On the Millian view, proper names and their co-extensional descriptions turn out to have the same referents (or denotations) but different contents. For example, 'Superman' and 'the boring newspaper reporter who works at Daily Planet' have the same referents but different contents. The content of the former just is the referent, whereas the content of the latter is a descriptive complex.

These two assumptions, however, could be questioned. If propositions ultimately derive from the cognitive acts of agents, then the nature of the relation of predication probably is not something we can determine on a priori grounds. Rather, the nature of the cognitive acts of agents should determine what the logical properties of the predication relation are. Soames states that there probably isn't such a thing as 'bare predication' (Soames 2013c, 4). Rather, predicating is one of the acts agents perform when they engage in cognitive events like perceiving, believing, asserting, judging, etc. Judging and believing, for example, involve predicating and assenting, and perhaps other mental doings as well. It could very well be that when we look closer at these cognitive events, the act of predicating involved in these events does not have the logical properties that Soames assumes that it does. It could be that when we truly say that we believe that o is F, the act of predicating involved consists in an operation on the Kaplanian character of 'F' and the Kaplanian character of 'o'. Or more realistically: It could turn out that agents predicate properties of mental representations of things. For example, if I think that Soames is a philosopher, then it might be that my thought involves predicating *being a philosopher* of whatever is depicted in a mental image I happen to have of someone who looks like Soames. If these acts of predicating turned out to be integral elements of beliefs and thoughts that we express using proper names, then either 'predicating of' should not be treated on the model of 'look for' (as Soames appears to read it) or we should question the second assumption.

The second assumption, viz. that the content of proper names are their referents, plays a role in how we understand the act of predicating, even assuming the logical properties Soames attributes to the predication relation. According to Soames, one can think of an object o simply by possessing a name for it, without knowing much about its referent (Soames 2013b, 23). So, I can predicate wisdom of Socrates by possessing the name 'Socrates' and then performing a certain cognitive operation. Because 'predicating of' is treated on the model of 'look for', predication is an operation on content. As the content of a Millian proper name is its referent, predicating wisdom of Socrates is an operation on an object, given the logical properties Soames attributes to the relation. If, however, one were to deny the assumption that proper names are Millian, this wouldn't automatically follow. If proper names had descriptive content, then predicating wisdom of Socrates would be an operation on descriptive content, not objects.

There are, of course, good arguments in the literature for thinking that proper names are Millian proper names. But many of those presuppose that we have already settled on what propositions are. Kripke's modal argument is familiar (Kripke 1980). Consider, for instance:

(5)
(a) Socrates is the teacher of Plato
(b) The teacher of Plato is the teacher of Plato

5(a) and 5(b) have different modal profiles: 5(a) expresses a proposition that is contingently true, whereas (5b) expresses a proposition that is necessarily true. Since 5(a) and 5(b) have different modal profiles, they have different contents. This shows that 'Socrates' and 'the teacher of Plato' cannot have the same content. Or so the argument goes.

This is a powerful argument, given a certain understanding of propositions as being both the bearers of modal properties and the entities expressed by utterances. Suppose, however, that it turns out that propositions are noncompositional assertoric contents, and that modal operators operate on compositional semantic values rather than assertoric contents (Stalnaker 1970, Lewis 1980, Salmon 1986, 1989; Dummett 1991, chap. 9; Stanley 1997a, 1997b; King 2003; Brogaard 2012, chap. 6). Then the modal profile of 5(a) and 5(b) that our intuitions track may well be a property of the compositional semantic values rather than a property of the assertoric content, in which case the modal argument is unsound. What this example is teaching us is that we cannot assume a particular theory of proper names prior to offering a theory of propositions. Given a cognitive theory of propositions, the nature of the content of proper names will turn out to depend on what the cognitive operations from which the intentionality of propositions derives are like.

Maintaining the two assumptions, in fact, does Soames a disservice. One of the advantages of his theory is that it solves certain semantic puzzles. But the solution to these puzzles is one-sided. It solves puzzles about beliefs that involve substituting a name for a description in a belief context. But it doesn't solve puzzles about belief that involve substituting one proper name for another. Consider:

(6)
(a) Lois Lane believes Superman can fly
(b) Lois Lane believes Clark Kent can fly

The puzzle here is to explain why 6(a) and 6(b) have different truth-values, if 'Superman' and 'Clark Kent' have the same content. The puzzle in 4(a)-(b) was solved because Mary might be able to predicate *being defended by Russell* of logicism without knowing that 'logicism' is a name for the proposition that arithmetic is reducible to logic. The two acts of predicating (i.e., predicating *being defended by Russell* of logicism and predicating that property of the view that arithmetic is reducible to logic) impose different constraints on the agent. Owing to these constraints, Mary might be able to perform one but not the other. But it is not clear that Soames can, or would want to, say something similar with respect to 6(a)-(b). On Soames' view, the act of predicating involved in believing that Superman can fly is an operation that predicates *being able to fly* of Superman, an external object. But Superman is Clark Kent. So this very operation of predicating *being able to fly* of Superman, then, also is an act of predicating *being able to fly* of Clark Kent. Furthermore, if Lois Lane assents to the instance of the proposition that results from that cognitive act, then she assents to both the proposition that Superman can fly and the proposition that Clark Kent can fly. So, Soames' theory predicts that 6(a) and 6(b) have the same truth-values, which clashes with most people's intuitions. If Soames had not made the assumption that proper names are Millian, he might have used his theory to explain the difference in truth-value in this case as well.

Another semantic puzzle which Soames' theory only partially avoids is the puzzle of empty names. Soames can explain why an agent can perform the act of predicating wisdom of the King of France, despite the fact that the King of France does not exist. This can be done because 'predicating of' is an intensional (but not hyperintensional) transitive, according to Soames. As 'the King of France' is a description, and intensional transitives operate on content rather than referents, there is something there to predicate wisdom of, viz. the descriptive complex *the King of France*. But Soames' theory cannot explain the many instances of empty names that purport to function as genuine proper names. Soames' own example is that of predicating *being a planet* of Vulcan (e.g., involved in the thought accompanying Urbain Le Verrier's utterance 'Vulcan is a planet'). Soames argues that since Vulcan doesn't exist, the cognitive act of predicating *being a planet* of Vulcan cannot be performed or it is incomplete in some way. This seems rather unsatisfactory. An agent who doesn't know that Vulcan doesn't exists and who has a good deal of scientific information about it appears to undergo perfectly complete cognitive events involving Vulcan, including believing, judging, asserting, etc., all events involving the act of predicating. Here Soames' claim that the act of predicating *being a planet* of Vulcan cannot be performed or is incomplete is clearly driven by the prior assumption that proper names are Millian. A more natural thing to do in this case would be to note that agents do engage in these cognitive events involving things that do not exist and then infer from that either that predicating is not an operation of the kind assumed in Soames' work or that proper names are not Millian.

The two assumptions prevent a solution to a host of other semantic puzzles. Here I will look at two puzzles related to each other as well as to the puzzle of belief, viz. the problem of cognitive significance and the problem of the contingent a priori. Consider:

(7)
(a) Hesperus is Hesperus
(b) Hesperus is Phosphorus

The problem here is to explain why 7(b) appears to be more informative than 7(a) if they express the same proposition. 7(a) is a priori in the sense that once one possesses the name 'Hesperus', it does not take any further engagement with one's environment to figure out that the proposition it expresses is true. But 7(b) is a posteriori in the sense that possessing the names 'Hesperus' and 'Phosporus' does not suffice for figuring out that it expresses a true proposition.

The related problem of the contingent a priori can be illustrated using the following example:

(8) Julius invented the zip (if someone did)

If 'Julius' is a genuine proper name introduced via the description 'the inventor of the zip', then (8) is a priori. If, on the other hand, the 'Julius' is acquired in a standard causal-historical way, then (8) is a posteriori. However, on most traditional views of propositions, (8) expresses the same proposition regardless of how the name is acquired. The problem is to explain how we can stand in different epistemic relations to one and the same proposition.

Given the assumptions Soames makes, it is not clear how the cognitive theory of propositions could solve these puzzles. In the first case, the act of predicating *being Hesperus* of Hesperus is the same act as that of predicating *being Phosporus* of Hesperus, because 'Hesperus' and 'Phosphorus' are proper names (or at least we can treat them as such), and when proper names are involved, the act of predicating predicates properties of objects. In the second case, things are similar. If 'Julius' is a genuine proper name, then there is only one act of predicating that produces an instance of the proposition that Julius invented the zip. So, it remains to be seen how we can stand in different epistemic relations to the act. If Soames' theory does offer an explanation of the epistemic differences in the two cases, he hasn't yet shown us what it is.

It should be emphasized that the problems with Soames' proposal that I have presented in this section are largely due to the reading Soames appears to attribute to 'look for' and hence to 'predicating of'. If Soames were to adopt Forbes' reading of 'look for' for the case of 'predicating of', my objections would be moot. Forbes' reading requires a semantics of the kind I am outlining at the end of the paper. So, the semantic proposal at the end can be understood as treating 'predicating of' as a hyperintensional transitive.

4. Traditional semantics and empirical evidence

Although I disagree about the details of Soames' new proposal, I agree that propositions derive their intentionality from agents who are engaged in representing things to be a certain way by performing cognitive operations like that of predicating. I also agree that propositions derive their intentionality from agents because they are (or are the result of) act types of predicating. However, I don't think that we can, or should, say much about the nature of the act of predicating prior to empirical investigation. If, indeed, propositions derive their intentionality from agents, then the common nature of cognitive operations and what they operate on ought to be determined empirically in cross-disciplinary work in, for example, perception, cognition, language production and language comprehension.

The main type of evidence for linguistic theories in philosophy of language and theoretical linguistics has traditionally consisted in two types of intuitions. Primary intuitions are introspective judgments about the acceptability or plausibility of a given linguistic expression, discourse fragment or inference. Secondary intuitions are introspective judgments explicitly about what a given linguistic expression refers to, what an utterance expresses or whether an inference is valid, or why the language works in those ways. Secondary intuitions are also sometimes called 'metalinguistic', because they are judgments explicitly about grammaticality, meaning and reference (Martí 2009). Primary intuitions, when collected carefully and systematically, constitute a much more robust kind of evidence for linguistic theories than secondary intuitions (Wasow and Arnold 2005). This is because unlike secondary intuitions, primary intuitions reflect how speakers use, or would use, an expression, and actual and potential language use fully determines meaning and reference. Of course, even when primary intuitions are collected carefully and systematically, they should not be considered a kind of irrefutable evidence, especially since even primary intuitions can vary considerably across speakers, perhaps partially because even this type of intuition can be difficult to access introspectively. However, in core cases at least we can hope to find some convergence in the primary judgments of speakers. Primary intuitions, of course, should not ultimately be the only kind of evidence for our theories. This type of evidence must eventually be supplemented by evidence from the cognitive sciences, which have used a range of different paradigms for testing cognitively-based semantic hypotheses, including reaction-time experiments, sentence completion tasks, eye-tracking, and neuroimaging. It is important to note, however, that the other types of evidence often incorporate reports of participants' primary intuitions (see e.g. Woodbury 2011).

In philosophy of language secondary intuitions have often been given more credit than primary intuitions. Secondary intuitions are typically used in verdicts about cases. The verdicts that are required in Kripke's Gödel case, for example, are not about the acceptability of sentences or inferences but about which person the name 'Gödel' refers to in a hypothetical scenario. Philosophers of language typically rely on their own secondary intuitions about this or similar cases to support their theories. It is also primarily philosophers' reliance on secondary intuitions that has been criticized by experimental philosophers (see e.g., Machery et al. 2004). Sometimes primary intuitions are explicitly set aside or ignored in order to give credit to secondary intuitions. A good example of this is the case of belief contexts. A lot of effort has gone into explaining why substituting one proper name for another in belief contexts seems unacceptable to many lay speakers when traditional semantics predicts that it should be valid. Primary intuitions have thus been set aside in favor of secondary intuitions in an effort to preserve the basics of traditional semantics. It is not difficult to see how philosophers taught to cherish a neo-Russellian account of propositions, which combines the Russellian account with a Millian theory of proper names, might be tempted to rely on this kind of methodology.

The cognitive theory has a major advantage compared to the neo-Russellian theory in this regard. The neo-Russellian theory of propositions has the answer to questions of reference and meaning built into it. The cognitive theory by its very nature demands empirical investigation as the only plausible way to settle questions about meaning and reference. If necessary, it could even accommodate significant inter- and intra-cultural differences in the cognitive acts of agents by sorting cognitive acts into cognitive subtypes.

If standard semantics is not empirically valid (or at least has not been shown to be), then the question arises what might take its place? We don't know yet. But if we look at the primary intuitions about the validity of inferences in ordinary language, the semantics that must accompany a cognitive theory of propositions will in all likelihood be radically different from the traditional framework. Though I hesitate to make any firm conclusions about what a correct semantics involving cognitive act types will look like once we look at a broader range of evidence, I will attempt to offer a semantic model of cognitive act types in the next section, relying on primary intuitions about cases.

5. A semantics for cognitive propositions

If we want to preserve the primary intuitions about cases outlined in the previous sections, it is clear that none of the standard ways of modeling propositions, or cognitive act types, is going to work. Consider first the suggestion that propositions can be modeled as intensions. The intension of an expression can be thought of as a function from worlds to extensions; it assigns, at each world, an extension to the expression. 'p' and 'q' express the same proposition iff they share a truth-value at every world. At first glance, this suggestion may seem to be ruled out by Soames' theory, as he states that possible world states conceptually depend on truth, propositions, and our ordinary modal notions (Soames 2013c). However, we can do without worlds altogether and construe intensions in terms of admissible extension-assignments, or interpretations. Typically, admissible extensions-assignments (for all the expressions) are precisely those that

(i) respect the classical valuation (truth) conditions for the logical constants and operators ($\sim$, &, $\forall$, $=$, $\Box$, etc.), and
(ii) agree with the actual extensions of every name.

Let's call these the *normal* interpretations (or normal extension-assignments).

The intension of an expression, then, is a function from normal interpretations to extensions. The intension of a given name is, by convention, a constant function from normal interpretations to the same individual. The intension of a predicate is a function from normal interpretations to sets of individuals. The intension of a whole sentence is a function from normal interpretations to truth-values. 'p' and 'q' express the same proposition iff they are assigned the same truth-values at every normal interpretation.

But intensions, of course, are not fine-grained enough to preserve even basic intuitions. If an agent A predicates evenness of the number 16, and another agent B predicates humanity of Socrates, they perform instances of very different act types of predicating. But if propositions are modeled on intensions, then there is only one necessary proposition and only one impossible proposition. So, this model wrongly predicts that A and B are performing instances of the same cognitive act type. Propositions modeled as intensions also lead to an inverted relations collapse and a collapse of certain contingent logically equivalent claims. For example, 'a is taller than b' and 'b is shorter than a' are strictly equivalent, as are 'p' and 'p & (q v ~ q)'.

Another traditional proposal is to model propositions as structured intensions. There are several ways to do this. One natural proposal is to define a notion of a structured extension for sentences. Structured extensions are based on extensions. Different types of expressions have different types of extensions, as illustrated below:[2]

Expressions	Their Extensions
Names, type e	individuals
Predicates, type < e,t >	sets of individuals
Sentences, type t	truth values

Instead of taking the extension of a sentence to be a truth-value, we can take extensions of sentences to be composed of the extensions of the sentence's parts. Let the structured extension of a sentence be the n-tuple that represents the set of extension-assignments to the sentence parts that are ordinarily assigned extensions. The following specifies the structured extensions for three types of sentences:[3]

Sentence	Sentence Structure	Structured Extension
'Al sits'	< a, S_, Sa >	< Al, set of sitters, true >
'2 equals 2':	< a, a, a = a >	< 2, 2, true >
'p implies p':	< p, p, p → p >	< false, false, true >

The structured intension of a sentence is a function from (normal) interpretations to structured extensions. Given this notion of a structured intension, we can say that two sentences, 'p' and 'q', express the same proposition iff they share a structured intension. This is equivalent to saying that 'p' and 'q' express the same proposition iff 'p' and 'q' share a structured extension on every (normal) interpretation.

This proposal avoids the problem outlined above. Since '2 = 2' and 'snow is white → snow is white' are necessarily co-extensional, they express the same unstructured intension. But because they do not have the same isomorphic structures, they express different structured intensions. So it will not generally be the case that strictly equivalent sentences express the same proposition.

However, this proposal cannot deal with the problems of cognitive significance and the contingent a priori. Consider again:

(7)
(a) Hesperus is Hesperus
(b) Hesperus is Phosphorus

The problem was this. Intuitively, 7(a) is less informative than 7(b); it's not just that an ordinary agent could believe the former without believing the latter, but there is also a sense in which the latter expresses something that is richer than the former.

Modeling act types as structured intensions cannot accommodate this intuition. As 7(a) and 7(b) have the same grammatical structure, *normal* interpretations assign the same extensions to the sentence's parts. Furthermore, *normal* interpretations always assign the same individuals to 'Hesperus' and 'Phosphorus'. So, 7(a) and 7(b) express the same proposition (qua structured intension), not a satisfactory result. Not only does believing one imply believing the other, but we also haven't uncovered a sense in which 7(b) is *more informative* than 7(a).

The related problem of the contingent a priori can be summarized as follows. Consider the following sentence, repeated from above.

(8) Julius invented the zip (if someone did)

If 'Julius' is introduced via the description 'the inventor of the zip', (8) is a priori. If, on the other hand, the name is acquired in a standard causal-historical way, then (8) is a posteriori. However, in each case, (8) has the same structured intension. So, this semantic framework has nothing to say about how to explain the epistemic difference between the two cases.

A further problem is provided by hyperintensional contexts. Some hyperintensional sentences 'O[p]' are special in that they can be true, even though there is no normal interpretation that makes 'p' true. Not all hyperintensional expressions work in this way. For example, 'Lois Lane believes Superman can fly' is hyperintensional but there is an actual normal interpretation that makes 'Superman can fly' true (within the story). But there is no normal interpretation that makes the following embedded sentences true.

(9)
(a) John entertained the possibility that $\sim(p \rightarrow p)$.
(b) John wanted it to be the case that a $\neq$ a.
(c) John said that a $\neq$ a.
(d) According to fiction F, a $\neq$ a.

(e) It's not the case that (if *a* had failed to be identical to *a*, then 'a = a' would have been true). [where the context is ' ~ (□→ q)'.]

It is not clear how any framework in terms of logically possible worlds or *normal* interpretations can provide a framework for explaining these contexts. The only option that seems to be left as a semantic model that captures our primary intuitions about cases is one that introduces the notion of a structured hyperintension. The hyperintension of an expression can be thought of as a function from possible and impossible worlds to extensions (Brogaard and Salerno 2013). Without invoking worlds-talk, the hyperintension of an expression can be thought of as assigning an extension from each normal or non-normal interpretation. For example, the hyperintension of 'Hesperus' maps the normal interpretations to Venus, but it may map the non-normal interpretations to some other object, and the hyperintension of 'Hesperus is Hesperus' maps normal interpretations to True, but may map non-normal interpretations to False (even if the non-normal interpretation assigns Venus to 'Hesperus'). An interpretation is non-normal either by (i) failing to respect the valuation conditions for the logical constants, or (ii) failing to agree with the normal interpretations on the extension of some name.

The logical constants and operators that occur in a sentence are defined only for normal interpretations by convention. So, they always get assigned a normal extension even on non-normal interpretations. Hyperintensional models for non-indexical sentences of the language will be n-tuples, M = <D, I, R>, consisting of a domain, a set of normal and non-normal interpretations and a binary relation on I, outlined as follows:

D = a domain of actual objects (to serve as normal and non-normal extensions)
I = a set of normal and non-normal interpretations assigning extensions to all the expressions (names, predicates and whole sentences). One interpretation, $i^@$, is the distinguished interpretation, and can be thought of as the actual assignment of extensions to the expressions. The normal interpretations, i, respect the valuation conditions (are compositional) and agree with $i^@$ on the extensions of all the names. The non-normal interpretations either violate the valuation conditions or disagree with $i^@$ on the extension of some name.
R = a binary relation on I. Specifically, it characterizes which normal and non-normal interpretations are admissible relative to a given normal interpretation

To deal with the indexicality involved in de se propositions we'll need further resources. Let interpretations be assignments at a centered point, viz. a world w, a time t, an individual i and a demonstration of an object d. A normal interpretation then assigns the individual i at the distinguished point to 'I', the time t at the distinguished point to 'now', the location of i at the distinguished point to 'here' and the object demonstrated at the distinguished point to 'this' and 'that'. A non-normal interpretation may assign arbitrary extensions to indexicals and demonstratives. This explains why it is possible for me to believe that I am not Brit. Some of my belief-worlds are non-normal interpretations. They assign Brit to 'Brit' but someone other than Brit to 'I'.

The valuation conditions for any 'universal' (hyper)intensional operator h can be given as follows.

$\Box^h$, $\Box^h F\phi$ is true just in case at every h-admissible interpretation i, i assigns True to ϕ.

Here are some examples:

(10)
(a) 'It is metaphysically necessary that ϕ' is true iff at every normal interpretation i, i assigns True to ϕ.
(b) 'It is a priori that ϕ' is true iff at every ideally conceivable interpretation i, i assigns True to ϕ.
(c) 'It is believed that ϕ' is true iff i assigns True to ϕ at every doxastically admissible interpretation i.

An example of an ideally conceivable interpretation that is not normal is the assignment of XYZ to 'water'. Every normal interpretation assigns H_2O to 'water' but empirical discoveries aside it is epistemically possible that 'water' is XYZ. Likewise, if all I know and believe about Violette Szabo is that she is a famous female spy and I don't have any spy-beliefs about Michelle or Barack Obama, then a non-normal but doxastically admissible interpretation with respect to my belief set is one that assigns Michelle Obama as an extension to 'Violette Szabo'. An assignment of Barack Obama to 'Violette Szabo', however, is inadmissible.

As noted above, the logical constants and operations are only defined for normal interpretations by linguistic convention, and therefore always get assigned a normal extension. So, 'every S is P entails that some S is P' is false on all interpretations. But consider now the following sentence:

(11) Bert believes that *every S is P* entails that *some S is P*

If the embedded sentence is false on all interpretations, how do we account for the potential truth of (11)? Here is how. (11) can be true, because there is a non-normal, doxastically permissible interpretation that assigns the truth-value True to *every S is P entails that some S is P*, regardless of which truth-values are assigned to *every S is P* and *some S is P*. If Bert irrationally believes that every S is P, disbelieves that some S is P and believes that *every S is P* entails *some S is P*, then the only doxastically permissible interpretations are those that assign True to *every S is P*, False to *some S is P*, and True to *every S is P entails that some S is P*.

On the hyperintensional semantics outlined here, 'p' and 'q' express the same cognitive act type (proposition) if and only if they are assigned the same structured extension on every normal and non-normal interpretation. For example, 'The article was written by Russell' and 'Russell wrote the article' are assigned the same structured extension on every normal and non-normal interpretation. Since not all strictly equivalent sentences express the same hyperintension, it should be clear that propositions are sufficiently fine-grained to do at least as well as structured intensions with respect to the problem of necessarily equivalent sentences.

But the proposed semantics is also equipped to deal with the problems of cognitive significance and the contingent a priori. 7(a) 'Hesperus is Hesperus' and 7(b) 'Hesperus is Phosphorus' express different structured hyperintensions, because all interpretations assign the same object to the two occurrences of 'Hesperus' in 7(a) but some of the non-normal interpretations assign different objects to the occurrences of 'Hesperus' and 'Phosphorus' in 7(b). This is why it is possible for someone to believe 7(a) but not 7(b). Moreover, 7(b) expresses something more informative than 7(a) in the sense that there are more distinct non-normal ways to interpret 7(b) and its components. Consequently, learning 7(b) 'rules out' more interpretations.

As an example of a contingent a priori sentence consider again:

(8) Julius invented the zip (if someone did)

If 'Julius' is a proper name, then (8) expresses the same structured hyperintension regardless of how the referent of 'Julius' is fixed. The proposition, however, may vary its epistemic status across contexts. If 'Julius' is stipulated to name the inventor of the zip (if there is one), then (8) is a priori. In the other case, it is a posteriori. The reason for this has to do with the nature of the epistemic modal operators. Certain non-normal interpretations of 'p' and its parts are ruled out when it is a priori that p. Interpretations that yield False for (8) are not a priori-admissible (ideally conceivable). For example, an assignment of Julius to 'Julius' and Scott Soames to 'invented the zip' is inadmissible. This is not so in the a posteriori case.

The model of proposition in terms of hyperintensions also provides a way to deal with hyperintensional contexts. Consider:

(12)
(a) John felt that $\sim(p \rightarrow p)$
(b) According to fiction F, $a \neq a$.

In 12(a), the John-felt-that-admissible interpretations include, say, an interpretation of 'p' as True and 'p $\rightarrow$ p' as False. In 12(b) the Fiction-F-admissible interpretations might include the non-normal assignment of the number 1 to 'a' and False to 'a = a'.

Finally, the present semantic framework allows that sentences containing proper names that refer to things that do not exist can express complete propositions. Consider:

(13) Vulcan is a planet

If propositions are structured hyperintensions, then there is no assumption to the effect that the only admissible extension-assignments are the actual referent of the name. While normal extension-assignments will be undefined, non-normal extension-assignments will assign existing entities to 'Vulcan'. So, the sentence will express a proposition that is a function from non-normal extension-assignments to extensions. This proposition, of course, is false.

A problem reminiscent of the original problem of empty names remains. Any sentence that results from substituting an "empty proper name" for Vulcan will express the same proposition, which may seem unintuitive. However, this is only a real problem for semantic frameworks that do not have a way of offering an adequate account of belief contexts. Consider:

(14)
(a) Urbain Le Verrier believes that Vulcan is a planet
(b) Scott Soames believes that Vulcan is a planet

Whereas traditional semantics predicts that 14(a)-(b) have the same truth-value (false), the present semantics predicts that they have different truth-values. As Urbain Le Verrier engaged in cognitive acts of believing that predicated *being a planet* of Vulcan, the only admissible (non-normal) assignments to 'Vulcan' are planets. So, 14(a) comes out true. As Soames has no belief involving Vulcan, there are no admissible assignments of an extension to 'Vulcan'.[4] So, 14(b) and its negation are false.

This semantics for cognitive act types (propositions) yields extremely fine-grained act types. For example, it predicts that the act of predicating *being Phosporus* of Hesperus and the act of predicating *being Hesperus* of Hesperus are different types of acts of predicating. But this is just the result we want. While some agents who perform these acts of predicating know that Hesperus is identical to Phosphorus, others do not. The act *types* abstract away from these individual differences and preserve only what the acts performed by actual and conceivable agents have in common, which means that we abstract away from the fact that some agents know that Hesperus is Phosphorus. So, at the abstract level of the *type* the two acts of predicating are distinct types of acts.

The feeling that we might have that the semantics makes act types too fine-grained further diminishes once we consider sentences embedded in hyperintensional contexts. Consider:

(15) Scott Soames believes Hesperus is Phosphorus

'Hesperus is Phosphorus' expresses an extremely fine-grained act type that encompasses the tokens of all conceivable agents. But once this sentence is embedded under 'Scott Soames believes' its admissible interpretations are narrowed down by Soames' belief set. Since Soames knows (and hence believes) that Hesperus is Phosporus, there is no admissible interpretation that assigns different extensions to 'Hesperus' and 'Phosphorus'. So, this particular belief context is not hyperintensional. This is another virtue of the semantics: It predicts that cognitive event types relativized to different individuals, such as *Soames-believings* and *Wedgwood-believings*, can come apart.

6. Conclusion

On Soames' new cognitive theory of propositions, the intentionality of propositions is derived from the intentionality of agents. It's agents who most fundamentally represent things as being a certain way. When agents represent, their acts of predicating (or cognizing) thereby become representational, and it's the intentionality of the act of predicating (e.g., predicating redness of o) and other mental operations that explain the intentionality of the event token and event types (e.g., seeing that o is red). Propositions just are the act type of predicating together with other types of cognitive operations, such as conjoining, disjoining, negating, etc. Even though propositions are ultimately derived from the mental doings of agents, Soames' framework may seem to allow us to *model* propositions in the standard way as n-tuples of objects and properties. I have argued, however, that Soames gets this result only by illicitly assuming (i) that the relation of predicating is an intensional but not a hyperintensional transitive and (ii) that proper names are Milliam. Both claims are unargued for and seem to presuppose a particular conception of propositions as n-tuples of objects and properties. But this presupposition is not valid, given a cognitive theory of propositions. I then briefly examined what can count as evidence for the nature of the constituents of the cognitive operation types that produce propositions and argued that the common nature of cognitive operations and what they operate on ought to be determined empirically in cross-disciplinary work in perception, cognition, language production and language comprehension. I concluded by offering a semantics for cognitive act types that accommodates one type of empirical evidence.[5]

Notes

1. It seems that Forbes would largely agree that if co-substitution of necessarily co-extensional terms is permissible, then we do not get the unspecific reading, and the existential commitments are normal. According to him, search verbs (e.g., 'look for'), depiction verbs (e.g., 'draw') and desire verbs are anomalous in all three ways. Evaluative verbs (e.g., 'admire') and emotion verbs (e.g., 'fear') are anomalous in the first and third way but do not typically have an unspecific reading. 'Need' as well as transaction verbs (e.g., 'owe') are atypical in that they allow for certain types of substitution but not others.
2. This, of course, could be extended to other types of expressions. For example, quantifier expressions can be treated as second-order predicates, or type $\ll e, t \gg$, $\ll e, t >$, $t \gg$, denoting relations between sets of individuals.
3. The extension of the whole sentence is taken to be a constituent of the structured extension. This move is redundant for structured intensions but will become important when we look at structured hyperintensions.
4. Of course, it could also be the case that Soames' belief set includes a belief that involves a descriptive name 'Vulcan' that is equivalent to something like 'the planet Urbain Le Verrier thought existed on the basis of peculiarities of Mercury's orbit'. In that case he might hold a belief to the effect that Vulcan doesn't exist.
5. I am grateful to David Hunter and Gurpreet Rattan for helpful comments on a previous version of this paper.

References

Brogaard, B. 2006. "The 'Gray's Elegy' Argument, and the Prospects for the Theory of Denoting Concepts." *Synthese* 152: 47–79.

Brogaard, B. 2012. *Transient Truths: An Essay in the Metaphysics of Propositions*. New York: Oxford University Press.

Brogaard, B., and J. Salerno. 2013. "Remarks on Counterpossibles." *Synthese* 190 (4): 639–660.

Dummett, M. 1991. *The Logical Basis of Metaphysics*. Cambridge, MA: Harvard University Press.

Forbes, G. 2003. "Verbs of creation and depiction: More events in the semantics of English.", Manuscript.

Forbes, G. 2013. "Intensional Transitive Verbs." In *The Stanford Encyclopedia of Philosophy*, edited by E. N. Zalta, Available at<http://plato.stanford.edu/archives/fall 2013/entries/intensional-trans-verbs/>. (Fall 2013 Edition).

Frege, G. 1892a. "Uber Sinn and Bedeutung." *Zeitschrift fur Philosophie und Philosophische Kritik* 100: 25–50.

Frege, G. 1892b. "On Concept and Object." *Vierteljahrsschrift fur wissenschaftliche Philosophie* 16: 192–205.

Frege, G. 1918. "Der Gedanke." *Beitrage zur Philosophie des deutschen Idealismus*, *1*. Translated by A Quinton and M. Quinton as "The Thought". *Mind* 1956 (65): 289–311.

King, J. C. 2003. "Tense, Modality, and Semantic Values." *Philosophical Perspectives* 17: 195–246.

Kripke, S. 1980. *Naming and Necessity*. Cambridge, MA: Harvard University Press.

Lewis, D. 1979. "Attitudes De Dicto and De Se." *The Philosophical Review* 88: 513–543.

Lewis, D. 1980. "Index, context and content." In *Papers on Philosophical Logic*, 1998 21–44. Cambridge: Cambridge University Press.

Machery, E., Mallon, R., Nichols, S., & Stich, SP. 2004. "Semantics, cross-cultural style." *Cognition* 92: B1–B12.

Martî, G. 2009. "Against semantic multi-culturalism." *Analysis* 69: 42–48.

Perry, J. 1979. "The Problem of the Essential Indexical." *Noûs* 13 (1): 3–21.

Russell, B. 1903. *The Principles of Mathematics*. New York: Norton.

Russell, B. 1905. "On Denoting." *Mind* 14: 479–493.

Russell, B. 1983-present. *Collected Papers*, The Bertrand Russell Editorial Project.

Salmon, N. 1986. *Frege's Puzzle*. Cambridge, MA: The MIT Press.

Salmon, N. 1989. "Tense and Singular Propositions." In *Themes From Kaplan*, edited by J. Almog, J. Perry, and H. Wettstein, 331–392. New York: Oxford University Press.

Soames, S. 2010. *What is Meaning?* Princeton: Princeton University Press.

Soames, S. 2012. "Propositions." In *Routledge Companion to the Philosophy of Language*, edited by D. Graff Fara, and G. Russell, 209–220. Routledge: New York.

Soames, S. 2013a. "Why the Traditional Conceptions of Propositions can't be Correct." In *New Thinking about Propositions*, edited by J. King, S. Soames, and J. Speaks. Oxford: Oxford University Press.

Soames, S. 2013b. "A Cognitive Theory of Propositions." In *New Thinking about Propositions*, edited by J. King, S. Soames, and J. Speaks. Oxford: Oxford University Press.
Soames, S. 2013c. "Clarifying and Improving the Cognitive Theory to Meet its Explanatory Burden." In *New Thinking about Propositions*, edited by J. King, S. Soames, and J. Speaks. Oxford: Oxford University Press.
Soames, S. 2013d. "For Want of Cognitively Defined Propositions." In To appear in *Act Based Conceptions of Propositional Content: Historical and Contemporary Perspectives*, edited by Moltmann Arapinis, and Textor.
Stalnaker, R. 1970. "Pragmatics." *Synthese* 22 (1–2): 272–289.
Stanley, J. 1997a. "Names and Rigid Designation." In *A Companion to the Philosophy of Language*, edited by B. Hale, and C. Wright, 555–585. Oxford: Blackwell Publishers.
Stanley, J. 1997b. "Rigidity and Content." In *Logic, Language and Reality: Essays in Honor of Michael Dummett*, edited by R. Heck, 131–156. Oxford: Oxford University Press.
Wasow, T., and J. Arnold. 2005. "Intuitions in Linguistic Argumentation." *Lingua* 115: 1481–1496.
Woodbury, R. 2011. *Behavioral and Neural Correlates of Deep and Surface Anaphora*, Doctoral Dissertation, Harvard University–MIT Division of Health Sciences and Technology.

ON ACT- AND LANGUAGE-BASED CONCEPTIONS OF PROPOSITIONS

What are the primary bearers of truth?

Peter Hanks

Department of Philosophy, University of Minnesota, Minneapolis, MN, USA

According to the traditional account of propositional content, propositions are the primary bearers of truth. Here I argue that acts of predication are the primary bearers of truth. Propositions are types of these actions, and they inherit their truth-conditions from their tokens. Against this, many philosophers think that it is a category mistake to say that actions are true or false. Furthermore, even if we grant that token acts of predication have truth-conditions, there are reasons for doubting that types of these actions also have truth-conditions. I respond to these objections in this paper. I also clarify what it means for propositions to *inherit* truth-conditions from token acts of predication.

1. Introduction

According to a traditional and widely held conception of propositional content, propositions are the primary bearers of truth. This is an explanatory claim. Propositions are the primary bearers of truth in the sense that when we explain why something else has truth-conditions we appeal to the truth-conditions of a proposition. The sentence 'Snow is white' is true iff snow is white because this sentence expresses the proposition that snow is white, and this proposition is true iff snow is white. Someone's assertion that snow is white is true iff snow is white because the speaker asserted the proposition that snow is white, and this proposition is true iff snow is white. To accept this traditional account is to treat propositions as a source of truth-conditions. Anything else that has truth-conditions, such as a sentence, assertion or belief, does so because of a relationship it bears to a proposition.

This conception of propositional content immediately leads to questions about whether it is possible to explain how propositions themselves have truth-conditions. This is the problem of the unity of the proposition – the problem of explaining how propositions have truth-conditions and other representational properties. Neither Frege nor Russell, the philosophers most responsible for the traditional account, were capable of solving this problem. Both tried to explain how propositions are unified into representational wholes by appealing to relationships between the internal constituents of propositions. So, for Frege, a name-sense *saturates* a predicate-sense in a thought, and for Russell a relation *relates* objects in a proposition. But saturation is mysterious and unhelpful, and Russell's relations-that-relate lead to intractable problems about false propositions.[1] A natural reaction to these difficulties is to abandon the search for an explanation for the truth-conditions of propositions. Perhaps it is a brute, unexplainable fact that propositions are bearers of truth-conditions. But this makes our explanations for the truth-conditions of sentences, assertions, and judgments utterly unsatisfying. If we find it puzzling how a sentence or assertion or judgment has truth-conditions it is no help at all to be told that it bears a certain relation to a proposition, and the proposition is a primitive bearer of truth-conditions. Whatever philosophical puzzlement we felt about the truth-conditions of the sentence or assertion or judgment will simply transfer over to the proposition. Taking propositions to be primitive bearers of truth-conditions sheds no philosophical light on how our sentences, mental states, and speech acts have truth-conditions.

In this paper I am going to argue that the primary bearers of truth-conditions are actions that subjects perform in thinking and speaking about the world. More specifically, they are acts of predication, in which, in the simplest cases, subjects attribute properties and relations to objects. Someone performs an act of predication when she judges that a is F or when she asserts that a is F. These actions are the proper source of truth-conditions. Propositions are types of these actions, and they owe their truth-conditions to them. This reverses the explanatory order of the traditional account. Instead of judgments and assertions deriving truth-conditions from propositions, propositions derive their truth-conditions from our acts of judging and asserting. The proper role for propositions is not to explain how our mental states and speech acts have their truth-conditions. Rather, propositions are types we use for the purposes of characterizing, individuating, and classifying the acts we perform in thought and speech.

To say this is not to adopt an instrumentalist or anti-realist attitude about propositions. Both the traditional account of propositions and my alternative treat propositions as abstract, objective entities. The disagreement is about the role or function that these entities play in thought and language. On the traditional account, we latch onto propositions by entertaining them, and then we deploy them in various ways in our thoughts and speech acts, e.g. by endorsing a proposition in a judgment, or putting one forward as true in an assertion. Our judgments and assertions acquire their truth-conditions from the propositions that are deployed in their performance. This is the sense in which, on the traditional account, propositions serve as a source of truth-conditions. By contrast, on my account, truth-conditions originate with our particular, token acts of predication. We abstract away from the details of these acts of predication to arrive at types, propositions, which we then use to classify and individuate our own and other's thoughts and speech acts. The types we arrive at are perfectly real and objective, and they serve an essentially classificatory role.

It won't be possible in this paper to give a full presentation of this alternative to the traditional account of propositional content.[2] My present aim is to get this approach off the ground by responding to some fundamental objections. First, many philosophers think that acts of judging or asserting are not the sorts of things that are true or false. Many think that it's a category mistake to attribute truth or falsity to judgments and assertions considered as actions. If that were so then my approach to propositional content would be a non-starter. Second, even if we grant that particular acts of predication have truth-conditions, one might still deny that types of these actions have truth-conditions. Perhaps a token act of predicating a property of an object has truth-conditions; according to the second objection, it is a mistake to think that this type of action also has truth-conditions. If that were right then, again, my approach to propositions would fail. Propositions are not the primary bearers of truth-conditions but they are still bearers of truth-conditions, a fact that any account of the nature of propositions must accommodate. I am going to argue, then, that not only are token acts of predication bearers of truth-conditions, but types of these actions are as well. Finally, I will show how the former explains the latter. Types of acts of predication have truth-conditions *because* their tokens do, and the types inherit their truth-conditions from their tokens. One of the goals of this paper is to clarify what this means.

2. Acts of predication

An act of predication, in the simplest case, is an act of sorting an object with other objects according to a rule determined by a property. To predicate the property of being green of an object x is to sort x with other green things. Such an act can be performed mentally, by judging that x is green, or in speech, by asserting that x green, or in other ways, e.g. by picking x up and putting it with other green things.[3] The property of being green provides a rule that determines whether these acts of predication are correct or incorrect. An act of predicating green of an object x is correct if and only if x is green. Correctness and incorrectness here are just truth and falsity. An act of predicating green of x is *true* iff x is green.

It follows that *acts* of judging or asserting have truth-conditions. As I mentioned earlier, many philosophers think that this is a mistake – in fact, a category mistake. This is the first point that Strawson makes in his reply to Austin in their symposium on truth:

> The words 'assertion' and 'statement' have a parallel and convenient duplicity of sense. 'My statement' may be either what I say or my saying it. My saying something is certainly an episode. What I say is not. It is the latter, not the former, we declare to be true. (Strawson 1950, 162)

My statement that x is green, considered as an episode, is my act of stating that x is green. Strawson thinks that it is a 'simple and obvious fact' (1950, 164) that when we attribute truth or falsity to statements, assertions, and the like, we are attributing truth and falsity to *what* is stated, asserted, etc. and not to the acts of stating, asserting, etc.[4] Bar-Hillel agrees:

> Since I find little, if any, point in talking about the truth of speech acts such as statings, assertings, or utterings, and of mental acts (or states) such as believings, I take it as close to self-evident that when one talks of true statements, assertions, utterances, and beliefs, one has the products of these acts in mind. (Bar-Hillel 1973, 304)

Bar-Hillel goes on to explain that by 'product' he means 'what is expressed' by a sentence – in other words, an abstract, non-linguistic proposition. Strawson and Bar-Hillel join the tradition in holding that it is propositions, and not the acts of stating or asserting propositions, that are the bearers of truth and falsity.

More recently, philosophers have begun to offer arguments for this view. These arguments point to the awkwardness of sentences in which 'true' and 'false' are combined with noun-phrases that denote actions. According to MacFarlane:

> We say 'His aim was true', but not 'His aim*ing* was true' or 'What he did in uttering that sentence was true.' This suggests that when we say 'His assertion was false' or 'That was a true utterance', we are using 'assertion' and 'utterance' to refer to what was asserted or uttered, not to the act of asserting or uttering. Characterizing relativism as a thesis about the truth of assertions or utterances in the 'act' sense looks like a category mistake. (MacFarlane 2005, 322)

King makes essentially the same point about event tokens instead of actions:

> Suppose I ask Vicky to think of o as red. As she is doing so, if I say 'The event of Vicky thinking of o as red is true (false)' or 'The event Vicky is now bringing about is true (false)' again this sounds like a category mistake. (King 2013, 90)

On the other hand, the sentence 'Vicky's assertion that o is red is true (false)' is 'immaculate', as King puts it, but this is because the noun phrase 'Vicky's assertion that o is red' denotes the proposition she asserted, not her act of asserting it.

This is a thin reed on which to hang a rejection of the view that acts of stating or asserting are true or false. The weight of the linguistic evidence is actually on the other side. First, consider cases of adverbial modification:

1a. Obama quickly stated that Clinton is eloquent.
 b. Obama loudly asserted that Putin is honest.
2a. Obama truly stated that Clinton is eloquent.
 b. Obama falsely asserted that Putin is honest.

Like 'quickly' and 'loudly', 'truly' and 'falsely' are verb modifiers that express properties of actions.[5] The mere fact that we have the adverbs 'truly' and 'falsely' in our language shows that we recognize properties of truth and falsity that apply to actions.

It is also easy to find examples in which truth and falsity are predicated of noun phrases for statements and assertions in their act senses. For example:

3a. Obama's statement lasted one minute and was true.
  b. Clinton's assertion occurred at the press conference and was false.
4a. Biden heard Obama's statement and thought it was true.
  b. Even though Clinton made her judgment very carefully, it was false.

The adjectives 'true' and 'false' can also occur attributively inside these noun phrases, as in:

5a. Obama's true statement took place at precisely 9:37 am.
  b. Clinton's false judgment occurred immediately after she got off the phone.

Or inside relative clauses:

6a. Obama's statement, which was false, made him exhausted.
  b. Clinton's judgment, which was true, caused her to cancel the meeting.

These are all perfectly fine.[6]

All the philosophers I quoted earlier recognize an act/object or act/content distinction in noun phrases like 'Obama's statement' or 'Clinton's assertion'. In the act sense these noun phrases denote acts of stating or asserting; in the object/content sense they denote the propositions stated or asserted. There is nothing wrong with this distinction (although, as I will argue in a moment, it is really just an instance of the token/type distinction). The problem occurs when these philosophers go on to claim that 'true' and 'false' can only be predicated of these noun phrases in the object/content senses, not in the act sense. Examples like (3)-(6) show that this is not so.

Bar-Hillel uses the terms 'act' and 'product' for what I am calling the act/object or act/content distinction (henceforth just the act/content distinction). This is confusing terminology, since the terms 'act' and 'product' are best reserved for a different distinction. In the product sense the noun phrase 'Obama's statement' denotes the concrete sentence token he produced in making his statement. This is clearest in the case of written language. Suppose Obama writes 'Clinton is eloquent' on a chalkboard. Then 'Obama's statement' in the product sense denotes the chalk marks on the chalkboard. Statements, assertions, and judgments considered as products become more fleeting, and more metaphysically suspect, the farther away we get from this paradigm. If Clinton's assertion is spoken, then 'Clinton's assertion' in the product sense denotes the sounds she produced. 'Clinton's judgment', in the product sense, denotes, I suppose, the brain events that constituted her judgment – although saying this requires a hair-splitting distinction between these brain events and her act of judgment. In any case, there is no denying that noun phrases like 'Obama's statement', at least in some cases, exhibit the same kind of act/product ambiguity that we find in noun phrases like 'Obama's building' or 'Obama's writing'.

The act/product distinction for 'Obama's statement' is genuine, but it provides no help for the philosopher who wants to deny that acts of stating or asserting are true or false. Even if the noun phrases in (3)-(6) can be read in the product sense, they do not have to be, and the act reading will be strongly preferred whenever the product reading is elusive or metaphysically questionable.

The act/product distinction is, of course, also subject to the token/type distinction. There are tokens and types of actions, and tokens and types of products. 'Obama's statement' is thus four-ways ambiguous:

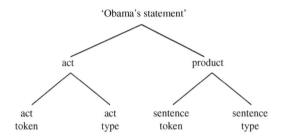

Adding the act/content distinction threatens to complicate the picture even further, but thankfully there's no need for that. The act/content distinction is already captured in our diagram in the form of the token/type distinction for the act reading of 'Obama's statement'. Obama's statement, in the content sense, is *what* Obama stated, and 'what Obama stated' typically (although not always) denotes the *type* of statement he made. We often use phrases of the form 'what S *v*'ed' to talk about types. For example, 'what Obama ate' can be used to denote a type of food he ate; 'what Obama wore' can be used to denote a type of clothing he wore, e.g. a blue suit. Now, compare these examples:

7a. Clinton did what Obama did.
 b. Clinton and Obama did the same thing.
 c. There's something Clinton and Obama both did.
8a. Clinton stated what Obama stated.
 b. Clinton and Obama stated the same thing.
 c. There's something Clinton and Obama both stated.

(7a-c), on their most natural readings, mean that Clinton and Obama performed the same type of action. 'What Obama did' in (7a), and 'the same thing' in (7b) denote this type of action. Similarly, 'what Obama stated' in (8a), and 'the same thing' in (8b), are naturally read as denoting a type, either the type of statement (action) that Obama performed, or perhaps the sentence type he produced. Given that propositions are not sentence types, if we use 'what Obama stated' to denote a proposition, then we should identify this proposition with the type of statement he produced – a type of action. Propositions are types of statements, assertions, judgments, and beliefs.

Note in addition that we happily predicate 'true' and 'false' of 'Obama's statement' in its act-type sense:

9a. Obama's statement, which is true, occurred seven times during the debate.[7]
b. Putin made Clinton's false judgment after reading the report.

My point here is two-fold. First, the act/content distinction is best assimilated to the token/type distinction for the act reading of 'Obama's statement'. Second, 'true' and 'false' can be predicated of 'Obama's statement' *in every one of its four senses*. This should be uncontroversial for the sentence-token and sentence-type readings, and examples (3)-(6) and (9) show that this is also the case for the act-token and act-type readings.

What about the examples MacFarlane and King use to argue that acts of stating and asserting are not true or false? Here are variations on their examples:

10a. *His stating that Clinton is eloquent was true.
b. *What he did in uttering that sentence was true.
c. *The act of Obama asserting that Clinton is eloquent was true.
d. *The act Obama is now performing is true.

I agree that all of these sound bad, but I don't think this poses any real threat to the view that acts of stating, asserting, or judging are true or false. There is a methodological point to be made here: negative results are less informative and carry less weight than positive ones. (Failed experiments are less informative than successful ones.) Our question is whether it makes sense to attribute truth and falsity to acts of stating or asserting. To answer this we look for examples in which 'true' or 'false' are felicitously predicated of noun phrases that denote actions. Examples (10a-d) are *not* such examples, but this doesn't give us an answer to our question. The fact that (10a-d) are not ways of predicating truth and falsity of actions does not tell us that it is nonsensical to do so. Examples like (2)-(6) are positive results, which carry more weight. These examples should be sufficient on their own to answer our question in the affirmative.

Let's also remember that a sentence can be unacceptable for any number of syntactic, semantic, or pragmatic reasons. Examples (11a-c) sound terrible, but it would be rash to conclude that hoping, fearing, and seeing are not propositional attitudes:

11a. *Obama hopes the proposition that the Republicans will compromise.
b. *Obama fears the proposition that the Republicans will compromise.
c. *Obama sees the proposition that the Republicans will compromise.

The problem for (11a) is most likely syntactic, and as King has argued (King 2002), the problems for (11b-c) are probably due to ambiguities in the verbs 'fear' and 'see'.[8] Whether or not this is right, the general point is that without an explanation for why a sentence sounds bad the mere fact that it does cannot be used to draw philosophical conclusions.

With that in mind, here are some tentative suggestions about what is wrong with (10a-d). First, (10a) has a possessive gerundive nominal in subject position, which often sounds awkward or marginally grammatical:

12a. *His moving attracted attention.
   b. *His investigating of the crime scene took two hours.
   c. *His reacting to the noise was unexpected.

If anything, these examples tell us something about the syntax and semantics of gerundive nominals, not whether actions can be true or false. Note that the problems disappear if we substitute the corresponding derived nominals for the gerundive nominals:

13a. His movement attracted attention.
   b. His investigation of the crime scene took two hours.
   c. His reaction to the noise was unexpected.
   d. His statement that Clinton is eloquent was true.

There is absolutely no temptation to read the nominals in (13a-c) as denoting anything other than actions, which makes it surprising that so many philosophers insist on reading (13d) in precisely that way.

The source of the problems for (10b-d) is subtler, I think. Obama's assertion, the token action he performed, is subject to both practical and theoretical norms. His assertion could be brilliant in a practical or pragmatic sense but false and theoretically unjustified. Conversely, it could be a tactical blunder but true and warranted. Some ways of talking about his action bring its practical side to the fore, while others bring out its theoretical side. When we describe Obama's action as something he *did* or as an *act* we highlight its practical aspects. When we describe it as something he *asserted* or as an *assertion* we highlight its theoretical aspects. Note the shift in the meaning of 'justified' between these two examples:

14a. What he did in uttering that sentence was justified.
   b. What he asserted in uttering that sentence was justified.

The justification in (14a) is practical justification; Obama had good reasons (or there are good reasons) for doing what he did. The justification in (14b) is theoretical justification; Obama had reasons (or there are reasons) that support the truth of his assertion. Similarly, the problems for (10b-d) disappear if we substitute predicates of practical rationality for 'true':

15a. What he did in uttering that sentence was irrational.
   b. The act of Obama asserting that Clinton is eloquent was clever.
   c. The act Obama is now performing is reasonable.

The problems also disappear if we substitute 'asserted' for 'did' in (10b), and 'assertion' for 'act' in (10d):

16a. What he asserted in uttering that sentence was true.
   b. The assertion Obama is now performing is true.[9]

Considered as something he *did*, as an *act*, Obama's assertion is subject to practical norms; considered as something he *asserted*, as an *assertion*, it is subject to theoretical norms. My suggestion, then, is that the reason (10b-d) sound bad is that they foreground the practical aspects of Obama's action, thereby making attributions of truth inappropriate.[10] This poses no threat to the claim that, when considered as an assertion, Obama's action is true or false and has truth-conditions.

3. Types of acts of predication

I have just been arguing that token acts of predication, which can be token acts of judging, stating, or asserting, are true or false and have truth-conditions. Someone might accept this and still deny that types of these actions have truth-conditions. We've already seen one bit of evidence against this objection, in the form of examples (9a-b). In the rest of this paper I want to consider a more theoretical, less example driven argument against the claim that types of acts of predication have truth-conditions.

The argument arises out of the metaphysical differences between tokens and types. Suppose we accept that token acts of predication are true or false. Any such token is true or false because it consists in a subject predicating a property of an object. When Obama asserts that Clinton is eloquent he predicates the property of being eloquent of Clinton. In doing so he sorts Clinton into the group of people who are eloquent. The truth-conditions for his act of predication are determined by a rule given by the property of eloquence: his assertion is true iff Clinton is eloquent.

This explanation for the truth-conditions of Obama's assertion depends on the fact that Obama performed an act of predication. He predicated eloquence of Clinton, and therefore his assertion is true iff Clinton is eloquent. But, of course, the *type* of action he performed doesn't predicate eloquence of Clinton. The type does not consist in a subject predicating a property of an object. If it did then it would be a token act of predication. Therefore, even if token acts of predication have truth-conditions, it doesn't make sense to say that types of these actions do as well.

To see what is wrong with this argument it helps to consider the following parallel argument. Types of material objects are not themselves material objects. Therefore, types of material objects do not have material properties:

Argument 1 P_1. Only token material objects have material properties.
                  P_2. Types of material objects are not token material objects.
                  Types of material objects do not have material properties.

This argument is unsound; premise 1 is false. Consider the Union Jack, the flag of the United Kingdom. Tokens of the Union Jack have material properties, but so does the type. The Union Jack, the type, is partly red, partly blue, and partly white. It is striped. It is rectangular. It is attached to flagpoles all over the United Kingdom. Works of art provide another rich source of examples. As Wollheim observes:

> For though they may not be objects but types, this does not prevent them from having physical properties. There is nothing that prevents us from saying that Donne's *Satires* are harsh on the ear, or that Dürer's engraving of St. Anthony has a

differentiated texture, or that the conclusion of "Celeste Aida" is pianissimo. (Wollheim 1980, 82)

In each of these examples a material property is attributed to a work of art considered as a type.

Let's stay with this analogy for a moment before returning to tokens and types of acts of predication. How could an abstract type of material object have material properties? There is really no great mystery here. Types of material objects have material properties in a secondary or derivative sense. Token material objects are the primary bearers of material properties, and types of material objects have material properties because their tokens do. The sense of 'because' here is metaphysical or constitutive. The fact that the Union Jack, the type, is flying from flagpoles all over the UK is constituted by the fact that tokens of the Union Jack are flying from flagpoles all over the UK. Dürer's engraving of St. Anthony has a differentiated texture in virtue of the fact that tokens of this engraving have differentiated textures.

In addition, for many material properties, the possession of the material property by the type does not depend on the existence of tokens of that type.[11] Suppose all the tokens of Dürer's engraving of St. Anthony are destroyed. We would still say that the engraving, the type, has a differentiated texture. In this case the fact about the type is constituted counterfactually. Dürer's engraving of St. Anthony has a differentiated texture in the sense that if there were tokens of this engraving then those tokens would have differentiated textures. We explain what it is for the type to have a material property by appealing to the possession of that property by its actual or possible tokens.

All of this is consistent with the fact that we can often explain why an object has some property by saying that it is a token of a certain type. Suppose someone wants to know why a particular engraving is worth, say, $400,000. We can explain this by saying that it is an instance of Dürer's engraving of St. Anthony, and this type of engraving is worth $400,000. Here we explain why the token has a certain property by locating it under a type. This doesn't threaten the constitutive dependence of facts about the type on facts about its tokens since the nature of this explanation is not constitutive. The fact that the token engraving is worth $400,000 is not constituted by a fact about the type. It is constituted by some complicated fact about the art market. Saying that the engraving is a token of Dürer's engraving of St. Anthony explains why it is worth $400,000 by telling us what kind of engraving it is. The explanation is classificatory, not constitutive. Compare explaining why this apple is green by appealing to its surface reflectance properties versus saying that it is a Granny Smith.

All of these points carry over in a straightforward way to tokens and types of acts of predication. Types of acts of predication are not particular acts of predication, but this is no barrier to their sharing truth-conditions with their tokens. Furthermore, the possession of truth-conditions by a type is constituted by the possession of truth-conditions by actual or possible tokens of that type. This is the sense in which a type of act of predication, a proposition, *inherits* truth-conditions from its tokens.[12]

Of course, the analogy between material objects and acts of predication is not exact. Acts of predication are not objects. What, then, is the analog of argument 1 for acts of predication? To answer this, we need an analog for material properties. In the case of acts of predication, that role can be played by the concept of an *evaluative* property. We evaluate token actions along rational, prudential, moral, and aesthetic dimensions, among many others. Actions are justified or unjustified, wise or foolish, morally right or wrong, beautiful or ugly. We apply these sorts of evaluative properties in the first instance to particular, token actions. In doing so, we evaluate what an agent did. This may lead one to think that, because types of actions are not constituted by agents performing actions, it is inappropriate to attribute evaluative properties to types of actions. Token actions may have evaluative properties, but types of actions do not. Here, then, is our analog for argument 1:

Argument 2 P_1. Only token actions have evaluative properties.
P_2. Types of actions are not token actions.
Types of actions do not have evaluative properties.

As before, premise 1 is false. We regularly attribute evaluative properties to types of actions. Consider a skillfully executed, elegant pirouette. The token movement performed by the dancer is skillful and elegant, but so is that type of movement. It is easy to multiply examples. There are mechanically sound and unsound ways to swing a baseball bat, healthy and unhealthy ways to make an omelet, easy and hard ways to change a bicycle tire, effective and ineffective ways to deliver a lecture. In each case, evaluative properties are applied to *ways* of doing something – types of actions.

Truth and falsity are evaluative properties. To say that a judgment or assertion is true is to give it a positive evaluation. Whatever other features a token act of predication may have, being true is a positive feature and being false is a negative feature. As we have just seen, we regularly attribute evaluative properties not only to token actions but also to types under which these actions fall. The metaphysical differences between tokens and types therefore present no barrier to holding that types of acts of predication are true or false. And, of course, in order to be true or false a type of act of predication must have truth-conditions.

Just as in the case of types of material objects and material properties, types of acts of predication inherit their truth-conditions from their actual or possible tokens. A type of act of predication need not have any actual tokens in order for it to have truth-conditions. Even if no one ever has or ever will predicate eloquence of Clinton, this type of act of predication is true iff Clinton is eloquent because if there were any tokens of this type, those tokens would be true iff Clinton is eloquent. The fact that types of acts of predication have truth-conditions is constituted by the possession of those truth-conditions by its actual or possible tokens.

The story is complicated by the fact that any token act of predication falls under an indefinitely large number of different types, only some of which inherit the truth-conditions of the token. Consider a case of moral evaluation. Suppose Obama lies to Clinton during a Cabinet meeting on a Thursday. This token action is morally wrong, and it falls under a large range of types that are also morally wrong, e.g. lying to Clinton during a Cabinet meeting on a Thursday, lying to Clinton during a Cabinet meeting, lying to Clinton on a Thursday, lying to Clinton, lying, intentionally deceiving Clinton on a Thursday, intentionally deceiving Clinton, etc. But there are other types under which Obama's action falls that are morally neutral, e.g. saying something to Clinton during a Cabinet meeting on a Thursday, saying something to Clinton during a Cabinet meeting, saying something to Clinton, uttering a sentence of English, making noises with one's mouth, doing something on a Thursday, etc. This raises a question about why some types inherit a property from their tokens and some do not. I do not know how to answer this question for the moral case, although I have the beginning of an answer for the case of truth and falsity. But let's first get a better sense of the range of available types pertaining to acts of predication.

Let's represent the proposition Obama asserts when he says that Clinton is eloquent as follows:

17 ⊢ < **Clinton**, ELOQUENT >

This is a type of action someone performs when she refers to Clinton, expresses the property of eloquence, and predicates this property of Clinton. '**Clinton**' stands for a type of reference act, 'ELOQUENT' stands for a type of expression act, and '⊢' stands for predication. Like its tokens, this type of action is true iff Clinton is eloquent.

This type, (17), sits roughly near the center of a range of types of varying degrees of fineness of grain. The reference type **Clinton** is an example of what I call a *semantic reference type*, which is more finely grained than the type that covers acts of reference to Clinton of any kind using any referential device whatsoever (see Hanks 2011, 2013). Semantic reference types are defined in terms of the concept of semantic competence. Very roughly, two token acts of reference employing the names n_1 and n_2 fall under the same semantic reference type just in case anyone who is semantically competent with the names n_1 and n_2 will know, just in virtue of their competence, that these tokens acts of reference co-refer. This entails that most acts of reference employing co-referential but distinct names, e.g. 'Mark Twain' and 'Sam Clemens', fall under different semantic reference types, since someone can be competent with both names and fail to realize that their uses co-refer. On the other hand, we can define a type of reference act solely in terms of the identity of the referent, in which case uses of 'Mark Twain' and 'Sam Clemens' would fall under the same reference type. Let's call this more coarsely grained type an *object dependent reference type*, since whether a token act of reference falls under it depends only on the identity of the object referred to. Uses of 'Mark Twain' and 'Sam Clemens' fall under different semantic reference types but the same object dependent reference type. Any token of a semantic reference type falls under the corresponding object dependent reference type, but not vice versa.

Let '**Clinton**$_{obj}$' stand for the object dependent reference type corresponding to the semantic reference type **Clinton**. Corresponding to (17), then, we have a more coarsely grained type:

18 ⊢ < **Clinton**$_{obj}$, ELOQUENT >

This is a super-type of (17): any token of (17) falls under (18), but not vice versa. In addition, there are indefinitely many sub-types of (17), each of which incorporates more details about how the reference act is performed. There is the type of act of referring to Clinton under the semantic reference type **Clinton** while thinking of her as Bill's wife, or while thinking of her as the 42nd First Lady of the United States, or during a Cabinet meeting on a Thursday, or etc. The more details we include the more finely grained the resulting type will be. This generates sub-types of (17):

19a. ⊢ < **Clinton**$_{thought\text{-}of\text{-}as\text{-}Bill's\text{-}wife}$, ELOQUENT >
   b. ⊢ < **Clinton**$_{thought\text{-}of\text{-}as\text{-}the\text{-}42nd\text{-}First\text{-}Lady}$, ELOQUENT >
   c. ⊢ < **Clinton**$_{during\text{-}a\text{-}Cabinet\text{-}meeting\text{-}on\text{-}a\text{-}Thursday}$, ELOQUENT >

Like (17), all of these types, (18) and (19a-c), are true or false depending on whether Clinton is eloquent. And there are many more that share these truth-conditions. Intuitively, the idea is that a type like (17) is surrounded by an array of less or more finely grained types, all of which share the same truth-conditions. I see no problem with calling all of the types in this array propositions. Propositions, on this approach, play a fundamentally classificatory role. In some contexts we want to classify a judgment or assertion quite broadly, in which case we will classify it under the type (18). In other contexts we want to classify a judgment or assertion more narrowly, in which case we could use the type (17), (19a-c), or any number of other more finely grained types. These acts of classification take the form of propositional attitude reports. When I say 'Obama asserted that Clinton is eloquent', the that-clause determines the type (17) and its surrounding array of less or more finely grained types. The truth of the attitude report in a context depends on whether Obama performed a token of one of the types in this array. So, in some contexts 'Obama asserted that Clinton is eloquent' is true iff Obama performed a token of (18), in others iff he performed a token of (17), or (19a-c), or some other more finely grained type. All of this allows us to capture the complicated and highly context sensitive facts about the truth-conditions of propositional attitude reports. This is just a sketch of how to use this approach to propositions to give a semantic account of propositional attitude reports.[13] The point to emphasize is that all of the above types, and many more, are useful for classifying attitudes and speech acts in propositional attitude reports. This is why all of these types deserve to be called propositions.

The types (18) and (19a-c) all share the truth-conditions of (17). By widening our scope we can arrive at super-types of (17) that do not share these truth-conditions. Consider the type of act of referring to someone or other, expressing the property of eloquence, and predicating that property of the person referred to. This is also a super-type of (17), but it does not have a truth-value or truth-conditions. This is because the reference type, the type of act of referring to someone or other, fails to determine a referent. There is also the type of act of referring to Clinton, expressing the property of eloquence, and combining that property with Clinton in some way or other – not necessarily by *predicating* eloquence of Clinton, but perhaps by *asking* whether Clinton has this property, or *ordering* Clinton to have this property. This super-type of (17) also lacks a truth-value and truth-conditions, because its tokens need not be cases of agents predicating eloquence of Clinton. There are many, many more such super-types. Why do some of these types have truth-conditions and others do not? At a minimum, in order to be true iff Clinton is eloquent, a type has to determine Clinton, determine the property of eloquence, and determine that this property is predicated of Clinton. Super-types of (17) that fail to meet one of these conditions are not true or false and do not have truth-conditions. More generally, in simple atomic cases, in order to inherit truth-conditions from its tokens a type needs to be finely grained enough to determine a property or relation, the right number of objects, and predication.[14] In more complicated cases involving connectives, quantification, and so on, the story has to be more complicated – but that takes us beyond the scope of this paper.

4. Conclusion

According to the traditional conception of propositional content, propositions are the primary bearers of truth and falsity, making them the source of truth-conditions. On the alternative that I have been defending in this paper, our acts of judging, stating, and asserting are the primary bearers of truth-conditions, making *us* the source of truth-conditions. Representation begins with our acts of thinking and speaking about the world. To say this, however, is not to eliminate the need for propositions. We use propositions to characterize, individuate, and classify our thoughts and speech acts. We do so by classifying these mental and spoken actions under types. When these types are sufficiently detailed they inherit the truth-values and truth-conditions of their tokens, in much the same way that types of acts inherit evaluative properties from their tokens, and types of material objects inherit material properties from their tokens.

Notes

1. See (Hanks 2007a, 2007b).
2. See (Hanks ms).
3. In performing acts of predication we exercise capacities for noticing similarities between objects and grouping them according to these similarities. Many of these

4. Echoing Strawson, Searle remarks that 'the view that it is the act of stating which is true or false is one of the most serious weaknesses of Austin's theory of truth,' (Searle 1968, 423).
5. See (Parsons 1990, ch.4). 'Truly' the verb modifier should not be confused with 'truly' the sentence modifier, as in 'Truly thou art damned, like an ill-roasted egg, all on one side,' (Shakespeare, *As You Like It*).
6. In assessing the naturalness of these examples it helps to imagine conversations in which they might occur. Here is a possible conversation for (3b):

    Reporter 1: Clinton and Obama both made assertions yesterday about the health care bill.
    Reporter 2: Where did Clinton's assertion take place, and was it true?
    Reporter 1: Clinton's assertion occurred at the press conference and was false.

    It is easy to devise similar conversations for any of the examples in (3)-(6).
7. Here is a context in which one might hear (9a):

    There was a debate last night in which the candidates spent a lot of time talking about how the government should respond to the current recession. Many years ago, Obama stated that deficit spending can pull the country out of a recession. Obama's statement, which is true, occurred seven times during the debate. Obama himself made it twice, as did five others.

    For this to make sense, 'Obama's statement' must be read as denoting a type of statement.
8. See (Hanks 2009) for a survey of the philosophical issues raised by these sorts of examples.
9. This doesn't work for (10c). '*The assertion of Obama asserting that Clinton is eloquent is true' is terrible. But again, this seems to be due to the gerundive nominal 'Obama asserting that Clinton is eloquent'. '*The movement of him moving attracted attention' and '*The reaction of him reacting to the noise was unexpected' are equally bad.
10. Thanks to Michelle Mason for insightful comments that led to this idea. Note that (10b-d) are about *token* acts of assertion. My suggestion is that these examples sound bad because they foreground the practical aspects of these token actions. Nothing I have said implies that propositions, considered as types of acts of assertion, are subject to practical norms.
11. This is true for many material properties, but not all. If no tokens of the Union Jack exist then the Union Jack, the type, is not flying from any flagpoles.
12. In their contribution to this special issue, Tillman, Caplan, Mclean and Murray criticize the inheritance model for not being able to explain why propositions inherit their semantic properties from their tokens. As they understand it, an answer to this question would provide a general principle that tells us which properties of token acts of predication are inherited by which types. Now, obviously it would be nice to have such a general principle, and later on in this paper I will offer a necessary condition on the inheritance of truth-conditions. But the success of the inheritance model does not depend on providing a general principle of this kind. The inheritance model is meant to answer the question about how propositions have truth-conditions, where this is understood as a metaphysical or constitutive question. The question is: what is it for a proposition to have truth-conditions? The answer given by the inheritance

model is that a proposition is a type of act of predication, and the possession of truth-conditions by this type is constituted by the possession of truth-conditions by its actual and possible tokens. There is no further need to provide a general principle indicating which properties of token acts of predication are inherited by which types. Consider, by way of comparison, the view that it is primitive that propositions have truth-conditions. This is a different answer to the constitutive question about how propositions have truth-conditions. This view holds that it is a brute, primitive fact that a proposition has truth-conditions, not constituted by any more basic facts. Clearly, the success of this answer does not depend on providing a general principle that tells us which properties of which propositions are primitive and which are not.

13. See (Hanks 2011, 2013).
14. When the relation involved is not symmetric then the type must also determine roles for the various objects to play in the relation. Compare asserting that Desdemona loves Cassio with asserting that Cassio loves Desdemona. Both of these assertions fall under the type of act of predicating the relation of loving of the two people Desdemona and Cassio, but this type does not have truth-conditions since it fails to specify who is the lover and who is the one being loved.

References

Bar-Hillel, Y. 1973. "Primary Truth Bearers." *Dialectica* 27: 303–312.
Hanks, P. 2007a. "The Content-Force Distinction." *Philosophical Studies* 134: 141–164.
Hanks, P. 2007b. "How Wittgenstein Defeated Russell's Multiple Relation Theory of Judgment." *Synthese* 154: 121–146.
Hanks, P. 2009. "Recent Work on Propositions." *Philosophy Compass* 4: 1–18.
Hanks, P. 2011. "Structured Propositions as Types." *Mind* 120: 11–52.
Hanks, P. 2013. "First-Person Propositions." *Philosophy and Phenomenological Research* 86: 155–182.
Hanks, P. ms. *Propositional Content*. Under contract with Oxford University Press.
King, J. 2002. "Designating Propositions." *The Philosophical Review* 111: 341–371.
King, J. 2013. "Propositional Unity: What's the Problem, Who Has It and Who Solves It?" *Philosophical Studies* 165: 71–93.
MacFarlane, J. 2005. "Making Sense of Relative Truth." *Proceedings of the Aristotelian Society* 105: 321–339.
Parsons, T. 1990. *Events in the Semantics of English: A Study in Subatomic Semantics*. Cambridge, MA: MIT Press.
Quine, W. V. O. 1969. "Natural Kinds." In *Ontological Relativity and Other Essays*, 114–138. New York: Columbia University Press.
Searle, J. 1968. "Austin on Locutionary and Illocutionary Acts." *The Philosophical Review* 77: 405–424.

Strawson, P. F. 1950. "Truth." In *Truth*, edited by S. Blackburn, and K. Simmons, 162–182. Oxford: Oxford University Press, 1999.
Tillman, C., B. Caplan, B. Mclean, and A. Murray. Forthcoming. "Not the Optimistic Type." *Canadian Journal of Philosophy*.
Wollheim, R. 1980. *Art and Its Objects*. 2nd Edition Cambridge: Cambridge University Press.

ON ACT- AND LANGUAGE-BASED CONCEPTIONS OF PROPOSITIONS
Not the optimistic type

Ben Caplan[a], Chris Tillman[b], Brian McLean[c] and Adam Murray[d]

[a]*Department of Philosophy, Ohio State University, Columbus, OH, USA;* [b]*Department of Philosophy, University of Manitoba, Winnipeg, MB;* [c]*Department of Philosophy, Ohio State University, Columbus, OH, USA;* [d]*Department of Philosophy, University of Toronto, Toronto, ON*

> In recent work, Peter Hanks and Scott Soames argue for the type view, according to which propositions are types whose tokens are acts, states, or events. Hanks and Soames think that one of the virtues of the type view is that it allows them to explain why propositions have semantic properties. But, in this paper, we argue that their explanations aren't satisfactory.

1. Introduction

In recent work, Peter Hanks (2007, 2011) and Scott Soames (2010b, 2014b) argue that propositions are types whose tokens are acts, states, or events. Let's call this view *the type view*. Hanks and Soames think that one of the virtues of the type view is that it allows them to explain why propositions have semantic properties. But, in this paper, we argue that their explanations aren't satisfactory. In Section 2, we present the type view. In Section 3, we present one explanation – due to Hanks (2007, 2011) and Soames (2010b) – of why propositions have semantic properties. We criticize this first explanation in Section 4. In Section 5, we present another explanation – due to Soames (2014b) – of why propositions have semantic properties. We criticize this second explanation in Section 6.

2. The type view

Hanks and Soames make two assumptions that, at least for the sake of this paper, we grant.[1] The first assumption is that there are *propositions*: that is, things that sentences express, that agents assert and believe, and that have truth-values. For example, the sentence 'Mother Teresa supplicates' expresses something – namely, the proposition that Mother Teresa supplicates – that some people believe and that is (or at least was) true. Let's call that proposition 'SUPPLICATE'.

The second assumption is that propositions have *semantic* properties. Among these semantic properties are *truth-conditional* properties. For example, SUPPLICATE is true if and only if Mother Teresa supplicates. This observation might seem banal. After all, SUPPLICATE just is the proposition that Mother Teresa supplicates, and it might seem obvious that the proposition that Mother Teresa supplicates is true if and only if Mother Teresa supplicates. But not everything has truth-conditions. Mother Teresa, for example, doesn't. And not everything that has truth-conditions has the same truth-conditions as SUPPLICATE does. The proposition that Ole-Kristian fights, for example, has truth-conditions; but it's not the case that it's true if and only if Mother Teresa supplicates. Rather, it's true if and only if Ole-Kristian fights.

Among the semantic properties that propositions have are also *representational* properties. For example, SUPPLICATE represents Mother Teresa as supplicating. Again, not everything has representational properties. Electrons, for example, don't. And not everything that has representational properties has the same representational properties as SUPPLICATE does. The proposition that Ole-Kristian fights, for example, has representational properties; but it's not the case that it represents Mother Teresa as supplicating. Rather, it represents Ole-Kristian as fighting.[2]

Hanks and Soames both accept versions of the type view, according to which propositions are act, state, or event types. For example, on the type view, SUPPLICATE is a type whose tokens are particular acts, mental states, or events that represent Mother Teresa as supplicating. On one version of the type view, agents who perform those acts or who are in those mental states all predicate the property *supplicating* of Mother Teresa. For example, when Ben asserts that Mother Teresa supplicates, when Chris judges that Mother Teresa supplicates, when Brian supposes that Mother Teresa supplicates, and when Adam believes that Mother Teresa supplicates, we all predicate *supplicating* of Mother Teresa.[3] So the acts that we perform or the mental states that we are in are all tokens of the type that, on one version of the type view, is SUPPLICATE.[4]

3. Inheritance

By itself, the type view doesn't explain the semantic properties of propositions. Indeed, the type view doesn't say anything about those properties. For all the type view says, Michael McGlone's (2012) view, according to which it is a brute fact about each proposition that it has the truth-conditional properties that it does, might be true.

But, unlike McGlone, Hanks and Soames think that it is not a brute fact that propositions have semantic properties; rather, they think that these properties can be explained. In this sense, Hanks and Soames are *optimists*. Hanks and Soames also think that it is agents or their activities that explain why propositions have semantic properties. In this sense, Hanks and Soames are *naturalists*.[5] For example, Hanks (2011, 48) 'locates the source of representation in the acts of predication that people perform.'[6] And Soames (2010b, 94) takes the alternative to optimistic naturalism to require accepting that propositions are '*intrinsically* representational': that they 'somehow predicate certain things of other things, entirely on their own, independent of any cognitive attitudes agents bear to them.'[7] But Soames finds this alternative unacceptable. He says, 'Since we have no idea how to make sense of this, we shouldn't accept it.'[8] Here Soames is echoing Hanks (2007, 143, 158), who considers 'the idea that there are propositional contents that represent states of affairs independently of what speakers do in making assertions or forming judgments' and ultimately concludes that 'there is no sense to be made of representations that are independent of what subjects do in judgment and assertion.'

In "The Content-Force Distinction" (2007) and "Structured Propositions as Types" (2011), Hanks offers the following explanation of why propositions have representational properties: they are types that inherit their representational properties from their tokens. In "The Content-Force Distinction," he says, 'propositions inherit their representational features from the actions subject perform in producing speech acts or forming attitudes.[9] And, speaking of 'the acts of predication through which speakers apply properties and relations to objects,' in "Structured Propositions as Types" he says, 'Propositions can be seen as abstractions from these acts, and they inherit their representational features from them.'[10] Let's call this explanation *the inheritance model*. On the inheritance model, the *source* of the properties that types end up with is their tokens, and the *mechanism* by which types end up with those properties is inheritance, which results in types having the same properties as their tokens. For example, on the inheritance model SUPPLICATE represents Mother Teresa as supplicating because it inherits *representing Mother Teresa as supplicating* from its tokens. To paraphrase what Hanks says about a different example, 'in asserting SUPPLICATE, a subject predicates the property *supplicating* of Mother Teresa and thus represents Mother Teresa as supplicating. The act type of which this is a token, i.e. SUPPLICATE, inherits this representational property. Because any token in which a speaker predicates *supplicating* of Mother Teresa represents her as supplicating, the type that unites these tokens also represents her as supplicating.'[11]

In *What is Meaning?* (2010b), Soames endorses Hanks's explanation of why propositions have representational properties. He says, 'propositions are representational *because* of their intrinsic connection to the inherently representational cognitive events in which agents predicate some things of other things.'[12] And, looking back in "Clarifying and Improving the Cognitive Theory" (2014b), he describes his earlier explanation as one according to which 'propositions *inherit* their representational properties from their possible instances.'[13]

Hanks (2007, 2011) and Soames (2010b) thus use the inheritance model to explain why propositions have representational properties. But the semantic properties that propositions have are not limited to representational properties;

propositions also have truth-conditional properties. And Hanks (2011) and Soames (2010b) offer different explanations of why propositions have truth-conditional properties.

In "Structured Propositions as Types," Hanks applies the inheritance model directly to explain why propositions have truth-conditional properties: propositions are types that inherit their truth-conditional properties from their tokens. For example, SUPPLICATE is true if and only if Mother Teresa supplicates because it inherits *being true if and only if Mother Teresa supplicates* from its tokens. To paraphrase what Hanks says about a different example, 'A token assertion that Mother Teresa supplicates is a paradigm of the sort of thing that can be true or false, and the type that is SUPPLICATE inherits its truth-value from its tokens. The reason that SUPPLICATE is true if and only if Mother Teresa supplicates is that tokens of this proposition, particular assertions that Mother Teresa supplicates, are true if and only if Mother Teresa supplicates.'[14]

By contrast, Soames (2010b) does not apply the inheritance model directly to explain why propositions have truth-conditional properties. Rather, he first uses the inheritance model to explain why propositions have representational properties and then uses those representational properties to explain why propositions have truth-conditional properties. According to the explanation that he offers, it is because they have representational properties that propositions have truth-conditional properties.[15] For example, SUPPLICATE is true if and only if Mother Teresa supplicates, because (*i*) it represents Mother Teresa as supplicating, and (*ii*) a proposition is true if and only if what it represents is the case.

In the next section, we criticize the inheritance model. Since Hanks (2011) applies the inheritance model directly to both representational and truth-conditional properties, we discuss both. Soames (2010b) doesn't apply the inheritance model directly to truth-conditional properties, but he does apply it directly to representational properties, so what we say about representational properties is relevant to the explanation that he offers.

4. Problems with inheritance

According to the inheritance model, propositions inherit their semantic properties from their tokens. But what can those who endorse the inheritance model say about why it is that propositions inherit their semantic properties from their tokens?

Those who endorse the inheritance model might start by saying that types inherit *all* of the properties that are shared by all of their tokens, or all of their possible tokens, or all of their conceivable tokens.[16]

> **Universal Inheritance:** For any property F and any type T, if every conceivable token of T has F (and it is conceivable that something is a token of T), then T itself has F.

But Universal Inheritance is false.[17] Here's a counterexample: every conceivable token of the act, state, or event type that on the type view is SUPPLICATE has the property *being a token of the act, state, or event type that on the type view is* SUPPLICATE; but the act, state, or event type that on the type view is SUPPLICATE doesn't have that property. It isn't a token of itself.[18]

Those who endorse the inheritance model might instead say that types inherit the *semantic* properties that are shared by all of their conceivable tokens. For example, Hanks (2011, 41) might have this sort of restriction to semantic properties in mind when he says, 'linguistic tokens are the primary bearers of semantic properties, and linguistic types inherit their semantic properties from their tokens.'

> **Semantic Inheritance:** For any **semantic** property F and any type T, if every conceivable token of T has F (and it is conceivable that something is a token of T), then T itself has F.

Semantic Inheritance is an improvement over Universal Inheritance, since *being a token of the act, state, or event type that on the type view is* SUPPLICATE is not a semantic property, while *representing Mother Teresa as supplicating* and *being true if and only if Mother Teresa supplicates* are.[19]

The counterexample to Universal Inheritance used above has to do with *which properties* types inherit. There might be counterexamples to Semantic Inheritance that have to do with which properties types inherit (for example, consider *non-derivatively representing Mother Teresa as supplicating* or *non-derivatively being true if and only if Mother Teresa supplicates*), but there are also counterexamples to Semantic Inheritance that have to do with *which types* inherit properties.[20] Suppose that, while eating a cookie, you predicate *supplicating* of Mother Teresa; and suppose that the act, state, or event in which you do so has the properties *representing Mother Teresa as supplicating* and *being true if and only if Mother Teresa supplicates*. That act, state, or event is a token of many different act, state, or event types: for example, act, state, or event types in which

(i) while eating a cookie, you predicate *supplicating* of Mother Teresa;
(ii) you predicate *supplicating* of Mother Teresa;
(iii) while eating a cookie, someone predicates *supplicating* of Mother Teresa; and
(iv) someone predicates *supplicating* of Mother Teresa.

The types (i)-(iv) are distinct, since they have different tokens. But it seems that, on the type view, at most one of them is SUPPLICATE, and the others are not propositions. So here's a counterexample to Semantic Inheritance: every conceivable token of the types (i)-(iv) has *representing Mother Teresa as supplicating* and *being true if and only if Mother Teresa supplicates*; but at least three of those types don't have those semantic properties, since at least three of them aren't propositions.

Hanks might reply that types (i)-(iv) are all propositions, so there is no problem if they all have semantic properties.[21] According to Hanks (2011, 12–23), SUPPLICATE is a type whose tokens are complex acts each of which consists in doing three things: referring to Mother Teresa, expressing the property *supplicating*, and predicating that property of her.[22] And, on his view, in the vicinity of SUPPLICATE are a range of further propositions that are sub-types of the type that is SUPPLICATE.[23] These sub-types usually have to do with ways of thinking about objects.[24] For example, in addition to SUPPLICATE, whose tokens are complex acts that consist in part in referring to Mother Teresa, there is one sub-type whose tokens are complex acts that consist in part in referring to Mother Teresa while thinking of her as the Albanian recipient of the 1979 Nobel Peace Prize, and there is another sub-type whose tokens are complex acts that consist in part in referring to Mother Teresa while thinking of her as the Roman Catholic founder of the Missionaries of Charity. But types (*i*) and (*iii*) aren't like those sub-types. Predicating a property of someone while eating a cookie is different than predicating a property of someone while thinking of them in a certain way. Even if it's plausible that sub-types that have to do with how agents think of objects have semantic properties, it's less plausible that sub-types that have to do with what agents are eating do, too.[25]

Finally, those who endorse the inheritance model might restrict inheritance to types that are propositions.

Propositional Semantic Inheritance: For any **semantic** property *F* and any type *T*, if every conceivable token of *T* has *F* (and it is conceivable that something is a token of *T*), and if ***T* is a proposition**, then *T* itself has *F*.

Propositional Semantic Inheritance is an improvement over Semantic Inheritance, since it doesn't require types that are not propositions to have semantic properties. But Propositional Semantic Inheritance is ad hoc. Propositional Semantic Inheritance, like Semantic Inheritance before it, trades on a distinction between *semantic* and *non-semantic* properties. According to Propositional Semantic Inheritance, semantic properties are inherited (by the relevant type under the right conditions), whereas non-semantic properties need not be. What is it about semantic properties in virtue of which they are inherited, while other properties need not be?[26]

In addition, Propositional Semantic Inheritance trades on a distinction between types that are propositions and types that are not. Types that are propositions inherit semantic properties (under the right conditions), whereas other types need not. What is it about types that are propositions in virtue of which they inherit semantic properties, while other types need not?[27]

Perhaps there isn't anything about semantic properties or types that are propositions in virtue of which the latter inherit the former. Perhaps it's just a brute fact that types that are propositions inherit semantic properties. While this proposal doesn't posit as many brute facts as does McGlone's view (which posits one brute fact for each proposition), it still posits a brute fact about propositions and their semantic properties where those who endorse the inheritance model, especially optimistic naturalists like Hanks (2007, 2011) and Soames (2010b), might have hoped to offer an explanation. We conclude, then, that the inheritance model does not offer a satisfactory explanation of why propositions have semantic properties. Those who accept the type view and who want to explain why propositions have semantic properties need another model.

5. Extension

According to the inheritance model, propositions are types that inherit their semantic properties from their tokens. Soames now favors a different model, one on which propositions are types that have extended versions of representational properties, while the agents of their tokens have non-extended versions of those properties. Soames (2014b, 235) says

> it is *not* the act itself that most fundamentally represents o as red, but the agents who perform it who do. Of course, the properties of agents-of doing this or that-are not literally *transferred* to the acts they perform .... For agents to predicate redness of o and thereby to represent o as red is for them *to do* something. Since acts don't *do* anything, but rather are the things done, this is *not* precisely the sense in which the act *predicating redness of o* represents o as red .... Rather, there is an extended sense of *representing o as red,* attributable to acts. (italics in original)

Here, the acts are types that, on the view that Soames currently favors, are propositions. On the inheritance model, things of one kind (act, state, or event types) inherit properties from things of another kind (act, state, or event tokens). On the new model, things of one kind (act, state, or event types) have extended versions of properties, while things of a third kind (agents of the tokens of the act, state, or event types) have non-extended versions of those properties.[28] Let's call this *the extension model.* For example, on the extension model SUPPLICATE represents Mother Teresa as supplicating because it has an extended version of *representing Mother Teresa as supplicating*; and it has an extended version of *representing Mother Teresa as supplicating* because agents of its tokens have a non-extended version of that property.

The inheritance model and the extension model disagree about the *source* of the properties that types end up with: on the inheritance model, the source is the tokens; whereas, on the extension model, the source is the agents of those tokens. And, more importantly, the inheritance model and the extension model disagree about the *mechanism* by which types end up with properties: on the inheritance model, the mechanism is inheritance, which results in types having the same properties as their tokens; whereas, on the extension model, the mechanism is extension, which results in types having extended versions of the properties that the agents of their tokens have non-extended versions of.

As before, Soames (2014b) does not apply the extension model directly to explain why propositions have truth-conditional properties. Rather, he first uses the extension model to explain why propositions have representational properties and then uses those representational properties to explain why propositions have truth-conditional properties. He still thinks that it is because they have representational properties that propositions have truth-conditional properties.[29]

In the next section, we accept Soames's explanation of why propositions have truth-conditional properties and criticize his explanation of why propositions have representational properties.[30]

6. Problems with extension

Soames (2014b, 241) now favors the extension model over the inheritance model and regards a principle like Universal Inheritance that the inheritance model relies on as 'absurd.' But it is not clear that saying that propositions have extended versions of representational properties explains what needs to be explained. What needs to be explained is why, for example, SUPPLICATE has *representing Mother Teresa as supplicating*, not why SUPPLICATE has an extended version of that property.

And it is hard to see how the extension model would be an improvement over the inheritance model, since it is hard to see how saying that types have extended versions of properties would be an improvement over saying that properties can be inherited. The counterexamples from Section 4 aren't avoided by saying that, although types don't have the wrong properties, they have extended versions of those properties; nor are those counterexamples avoided by saying that, although the wrong types don't have representational properties, they do have extended versions of those properties.

Let's go through this in more detail. According to the extension model, propositions have extended versions of the representational properties of the agents of their tokens. What can Soames say about why it is that propositions have extended versions of those properties? Soames could start by saying that act, state, or event types have extended versions of all of the properties that are shared by every conceivable agent of every conceivable token.

Agent-Based Universal Extension: For any property F and any act, state, or event type T, if every conceivable agent of every conceivable token of T has F (and it is conceivable that something is a token of T that has an agent), then T has an extended version of F.

But Agent-Based Universal Extension is false. Here's a counterexample: every conceivable agent of every conceivable token of the act, state, or event type that on the type view is SUPPLICATE has the property *being an agent*; but the act, state, or event type doesn't have an extended version of that property. It's (supposed to be!) a proposition; and propositions are not agents, not even extended ones.

Soames could say that act, state, or event types have extended versions of the *representational* properties that are shared by every conceivable agent of every conceivable token.

Agent-Based Representational Extension: For any **representational** property F and any act, state, or event type T, if every conceivable agent of every conceivable token of T has F (and it is conceivable that something is a token of T that has an agent), then T has an extended version of F.

68

Agent-Based Representational Extension is an improvement over Agent-Based Universal Extension, since *being an agent* is not a representational property, while *representing Mother Teresa as supplicating* is.

But Agent-Based Representational Extension conflicts with Soames's account of entertaining. On Soames's account, entertaining is essentially representational: to entertain SUPPLICATE is to predicate *supplicating* of Mother Teresa and thereby represent Mother Teresa as supplicating.[31] And every conceivable agent of every conceivable token of the act, state, or event type that on the type view is SUPPLICATE entertains that proposition.[32] For every conceivable agent of every conceivable token of that act, state, or event type predicates *supplicating* of Mother Teresa and thereby entertains SUPPLICATE.[33] So here's a counterexample: every conceivable agent of every conceivable token of the act, state, or event type that on the type view is SUPPLICATE has the property *entertaining SUPPLICATE*; but SUPPLICATE doesn't have that property, nor does it have an extended version of that property. Entertaining is an attitude one stands in to a proposition, not an inward-gazing attitude that a proposition stands in to itself; nor is it an extended version of such an inward-gazing attitude.

And there are still counterexamples that have to do with which types inherit properties rather than with which properties are inherited. Suppose that, as before, you predicate *supplicating* of Mother Teresa while eating a cookie and thereby represent her as supplicating. That act, state, or event is a token of many different act, state, or event types, including act, state, or event types in which (*i*) while eating a cookie, you predicate *supplicating* of Mother Teresa; (*ii*) you predicate *supplicating* of Mother Teresa; (*iii*) while eating a cookie, someone predicates *supplicating* of Mother Teresa; and (*iv*) someone predicates *supplicating* of Mother Teresa. The types (*i*)-(*iv*) are distinct. But, on the view that Soames currently favors, only type (*iv*) is a proposition. So here's a counterexample to Agent-Based Representational Extension: every conceivable agent of every conceivable token of the types (*i*)-(*iv*) has the property *representing Mother Teresa as supplicating*; but, on the view that Soames currently favors, only type (*iv*) has an extended version of that property, since only type (*iv*) is a proposition.

Soames replies to this counterexample. He says

> The reason that [some types] are not good candidates for propositions, and are not naturally assigned representational content that makes them bearers of truth conditions, is that they are not connected closely enough to the cognitive lives of agents to serve the function that is the *raison d'être* of this extended sense of *representing*.[34]

This suggests that we should restrict Agent-Based Representational Extension in some way.

Relevant Agent-Based Representational Extension: For any **representational** property F and any act, state, or event type T, if every conceivable agent of every conceivable token of T has F (and it is conceivable that something is a token of T

that has an agent), and if **T is relevant to the purposes for which we might want to extend F**, then T has an extended version of F.

For Relevant Agent-Based Representational Extension to avoid the counterexamples, it would have to be that type (*iv*) is relevant to the purposes for which we might want to extend *representing Mother Teresa as supplicating* in a way in which types (*i*)-(*iii*) are not. Consider types (*ii*) and (*iv*). They are both types whose tokens are acts of predicating *supplicating* of Mother Teresa. The difference between them is that the agent of the tokens of type (*ii*) is you, whereas tokens of type (*iv*) have other agents. It is not obvious to us that, because of this, type (*iv*) is relevant to the purposes for which we might want to extend *representing Mother Teresa as supplicating* in a way in which type (*ii*) is not. (For example, is type (*iv*) more closely connected to the connected lives of agents than type (*ii*) is, simply because it's connected to the cognitive life of more than one agent?)

But set this worry aside. There is still the previous counterexample, the one about *entertaining* SUPPLICATE. For Relevant Agent-Based Representational Extension to avoid that counterexample, it would have to be that the act, state, or event type that on the type view is SUPPLICATE is relevant to the purposes for which we might want to extend *representing Mother Teresa as supplicating* in a way in which it is not relevant to the purposes for which we might want to extend *entertaining* SUPPLICATE: that is, *entertaining the proposition that Mother Teresa supplicates*. It's not obvious to us that this is so.

But set this worry aside, too. A deeper worry remains: Relevant Agent-Based Representational Extension is ad hoc. Relevant Agent-Based Representational Extension trades on a distinction between *representational* and *non-representational* properties. According to Relevant Agent-Based Representational Extension, extended versions of representational properties are had (by the relevant type under the right conditions), whereas extended versions of non-representational properties need not be. What is it about representational properties in virtue of which extended versions of them are had, while extended versions of other properties need not be?

In addition, Relevant Agent-Based Representational Extension trades on a distinction between types that are relevant to the purposes for which we might want to extend a property and types that are not. Types that are relevant to the purposes for which we might want to extend a property have extended versions of representational properties (under the right conditions), whereas other types need not. Can relevance to our purposes really be such that types that are relevant to the purposes for which we might want to extend a property have extended versions of properties, while other types need not?

Perhaps it's a brute fact that representational properties are such that extended versions of them are had. And perhaps relevance to our purposes really is such that types that are relevant to the purposes for which we might want to extend a property have extended versions of properties. This second claim doesn't strike us as particularly plausible, but perhaps it's something that Soames would be happy to accept. Still, the first claim, which requires there to be a brute fact about representational properties, does not strike us as the sort of claim that an optimistic naturalist like Soames would be happy to accept. So we conclude that the extension model does not offer a satisfactory explanation of why propositions have representational properties and hence does not offer a satisfactory explanation of why propositions have truth-conditional properties either. In the end, those who accept the type view don't yet have a satisfactory explanation of why propositions have semantic properties.

Now we grant that, in some cases, it seems that types inherit properties from their tokens. For example, maybe the word 'supplicate' has ten letters because all of its tokens do. But types don't inherit properties from their tokens in all cases. For example, even if every token of the word 'supplicate' is composed of ink, it doesn't follow that the type is, too. So one can't simply say that types inherit properties in any particular case and leave it at that. This means that, without a general principle governing inheritance that is not ad hoc, optimistic naturalists lack an *explanation* of why propositions have the semantic properties that they do. And, as far as we can tell, this point extends to any version of the type view. So we think that the best option is to abandon the type view and instead endorse something more like the view that it's a brute fact about propositions that they have the semantic properties that they do.[35] Sometimes you should abandon your optimism.

Acknowledgements

For comments and discussion, thanks to participants in seminars at Ohio State and the University of Manitoba; to participants at talks at the CPA, CSMN at the University of Oslo, the Semantics Workshop of the American Midwest and Prairies, the Society for Exact Philosophy, SPAWN, and the WCPA; to Scott Brown, Einar Duenger Bøhn, Sam Cowling, Wesley Cray, Olav Gjelsvik, Jill Isenberg, Ali Kazmi, Sandra Lapointe, Kirk Ludwig, Cathy Muller, Anders Nes, Greg Ray, Georges Rey, Craige Roberts, David Sanson, Andreas Stokke, Judith Tonhauser, and the editors of this volume; and especially to Peter Hanks, David Liebesman, Jeff Speaks, and Joshua Spencer. Thanks also from the first author to CSMN for hospitality in Spring 2012.

Notes

1. See, for example, Hanks 2007, 157–159; 2011, 13, 17, 41, 48; Soames 2010b, 2–3, 6–7; 2014b, 226.
2. Some think that propositions have truth-conditional, but not representational, properties. See, for example, Speaks 2014. We think that Speaks is right about this, but we set that aside in the text. Even if propositions don't have representational properties, they still have semantic properties, since they still have truth-conditional properties; so there is still a need to explain their semantic properties.
3. See, for example, Hanks 2007, 153; Soames 2010b, 114. For a different view of predication, see Hanks 2011, 14–16, 2013, 161–164.

4. There are differences among Hanks's initial view (see Hanks 2007, 151–152); the view that Hanks currently favors (see Hanks 2011, 12–23, 2013, 156–165, this volume); Soames's initial view (see Soames 2010a, 116–123, 2010b, 99–107, 2012, 216–219, 2014a); and the view that Soames currently favors (see especially Soames 2014b, 241 n. 16). Hanks's initial view is one on which propositions are types whose tokens are acts and states; the view that Hanks currently favors and the view that Soames currently favors are views on which propositions are types whose tokens are only acts; and Soames's initial view is one on which propositions are types whose tokens are only events. But, when it comes to explaining the semantic properties of propositions, these differences don't matter. So, in the text, we consider Hanks's initial view, the view that Hanks currently favors, Soames's initial view, and the view that Soames currently favors together as instances of the type view, according to which propositions are act, state, or event types.
5. King (2007, 2009, 2013, 2014) is also an optimistic naturalist. (But he does not accept the type view.) For a criticism of King's view, see Caplan and Tillman forthcoming.
6. Hanks (2013, 161) makes a parallel claim about truth-conditions.
7. Italics in original.
8. Soames 2010b, 94.
9. Hanks 2007, 159.
10. Hanks 2011, 48.
11. What Hanks (2007, 159–160) says is the following: 'in asserting that Smith is tall a subject applies the property of tallness to Smith and thus represents the state of affairs that Smith is tall. The type of speech act of which this is a token, i.e. the assertive proposition that Smith is tall, inherits this representational content. Because any instance of a speaker applying the property of tallness to Smith represents a certain state of affairs, the type that unites these instances also represents that state of affairs.' (Hanks (2007, 151–152, 2011, 16–17) distinguishes assertive, interrogative, and imperative propositions. In this paper we are focusing on what he regards as assertive propositions, which include the propositions expressed by declarative sentences such as 'Mother Teresa supplicates'.)
12. Soames 2010b, 107; italics in original. See also Soames 2010b, 7.
13. Soames 2014b, 230; italics in original. See also Soames 2014b, 234 n. 5, 235, and 239.
14. What Hanks (2011, 41) says is the following: 'A token assertion that Le Carré is a novelist is a paradigm of the sort of thing that can be true or false, and the type [that Hanks identifies with the proposition that Le Carré is a novelist] inherits its truth-value from its tokens. ... The reason the proposition that Le Carré is a novelist is true if and only if Le Carré is a novelist is that tokens of this proposition, particular assertions that Le Carré is a novelist, are true if and only if Le Carré is a novelist.' See also Hanks 2013, 161.
15. See, for example, Soames 2010b, 6.
16. Soames (2014a, 96–97) talks of 'conceivable instances.' When he says that every (possible or) conceivable token or instance of T has F, he presumably means that the following is (impossible or) inconceivable: x is a token or instance of T, and x lacks F.
17. This problem is noted in King 2013, 91 and Speaks 2014, 165. Speaks attributes the problem to Caplan. The problem is discussed in Tillman and Caplan 2011.
18. Kleinschmidt and Ross (2012, 134–135) offer a related counterexample to an inheritance principle that they attribute to Liebesman 2011.
19. Elsewhere, Hanks (this volume) might have in mind a restriction to evaluative properties. Such a restriction still faces the problem of sub-types discussed below in

the text (and the problem of super-types discussed below in note 25). In addition, the worry about ad hocness might remain. See note 26.

20. We owe this point to Jeff Speaks. See Speaks 2014, 165.
21. Hanks suggested this reply in correspondence.
22. See also Hanks 2013, 156–165, this volume. On the view that Hanks currently favors, not any act of referring to Mother Teresa will do; only acts of referring to Mother Teresa that are tokens of the relevant semantic reference type will do. See Hanks 2011, 26–32, 2013, 157–161.
23. T is a sub-type of $T*$ if and only if, necessarily, any token of T is also a token of $T*$.
24. See Hanks 2011, 37, 47; 2013, 176; this volume. According to Hanks, these sub-types might not be expressed by 'Mother Teresa supplicates' or referred to by 'that Mother Teresa supplicates' relative to any context, but there are contexts relative to which 'Sam believes that Mother Teresa supplicates' is true if and only if Sam stands in the belief relation to one of these sub-types. See Hanks 2011, 36–38, 2013, 176–177; this volume.
25. Nor does it seem plausible that there are contexts relative to which 'Sam believes that Mother Teresa supplicates' is true if and only if Sam stands in the belief relation to one of these gastronomical sub-types. (See note 24.)

    Hanks (2011, 23) acknowledges that there are sub-types of propositions whose tokens are complex acts that consist in part in referring to objects in very specific ways: for example, 'referring to George in a loud voice using one of his nicknames while holding an umbrella and standing at a train station.' But it doesn't seem plausible that such sub-types have semantic properties. Nor does it seem plausible that there are contexts relative to which belief ascriptions are true if and only if agents stand in the belief relation to such sub-types. For a contrary position, at least about a sub-type whose tokens are complex acts that consist in part in referring to Hillary 'during a Cabinet meeting on a Thursday,' see Hanks, this volume.

    Here's a related problem. Consider act, state, or event types in which (v) someone predicates something of Mother Teresa, (vi) someone predicates something of someone, or (vii) someone does some predicating. Every conceivable token of types (v)-(vii) has the properties *representing something* and *having truth-conditions*; so, by Semantic Inheritance, types (v)-(vii) have those properties, too. But it seems that, on the type view, types (v)-(vii) are not propositions. So presumably types (v)-(vii) should not have any semantic properties. See Speaks 2014, 165.

    Hanks allows that in the vicinity of SUPPLICATE are super-types that are also propositions, where $T*$ is a super-type of T if and only if, necessarily, any token of T is also a token of $T*$. But these super-types usually have to do with referring to objects using any referential device whatsoever. (See Hanks 2011, 35, 2013, 174. See also note 22.) So the super-types that Hanks discusses don't include types like (v)-(vii). (See also Hanks, this volume.)
26. Or, if we restrict inheritance to evaluative properties (see note 19), what is it about evaluative properties in virtue of which they are inherited, while other properties need not be? This question retains at least some of its force, we think, even if types other than propositions inherit evaluative properties, provided that they need not inherit other properties.
27. Hanks (this volume) might say that evaluative properties are inherited by all types alike (see note 19). But that leaves the problems of sub- and super-types. (On super-types, see note 25.) And, in any case, Propositional Semantic Inheritance would still be subject to the counterexamples to Semantic Inheritance that we discussed above in the text: that is, *non-derivatively representing Mother Teresa as supplicating* and *non-derivatively being true if and only if Mother Teresa supplicates*.

28. Soames speaks of having (non-extended versions of) properties 'in an extended sense' where we speak of having (in a non-extended sense) extended versions of properties. We're not sure what, if anything, this difference amounts to. In any case, we don't think that anything hangs on it.
29. See, for example, Soames 2014b, 235.
30. Of course, we are accepting Soames's explanation merely for the sake of argument, since we don't think that propositions really have representational properties. See note 2.
31. Entertaining is predicating: 'What is it to entertain a proposition? It is, I suggest, to predicate something of something else.' (See Soames 2010b, 81; italics in original.) And predicating is representing: 'To *predicate* a property *being P* of an object o is to represent o as *being P*.' (See Soames 2010b, 114; italics in original.) It seems that Soames (2014b) has not changed his mind about entertaining. See note 32.
32. Soames (2014b, 230) accepts this consequence. He says that the types T and *entertaining T* are identical. See also Speaks 2014, 164.
33. Predicating is entertaining. See note 31.
34. Soames 2014b, 235 n. 7; italics in original.
35. Of course, there's brute and then there's *brute*. On some views, each proposition is a primitive entity, and it is a brute fact about it that it has the truth-conditional properties that it does. (See McGlone 2012, Merricks ms.) By contrast, the brutal view we prefer invokes one primitive entity and one brute fact about it. (See Caplan and Tillman ms.)

References

Caplan, Ben, and Chris Tillman. forthcoming. "Benacerraf's Revenge." *Philosophical Studies*. doi: 10.1007/s11098-012-0064-8. http://link.springer.com/article/10.1007/s11098-012-0064-8

Caplan, Ben, and Chris Tillman. ms. "Brutal Propositions."

Hanks, Peter W. 2007. "The Content-Force Distinction." *Philosophical Studies* 134 (2): 141–164.

Hanks, Peter W. 2011. "Structured Propositions as Types." *Mind* 120 (477): 11–52.

Hanks, Peter W. 2013. "First-Person Propositions." *Philosophy and Phenomenological Research* 86 (1): 155–182.

Hanks, Peter W. this volume. "What are the Primary Bearers of Truth?".

King, Jeffrey C. 2007. *The Nature and Structure of Content.* Oxford: Oxford University Press.
King, Jeffrey C. 2009. "Questions of Unity." *Proceedings of the Aristotelian Society* 109 (3): 257–277.
King, Jeffrey C. 2013. "Propositional Unity: What's the Problem, Who Has It and Who Solves It?" *Philosophical Studies* 165 (1): 71–93.
King, Jeffrey C. 2014. "Naturalized Propositions." In King, Soames, and Speaks 2014, 47–70.
King, Jeffrey C., Scott Soames, and Jeff Speaks. 2014. *New Thinking about Propositions.* Oxford: Oxford University Press.
Kleinschmidt, Shieva, and Jacob Ross. 2012. "Repeatable Artwork Sentences and Generics." In *Art and Abstract Objects*, edited by Christy Mag Uidhir, 125–157. Oxford: Oxford University Press.
Liebesman, David. 2011. "Simple Generics." *Noûs* 45 (3): 409–442.
McGlone, Michael. 2012. "Propositional Structure and Truth Conditions." *Philosophical Studies* 157 (2): 211–225.
Merricks, Trenton. ms. *Propositions.*
Soames, Scott. 2010a. *Philosophy of Language,* Princeton Foundations of Contemporary Philosophy. Princeton, NJ: Princeton University Press.
Soames, Scott. 2010b. *What is Meaning?* Soochow University Lectures in Philosophy. Princeton, NJ: Princeton University Press.
Soames, Scott. 2012. "Propositions." In *The Routledge Companion to the Philosophy of Language*, edited by Delia Graff Fara and Gillian Russell, 209–220. New York: Routledge.
Soames, Scott. 2014a. "Cognitive Propositions." In King, Soames, and Speaks 2014, 91–124.
Soames, Scott. 2014b. "Clarifying and Improving the Cognitive Theory." In King, Soames, and Speaks 2014, 226–244.
Speaks, Jeff. 2014. "Representational Entities and Representational Acts." In King, Soames, and Speaks 2014, 144–165.
Tillman, Chris, and Ben Caplan. 2011. "Russellianism and Representation." Presented at SPAWN at Syracuse University.

ON ACT- AND LANGUAGE-BASED CONCEPTIONS OF PROPOSITIONS

Why it isn't syntax that unifies the proposition

Logan Fletcher

Department of Philosophy, University of Maryland, MD, United States

King develops a syntax-based account of propositions based on the idea that propositional unity is grounded in the syntactic structure of the sentence. This account faces two objections: a Benacerraf objection and a grain-size objection. I argue that the syntax-based account survives both objections, as they have been put forward in the existing literature. I go on to show, however, that King equivocates between two distinct notions of 'propositional structure' when explaining his account. Once the confusion is resolved, it is clear that the syntax-based account suffers from both Benacerraf and grain-size problems after all. I conclude by showing that King's account can be revised to avoid these problems, but only if it abandons its motivating idea that it is syntax that unifies the proposition.

1. Introduction

In a recent book and series of articles, Jeffrey King (2007, 2009, 2013a, 2013b) advances a theory of propositions that offers a novel solution to the old puzzle of the 'unity of the proposition': If we regard the individual Sophie and the property of swimming as the *constituents* of the proposition that Sophie swims, what serves to bind these constituents into the representational unity of the proposition? King's proposal is that it is the *syntax* of the sentence 'Sophie swims' that supplies this unifying structure. King attempts to secure this result by building syntax directly into the metaphysical nature of the proposition itself, yielding an account that identifies propositions as *facts* about natural-language sentences. While this metaphysical identification of propositions with facts is itself controversial, I regard it as plausible, and I accept it here as a working assumption, in order to criticize King's central idea: that it is syntax that unifies the proposition. I think that this idea cannot be right, because (on the plausible assumption that unity is intrinsic to propositions) making good on it requires an account that includes particular syntactic structures in the metaphysical makeup of propositions, and such an account will suffer from two fatal problems: a Benacerraf problem and a grain-size problem. I will argue that King's account in particular suffers from both problems, but that these can be avoided by excising the direct appeal to syntax from the account; this leaves us with a revised account that retains the identification of propositions with facts about natural-language sentences, but which abandons the original idea that syntax unifies the proposition.

The paper proceeds as follows. Section 2 introduces the Benacerraf and grain-size problems, showing how they arise for previous theories of propositions. Section 3 then sets out King's syntax-based account in detail. In order to explain why his account ultimately suffers from Benacerraf and grain-size problems, it is necessary first to examine how previous attempts to pin these problems on his account miss the mark. This task is taken up in Sections 4 and 5, which respectively consider the Benacerraf and grain-size objections as posed by King's critics, and offer a provisional defense of the syntax-based account against both objections. Section 6 then argues that King's account faces Benacerraf and grain-size problems after all, and considers the negative implications for the idea that it is syntax that unifies the proposition.

The key argumentative move of Section 6 is worth previewing at the outset. As we'll see in Section 5, King's natural response to the grain-size objection appeals to his claim MIRROR, which states that propositional structure is identical to syntactic structure. Section 6 argues, however, that MIRROR is ambiguous as it stands, for King's metaphysical identification of propositions with facts has the consequence of putting into play two distinct notions of 'propositional structure': the structure of the proposition considered as *content*, and the structure of the proposition considered as *fact*. I will argue that King equivocates between the two interpretations of MIRROR, establishing it as a claim about fact-structure, but then appealing to it as a claim about content-structure. Once the confusion is resolved, and it is clear that the structure of propositional *content* need not mirror the structure of syntax, it also becomes clear that the syntax-based account faces both Benacerraf and grain-size problems after all.

2. Two problems facing a theory of propositions

King's syntax-based theory can be framed as an attempt to resolve two problems facing theories of propositions: a grain-size problem and a Benacerraf problem. The grain-size problem arises for the 'possible-worlds' account that held sway until the 1980s (e.g., Stalnaker 1976). Roughly, this account identifies the proposition expressed by a sentence with the set of possible worlds at which the sentence is true. The familiar difficulty with the possible-worlds account is that its propositions are too coarse-grained to capture differences in content between truth-conditionally equivalent sentences, such as 'bachelors are unmarried' and '199 is prime'. Plausibly, these sentences, being *about* different objects and properties, ought to come out as expressing distinct propositions. In general, I will say that a theory of propositions suffers from a grain-size problem when it individuates propositions in a way that is either too coarse-grained or too fine-grained.

It was in part the grain-size problem that motivated the neo-Russellian 'structured propositions' approach of Salmon (1986) and Soames (1987). This approach views propositions as complex entities possessing *constituents*: the objects, properties, and relations the proposition is *about*. The constituent structure of neo-Russellian propositions makes them sufficiently fine-grained to capture the differences in content that pose a problem for the possible-worlds account. King therefore embraces the neo-Russellian approach, but argues that it faces a problem of its own, which serves to motivate his own account. For neo-Russellians typically represent propositions using set-theoretic devices such as ordered *n*-tuples – representing, for instance, the propositions *John loves Mary* and *Mary loves John* (respectively) as follows:

(1) < John, loving, Mary >
(2) < Mary, loving, John >

As King (2007, 9) notes, these theorists don't indicate whether they consider these *n*-tuples to *be* the propositions in question, or whether they are merely using the *n*-tuples to *model* the propositions – if the latter, then the question of the propositions' full ontological nature remains unanswered.

King (2007, 9–10) argues that ordered *n*-tuples could not actually *be* propositions. His main argument derives from Benacerraf (1965), who argues that numbers could not be ontologically identical to sets, given the parity between alternative codes for assigning numbers to sets. The attempt to identify propositions with ordered *n*-tuples faces the same problem. On a standard code, ordered triple (1) is identified with the proposition that John loves Mary, (2) with the proposition that Mary loves John. On an alternative code, however, (1) becomes the proposition that *Mary* loves *John*, (2) the proposition that *John* loves *Mary*. Since the choice of code is extrinsic to the *n*-tuples themselves, *n*-tuples cannot actually *be* propositions, since no particular *n*-tuple is *intrinsically* best suited to play the role of a given proposition, with its characteristic truth conditions. In general, I will say that a theory of propositions faces a Benacerraf problem when it fails to motivate the *unique* identification of a particular entity with a given proposition.

Since *n*-tuples are, then, at best *models* of structured propositions, the neo-Russellian account remains crucially incomplete as an ontological theory: It specifies the propositional constituents, but leaves unresolved the question of what it is that imposes structure on the constituents, binding them into a unified proposition with intrinsic representational properties. As King (2007, 8) puts it, the question is what it is the corner brackets and commas of an *n*-tuple are taken to *represent*, when the *n*-tuple as a whole is taken to represent a proposition. Of course, this question is recognizable as a version of Russell's puzzle of the 'unity of the proposition'.[1] The task King sets himself is to complete the neo-Russellian account of propositions, by specifying the 'propositional relation' that serves to integrate the constituents into a unified proposition. If King's account of propositions is to improve over its predecessors, it will need to avoid both the grain-size and Benacerraf problems.

It is worth noting at the outset that there are *prima facie* reasons to doubt that King's syntax-based account will be able to avoid *either* problem. For as we will see in Section 3, the structures King identifies as the propositional relations include as proper parts the *syntactic* relations of the associated natural-language sentences. One might worry that this inclusion of syntax in the proposition's ontological nature will make propositions *too* fine-grained, since it will preclude that syntactically different sentences might express the same proposition. One might also expect the inclusion of syntax to generate a Benacerraf problem, since one might think that syntax, like *n*-tuple structure, will be subject to alternative codes that ascribe to it different semantic interpretations. Ultimately, I argue that both of these *prima facie* worries turn out to be justified.

3. King's syntax-based account

The central idea motivating King's account is that the proposition inherits its unifying structure from the syntax of the sentence expressing it. King's key insight is that syntax relates not only the lexical items of a sentence, but also, by extension, the entities they designate. Composing the syntactic relation with the *designation* relations that map lexical items to their semantic values (i.e., the propositional constituents), while existentially generalizing over the particular lexical items, yields a complex relation that holds among the propositional constituents themselves – on King's account, this is the 'propositional relation' that binds them into a unified proposition. What the proposition *is*, on his account, is the *fact* of the constituents standing in this relation. The fact that *is* the proposition that Sophie swims, for instance, is the fact of there being lexical items a and b in some language such that a designates the individual Sophie, b designates the property of swimming, and a stands in R to b – where R is the syntactic relation in which 'Sophie' stands to 'swims' in the English sentence 'Sophie swims' (King 2007, 31–32).[2] On this picture, syntax serves as the structural core of the proposition, the addition of the designation relations merely 'extending its reach' to the propositional constituents. Because of the way propositional relations are constructed as extensions of syntactic relations, King claims that it is the syntactic relations that 'provide all the significant structure ... to propositions' (32). King takes this to establish an important claim I call MIRROR: that 'the structure of a proposition will be identical to the syntactic structure of the sentence expressing it' (57).[3]

Two central notions bear clarification: *facts* and *syntax*. A fact is composed of some objects, properties, or relations (the 'components' of the fact) standing in the (metaphysically basic) *instantiation* relation, so that an object instantiating a property is a fact, two properties instantiating a relation is a fact, and so on; all facts by definition obtain (King 2007, 26).[4] Facts play a dual role in King's theory, for his propositions not only *represent* facts but also *are* facts of a certain kind. The proposition that Sophie swims, for example, represents the fact of Sophie instantiating the swimming property, and is true on condition that this fact obtains (27). The fact that *is* the proposition that Sophie swims is the fact of Sophie standing in the complex propositional relation to the swimming property (32).

It is, of course, not *obvious* that the facts King identifies as propositions should have truth conditions at all, yet grasping a proposition seems inherently to involve a grasp of its truth conditions. King addresses this potential puzzle by proposing that there are two ways we can be acquainted with the proposition that Sophie swims. When we are acquainted with the proposition *qua* content,[5] we immediately grasp it as *representing* Sophie instantiating the swimming property; here Sophie and swimming are viewed as *constituents* of a proposition. When we grasp the same proposition *qua* fact, Sophie and swimming are apprehended merely as *components* of a fact, alongside the syntactic and designation relations; so regarded, the fact is not obviously the kind of thing that would possess representational properties. Nevertheless, the fact that *is* the proposition is ontologically single (King 2007, 52).

The second point of clarification concerns *syntax*. For King, the relevant sort of natural-language syntax will consist in the 'deep' syntactic representations over which semantics is defined. On the minimalist framework proposed by Chomsky (1995), which King (2007, 27–28) adopts as a working assumption, these will be representations at the 'LF' level, which are viewed as the inputs to conceptual-intentional systems. LF representations are constructed by successive applications of the *Merge* operation, which in each case combines a pair of sentential constituents (either lexical items or phrases) into a complex phrasal constituent, eventually resulting in the hierarchical organization of all the *basic* sentential constituents – i.e., the lexical items (47–48). Since 'Sophie swims' contains just two lexical items, the syntactic relation R in which they stand will result from a single application of *Merge*, applied to a name and a monadic predicate, and will have the following (degenerate) hierarchical structure:

[Sophie swims]

The LF representation of the sentence 'Shane runs down the street', on the other hand, will have the hierarchical structure:

[Shane [runs [down [the street]]]]

In general, representations at the LF level embody the complete disambiguation of syntactic structure, including the structure internal to the complex phrasal constituents.

Now that the basic features of King's account are on the table, it is necessary to introduce some refinements, in several stages. Here, again, is the fact identified above as the proposition expressed by the English sentence 'Sophie swims':

SWIMS-1: The fact of there being some language L and lexical items a and b such that a designates Sophie (in L), b designates the property of swimming (in L), and a stands in R to b.

The original version of King's account identifies SWIMS-1 as the fact that is the proposition that Sophie swims (see King 1995). This version of the account suffers from two defects, however. First, it is unable to accommodate lexical items, such as indexicals, that designate entities in a contextually sensitive manner. The straightforward solution to this problem is to build contexts directly into the fact identified as the proposition (while existentially generalizing over them), so that the proposition becomes the fact of there being some *context*, some language, and some lexical items, such that the lexical items designate certain entities and stand in a certain syntactic relation, in that language and in that context (King 2007, 38–39).

The second defect, more important for our purposes, concerns the *semantic significance* of the syntax. As King notes, the proposition expressed by 'Sophie swims' possesses its familiar truth conditions, instead of different ones (or none at all), in virtue of the significance assigned to R in English – that is, due to the semantics of English being such that, when a name and a monadic predicate are concatenated to form a sentence, the sentence as a whole is evaluated as true just in case the individual that is the semantic value of the name instantiates the property that is the semantic value of the predicate; as King (2007, 34) puts it, the syntactic relation R 'provides an instruction' to evaluate the sentence for truth according to this rule. The problem is that the significance of R is not intrinsic to SWIMS-1, and hence, neither are the truth conditions that depend on it.

To illustrate this point, King (2007, 35–36) considers two imaginary languages that differ from English only in the semantic significance assigned to R. In Nenglish, the concatenation of 'Sophie' with 'swims' provides an instruction to evaluate the sentence 'Sophie swims' as true just in case Sophie *fails* to instantiate the property of swimming. In Englist, this same concatenation has the significance of a *list*, so that the sentence 'Sophie swims' fails to express a proposition at all. Since in all three languages 'Sophie' and 'swims' designate the same entities, and stand in the same syntactic relation R, the account of SWIMS-1 implies that the sentence 'Sophie swims' expresses the same proposition in each case.

King's solution is to build the semantic significance of the syntax directly into the fact that is the proposition, as an additional component. King synoptically expresses the significance (in English) of the syntax of 'Sophie swims' by saying that it 'encodes the instantiation function' (2007, 34) or that it 'encodes ascription' (2009, 262; 2013b, 74). That is, in English, the syntactic relation R provides the instruction to evaluate the sentence as true just in case the semantic value of the name instantiates the semantic value of the predicate; the same syntactic relation R 'encodes the anti-instantiation function' in Nenglish and encodes no function in Englist (King 2007, 36). Incorporating the necessary revisions, the proposition that Sophie swims is now identified as:

SWIMS-2: The fact of there being some context c, language L, and lexical items a, b such that a designates Sophie (in c), b designates the property of swimming (in c), a stands in R to b, and R encodes instantiation in L.

On the account of SWIMS-2, the propositional relation that binds the constituents *Sophie* and *swimming* into the proposition that Sophie swims, then, is just the relation in which these two constituents stand within the fact SWIMS-2: that of being, respectively, the semantic values of some lexical items standing in the syntactic relation R, which encodes instantiation. As King notes, the one component of this relation that might seem obscure is the property R possesses of 'encoding instantiation,' or 'providing instructions' regarding the evaluation of the sentence for truth or falsity; he defers explanation on this point, however, noting that

> on any approach to compositional semantics for natural languages, even one that eschews propositions altogether, one will have to invoke this idea.... Semantic approaches differ only on what they claim *is* the instruction that a given bit of syntax provides. They are all stuck with the idea of syntax providing instructions. (King 2007, 34)

This is true, but while King places genuine metaphysical weight on the idea of syntax 'providing instructions,' semanticists are committed only to the idea that syntax *can be thought of* as providing instructions to conceptual-intentional systems (e.g., Chomsky 1995, 168). Nonetheless, there is a natural way to cash out King's appeal to syntax 'providing instructions,' which is in terms of the *reception* of syntax by conceptual-intentional systems, consisting in computational procedures for the truth-evaluation of the sentence. This interpretation strikes me as not only independently plausible but also consonant with the standard picture in contemporary semantics, and so I will assume that the component of SWIMS-2 that consists in R encoding instantiation is ultimately to be understood in those terms.

There is a final complication to be considered in connection with King's account. Surprisingly, King says that the account as it stands (in SWIMS-2) fails to determine the truth conditions of the proposition. On his view, the proposition will only have the truth condition *True IFF Sophie swims* provided that the propositional relation of SWIMS-2 (call it *PR-2*) *itself* encodes instantiation, just as the syntactic relation R already does. Therefore, a complete account requires the further stipulation that *PR-2* 'inherits its semantic significance' from R (King 2007, 59–60).[6] On this final revision, the proposition that Sophie swims is identified with the following fact:

SWIMS-3: The fact of there being some context c, language L, and lexical items a, b such that a designates Sophie (in c), b designates the property of swimming (in c), a stands in R to b, R encodes instantiation in L, and *PR-2* encodes instantiation.

4. The Benacerraf objection

In this section I consider the objection, raised by Caplan and Tillman, that King's account faces a Benacerraf problem. In particular, they claim that SWIMS-2 and SWIMS-3[7] are distinct yet equally good candidates for being (the fact that is) the proposition that Sophie swims (Caplan and Tillman 2012, 10). For both include the same constituents and syntax, both are facts that plausibly obtain, and both seem equally suited to serve as objects of attitudes and as the content of the sentence 'Sophie swims'. Moreover, provided that *PR-2* does in fact come to encode instantiation, as King proposes, both SWIMS-2 and SWIMS-3 will end up having the right truth conditions. This follows because on King's view, *PR-2* comes to encode instantiation when language users implicitly *take* the fact SWIMS-2 to have the appropriate truth conditions, and thereby interpret *PR-2* as ascribing the property of swimming to Sophie (King 2007, 60–61; 2009, 265–267; 2013b, 76–77). By taking SWIMS-2 to have these truth conditions, language users thereby *endow* it with those truth conditions, and thereby also bring into existence the *new* fact SWIMS-3, which will possess the very same truth conditions, but (unlike SWIMS-2) will possess them *intrinsically*.

Now, there might seem to be an important asymmetry between SWIMS-2 and SWIMS-3, namely that only the latter possesses *intrinsic* truth conditions. This might be thought to break the tie in favor of SWIMS-3, but Caplan and Tillman regard it as insufficient to resolve the Benacerraf dilemma, arguing that since SWIMS-2 is *simpler* than SWIMS-3, 'simplicity and intrinsicality pull in opposite directions here, and it seems there is no clear winner' (2012, 11). This is unconvincing, however, because simplicity only plausibly bears on a choice between candidates that are *otherwise* eligible to be the proposition. Since propositions are generally regarded as the primary bearers of truth and falsity, it is reasonable to take it as a constraint on eligibility that the candidate for being the proposition should possess its truth conditions intrinsically (King 2007, 64).

In any case, Caplan and Tillman (2012, 16–18) raise a second Benacerraf problem that is more convincing. The Benacerraf problem they now raise does not (at least not initially) involve a dilemma regarding which fact is the *proposition*, but instead a dilemma regarding which fact best serves as the *proto-proposition* – that which on King's story is implicitly *taken* by language users to have truth conditions, thereby bringing into existence the fact that *is* the proposition. On King's story, it is SWIMS-2 that serves as the proto-proposition; by taking SWIMS-2 to have truth conditions, language users endow its associated 'propositional relation'[8] *PR-2* with the significance of encoding instantiation, thereby bringing about the fact SWIMS-3, which *is* the proposition. Caplan and Tillman now claim, quite plausibly, that SWIMS-1 is just as eligible as SWIMS-2 to play this role of proto-proposition. As they correctly note, this gives rise to a Benacerraf problem that occurs within King's explanation of how propositions come to acquire truth conditions. What they don't point out, however, is that it also generates a Benacerraf problem concerning which facts *are* propositions.

If it is SWIMS-1 that plays the role of proto-proposition, then it will be *PR-1*, the 'propositional relation' associated with that initial iteration of King's account, which will come to encode instantation. If so, the proposition will be identified, not with SWIMS-3, but with the following fact:

SWIMS-2.5: The fact of there being some context c, language L, and lexical items a, b such that a designates Sophie (in c), b designates the property of swimming (in c), a stands in R to b, and *PR-1* encodes instantiation.

SWIMS-2.5 differs from SWIMS-3 only in that it omits the provision that R encodes instantiation, and skips straight to the requirement that the 'propositional relation' of the proto-proposition (*PR-1* in this case) does so. It is clear upon examination that SWIMS-2.5 is just as qualified as SWIMS-3 to play the role of the proposition that Sophie swims.[9] After all, it has identical constituents and syntax, as well as the same intrinsic truth conditions. It appears, then, that King's account does face a Benacerraf problem.

In fact, I think that *neither* SWIMS-2.5 nor SWIMS-3 is most eligible to be the proposition that Sophie swims, for two reasons: First, neither fact *is* eligible, and second, SWIMS-2 (which is in any case the simplest) is *already* fully eligible. The reason I think neither SWIMS-2.5 nor SWIMS-3 is eligible is that King regards it as a constraint on a plausible theory of propositional structure that it 'should give us confidence that propositions so construed really exist' (2007, 25). I claim that neither of these facts will plausibly obtain, because both include as a component that some proto-propositional relation (either *PR-1* or *PR-2*) encodes instantiation, and this is itself implausible. Recall from Section 3 that the claim that syntactic relation R 'encodes instantiation' is most plausibly understood in terms of the claim that this significance is implicit in the way R is received by conceptual-intentional systems. This explanation only makes sense because syntax is represented locally and concretely within language systems, and hence is capable of entering into the sorts of computational relations that would constitute its reception by conceptual-intentional systems. The same explanation won't work in the case of *PR-1* or *PR-2* 'encoding instantiation', because the semantic components of these proto-propositional relations aren't locally accessible for computation – they include, for instance, designation relations that link lexical items to objects in the external world. Such external semantic relations might be partly *maintained* by computations, but they aren't themselves the sorts of things that are capable of *entering into* computations.

An alternative explanation, perhaps more in keeping with King's story about how (proto-) propositions come to acquire their truth conditions, might be that it is *language users* (rather than subpersonal cognitive systems) whose reception of the proto-propositional relations endows these relations with the significance of encoding instantiation. This is sensible insofar as language users *are* presumably capable of representing to themselves external semantic relations. It is, however, quite psychologically implausible to suppose that language users are apt to interpret external semantic relations themselves as encoding any *further* semantic properties, beyond the semantic relations they already *are*. The word 'Sophie' may well be thought to represent Sophie, but the *fact* of 'Sophie' representing Sophie is not *itself* likely to be thought of as representing anything at all. Yet the explanation under consideration is that language users will interpret either *PR-1* or *PR-2* (both of which include the fact of Sophie being represented by some lexical item) as carrying semantic significance. Since there appears to be no plausible explanation for how *PR-1* or *PR-2* could come to encode instantiation, then, it looks highly unlikely that either SWIMS-2.5 or SWIMS-3 is a fact that might actually obtain.

In contrast, SWIMS-2 *does* appear eligible to be the proposition that Sophie swims. King denies this because on his view, SWIMS-2 fails to possess its truth conditions intrinsically. As far as I can discern, however, King is simply mistaken about this. It appears that the truth-conditional properties of SWIMS-2 are already determined by its two semantic components, operating in combination. These are: (i) the semantic significance of the syntax, and (ii) the designation relations. As we saw in Section 3, King claims that the syntax provides the instruction to evaluate the sentence as true just in case the semantic values of the lexical items occupying the relevant positions in the syntactic relation stand in the appropriate relations in the world. This instruction, citing the propositional constituents obliquely *via* the syntactic positions of the lexical items designating them, effectively enlists the designation relations to resolve the reference, deferring to them to supply the semantic values of the positions' lexical occupants. Since it is included in the fact SWIMS-2 that there actually *are* lexical items at these positions, and that they *do* designate the appropriate entities, the 'imperative content' of the syntax – to evaluate the sentence for truth by assessing whether the semantic value of the name instantiates the semantic value of the predicate – makes contact with its intended target. I fail to see any respect in which this leaves the truth conditions undetermined. Of the candidate facts so far considered, then, there *is* one most eligible to be the proposition, namely SWIMS-2. I conclude that while Caplan and Tillman have indeed uncovered a Benacerraf problem in King's account *as he presents it*, the syntax-based account is capable of surviving their challenge.

5. The grain-size objection

In this section I consider the objection, raised by a number of King's critics, that the syntax-based account individuates propositions too finely.[10] Since on King's account, the syntax of the sentence is a component part of the fact that is the proposition, sentences differing in syntax will necessarily express different propositions. Since intuitively, syntactically different sentences can sometimes express the same proposition, King's account does indeed individuate propositions in an unusually fine-grained manner. Accordingly, King (2007, 95–101; 2013a) goes to considerable lengths to respond to various versions of the grain-size objection.

An initial version of the objection is raised by Collins (2007, 820), who observes that 'there are indefinite ways of "saying the same thing" with distinct syntactic structures' – for instance, 'Bill kicked the ball' *vs*. 'The ball was kicked by Bill' – and claims that it is this intuitive synonymy that an account of propositions ought to capture. Burgess raises a related point:[11] It is plausible that across languages, there are syntactically different sentences that are nonetheless standard translations of each other, and hence which, intuitively, ought to come out as expressing the same proposition. The general response King offers to both is that *proposition* is a theoretical notion that need not align with our *pre*theoretical intuitions about sentences 'saying the same thing'.[12] King offers examples for which he claims our pretheoretical intuitions of 'saying the same thing' demonstrably fail to track propositional identity. For instance, utterances of 'I am hungry' by different speakers express different propositions, as do utterances of 'Today is going to be a great day' on different occasions. Nonetheless, both utterance-pairs are intuitively cases of 'saying the same thing' (King 2007, 101; 2013a, 767). I find King's examples here unconvincing, because *these* intuitive judgments that 'the same thing' is said (which, unlike Collins' examples, turn on the context-sensitivity of indexicals) are plausibly understood as judgments that the same *sentence* has been uttered, rather than judgments that the same *proposition* has been expressed. Nonetheless, I am sympathetic to King's general methodological point, that theoretical motivations for individuating propositions should outweigh our pretheoretical intuitions about whether or not 'the same thing' is expressed by different sentences. It is thus important to consider what theoretical motivations King can offer for his fine-grained individuation policy.[13]

It is pairs like '1 = 2' and '2 = 1' that pose a genuine problem for King. On King's account, these sentences express distinct propositions, because the lexical items denoting the numbers occupy different positions within the syntactic structures of the respective sentences:

[1 [= 2]]
[2 [= 1]]

The standard view that these sentences express the same proposition is motivated by more than merely an appeal to intuition. We might reason as follows: Since propositions are essentially semantic entities, they should be individuated precisely as finely as their semantic properties, which are exhausted by: (i) their truth-conditional properties and (ii) their 'aboutness' properties (i.e., which objects and properties a given proposition is about). Call this principle of individuation GRAIN. GRAIN cuts propositions finely enough to avoid the grain-size problem of the possible-worlds account. It seems to imply, however, that King's account cuts propositions *too* finely, since the propositions expressed by '1 = 2' and '2 = 1' are not only truth-conditionally equivalent but are also *about* the same entities, in that they share the same basic constituents: the equality relation and the numbers 1 and 2.

King (2013a, 774–777) provides a forceful argument that, in spite of appearances, '1 = 2' and '2 = 1' do express distinct propositions. His argument assumes two plausible theoretical principles, SSSS and DCDP:

Same Syntax, Same Structure: Sentences of a given language with the same syntactic structure and that differ only in having lexical items with different semantic values occurring at the same places in their syntactic trees express propositions with the same structure that differ at most in having different constituents... occurring in the same places in those propositions.[14]

Distinct Combination, Distinct Propositions: Two propositions P and Q with the same structure and the same constituents are distinct iff those constituents are combined differently (occupy different 'places') in P and Q.

Consider that the propositions expressed by '1 = 2' and '2 = 1' have the same structure (by SSSS) and the same constituents. Suppose for *reductio* that these propositions are identical. Then by DCDP their constituents do not occupy different places within their propositional structures. Since the lexical items designating these constituents (the numerals '1' and '2') *do* occupy different places within the syntax of the sentences, it follows that the propositional structures must be more coarse-grained than the syntactic structures, for instance:

'1 = 2' expresses = *{1*, 2*};
'2 = 1' expresses = *{2*, 1*},

where the right-hand side displays the propositional structures, with $x*$ denoting the semantic value of any lexical item x and the braces indicating *un*ordered pairs. But now consider '1 < 2' and '2 < 1', which we can assume have the same syntax as '1 = 2' and '2 = 1'. By SSSS, the propositions they express therefore have the same structures as the propositions expressed by '1 = 2' and '2 = 1':

'1 < 2' expresses <*{1*, 2*};
'2 < 1' expresses <*{2*, 1*}.

Since the pairs are unordered, the semantic values of '1' and '2' occupy the same positions within the common propositional structure. Since these propositions share a common set of constituents, by DCDP they are identical. But this is absurd, since the proposition that 1 < 2 is true and the proposition that 2 < 1 is false.[15]

I agree that this argument is valid, and that the principles it assumes, SSSS and DCDP, are plausible. Nevertheless, since GRAIN seems no less plausible, and GRAIN seems to imply quite directly that '1 = 2' and '2 = 1' express the same proposition, the overall case appears inconclusive. Below I explain how this antinomy can be resolved. In the meantime, we can note that King's argument is limited in scope, since SSSS requires only that identical syntax should correspond to identical propositional structure *within a given language*. If we were to consider a similar pair of sentences from different languages, SSSS would no longer apply. Moreover, a stronger version of SSSS, which would require *any* syntactically identical sentences (in whatever languages) to express structurally identical propositions, would not have the same degree of plausibility as SSSS itself.

Let's consider, then, a cross-language variation on the '1 = 2'/'2 = 1' case. Take the pair of sentences with syntactic structures as follows:

[John [loves Mary]]
[[John loves] Mary]

The first is a sentence of English, the second a sentence of English∗. Let's suppose that both sentences have lexical items with the usual (English) semantics, and that they share the same truth conditions: Both are true IFF John loves Mary. They differ only in the way their lexical items are syntactically combined: In the English sentence, the lexical items designating John, the loving relation, and Mary (in that order) stand in syntactic relation S; in the English∗ sentence, they stand in syntactic relation T. Since we're supposing that the two sentences have the same truth conditions, it seems to follow that the significance of concatenating a name, a dyadic predicate, and another name in the syntactic relation S in English is the same as the significance of concatenating the identical ordered triple in the syntactic relation T in English∗. Specifically, it seems that both syntactic relations provide the instruction: Map to True IFF the semantic values of the first name stands in the relation that is the semantic value of the predicate to the semantic value of the second name. On King's account, these sentences will express different propositions because they differ syntactically. The two propositions, however, seem to have all their semantic properties in common, since in both sentences, the lexical items *and* the syntactic relations carry the same semantic significance. Since propositions *are* the semantic contents of sentences, it seems reasonable to expect this semantic identity to imply identity of propositions. But that is not the result that King's account provides. This suggests that his account may indeed individuate propositions too finely.[16]

While this case poses a serious challenge to King's account, it seems to me that there is a natural way for King to respond to it. In particular, the natural move for King will involve an appeal to MIRROR: the claim that propositional structure is identical to the syntactic structure of the sentence that expresses it. For King takes MIRROR to establish that the propositional *content* will have a hierarchical structure identical to that of the sentential syntax. If that's right, then the semantic significance of the syntax will have to reflect the full structure of the syntax itself, and hence it will be impossible for the distinct syntactic structures of the English and English∗ sentences to encode the same semantic significance.

That King is indeed inclined to reason in this manner is suggested by his discussion of the contribution that complex phrases make to propositional contents (King 2007, 54–55; 202–204). He considers the English sentence 'Shane runs down the street', which has syntactic structure:

[Shane [runs [down [the street]]]]

Here the hierarchical structure of the syntax reflects its construction by successive applications of the *Merge* operation, generating at each stage a complex phrasal constituent: 'the street', 'down the street', 'runs down the street', and finally the entire sentence. King (2007, 54–55) claims that since MIRROR is true, each of these complex phrasal constituents will contribute to the proposition a complex 'sub-propositional constituent' (SPC), which, like the proposition as a whole, is a fact composed of a semantically significant syntactic relation, together with a set of designation relations from lexical items to semantic values. The complex predicate 'runs down the street', then, contributes to the proposition an SPC that *represents* the complex property of running down the street. This implies that the phrase-structure of the sentence will be mirrored by the proposition's representational content, which will possess a corresponding structural hierarchy:

[Shane* [runs* [down* [the* street*]]]][17]

Here the constituents (indicated with *s) are not lexical items, but rather their semantic values, and the brackets represent not the syntactic relation, but the complex propositional relation. King states that the SPC contributed by a complex phrase *represents* the associated complex property 'in the sense that the definition of truth for propositions maps this sub-propositional constituent to the ... property' (2007, 211). I interpret this to mean that the complex property of running down the street– call it STREET – becomes part of the representational content of the proposition in virtue of its being (as we might say) *cited* in the 'instruction' the syntax provides for the truth-evaluation of the sentence.[18] In contrast, the property SHANE, which x instantiates just in case Shane runs down x, is not part of the content of this proposition, because 'Shane runs down' is not a phrasal constituent of the sentence, and hence the syntactic relation of the sentence will not cite SHANE in the instruction for truth-evaluation of the sentence. The upshot is that on King's view, the hierarchical phrase-structure of the sentential syntax will be reflected in the *instructions* the syntax provides for the truth-evaluation of the sentence:

Map to True IFF [Shane* *I* [runs* *I* [down* *I* [the* *I* street*]]]]

Here *I* represents the (metaphysically basic) instantiation relation that holds together the components of the fact of Shane running down the street (as it is represented by the proposition).

This proposal explains why the proposition that Shane runs down the street should have *content* with hierarchical structure, and should so represent the complex property STREET (but not SHANE). It does so because the instruction for truth-evaluation is itself hierarchically structured, so that the truth-evaluation procedure will consider whether the semantic value of 'Shane' instantiates STREET (instead of considering whether the semantic value of 'the street' instantiates SHANE). So on King's view, the syntactic structure of the sentence is reflected in the structure of the 'instruction' provided by the syntax, which in turn determines the representational structure of the proposition expressed, by prescribing a truth-evaluation procedure that involves the representation of complex properties.

This also explains how King can hold that the English sentences '1 = 2' and '2 = 1' express different propositions without violating GRAIN, the principle that propositions should be individuated precisely as finely as their truth-conditional *and* aboutness properties. For even though the propositions expressed by these sentences are about precisely the same *basic* constituents, their *total* content is hierarchical: The proposition expressed by '1 = 2' is partly about the complex property *being equal to 2*, while the proposition expressed by '2 = 1' is partly about the complex property *being equal to 1*. This is because, in accordance with MIRROR, the different syntactic structures lead to the contribution of different content-bearing SPCs to the propositions. By appealing to MIRROR in this way, King is thereby able to motivate the idea that the semantic structure of the proposition is precisely as fine-grained as the syntactic structure of the sentence expressing it.

The same result applies to the English/English* case. While the two propositions in this case are indeed truth-conditionally equivalent, and also share the same *basic* constituents, King can claim that they have different *complex* constituents, in virtue of their different syntactic structures providing differently structured instructions for truth-evaluation. On the assumption that MIRROR is true, the syntax of the English sentence

[John [loves Mary]]

will provide the instruction

Map to True IFF [John* *I* [loves* *I* Mary*]]

and so the proposition expressed will represent John as instantiating the complex property *loving Mary*. In contrast, the syntax of the English* sentence

[[John loves] Mary]

will provide the instruction

Map to True IFF [[John* *I* loves*] *I* Mary*]

and so the proposition expressed will represent Mary as instantiating the complex property *being loved by John*. The mere difference in syntax amounts to a semantic difference after all.

6. Syntax and propositional structure

Or does it? In this section, I argue that the response just provided to the English/English* challenge on behalf of King depends on an assumption to which he is not entitled: that the representational *content* of the proposition is structurally identical to the syntax of the sentence expressing it. King takes this to follow straightforwardly from the way his account constructs (the fact that is) the proposition around the syntax of the sentence, but this is a mistake. The way King sets up his account *does* guarantee that syntactic structure is identical to the component structure of the *fact* he identifies as the proposition, but the constituent structure of the propositional *content* is a separate matter. The confusion arises because MIRROR, which states that propositional structure is identical to syntactic structure, is ambiguous as it stands. As I will argue, there are actually two distinct notions of 'propositional structure' in play: the structure of the propositional *fact* and the structure of the propositional *content*. Let's call MIRROR-F the claim that the *fact* (the one King identifies as the proposition) is identical in structure to the syntax of the sentence, and MIRROR-C the claim that the representational *content* of the proposition is identical in structure to the syntax. When King *argues* that MIRROR is true on his account, the argument applies to MIRROR-F, but when he *appeals* to MIRROR in his discussion of SPCs, it is MIRROR-C that is assumed. Once the confusion is resolved, and the apparent motivation for accepting MIRROR-C is dispelled, it becomes clear that King's account does suffer from both Benacerraf and grain-size problems after all.

In making this case, the key point to establish is that there are, in fact, two distinct notions of propositional structure in play. Fortunately, King himself has already laid the necessary groundwork for drawing the distinction. Recall from Section 3 that on King's account, we can be acquainted with the fact that *is* the proposition in two different ways: *qua* fact or *qua* content. When we are acquainted with it *qua* fact, what we grasp is the way that certain objects and properties are aligned with certain positions within the syntactic structure, in virtue of the designation relations that link those objects and properties to the lexical items occupying those positions. In considering the proposition in this manner, *qua* fact, we grasp the relations of the fact's components to one another, where the structured arrangement of these components is determined (at least primarily) by the structure of the syntactic relation. When we are acquainted with the proposition in this way, we 'need only see it as another fact in the world, and so need not see it as representing anything or having truth conditions' (King 2007, 52).

When we are acquainted with it *qua* content, on the other hand, what we grasp is the way in which the proposition *represents* its constituents as being related to one another. From this vantage point, we 'cannot help but see [the proposition] as having truth conditions,' but the underlying metaphysical makeup of the proposition is entirely nonobvious: As King says, we 'need not know about the nature of the complex relation (the propositional relation) binding together [Sophie] and the property of swimming in the proposition, nor what the components of that relation are' (2007, 52). That is to say that when we grasp the proposition *qua* content, this need involve no awareness of the fact-structure of the proposition, considered as such. But the unified structure of the proposition, in the most familiar sense of that term, is of course something we can readily apprehend without needing to think of propositions as facts; it is immanent in the propositional content itself. To put the point a bit differently, the propositional relation that binds the constituents into a unified proposition is something that we grasp *directly* when we are acquainted with the proposition *qua* content. For when we grasp that content, we grasp it as *representing* Sophie instantiating the swimming property, and for the propositional content to represent Sophie and swimming as so related just *is* for them to stand in the propositional relation to one another. But since we need not have the underlying fact-structure in mind when we grasp the content-structure of the proposition, it is clear that these are distinct *notions* of 'propositional structure'.

Of course, since King's view is that the fact and the proposition are metaphysically identical, he will regard this distinction between fact-structure and content-structure as *merely* notional; ontologically, there is just a single structure, differently regarded. That identity cannot be simply assumed, however, since what is in question here is precisely the viability of King's proposed identification of propositions with certain facts. If King were to defend his account against the grain-size objection by invoking the identity of fact-structure and content-structure, the defense would be viciously circular. So even though King might well regard MIRROR-F and MIRROR-C as equivalent, given the assumption that his account of propositions is *true*, for the purpose of considering *whether* his account is true, it is of course necessary to regard MIRROR-F and MIRROR-C as independent claims.

Now, King is right to think that MIRROR-F follows trivially from the way the fact he claims *is* the proposition is constructed around the syntax of the sentence. For as we saw in Section 3, the fact-structure King identifies as the propositional relation merely 'extends the reach' of the syntactic relation by composing it with the designation relations linking lexical items to their semantic values.[19] MIRROR-C, on the other hand, is far from trivial; indeed, the whole point of King's distinction between modes of acquaintance is to account for how *un*obvious is his identification of propositional contents with facts. King has, in fact, provided no independent motivation at all for accepting MIRROR-C, aside from the spurious motivation that results from its conflation with MIRROR-F.

Without the assumption that MIRROR-C holds, it becomes clear (contrary to what King supposes in his discussion of SPCs) that the semantic significance of the syntax is not constrained to reflect the structure of the syntax itself. For the syntactic relation and the significance it encodes are independent components of the fact King identifies as the proposition, and so in principle one can vary independently of the other. Let's reconsider the English/English* case in this light, stipulating that the English* syntactic relation T encodes the very same instruction that the English syntactic relation S will encode, on King's own view:

Map to True IFF [John* *I* [loves* *I* Mary*]]

I claim that *both* sentences will then express the same hierarchical propositional content, which ascribes to John the complex property *loving Mary*. This follows directly from King's own claim that the structure of content is determined by the way the procedure for the truth-evaluation of the sentence is structured, which I am happy to grant. As we saw in Section 5, it is this claim that allows King to explain why propositional content should have hierarchical structure in the first place.

Admittedly, the possibility here under consideration, that the syntax of the English* sentence

[[John loves] Mary]

will encode an instruction with the above hierarchical structure, and will thereby determine a propositional content with that same structure, is somewhat perverse, since in this case the structure of the instruction/content effectively *inverts* the structure of the syntax. But the possibility cannot be dismissed merely on grounds of perversity. Recall from Section 3 that King himself takes seriously the possibility of the Nenglish sentence 'Sophie swims' expressing the content that Sophie *fails* to instantiate swimming, due to the perverse instruction encoded by its syntax. The possibility considered here must be taken seriously as well, at least in the absence of any theoretical motivation for supposing that the structural relation of syntax to propositional content must be well behaved. MIRROR-C would provide such motivation, but as we've seen, King has offered no legitimate basis for accepting MIRROR-C in the first place. MIRROR-F, the version of the MIRROR claim that King *has* succeeded in motivating, *is* satisfied by the fact constructed around the English* sentence, since that fact-structure will inherit the structure of the syntactic relation that forms its core.

What we have in the English/English* case, then, are two sentences that differ syntactically, but which express propositions that share all their semantic properties. Since propositions just *are* the semantic contents of sentences, this semantic identity provides compelling reason to regard the propositions themselves as identical. Since King is committed to distinguishing them, due to the difference in syntactic structure, it is clear that in the end his account does individuate propositions too finely.[20] So King's account does ultimately suffer from a grain-size problem. In addition, it suffers from a Benacerraf problem: For which fact is best qualified to be the proposition that John loves Mary? Either of the facts constructed around the English and English* sentences in the manner of SWIMS-2 will do just as well. In fact, since the assignment of significance to a given syntactic relation is in principle arbitrary, there will be indefinitely many such facts equally qualified to play the role of this proposition.

This might seem like a disastrous consequence for King's account, but in fact there is a simple modification to the account that will avoid both grain-size and Benacerraf problems. Since both problems result from the possibility of different syntactic relations encoding the same semantic significance, the obvious fix is to revise the fact identified as the proposition, so that it existentially generalizes over syntactic structures, just as it already does over lexical items.[21] This yields:

SWIMS-4: The fact of there being some context c, language L, syntactic relation X, and lexical items a, b such that a designates Sophie (in c), b designates the property of swimming (in c), a stands in X to b, and X encodes instantiation in L.

This final version of the account suffers from neither a Benacerraf nor a grain-size problem. Indeed, it strikes me as a plausible account of the nature of the proposition that Sophie swims. But notice that what has been given up is any direct appeal to syntax as a basis for propositional unity. It is true that syntactic relation X still appears in the formulation of SWIMS-4, but here X could be any syntactic relation at all, so long as it can encode instantiation. On this revised account, it is clear that it is not *syntax*, but rather the property of *encoding instantiation* that really unifies the proposition. In fact, now that all appeal to *particular* syntactic relations has been excised from the account, there is no restriction on the kind of thing X can be – it merely needs to relate the lexical items and to encode instantiation; otherwise, it needn't be recognizably 'syntactic'.

Moreover, now that we are existentially generalizing over *both* the lexical items *and* the syntactic relation they stand in, there is no motivation for distinguishing these as separate components of the fact that is the proposition. Consider that, as we have seen, for X to 'encode instantiation' is really just shorthand for X being *interpreted* as signifying that the semantic value of a instantiates the semantic value of b. If we take a *phrase* to be any syntactic concatenation of lexical items, we can therefore simplify SWIMS-4 as follows:

SWIMS-4*: The fact of there being some context c, language L, and phrase P such that P is interpreted as signifying that Sophie instantiates the property of swimming, in c, in L.

It should be clear that any circumstance in which the fact SWIMS-4 obtains is a circumstance in which the fact SWIMS-4* obtains as well. I claim that the fact SWIMS-4* is identical to the fact SWIMS-4, differing only in being more concisely stated. But suppose I am wrong, and the facts are actually distinct. In that case, considerations of simplicity should lead us to regard SWIMS-4* as *more* eligible than SWIMS-4 to play the role of the proposition that Sophie swims. For in all other respects, SWIMS-4* is just as eligible as SWIMS-4: It is a fact that plausibly obtains, it has its truth conditions intrinsically, and it is suited to serve as the content of the sentence and as an object of propositional attitudes. Once King's account is revised so as to avoid the Benacerraf and grain-size problems, then, it is SWIMS-4* that emerges as the fact that is the proposition.

It is clear that what is lost in this revision is not only a distinctive role for syntax in providing propositional structure, but also the impression that the account offers any informative explanation of the unity of the proposition. The proposition that Sophie swims *is*, of course, unified on the revised account – that is guaranteed by its intrinsic possession of truth conditions. But the true explanation of this propositional unity rests in the unknown processes by which significance is *endowed* upon the phrase P (the sentence 'Sophie swims') through its *reception* by the conceptual-intentional systems that take such linguistic forms as input.

7. Conclusion

I have argued that previous attempts to show that King's syntax-based account of propositions faces either a Benacerraf problem or a grain-size problem have been unsuccessful. Nevertheless, I have argued that King's account as it stands is vulnerable to both problems, and I have identified the revision that is necessary to avoid these problems. The revised account provides a plausible identification of propositions with certain facts about natural-language sentences, but it is strikingly uninformative on the question of how propositional unity is achieved. In particular, it fails to establish the view that it is syntax that unifies the proposition.[22]

Notes

1. 'A proposition, in fact, is essentially a unity, and when analysis has destroyed the unity, no enumeration of constituents will restore the proposition. The verb, when used as a verb, embodies the unity of the proposition, and is thus distinguishable from the verb considered as a term, though I do not know how to give a clear account of the precise nature of the distinction' (Russell [1903] 2009, 51).
2. This initial statement of the account will be subject to several refinements as we proceed, along the lines of King's own exposition.
3. King indicates that MIRROR is subject to a slight qualification, resulting from a later refinement to his account: the additional provision, included within the propositional relation, that R 'encodes the instantiation function'. Under this refinement, MIRROR is 'not quite true' since 'propositions have an extra bit of structure not had by the sentences expressing them' (King 2007, 30).
4. Facts are taken to be individuated independently of their descriptions; for example, 'o instantiating P', 'P being instantiated by o', 'o standing in the instantiation relation to P' are descriptions of the same fact (King 2007, 63–64, note 69).
5. King refers here to acquaintance with the proposition 'qua proposition' (2007, 52). My terminology of 'acquaintance with the proposition *qua* content' is intended to preserve the primacy that King's terminology imputes to this mode of acquaintance.
6. King's explanation of how *PR-2* comes to inherit its significance from R is briefly discussed in the next section.
7. They call these, respectively, the 'plain propositional fact' and the 'augmented propositional fact'; SWIMS-1 is the 'diminished propositional fact'.
8. I put the term 'propositional relation' in scare-quotes here because the propositional relation is *by definition* that which binds the constituents together into the proposition. If on the correct account, SWIMS-2 were identified as the proposition, then *PR-2* would indeed be the propositional relation. But here the proposal under consideration is that SWIMS-2 is merely the *proto*-proposition; the *genuine* propositional relation on this story would be *PR-3* (the propositional relation of the SWIMS-3 account), which itself includes as a component that *PR-2* encodes instantiation. Similar comments apply to the discussion of *PR-1* below.
9. I ignore here the possibility that considerations of simplicity might break the tie in favor of SWIMS-2.5.
10. See, e.g., Collins (2007), Hanks (2009), and Speaks (2011).
11. This is in a personal communication cited by King (2013a, 769).
12. King's response to Burgess' objection is more nuanced than this remark suggests; see King (2013a, 769–773).
13. I omit discussion of another version of the grain-size objection, which is based on the observation that it seems possible to substitute syntactic variants of embedded

14. Note that SSSS only requires that syntactically identical sentences express structurally identical propositions. It does not itself require MIRROR, the claim that propositional structure is identical to syntactic structure. See King (2013a, 775).
15. King develops the argument in a different way from the presentation provided here, but the underlying idea is the same. See King (2013a, 774–777).
16. While to my knowledge, this challenge to King's account has not appeared anywhere in print, a very similar challenge is put forward in an unpublished paper by Speaks (2011, 8–9). In Speaks' example, the English sentence 'John loves Jane' is contrasted with the Reverse-English sentence 'Jane loves John', which has identical truth conditions.
17. This follows the diagram from King (2007, 54).
18. There is a subtlety here, because on King's account, the instruction provided by the syntactic relation will refer to the basic propositional constituents obliquely, that is, *via* the syntactic positions of the lexical items that designate them, and the instructions' reference to complex properties will therefore be oblique in a corresponding way. I ignore this complication here for ease of exposition.
19. At least this is true on the SWIMS-1 model. Since the account of SWIMS-2 introduces the additional component that R encodes instantiation, that fact will have some additional structure, which as King admits, makes MIRROR-F subject to a 'slight qualification' (King 2007, 54, note 59). Since as we've seen, for R to 'encode instantiation' is actually for R to bear some complicated relation to the conceptual-intentional systems that receive it, one might wonder whether the additional component actually introduces a lot of hidden complexity into the fact SWIMS-2, making the qualification to MIRROR-F not so slight after all. See note 3.
20. Note, however, that this is not because the syntactic structure of the sentence is *more* fine-grained than the content-structure of the proposition. In the case under consideration, the shared content-structure is precisely as fine-grained as the two syntactic structures.
21. While the proposal that King's account be amended so as to existentially generalize over particular syntactic relations has not to my knowledge appeared anywhere in print, it has been suggested in an unpublished paper by Speaks (2011, 9).
22. I would like to thank David Hunter and Gurpreet Rattan for very helpful comments on an earlier version of this paper.

References

Benacerraf, P. 1965. "What numbers could not be." *Philosophical Review* 74 (1): 47–73.
Caplan, B., and C. Tillman. 2012. "Benacerraf's revenge." *Philosophical Studies*. doi:10.1007/s11098-012-0064-8.
Chomsky, N. 1995. *The Minimalist Program*. Cambridge, MA: MIT Press.
Collins, J. 2007. "Syntax, More or Less." *Mind* 116 (464): 805–850.
Hanks, P. 2009. "Recent Work on Propositions." *Philosophy Compass* 4 (3): 469–486. doi:10.1111/j.1747-9991.2009.00208.x.

King, J. C. 1995. "Structured Propositions and Complex Predicates." *Noûs* 29 (4): 516–535.
King, J. C. 2007. *The Nature and Structure of Content*. Oxford: Oxford University Press.
King, J. C. 2009. "XIII—Questions of Unity." *Proceedings of the Aristotelian Society* 109 (3): 257–277.
King, J. C. 2013a. "On fineness of grain." *Philosophical Studies* 163 (3): 763–781.
King, J. C. 2013b. "Propositional unity: what's the problem, who has it and who solves it?" *Philosophical Studies* 165 (1): 71–93.
Russell, B. (1903) 2009. *Principles of Mathematics*. Reprint. Abingdon: Routledge.
Salmon, N. 1986. *Frege's Puzzle*. Cambridge, MA: MIT Press.
Soames, S. 1987. "Direct Reference, Propositional Attitudes, and Semantic Content." *Philosophical Topics* 15 (1): 47–87.
Speaks, J. 2011. "Facts, properties, and the nature of the proposition." Unpublished ms. http://www3.nd.edu/~jspeaks/papers/facts-properties-propositions.pdf
Stalnaker, R. 1976. "Possible Worlds." *Noûs* 10 (1): 65–75.

ON ACT- AND LANGUAGE-BASED CONCEPTIONS OF PROPOSITIONS

Why we should not identify sentence structure with propositional structure

Thomas Hodgson

It is a common view among philosophers of language that both propositions and sentences are structured objects. One obvious question to ask about such a view is whether there is any interesting connection between these two sorts of structure. The author identifies two theses about this relationship. *Identity* (ID) – the structure of a sentence and the proposition it expresses are identical. *Determinism* (DET) – the structure of a sentence determines the structure of the proposition it expresses. After noting that ID entails DET, the author argues against DET (and therefore also against ID). This argument is based on considerations to do with unarticulated constituents, but it is not ultimately empirical. As well as answering a question suggested by contemporary theories of propositions, the conclusion is significant because some, but not all, of the theories of propositions currently popular entail ID and/or DET. Unless there is a response to the argument here, those theories are refuted.

1. Introduction

Many philosophers of language claim that sentences express propositions. In this paper I will be interested only in structured propositions; I will assume that propositions are objects with constituents. I will also assume that these propositions are genuine existents in whatever precise sense that is to be understood; they are neither theorists' constructs nor creatures of fiction. The question of what sorts of things propositional constituents are is difficult and important, but it has no bearing on any of my arguments so I will take no view on it here.

Here is an idea that I think many philosophers would find congenial. Sentences are complexes with words as constituents. Sentences have a structure, and this structure is a key ingredient of their meaning as can be seen from the fact that there are distinct sentences with identical constituents as in:

(1) John loves Mary.
(2) Mary loves John.

The same can be said of propositions: they have a structure that is a key ingredient of their meaning. There are difficult metaphysical questions that need to be answered about both sentences and propositions, but I will assume that the thought just described is basically right. I will be focusing on a question that arises once it is accepted: what is the relationship between the structure of a structured proposition and the structure of the sentence that expresses it? One view, which I will called *Identity* (ID) is that, necessarily, the structures are identical. Another, *Determinism* (DET), which is weaker than ID, is that, necessarily, the structure of the sentence fixes the structure of the proposition. I will argue against DET. The argument, in Section 3, has two parts. (i) If English is a language that has unarticulated constituents, then a theory of propositions entailing DET is inadequate for theorising about linguistic communication using English. (ii) If it is merely possible that there is a language, L, that has unarticulated constituents then such a theory of propositions is inadequate for theorising about linguistic communication *tout court*. Because ID entails DET my argument against the latter is *ipso facto* an argument against the former.

2. Identity, determinism, structure, and expression

I will now spell out three key ideas that play a role in my argument. (i) What it is for the structure of a sentence and the structure of a proposition to be identical. (ii) How ID and DET should be understood. (iii) How the technical sense of *expression* that is operative here should be understood.

2.1. Identity

It is not entirely easy to explain what it is for a proposition to have the same structure as a sentence in a way that is clear, general, and does not presuppose anything about what propositions are. Fortunately, it is not so hard to say something about what it is for two sentences to have the same structure; I will start with that and then move on to dealing with propositional structure. Assuming some account of what the structures of sentences are, and that these structures can be represented as trees, one might be in the position of comparing the following:

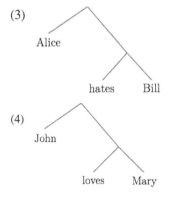

These two trees differ only in which lexical items occupy their nodes. That would be a good enough definition of what it is for two syntactic structures to have identical structures. If propositions were also trees then this account of identity could be extended to them without any difficulty, and it would allow for identity judgements to be made about pairs of sentences, pairs of propositions, and mixed pairs of propositions and sentences. If propositions are not trees then the situation is more complicated. Other sorts of structured object such as *n*-tuples or facts do not have nodes. If a definition in terms of nodes is used for ID then it looks like ID is trivially false unless propositions are trees. And, as far as I know, no philosophers think that propositions are trees even though some think that propositions can be represented by trees. What is needed is a general account of both propositional and sentential structures such that they can be compared with each other.

The closest thing to such an account is found in Jeffrey C. King's work. King employs two notions that are relevant, that of *sentential relations* and *propositional relations*. He writes about the former: 'I call relations ... that lexical items stand in to form sentences *sentential relations*' (King 2013a, 73). The propositional relation is described in the same paper as 'the relation that holds Michael and the property of swimming together in the proposition that Michael swims' (King 2013a, 75). I think that it is clear from King's overall picture that were the same lexical items to form a different sentence, or the same constituents to be combined in a different proposition, they would stand in different sentential/propositional relations.

According to this picture, there are relations corresponding to each distinct sentence structure and propositional structure. This suggests that a sentence and proposition can be compared in terms of their respective sentential and propositional relations. Here is one way that might be done. Let F be a function that maps lexical items to their denotations. Sentence S and proposition P will have an identical structure just in case the following conditions hold:

(i) The sentential relation of S relates lexical items $s_1, \ldots, s_n$ in that order.
(ii) The propositional relation of P relates lexical items $p_1, \ldots, p_n$ in that order.
(iii) For all i, $F(s_i) = p_i$.

This suggestion would make ID non-trivial and would allow us to compare sentence structure to propositional structure regardless of what propositions are. I propose adopting it as a working definition of what it is for two distinct structured objects, which may well not be unified by the same relation, to have the same structure in an appropriately abstract sense.

With a definition of sameness of structure in place, it is possible to define ID:

(ID) Necessarily, if sentence S expresses proposition P, then the structure of S is the same as the structure of P.

Note that this is not merely a possible position in logical space: one of the more prominent recent theories of propositions entails ID, i.e. the theory defended in

King (2007, 2009, 2013a). According to King's view, propositions are facts that have the same structure as the sentences that express them, and because this follows from the very nature of propositions it follows that ID is a necessary truth. (There is a possible complication here, to do with the particular notion of expression, described in Section 2.4, that I will be working with. It might be that King has something else in mind. In Section 4, I will explicitly connect my argument to one he makes where he uses the term 'expression'.) ID would also hold of certain Fregean views, as pointed out by an anonymous commentator; see Heck and May (2011). However, even if nobody had actually held a view that entails DET, it would still be worthwhile to show that one possible substantive connection between propositions and the sentences that express them cannot hold.

2.2. Determinism

Even if one doesn't think that the structure of a sentence and a proposition that it expresses are identical, there are other ways in which they might be systematically related. One such view is that the structure of a sentence fixes the structure of the proposition that it expresses. ID entails this, although not vice versa. I suggest the following as a way of capturing this idea:

> (DET) If sentence S expresses proposition P, then (i) S having the structure it has, and (ii) S expressing P entails that P has the structure it has.

This does not require that the structures are the same, merely that the structure of the sentence that expresses the proposition fixes the structure of the proposition expressed; the latter has the structure it has because the former has the structure it has. In Section 3, I will argue against it, or rather that theories of propositions that entail it are unacceptable. For the sake of brevity I will speak of DET as if it is a theory, i.e. I will speak as if I am arguing against philosophers who endorse DET rather than philosophers who endorse a theory that entails DET. For an example of a view that entails DET (but not ID) see Soames (1987).

I will not offer additional arguments against ID. Instead, I will rely on the fact that ID entails DET, therefore if DET is refuted then so is ID. To see that ID entails DET it is sufficient to note that, if the structure of a sentence and a proposition expressed are necessarily identical, then the former fixes the latter. The structure of the proposition could not have been different unless the structure of the sentence was and this is sufficient for DET.

2.3. Structure

Both ID and DET presuppose not only that propositions have structure, and that sentences and propositions can have the same structure, but also that sentences have structure. This is of course an absolutely standard view, but I think that it is worth pointing out that there is not one notion of sentence structure that is common to all theories of language. A discussion of arguments for and against

DET would be incomplete, to the point of uselessness, without some idea of what notion of sentence structure is supposed to be in play. In this section, I will briefly describe the notion of sentence structure that I have in mind, and that I think that many of the theorists involved in these debates have as well.

As said in Section 1, the idea that sentences are complexes with words as constituents is widely held. It is not a trivial question to fix on what words are, see for example Kaplan (1990) and Hawthorne and Lepore (2011) for some of the debate over this question. That sentences are structured, with different structures corresponding to certain sorts of disambiguations, is a standard idea. This structure is sometimes called the *logical form* (LF) of a sentence, as in this representative quote from Jason Stanley:

> According to the second tradition of usage, which one might call the *descriptive* conception of logical form, the logical form of a sentence is something like the 'real structure' of that sentence (e.g., [Harman (1970)][1]). On this approach, we may discover that the 'real' structure of a natural language sentence is in fact quite distinct from its surface grammatical form. Talk of logical form in this sense involves attributing hidden complexity to sentences of natural language, complexity which is ultimately revealed by empirical inquiry. (Stanley 2000, 392)

Stanley is not using the term 'logical form' idiosyncratically; there is a tradition of framing certain issues this way. For example, in the paper I cite he defends the view that every constituent of a proposition expressed by an utterance can be traced to some element of the uttered sentence's LF. Opponents of that claim (e.g. Recanati 2002, 2004, 2007, 2010), have tended to accept the terms in which it is made while they argue against it. In other words they accept that there is an interesting notion of LF along these lines, but they deny that every constituent of what is expressed is present (*articulated*) at LF. I think that all these theorists would be happy to accept the following two theses about LF. (i) LF is there to be discovered by the methods of linguistics. (ii) LF is the input to semantic interpretation. It is worth noting that (i) leads to the situation that any very strong or specific claim about the nature of LF is a hostage to empirical fortune. A striking illustration of this fact can be given using the observation that most of the technical vocabulary used by Harman in the paper cited by Stanley is not used in the dominant *minimalist* grammars associated with recent work by Noam Chomsky and those he has influenced. There is, of course, still a notion of sentence structure to be found in such theories; my point is just that it is both terminologically and substantively different to that found in Stanley's work and those who engage with it. For a discussion of this and related points in the context of the debate over structured propositions see Collins (2007). In any case, I will be assuming that there is some sense in which sentences have structures, and that we can come to know about their nature. My arguments against DET will not presuppose anything substantive about the nature of such structures.

The second thesis about LF is extremely common. It is presupposed in the debate about the articulation or otherwise of constituents, and it is a central part of the sort of approach to formal semantics found in textbooks such as Heim and

Kratzer (1997). It is worth noting that use of the term 'logical form' does not always track such an input. For example *relevance theorists* use the term to refer to the meaning encoded by a sentence relative to a context (Sperber and Wilson 1995; Carston 2002). This is a kind of structured representation and, in this, relevance theory and the Chomskyan approach to syntax agree. But a LF, on this account, is not something that can receive interpretation: it is already interpreted. Nor is it essentially syntactic; it is already in the same 'format' as other thoughts (see Carston 2002, 89, endnote 26). Leaving that alternative view aside, I will be assuming the notion of logical form that is synonymous with sentence structure in the sense described in Stanley (2000). I think that this is what proponents of DET likely have in mind. If not, then it is at least clear exactly where my discussion of the relationship between sentence structure and propositional structure fails to connect with theirs.

2.4. *Expression*

The notion of *expression* will be extremely important in what follows; it will appear in the premises of arguments in Section 3. I have chosen 'expression' as a relatively neutral term, but it will perhaps be helpful to explain what I mean by it with reference to some standard technical terminology. What I mean by expression is the thing targeted by relevance theorists as *explicature*, by Kent Bach as *impliciture*, by and François Recanati as *what is said* in his version of truth-conditional pragmatics (Bach 1994; Sperber and Wilson 1995; Recanati 2004, 2010). Common to all these views is the claim that propositions are communicated by the utterance of sentences. But not every proposition that is communicated is done so in a like manner. For example, borrowing Gricean terminology, some of the propositions that are communicated by utterances are *implicated* (Grice 1989). The terminology I have just mentioned is designed to pick out a proper subset of the class of communicated propositions, i.e. those that are not implicated. I mean 'expression' to track that subset as well. On this taxonomy, utterances may express one or more propositions, and they may implicate one or more further propositions. (It doesn't matter for present purposes whether more than one proposition can be expressed, or whether one proposition can be both expressed and implicated. My way of speaking so far is compatible with any answer to the first question. It would have to be amended slightly to accommodate the second possibility.)

It will become important in what follows that expression is primarily a psychological notion. A proposition P being expressed depends on language users taking it to be communicated in a certain sort of way. In putting things in these terms I am especially following Recanati (2004, 2010) although I think that the other theorists mentioned above also hold this view. The proposition expressed must be something that speakers take to be communicated by the utterance in question. The point is that speakers' judgements about what has and has not been communicated by a particular utterance play the main role in fixing what has been expressed, although there are, of course, other factors that are relevant, including those that make the difference between expression and implicature. This is not supposed to be a diagnostic for expression, and I hope that it does not beg any questions. The point is just that: (i) speakers have access to the contents that are expressed, and (ii) speakers' judgements about these contents are a way for theorists to get a grip on what is or is not expressed by an utterance. When I come to make my main argument I will make use of this notion of expression. I will also indicate where someone who wanted to resist my argument might try to reject the notion of expression on which I rely. The point of the preceding discussion is to show that a notion like mine, in the respects that are relevant for this paper, is a popular view in philosophy of language and linguistics, and that it has been defended by prominent theorists working in those fields. I hope that this goes some way to justify my reliance on it.

3. Against determinism

In this section I will present my argument against DET. In Section 3.1, I describe the phenomenon of *(communicational) unarticulated constituents*. In Section 3.2, I argue that, if there is such a phenomenon, then DET is refuted. Finally, in Section 3.3, I make an argument that does not rely on the empirical premise that unarticulated constituents are actual. This matters dialectically, because that thesis is controversial and has been denied by at least one proponent of an account of propositions entailing DET, i.e. King (King and Stanley 2005).

In what follows I will be focusing on one among many of the roles that propositions have been supposed to play in the philosophy of language: being the things that are expressed by utterances. This might be called the *communicational role*. The importance of the communicational role is the part that it plays in theories of linguistic communication, for example disputes about the various contributions of semantics and pragmatics. I am not interested here in other roles propositions might be wanted for, such as being the primary bearers of truth, the objects of psychological attitudes, or the referents of that-clauses. This is not because I am not interested in these questions, but because they are not directly relevant to the present argument.

3.1. Communicational unarticulated constituents

The term *unarticulated constituent* was introduced by John Perry (1986). The example that Perry used, which has been ubiquitous in the literature ever since, is:

(5) It is raining.

Here is what Perry says about the example:

> It is a rainy Saturday morning in Palo Alto. I have plans for tennis. But my younger son looks out the window and says, 'It is raining'. I go back to sleep. What my son said was true, because it was raining in Palo Alto. There were all sorts of places

where it wasn't raining: it doesn't just rain or not, it rains in some places while not raining in others. In order to assign a truth-value to my son's statement, as I just did, I needed a place. But no component of his statement stood for a place. The verb 'raining' supplied the relation *rains (t,p)* – a dyadic relation between times and places ... [.] The tensed auxiliary 'is' supplies a time, the time at which the statement was made. 'It' doesn't supply anything, but is just syntactic filler. So Palo Alto is a constituent of the content of my son's remark, which no component of his statement designated; it is an *unarticulated* constituent. (Perry 1986, 138)

In this paper, I am interested in the data Perry noted, rather than the analysis he gave. Here is what I take to be a relatively neutral characterisation of what the observation is supposed to be, in a form that should be acceptable to all of those who believe in unarticulated constituents. (i) An utterance of sentence (5) relative to a certain context expresses the proposition that it is raining in Palo Alto. (ii) Palo Alto is not the semantic-value of any constituent of the sentence (5). Note that knowing (i) requires having access to the content expressed in one way or another. Knowing (ii) requires knowing what the semantic-values of the constituents of the sentence are. This in turn requires knowing what the constituents are.

Here is one way to characterise the claim that there are unarticulated constituents:

(UC) A constituent O of the proposition P expressed by utterance U of sentence S is *unarticulated* if O is not the semantic-value relative to the context of U of any element of S's LF.

This condition is sufficient, although arguably it is not necessary. Adam Sennet has recently argued that there are cases where what is intuitively an unarticulated constituent is in fact the semantic-value of a constituent of the sentence uttered. In his examples the constituent appears twice in the proposition, but only once is it articulated (Sennet 2011); sentence (5) is not one of those cases. I only need a sufficient condition to make my point. If something like UC is a sufficient condition for unarticulated constituency the claim being made by those influenced by Perry is that there are cases, such as (5), that meet that condition. In what follows, I will sometimes talk about a language having unarticulated constituents, or about UC being true of a language. I intend that as a shorthand way of saying that the language in question is such that UC is true of at least some of its sentences as they are used by its speakers.

While it was Perry who introduced the idea of an unarticulated constituent into the philosophical literature, at least under that name, an important distinction needs to be drawn between his proposal and the version of the claim that I am concerned with in this paper. I will follow Recanati in labelling the distinction as one between *communicational* and *metaphysical* unarticulated constituents. Recanati introduces the distinction like this:

[T]here is an important distinction between the metaphysical variety and the communicational variety. An unarticulated constituent belongs to the communicational variety to the extent that it is part of the interpretation of an utterance and, as such, is 'available' to whoever fully understands the utterance.

> This feature is best appreciated by contrast to the other sort of unarticulated constituents — the metaphysical sort, for which no such constraint holds. (Recanati 2002, 305)

I take Recanati to be making the following distinction. One might, following Perry's original statement, hold that because certain sorts of event necessarily take place in some location, the content expressed by certain utterances must include that location. That is a metaphysical claim aimed at avoiding the consequence that such utterances lack truth-values. The argument in question is an argument for metaphysical unarticulated constituents. The argument for communicational unarticulated constituents is different. That argument is based on observations about the content that those who encounter utterances of sentences like (5) typically take to be communicated by them.

The communicational version of UC, which is what I will be focusing on, is closely connected to the notion of expression discussed in Section 2.4. That a proposition with certain constituents is expressed in this sense is part of the evidence for UC, along with the additional premise that one or more of its constituents is not the semantic-value of some element of the structure of the sentence uttered. There is an epistemological consequence to this way of setting up UC. If we have reason to think that UC is true, that must be because we have reason to think that we know what is expressed. I don't think that this claim is particularly controversial, but it does play a role in the argument I am about to give. That is because the argument uses UC as a premise, and therefore presupposes that we have access to what is expressed (and that it is as UC requires). One might object to this, but only by rejecting UC itself. This would be an objection to the soundness of the argument I am about to give, rather than its validity. This in turn matters dialectically because I will go on to argue that the mere validity of the argument I am about to give can be used as a premise in a further argument against DET.

3.2. Unarticulated constituents refute determinism

Many philosophers of language endorse UC, and given that UC is framed in terms of propositions and their constituents, those who endorse UC are committed to structured propositions. It is surprising that there has not been more discussion of the relationship between these two views. I have been able to find only two discussions; one is Sennet (2011, 423, footnote 15), and the other is King (2012, §1); in both cases the possibility of a problem is raised in passing rather than being fully discussed. I will now argue that UC is incompatible with a certain sort of account of structured propositions, namely one that entails DET. Among other things I intend this as an illustration of the importance of UC, a thesis about how natural languages are used to communicate, for theories of the metaphysics of content.

In order to make my argument, one final feature of UC needs to be emphasised: unarticulated constituents are *optional* in a sense that I will now explain. A genuine unarticulated constituent does not merely have different contents relative to different contexts, but appears at all only in certain contexts. This claim has been defended mainly in Recanati (2002, 2004, 2007), and also in Martí (2006). To illustrate, one might compare:

(5) It is raining.
and
(6) It is raining here.

An utterance of (6) always expresses a proposition with some location in it. An utterance of (5) might express a proposition that does not or one that does. Note that without optionality it is not clear that UC is interestingly different from some of its competitor views, for example it is not clear why one would posit non-optional unarticulated constituents rather than covert elements of logical form. As a matter of fact, optionality has been taken as a central part of the view by defenders such as Recanati; the work cited above also contains empirical arguments for the claim that UCs are optional. The following argument should be read as an argument based on (communicational, optional) unarticulated constituents. If UCs weren't optional then the argument would be weakened. The optionality shows that, unlike for example (6), the very structure of the proposition expressed by (5) depends on the context in which it is uttered.

Taking as granted the claim that in some context an utterance of (5) expresses a proposition containing Palo Alto, and in another it does not, and that this is not because there is unpronounced structure in both that simply takes a different contextually fixed value, one can argue as follows.

(i) Relative to context C, the proposition expressed by sentence S with structure Θ has propositional structure Λ.
(ii) Relative to context C', the proposition expressed by sentence S with structure Θ has propositional structure Λ'.
(iii) $\Lambda \neq \Lambda'$.
(iv) So, it is not the case that the structure of S determines the structure of the proposition it expresses.

Premises (i)–(iii) can be established for (5) by looking at its utterance in the context originally described by Perry and one in which it expresses a proposition that has no location as a constituent. Note that there must be such cases if unarticulated constituents are genuinely optional; see especially Recanati (2007) for discussion of some plausible candidate contexts. In these two contexts, propositions with different structures are expressed, but the sentences that express them have the same structure. The propositions in question must have different structures, not because they have different constituents, but because they have different numbers of constituents (cf. my discussion of identity conditions for propositional structures in Section 2.3). Conclusion (iv) follows because, if the same sentence structure allows for the expression of different propositional structures, then sentence structure cannot be determining propositional structure. The conclusion of the argument is just the denial of DET as described in Section 2.2.

A defender of DET might respond that the problem arises from the conflation of two notions of expression. The objection would begin by noting that the unarticulated constituent theorist has used a notion of expression that tracks the content that speakers take to be communicated by an utterance. That is the sense of 'expression' they appeal to in the formulation of their view. The defender of DET might then argue that she does not need to accept that that is the thing that her notion of expression tracks. For instance, she might claim that her theory just is a theory of the contents composed from the structure and constituents of the LF. Such a thing need not be identical to what is expressed in the first, communicative, sense. Here is how the two notions might be formulated.

(E1) A sentence S relative to a context C expresses, in the communicational sense, that proposition which competent hearers take to be communicated by the utterance of S.

(E2) A sentence S relative to a context C expresses, in the semantic-value sense, the proposition that consists of the semantic-values of the terminal nodes of S composed according to the structure of S.

The defender of DET might try to avoid the problem with unarticulated constituents by making this sort of distinction and holding that her theory is a theory of E2. The theory will no longer make problematic claims about E1. In fact it will not make any claims about what is communicated, so this version of DET will be compatible with the unarticulated constituency theorist's claim about what is communicated, as well as her claim about the LF of sentences such as (5). In terms of the argument presented in this section, the response amounts to denying that such an argument would ever be sound. If expression is just the relation between an LF and a (skeletal) proposition that holds when the proposition is constructed out of the semantic-values of the lexical items and combined as the lexical items are combined, then there will be no cases where structurally identical sentences express, in the E2 sense, structurally distinct propositions.

This response on behalf of DET is ultimately unsatisfactory. Propositions are supposed to be part of our theories of communication. Those theorists who employ them typically identify them as what is communicated, or what is said, and that just is what is expressed in the sense that I have been using the term. This proposal on behalf of DET requires breaking that link; using 'expression' in a different sense does not make this move more appealing. So, the amended version of the theory cannot do what a theory of its type is supposed to. Perhaps some defenders of DET will be prepared to bite that bullet; possibly motivated by some consideration such as the following. It is true that a proposition communicated is not related to the sentence used to express it in the way described by DET. But there is an important theoretical role for a class of propositions that are related in that way to a class of sentences. Endorsing DET in its restricted form is therefore a viable theoretical option. The kind of view I have in mind is one where there are (skeletal) propositions that are the semantic values of sentences in context. They are not what is communicated, but they play a role in the explanation of communication (precisely what that role is doesn't matter here). Furthermore, the relationship between a sentence in context and the relevant skeletal proposition satisfies DET, for views of this sort see for example Bach (2001) and Soames (2008). The problem is that, whatever else one thinks of such theories, they have the consequence that the semantic values of sentences relative to contexts are sometimes incomplete i.e. not fully propositional in the sense of having truth-conditions. (This point is emphasised more by Bach than Scott Soames, although both endorse it.) This fact puts the defender of DET in a very uncomfortable position. Propositions are posited because we need structured entities with truth-conditions in order to give theories of linguistic communication. However, because the theory entails DET and given UC, their version of the theory cannot have propositions be the things that are communicated. To say that they are playing some other role, i.e. that of the semantic-values of sentences, would be reasonable if we needed structured entities with truth-conditions to play that role. But if semantic-values need not have truth-conditions then it is unclear why we need propositions to play that role. Furthermore, if some semantic-values do not have truth-conditions but all propositions do then it is not just that propositions have properties that they would not need to have in order to play this role; they have properties that preclude them from playing that role. If we do not need propositions to play that role then there is no reason to defend DET as a theory of propositions; one might as well defend the view that an equivalent principle to DET governs the relationship between semantic-values and sentences. There is no objection to adopting that view, but it is not a defence of DET in any interesting sense, because it is not a defence of a theory of propositions. This concludes my argument that, if UC is true, any theory of propositions that entails DET is refuted.

3.3. *Doing without the empirical premise*

The argument in Section 3.2 is empirical in the following way. UC is a claim about English, although presumably it is intended to apply to other natural languages. Those who think it is true do so because they think that the sentences produced by speakers are a certain way, and that the thoughts they communicate by uttering such sentences are a certain way. If things had been different, and to my knowledge no defender of unarticulated constituents has argued that they could not have been, the thesis would be false. Because the argument against DET relies on the premise that there are unarticulated constituents in English, that argument's soundness depends on an empirical claim.

It is not insignificant to show that two views are incompatible, especially if both are interesting and are actually held by some people working in the field. However, resting on an empirical premise in this way means that a defender of

DET has an obvious strategy for avoiding the argument: she can simply deny the empirical claim. Furthermore, as said above, King defends a view that entails DET and also rejects UC. So, at least one of the philosophers who I am trying to argue against in this paper has so far been given no reason to think that his view has unacceptable consequences. One way to proceed would be to argue that UC is in fact true. I won't pursue that line here partly because I think that the question remains open. I will also not try to find some other empirical phenomenon on which to rest the premise in Section 3.2 because the same response could be made to that. If one wanted to pursue that line the most promising example would be non-sentential assertion, as described and defended in for example Stainton (2005).

Instead I will argue that views entailing DET are refuted even if UC is merely possible, and that it is possible. In order to make this argument I will need to introduce the notion of a *linguistic practice*. By this I intend to pick out the sort of thing covered by the rough and ready folk idea of *speaking English*. Roughly speaking, a group of human beings are speaking English when they are uttering sentences of a certain sort in order to communicate with one another. There are a lot of actual linguistic practices, and also many non-actual but possible ones. Examples would be languages that were once spoken but are no longer, but also various alternative ways that actual languages might have been that have simply not been realised. Note that nothing much depends on how finely or coarsely the idiolects of speakers at times are grouped into languages, nor is there a particular ontology of language being assumed in this description. I am interested in whatever it is that turns out to be what ordinary reflective people are tracking when they say in ordinary clear cases that, for example the language of instruction for a course is English. Theories of (linguistic) communication are in part theories of linguistic practices. And theories of propositions are supposed to be part of our theories of communication, propositions are introduced in part in order to be the things that are communicated. In particular they are introduced as part of a theory of what is expressed by utterances of sentences.

The argument can be put like this.

(i) If a theory of propositions is not applicable to any possible linguistic practice, then it is unacceptable.
(ii) A theory of propositions entailing DET is not applicable to a linguistic practice of which UC is true.
(iii) Linguistic practices of which UC are true are possible.
(iv) So, a theory of propositions entailing DET is unacceptable.

My argument for premise (ii) is just to appeal to the argument in Section 3.2. Note that the argument does not need to be sound in order to establish premise (ii), merely valid. What is required is the incompatibility of UC and DET, which is established by an argument with the truth if UC as a premise and the rejection of DET as its conclusion. So this argument does not carry any commitment to the empirical premise that UC is true of English, or any other (actual) natural language.

Premise (iii) requires a defence I will now provide. First, I would like to note that no opponent of UC has denied premise (iii). This is not particularly surprising given that UC is based in part on claims about the psychologies of groups of speakers, and the sentences they use to communicate. In other words, it is the kind of claim that it is very easy to suppose could have been false if certain things had turned out differently, in this case the psychologies of the speakers and/or the nature of the sentences that they produce. That the ultimate correctness of UC is bound up with this sort of empirical, and presumably contingent, claim, has been put by two prominent opponents of UC as follows: '[These debates over UC] are largely empirical disputes, the resolution of which will require decades of cross-linguistic syntactic and semantic research, together with psychological studies' (King and Stanley 2005, 137). That this is so follows from the nature of (communicational) unarticulated constituents.

Of course it does not follow from the fact that nobody seems to deny premise (iii) that it is true, and for obvious reasons it will not do to defend the premise by arguing that unarticulated constituents are possible because they are actual. That would be to return the argument to that of Section 3.2, which is just what I am trying to avoid. My reason for thinking that premise (iii) is true is that linguistic practices that would be sufficient for its truth can be perfectly coherently supposed. To illustrate the point, I will focus on a linguistic practice that I will call *speaking English'* which is one where (by stipulation) the conditions required for UC being true of that practice are met. My claim is that one can perfectly coherently suppose the existence of a community of humans who speak English'. Because of the way I have defined linguistic practices, and because of the nature of UC and therefore what it would take for it to be true of a community's linguistic practice, what is being supposed can be divided naturally into two parts. (i) That the members of the supposed community express certain thoughts (e.g. that it is raining in such-and-such a place). (ii) That they sometimes do so by uttering sentences that do not articulate all of the places that the thoughts communicated are about (e.g. tokens of 'It is raining' where there is no covert location in their LFs). One must deny that there could be a linguistic practice with these two properties in order to deny that there could be a linguistic practice of which UC was true. I will now argue in turn that both denials would be implausible, or at least that the cost of either denial is extremely high.

Before making that argument I will provide a brief defence of my methodology. First, I would like to point out that I am not attempting to make use of a principle such as: if I can imagine *P*, then *P* is possible. Rather, I wish to exploit a more specific feature of the debate over unarticulated constituents. In that debate it is accepted that UC is a claim about various features of a community of speakers, including facts about their psychologies and the sentences they utter. There is a dispute about how the actual community of English speakers is regarding those features, and therefore whether or not UC is true of their practice. Neither side claims that the claim they take to be actually true is metaphysically necessary. I am now engaged in explaining why it would be a mistake to make that claim. I propose to do so by drawing attention to the problems that arise from denying that various things necessary for making UC true might obtain.

The problem with denying that component (i) is a property of a possible linguistic practice is that it is clearly possible to describe a practice that has all the properties that lead us to say, of actual practices, that they involve the communication of that sort of thought. Note that here it is better to talk about an intuitive notion of communicating a thought, i.e. what we mean when we judge that the son in Perry's example has said something about Palo Alto, rather than a technical notion of expressing a proposition. That is because what is of interest now is the pre-theoretical data that a theory of communication is supposed to regiment, and propositions *qua* structured objects are not part of that data. Recall that English and English' cannot be distinguished simply by listening to the utterances made by their speakers. Even if English is a language of which UC is false and English' is one of which UC is true, the difference between them is solely in the unpronounced structure of the sentences that their speakers utter. So, all the evidence we have that English speakers communicate a certain thought is also evidence that in equivalent circumstances English' speakers communicate that same thought. In particular, the kind of behavioural evidence used in Perry's original example can be supposed to be the same.

Unless some reason is given to think that it is impossible that utterances of the two languages would have all the same sorts of psychological effects on their audiences, I take it that it is reasonable to hold that they could at least possibly be used to communicate the same things. Denying that would have the following odd consequence. Two linguistic practices that cannot be told apart by attending to the utterances of the speakers involved, nor by their psychological states, can nonetheless differ in what is communicated by those speakers. This would be to draw a distinction between sets of practices that seem to be best treated alike by a theory of communication. For this reason, I conclude that it would be a cost for an account of propositions if it could only be saved from an objection by appealing to such a distinction.

To make the argument in the preceding paragraph I have used the notion of *expressing a thought*. I have done this so as to avoid closing off by stipulation another possible response that the defender of DET might consider making. That response would be to argue as follows. One can concede both (i) and (ii), but hold that in such cases propositions are not what is expressed; i.e. that we should not theorise about those cases using a theory that models the communication of thoughts with the expression of propositions. One way to do this would be to propose a theory where some other entities, distinct from propositions, are expressed (or perhaps stand in some other relation to utterances entirely). This allows the proponent of DET to hold that when propositions are in play (i.e. when they are what is expressed) the principle relating sentence structure to propositional structure holds, while accepting that there are cases where what is expressed does not obey that principle. DET is not refuted by these cases because the things that do not obey the principle are not propositions.

The problem with this response is that it is a retreat from the basic motivation for positing propositions in the first place. The idea was to posit a class of objects that are the things expressed and use them in a theory that explained various linguistic phenomena, such as the communication of thoughts. Saving DET in this way means restricting the theory of propositions to a limited class of cases, and, even worse, based on a separation that does not seem to carve linguistic reality at its joints. The separation is not joint-carving because there is no reason to think that linguistic practices that seem to differ only in whether UC is true of them will also differ in what their speakers express independently of an attempt to save certain theories of the objects of expression. This is because the intuitive data about the thoughts communicated will be the same for the two practices; the defender of DET is now proposing an *ad hoc* distinction in the way we should model the two classes of practice in a theory of communication.

As far as I can see, the only way to deny component (ii) would be to deny that there could be an LF assigned to (5) with the property of lacking a location. The idea would be that 'rain' requires a location argument, and therefore that where a location is unpronounced a covert argument of some kind must be generated. (Whatever this is it must be an argument, not an adjunct, because it must be non-optional.) If so, UC is necessarily false rather than merely contingently false as its opponents have tended to claim.

The problem with this line of thought is that it is hard to see how it could be principled. Actual languages contain predicates with a single argument. So such predicates are possible. Someone who proposed the sort of denial of component (ii) that I am considering would have to explain why there could not be a predicate with a single argument that had the kind of meaning that those who think that UC is true of English take 'raining' to have in (5). Note that it will not do to say that 'raining' must have a location argument because it denotes a type of event that as a matter of metaphysical necessity happens at a location. This is for a reason familiar from the debate over UC. Many other predicates, e.g. 'dancing', denote types of event that happen at some location or other, but they do not show any sign of an extra argument; see Cappelen and Lepore (2007) for an argument of this type against the metaphysical version of UC. This is not to say that the opponents of UC cannot consistently hold that 'raining', but not 'dancing', has exactly the necessary property, i.e. being such that any predicate denoting an event of the same type must have a location argument, and that any predicate of English[′] will have it as well. My point is that there is no obvious motivation for that claim, and that without such a motivation it would be *ad hoc* to endorse it in order to preserve a certain account of propositions.

Even granting the points just made, someone might object to premise (iii) in the following way. It is all very well to hold that one can suppose a practice in which the right sort of thoughts are communicated, and one where the right sort of sentences are used. But it does not follow that there is one joint practice of which both these suppositions hold. I agree that this does not follow from the fact that the two components can each be supposed to hold of a practice. But, given that, I claim that the burden of proof is on those who hold that something about their interaction rules out a practice of which they both hold.

This position can be supported by the following consideration. If one is interested in whether a linguistic practice can have a range of properties, one way to provide evidence is through a thought-experiment in which a practice is stipulated to have one of them, and then to gradually acquire the other. In the scenario I have in mind there is a community of speakers who utter sentences of the type 'It is raining', where there is no covert location, and thereby communicate thoughts that are about no location. Over time they come to use these utterances to communicate thoughts about locations, typically the location of utterance, in just the way that defenders of UC claim is true of English speakers, and which is true by stipulation of English′ speakers. In this scenario, component (ii) was stipulated to obtain, and then it was supposed that the psychologies of the speakers changed in such a way that component (i) came to obtain. There is no reason to think that adding component (i) can plausibly be thought of as a dividing line between a practice that can coherently be supposed and one that cannot be, because all that is being supposed is that speakers take certain thoughts to be expressed by their utterances. Such facts about communication presumably supervene on those speakers' beliefs and intentions. The beliefs and intentions they would have to have in this case are ones that they might perfectly well have; after all they are the same beliefs and intentions as English speakers have.

Another objection, on behalf of a defender of a view that entails DET, has been suggested to me by an anonymous commentator. Suppose that linguistic practices are natural kinds. It is widely believed that at least some of the properties of a given natural kind are such that anything that did not possess them would not count as a member of that kind. According to a popular instantiation of this view, it is an empirical discovery that gold has atomic number 79. So something that didn't have this property just isn't gold, even if it is very like gold in other respects. (The literature on natural kinds and the semantics of terms that might denote them is vast; for a survey see Bird and Tobin 2012.) Perhaps the status of unarticulated constituents is like that, i.e. perhaps it is both the case that actual linguistic practices are not UC practices and that something that seemed like a linguistic practice but did involve UCs would *ipso facto* not be a linguistic practice. In that case, the defender of a view entailing DET could say that her view does apply to all linguistic practices, even though it doesn't apply to certain things that are superficially like linguistic practices but are in fact not linguistic practices.

This objection is promising for the defender of DET. One advantage it offers to the defender of DET is that it would allow her to explain in a principled way why some cases that look like they ought to fall under the scope of a theory of communication in fact do not. The cases that her theory of propositions cannot apply to would be just those cases that are apparent, but not genuine, linguistic practices. This would rebut my argument against the move presented above. That being said, I think that much work would be needed in order to flesh out the objection. In particular it rests on two claims that would need to be argued. (i) Linguistic practices are natural kinds. (ii) The property of having UCs is the sort of property (like an element's atomic number) that supports the argument. Neither of these claims is obvious. I would like to note, in response to the commentator, that nothing would be gained by putting the point in terms of natural languages rather than linguistic practices. There are things that philosophers and linguists have called 'language' that are more plausible candidates for being natural kinds than linguistic practices as I have defined them. I have in mind the I-languages found in Chomskyan theory (Chomsky 1986); see Collins (2010) for a recent philosophical discussion. But such things are not what theorists of communication study, and they are not the sort of thing that theories of propositions can do much to illuminate. I think that this point will generalise. I am open to the suggestion that the defender of DET might object to my use of linguistic practices and propose an alternative definition. But, I conjecture, any proposal she makes will not both pick out something that is more plausibly a natural kind than my definition, and also pick out something that is in the domain of a theory of communication. In that case pursuing the response will entail conceding my point, which is that theories of propositions that entail DET cannot be used as part of a theory of communication.

I have now presented an argument against theories of propositions that entail DET that does not carry the empirical commitment that the argument if Section 3.2 does. This shows that a proponent of a view entailing DET cannot respond by simply denying that empirical claim. Unless it turns out that UC is necessarily false, something which may well be proved by future research but which is currently not even suggested by anybody working in the field, DET is an unacceptable consequence for a theory of propositions to have.

4. Same syntax, same structure?

In this final section I will now discuss a thesis defended in King (2013b, §3) that is related to DET but distinct from it. King formulates the principle *Same Syntax, Same Structure* (SSSS) as follows:

> Sentences of a given language with the same syntactic structure and that differ only in having lexical items with different semantic values occurring at the same places in their syntactic trees express propositions with the same structure that differ at most in having different constituents, corresponding to the lexical items with different semantic values, occurring in the same places in those propositions. (King 2013b, 775)

ID, as I have defined it, is the claim that syntactic structure and propositional structure are identical. This entails that if two sentences have the same structure then the propositions they express have the same structure. It also entails the converse of this, i.e. it entails both SSSS and what might be called the *same structure, same syntax* principle. ID also entails DET. In Section 3 I argued against DET, which can straightforwardly be turned into arguments against ID. If SSSS also entails DET then arguments against DET will also count against SSSS. That this is so can be shown easily. Suppose that, as SSSS claims, it is necessary that all sentences with a certain syntactic structure express propositions with a certain propositional structure. It follows that if the structure of a sentence is fixed then the structure of the proposition it expresses is fixed, i.e. it is the structure that all the propositions expressed by sentences with that particular structure have.

A worry that might arise at this point is whether my argument against DET is talking past King's use of SSSS. Perhaps the intended sense of expression there is more like the E2 sense, i.e. compositional semantic-value, from Section 3.2, than the E1 communicated content sense. My reason for thinking that the sense operative in SSSS must be the E1 sense is that the E2 semantic-value sense trivialises the principle. King must intend SSSS to be substantive, which suggests that when he formulates it in terms of expression he means the same notion as is used in ID. With that in mind I will now return to the main point.

SSSS is used as a premise in an argument King makes in the course of defending his view of propositions. That view entails that propositions are individuated very finely. It is a common objection to the view that ordinary intuitions about sameness and difference of content do not individuate so finely. Several examples of this line of criticism are discussed in King (2013b) including Collins (2007); John Collins has pursued his criticism in Collins (2013). (Collins also rejects the argument I am discussing here, although he denies a different premise.) If this critical point is right then it would motivate a view that 'collapses' the propositions expressed by sentences with different syntactic structures into identical structured propositions. King uses SSSS as part of an argument against such collapse views. I will briefly summarise his argument in this subsection, but the more important point is that arguments against DET also threaten SSSS. While the failure of SSSS does not entail that King's position is false, it does refute his main positive argument against the collapse view.

King's argument proceeds by taking two pairs of sentences with the following properties. (i) All four plausibly have the same syntactic structure. (ii) One pair is a plausible candidate for collapse while the other is not. I will borrow one of King's sets of examples:

(7) $1 = 2$
(8) $2 = 1$
(9) $1 < 2$
(10) $2 < 1$

King's view entails that because the sentences (7) and (8) are distinct, the propositions that they express are too. A proponent of a collapse view might well claim that the proposition expressed by (7) = the proposition expressed by (8).

As (9) and (10) express different propositions, despite having the same constituents, the propositions they express must differ in the way those constituents are combined. So, these propositions must have distinct structures. By SSSS, the way the constituents are combined must be the same in (7) and (9), and (8) and (10) because the syntax of both pairs is the same, i.e. they differ only in their constituents not the way in which they are combined. That leads to a contradiction because the proponent of collapse is now committed to all of the following.

1. The structure of the proposition expressed by (7) = the structure of the proposition expressed by (8).
2. The structure of the proposition expressed by (7) = the structure of the proposition expressed by (9).
3. The structure of the proposition expressed by (8) = the structure of the proposition expressed by (10).
4. The structure of the proposition expressed by (9) ≠ the structure of the proposition expressed by (10).

King takes this to refute the collapse view: 'This argument shows that anyone who holds DCDP and SSSS is going to have to distinguish the propositions expressed by the pair [(7)]/[(8)]' (King 2013b, 777). My point is that this argument only goes through if SSSS can be appealed to in generating the contradiction. Without SSSS it would be open to the proponent of the collapse view to deny any of claims (ii)–(iv) from the contradictory set above and so avoid a contradiction; she would only be committed to (i) by her view that the propositions in question are identical. King thinks that SSSS is both widely believed and well-motivated. But SSSS is not well-motivated, because it entails DET and DET is vulnerable to the objections I make in Section 3.

It may well be that a similar argument can be formulated without SSSS, or DET. King does not provide one. The collapse view might be untenable for other reasons. My point is just that if there is no argument against the collapse view the dialectic returns to the counter-intuitive consequences of King's view. This illustrates one important consequence of my argument against DET: if it is successful, then the collapse view is saved from King's objection.

5. Conclusion

In this paper I have attempted to both raise and answer an important question for philosophers of language who are developing theories of propositions. Given that both sentences and propositions are structured objects it makes sense to ask what sort of relationship holds between the two structures. I have argued against two possible claims about what this relationship is: that it is necessarily one of identity, and that it is necessarily one of determination. I hope therefore to have made a contribution to the debate over the nature of propositions, and also to have illustrated the importance of theories of linguistic communication for that debate.

Acknowledgements

I thank Herman Cappelen, Ephraim Glick, Matthew McGrath, and audiences at Arché and CSMN for helpful comments on earlier versions of the ideas presented here. I also thank David Hunter and Gurpreet Rattan, the editors of the *Canadian Journal of Philosophy* special issue in which this paper is published, for useful suggestions and comments. Some of this paper is based on Hodgson (2013).

Note

1. Stanley cites a reprint of Gilbert Harman's paper.

References

Bach, Kent. 1994. "Conversational Impliciture." *Mind and Language* 9 (2): 124–162. doi:10.1111/j.1468-0017.1994.tb00220.x.

Bach, Kent. 2001. "You Don't Say?" *Synthese* 128: 15–44. doi:10.1023/A:1010353722852.

Bird, Alexander, and Emma Tobin. 2012. "Natural Kinds." In *The Stanford Encyclopedia of Philosophy*, edited by Edward N. Zalta, 2012 edn. http://plato.stanford.edu/archives/win2012/entries/natural-kinds/.

Cappelen, Herman, and Ernie Lepore. 2007. "The Myth of Unarticulated Constituents: Essays on the Philosophy of John Perry." In *Situating Semantics*, edited by Michael O'Rourke, and Corey Washington. Cambridge, MA: MIT Press.

Carston, Robyn. 2002. *Thoughts and Utterances: The Pragmatics of Explicit Communication*. Oxford: Blackwell.

Chomsky, Noam. 1986. *Knowledge of Language: Its Nature, Origin, and Use*. New York: Praeger.

Collins, John. 2007. "Syntax, More or Less." *Mind* 116 (464): 805–850. doi:10.1093/mind/fzm805.

Collins, John. 2010. "Naturalism in the Philosophy of Language; Or Why There is No Such Thing as Language." In *New Waves in Philosophy of Language*, edited by Sarah Sawyer. Basingstoke: Palgrave Macmillan.

Collins, John. 2013. "Cutting it (too) Fine." *Philosophical Studies*. doi:10.1007/s11098-013-0163-1.

Grice, Herbert Paul. 1989. "Logic and Conversation." In *Studies in the Way of Words*. Cambridge, MA: Harvard University Press.

Harman, Gilbert. 1970. "Deep Structure as Logical Form." *Synthese* 21: 275–297. doi:10.1007/BF00484801.

Hawthorne, John, and Ernie Lepore. 2011. "On Words." *The Journal of Philosophy* 108 (9): 447–485.

Heck, Richard G., and Robert May. 2011. "The Composition of Thoughts." *Noûs* 45 (1): 126–166. doi:10.1111/j.1468-0068.2010.00769.x.

Heim, Irene Roswitha, and Angelika Kratzer. 1997. *Semantics in Generative Grammar*. Oxford: Wiley-Blackwell.

Hodgson, Thomas. 2013. "Propositions: An Essay on Linguistic Content." PhD diss., University of St Andrews.

Kaplan, David. 1990. "Words." *Proceedings of the Aristotelian Society* 64: 93–119. doi:10.2307/4106880.

King, Jeffrey C. 2007. *The Nature and Structure of Content*. Oxford: Oxford University Press. doi:10.1093/acprof:oso/9780199226061.001.0001.

King, Jeffrey C. 2009. "Questions of Unity." *Proceedings of the Aristotelian Society* 109: 257–277. doi:10.1111/j.1467-9264.2009.00267.x.

King, Jeffrey C. 2012. "Structured Propositions." In *The Stanford Encyclopedia of Philosophy*, edited by Edward N. Zalta, 2012 edn. http://plato.stanford.edu/archives/win2012/entries/propositions-structured/.

King, Jeffrey C. 2013a. "Propositional Unity: What's the Problem, Who Has it and Who Solves it?" *Philosophical Studies* 165: 71–93. doi:10.1007/s11098-012-9920-9.

King, Jeffrey C. 2013b. "On Fineness of Grain." *Philosophical Studies* 163 (3): 763–781. doi:10.1007/s11098-011-9844-9.

King, Jeffrey C., and Jason Stanley. 2005. "Semantics, Pragmatics, and the Role of Semantic Content." In *Semantics versus Pragmatics*, edited by Zoltán Gendler Szabó. Oxford: Oxford University Press. doi:10.1093/acprof:oso/9780199251520.003.0005.

Martí, Luisa. 2006. "Unarticulated Constituents Revisited." *Linguistics and Philosophy* 29: 135–166. doi:10.1007/s10988-005-4740-4.

Perry, John. 1986. "Thought without Representation." *Proceedings of the Aristotelian Society Supplementary Volumes* 60: 137–152. doi:10.2307/4106900.

Recanati, François. 2002. "Unarticulated Constituents." *Linguistics and Philosophy* 25: 299–345. doi:10.1023/A:1015267930510.

Recanati, François. 2004. *Literal Meaning*. Cambridge: Cambridge University Press. doi:10.1017/CBO9780511615382.

Recanati, François. 2007. "It is Raining (Somewhere)." *Linguistics and Philosophy* 30: 123–146. doi:10.1007/s10988-006-9007-1.

Recanati, François. 2010. *Truth-conditional Pragmatics*. Oxford: Oxford University Press. doi:10.1093/acprof:oso/9780199226993.001.0001.

Sennet, Adam. 2011. "Unarticulated Constituents and Propositional Structure." *Mind and Language* 26 (4): 412–435. doi:10.1111/j.1468-0017.2011.01423.x.

Soames, Scott. 1987. "Direct Reference, Propositional Attitudes, and Semantic Content." *Philosophical Topics* 15 (1): 47–87. doi:10.5840/philtopics198715112.

Soames, Scott. 2008. "The Gap between Meaning and Assertion: Why What We Literally Say Often Differs from What Our Words Literally Mean." In *Philosophical Essays*. Vol. 1. Princeton, NJ: Princeton University Press.

Sperber, Dan, and Deirdre Wilson. 1995. *Relevance: Communication and Cognition*. 2nd edn Oxford: Blackwell.

Stainton, Robert J. 2005. "In Defense of Non-sentential Assertion." In *Semantics versus Pragmatics*, edited by Zoltán Gendler Szabó. Oxford: Oxford University Press. doi:10.1093/acprof:oso/9780199251520.003.0011.

Stanley, Jason. 2000. "Context and Logical Form." *Linguistics and Philosophy* 23: 391–434. doi:10.1023/A:1005599312747.

CONSTITUENTS AND CONSTITUENCY
Individuating Fregean sense

Jeff Speaks

Department of Philosophy, University of Notre Dame, Notre Dame, IN 46556, USA

> While it is highly controversial whether Frege's criterion of sameness and difference for sense is true, it is relatively uncontroversial that that principle is inconsistent with Millian–Russellian views of content. I argue that this should not be uncontroversial. The reason is that it is surprisingly difficult to come up with an interpretation of Frege's criterion which implies anything substantial about the sameness or difference of content of anything.

Propositions are the entities which are expressed by sentences in contexts and the entities to which subjects stand in the belief and other propositional attitude relations. One central question about these entities is whether they are individuated according to Frege's criterion for sameness and difference of sense, or not. Roughly speaking, and setting aside complications to which we will return, that criterion says that a pair of sentences differ in sense iff a certain sort of subject could be unsure whether they have the same truth-value.

It might seem puzzling that many think that this criterion could individuate *propositions*; for as stated it makes a claim, not directly about the sameness and difference of propositions, but about the conditions under which a pair of *sentences* express the same, or different, propositions.[1] But it is not hard to see why the truth or falsity of Frege's criterion has been thought to be of fundamental importance for questions about the nature of propositions. And that is because there is a plausible argument from the truth of Frege's criterion to the falsity of a widely held view of propositions: the Millian–Russellian view that the constituents of propositions are objects, properties and relations, and that the propositions expressed by sentences containing simple singular terms (including names, demonstratives and indexicals) will typically have the object which is the referent of the relevant singular term as a constituent.

The argument runs as follows: if Frege's criterion is true, then in general a pair of sentences which differ only in the substitution of simple coreferential singular terms will differ in sense. This follows from the fact that we can always find a subject of the appropriate sort who, while understanding the relevant terms, is unsure whether they are coreferential – and hence is unsure about whether the relevant sentences have the same truth-value. But then, given a plausible, if not uncontroversial, compositionality principle, it follows that the relevant singular terms must not have their referent as their content – for, if they did, then contra the argument just sketched, the sentences which differ only via substitution of those terms would *not* differ in sense. But surely if objects could ever be among the constituents of propositions, they would sometimes be the contents of simple singular terms. So objects are never among the constituents of propositions, and Millian–Russellian views of the nature of content are false. The constituents of propositions, our argument seems to show, are never simply objects, but are always more fine-grained 'ways of thinking about' or 'modes of presentation of' objects.

So, I think, goes the standard implicit argument from the truth of Frege's criterion to the falsity of Millian–Russellian views of content. I think that the validity of this argument has been, basically, common ground between Fregeans and Millian–Russellians – each agree that if Frege's criterion is true, then Millian–Russellian views of content have to go. The premise of that argument has not, of course, been so uncontroversial.

Fregeans defend the truth of Frege's criterion, largely on the basis of the claim that any theory which falsifies the criterion will leave Frege's puzzle – the task of explaining the difference between trivial, uninformative identities like

Hesperus is Hesperus

and non-trivial, potentially informative identities like

Hesperus is Phosphorus

–unsolved. Millian–Russellians typically concede that the truth of Fregean views of content would solve Frege's puzzle, but hold that such views are not the best to such explanation, for two sorts of reasons. First, there are other, equally plausible accounts of the data which do not involve positing Fregean senses (e.g. attempts to explain differences in informativeness in terms of facts about what sentences are typically used to pragmatically convey, or in terms of coordination relations between expression tokens).[2] Second, the view that the contents of expressions are Fregean senses might lead to other problems which are far worse than the inability to explain the relevant differences in informativeness (like, e.g. placing implausibly strong requirements on the truth conditions of attitude ascriptions, or leading to problems with the semantics of indexicals or variables, or entailing that names are non-rigid).

My aim in this paper is not to engage these much-discussed questions; in fact, my aim will not be, in the first instance, to figure out whether Frege's criterion for the sameness and difference of sense is true. Instead, I want to argue that any plausible interpretation of Frege's criterion will be vacuous, in the sense that it will not entail anything about the sameness or difference in sense of any actual sentences, and hence will not be inconsistent with Millian–Russellian views of content.

1. Conditions for sameness and difference of Fregean sense

Let's start with the question of how, exactly, Frege's criterion should be formulated. As is well known, Frege suggested that we can give conditions for the sameness and difference of sense as follows:

> Now two sentences A and B can stand in such a relation that anyone who recognises the content of A as true must thereby also recognise the content of B as true and, conversely, that anyone who accepts the content of B must straightway accept that of A. (Equipollence)[3]

Other passages in 'A brief survey of my logical doctrines' and elsewhere suggest that Frege took the relation of equipollence in the above sense to be equivalent to the relation of having the same sense.[4] One might, at a first pass, formulate this criterion for the sameness and difference of sense as follows:

S_1 and S_2 differ in sense iff $\Diamond \exists x$ (x is unsure whether S_1 and S_2 have the same truth-value)

But, as others have recognized, this claim needs qualification, because we need to put some constraints on the sort of subjects whose judgements can be used to test the sameness of sense of a pair of sentences.

We cannot, obviously, show that two sentences in German differ in sense by pointing out that someone who does not speak German might well be unsure whether they have the same truth-value; we need to at least require that the relevant subjects understand the sentences. This is not the only qualification we need; surely a subject who understood two sentences with the same sense might be unsure about whether they have the same truth-value if that subject was drunk, or very tired, or confused, or distracted, or in any one of the myriad conditions which might cause us to make mistakes about even very simple matters. Later I will return to some questions about what, exactly, these conditions involve; but for now let us set this question to the side, and simply abbreviate these conditions by saying that a subject who meets these conditions of understanding, rationality and reflectiveness is 'ideal'.

Then we might state our modified version of Frege's equipollence criterion roughly as follows:

S_1 and S_2 differ in sense iff $\Diamond \exists x$ (x is ideal & x is unsure whether S_1 and S_2 have the same truth-value)

As is well known, problems can also be raised for this modified criterion. For example, sentences which are such that any reflective and rational subject who understands them will see that they are true pose a problem for this principle, as the principle will entail – falsely, it seems – that they have the same sense. Let us just assume that this sort of problem has a solution.[5] For now, I want to bracket this kind of question and focus on the prior question of how our principle is to be interpreted.

In particular, I want to ask whether we should understand the values of 'S_1' and 'S_2' to be sentence tokens or sentence types.

A plausible argument can be made that certain versions of Frege's puzzle force us to take the former option. Consider, in particular, one of the instances of Frege's puzzle discussed by Kripke in 'A Puzzle About Belief'. There Kripke discusses the example of Peter, who hears the name 'Paderewski' on two different occasions, once as a name for a famous pianist, and once as a name for a statesman. Peter, Kripke points out, may well wonder whether the two are the same, and hence may be unsure whether a token of 'Paderewski is Paderewski' is true.

Such a use of 'Paderewski is Paderewski' seems to me plainly relevantly like the stock example of 'Hesperus is Phosphorus' rather than the usual understanding of 'Hesperus is Hesperus' — like the former, and unlike the latter, it is informative and non-trivial. But now consider Paul, who is under no such confusion. *His* tokens of 'Paderewski is Paderewski' are plainly relevantly like the stock example of 'Hesperus is Hesperus'. Hence, if we want our Fregean theory to provide a general solution to Frege's puzzle, that theory had better be able to assign a different sense to Peter's tokens of this sentence than it assigns to Paul's. But it is hard to see how our principle for the sameness and difference of Fregean sense could do that, unless it is a principle about the sameness and difference of the senses of sentence tokens.

Let us then revise our statement of that principle to make this explicit:

Sentence tokens s_1 and s_2 differ in sense iff $\Diamond \exists$ x (x is ideal & x is unsure whether s_1 and s_2 have the same truth-value)

But it is not clear that this at all fits with what we want our criterion or the sameness and difference of Fregean sense to do. The idea is supposed to be that if we want to figure out whether two sentence tokens that I utter have the same sense, we look at the attitudes which other speakers might take to those sentences; we imagine, for example, our 'Hesperus' and 'Phosphorus' sentences being considered by someone before the discovery that the bright object visible in the evening — the bright object visible in the morning. But these people are not considering *the very sentence tokens* that I consider; we do not, for example, require that they be encountering the very same sound waves, or bits of ink on paper, that I am.

What we presumably want, instead, is that their tokens of this name bear some important relation R to the tokens of the name which we wish to evaluate. To give a clear statement of a principle for the sameness and difference of Fregean sense which incorporates this thought, it will be useful to adopt a few abbreviations:

?(s_1, s_2) iff an ideal subject considers s_1, s_2 and is unsure whether s_1, s_2 have the same truth-value

$[\![s_1]\!]$ = the sense of s_1

Then we might state our principle of sameness and difference of sense as the claim that some instance of the following schema is true:

Sameness & Difference

$[\![s_1]\!] \neq [\![s_2]\!]$ iff $\exists s_1^* \exists s_2^*$ (R(s_1, s_1^*) & R(s_2, s_2^*) & ?$(s_1^*, s_2^*))$[6]

I will return below to the question of whether *Sameness & Difference* really is the best way to formulate the intuitive principle about the sameness and difference of

Fregean sense with which we began. For our purposes, though, it will be convenient to put those questions on hold for a moment to bring out a problem with the interpretation of *Sameness & Difference*.

This problem arises when we consider the interpretation of the schematic letter 'R' – when, that is, we consider the question of which relation R gives us the relevant (intended) instance of *Sameness & Difference*. We can state a kind of dilemma for candidates for this relation by asking: is R sufficient for sameness of sense, or not?

Intuitively, it seems clear that R *should* be sufficient for sameness of sense. For think about what the point of R is: the point of this relation is to tell us which sentence tokens we can look at to determine whether some pair of sentence tokens in which we are interested differs in sense. But it would be bizarre if we could derive conclusions about whether s_1 and s_2 differ in sense by looking at a pair of sentence tokens which do not even have the same sense as s_1 and s_2. How could we ever expect to get information about whether s_1 and s_2 have the same sense by seeing whether an ideal subject could be unsure whether some pair of sentences *which differ in meaning from s_1 and s_2* differs in truth-value?

This seems to me pretty persuasive; but in this case, we can do better than intuition, and can provide a kind of reductio of the thesis that R is not sufficient for sameness of sense. Suppose that it is not; then we can have a situation in which $R(s_1, s_2)$ but $[\![s_1]\!] \neq [\![s_2]\!]$. I suggest that the following assumptions are quite plausible:

(i) If some expression is R-related to some expression from which it differs in sense,
then every expression is R-related to some expression from which it differs in sense.
(ii) If an expression is R-related to some expression from which it differs in sense,
then it is R-related to at least two expressions which themselves differ in sense.
(iii) R is transitive.

I certainly do not claim that (i) is obvious – and still less that it logically follows from the supposition that R is not sufficient for sameness of sense. But I do find it hard to see how, given that supposition, (i) could be false. This is just because it is hard for me to see how some expressions could be special – if R is not in general a guarantor of sameness of sense, why should it guarantee sameness of sense in the case of some particular class of expressions?

Assumption (ii) – given (i) and our assumption that R is not sufficient for sameness of sense – is not negotiable. For the negation of (ii) plus that assumption entails not just that R is not sufficient for sameness of sense, but that it is sufficient for difference in sense. For if any expression is R-related to at least one expression with which it shares a sense and is R-related to at least one expression with which it differs in sense, then it is R-related to a pair of expressions which differs in sense. But if R were sufficient for difference in sense, then it would be doing part of the job that we wanted *Sameness & Difference* to do, with R's help.

It is harder to argue directly for (iii); but, given the role that R is supposed to be playing, it is also a bit hard to see how (iii) could be false. Suppose that R is not transitive, and that we have three pairs of sentence tokens A, B and C, such that the first member of A is R-related to the first member of B, the second pair of A is R-related to the second member of B and analogously for B and C, but that the members of A are not R-related to the members of C. Suppose now that the C-pair, but not the A- or B-pair, is ?-related. This would then entail that the B-pair differed in sense – but would, on the assumption that R is not transitive, be consistent with the A-pair having the same sense. But this is very odd. After all, given that A, B are R-related, if the B-pair were ?-related, this *would* be sufficient for the A-pair to differ in sense; surely, given this, the fact that the B-pair differs in sense should also be sufficient for the A-pair to differ in sense. But this would make R transitive. (Furthermore, as we will see below, a version of the argument to follow can be run without the transitivity assumption.)

Given the supposition that R is not sufficient for sameness of sense, and assumptions (i) and (ii), we know that for any sentence s_1, there is a pair of sentences s_2 and s_3 such that

1. $R(s_1, s_2)$
2. $R(s_1, s_3)$
3. $[\![s_2]\!] \neq [\![s_3]\!]$

From 3 and left-to-right direction of *Sameness & Difference*, it follows that there are sentence tokens s_4, s_5 such that

4. $R(s_2, s_4)$
5. $R(s_3, s_5)$
6. $?(s_4, s_5)$

From 1, 4, and the transitivity of R it follows that

7. $R(s_1, s_4)$

From 2, 5, and the transitivity of R it follows that

8. $R(s_1, s_5)$

But then it follows from 6, 7, 8, and the right-to-left direction of *Sameness & Difference* that

9. $[\![s_1]\!] \neq [\![s_1]\!]$

As s_1 was an arbitrarily chosen sentence token, this line of reasoning can be used to show that every sentence token differs in sense from itself, which is absurd.

It is worth emphasizing that the assumptions used in the above are, in a sense, stronger than they need to be. After all, for a reductio, we do not need to show that *every* sentence differs in sense from itself; it would be enough to show that one sentence token differs in sense from itself. But then we do not really need the assumption of transitivity. We could use instead the quite plausible assumption that there is at least one sentence token s_1 which is R-related to distinct sentence tokens s_2 and s_3 such that ?(s_2, s_3). This assumption is plausible given that we know that every sentence token is R-related to a pair of sentence tokens which themselves differ in sense. It would be somewhat mysterious if none of the ?-related sentence tokens were pairs to which a single sentence token is R-related.

The preceding argument was meant to support the anyways plausible view that any reasonable candidate for R must be sufficient for sameness of sense. But, you might ask, what is to stop the proponent of *Sameness & Difference* from simply conceding that R must be sufficient for sameness of sense? The problem is that *Sameness & Difference* is supposed to be providing necessary and sufficient conditions for sameness of sense; if we concede that R must be sufficient for sameness of sense, then we are conceding that we cannot interpret *Sameness & Difference* without some independent sufficient condition for sameness of sense – so *Sameness & Difference* cannot do the job for which it was introduced without some other theory which does half of that job.

I think that there are three main lines of reply to this argument. The first is to resist the line of thought which led to my claim that Fregean conditions for sameness and difference of Fregean sense are best articulated by *Sameness & Difference*. The second is to simply give up on the attempt to provide necessary *and* sufficient conditions for sameness in something like the way Frege seems to have envisaged – perhaps, one might think, sufficient conditions for difference of sense are enough. The third is to stick with *Sameness & Difference*, and look for some independent criterion for sameness of sense to give us an interpretation of 'R'. I consider the second and third options at some length below; but before going on to those, I would like to briefly consider some ways of blocking the argument for the conclusion that we should understand Frege's criterion in terms of *Sameness & Difference*.

First, one might resist the idea that our criterion has to be formulated in terms of sentence tokens. Might we, perhaps, simply deny that the 'Paderewski' case is a genuine instance of Frege's puzzle, and formulate our criterion in terms of sentence types? Then we would be rid of the need to find the troublesome relation R between sentence tokens.

In the end, though, the use of the 'Paderewski' example is dispensable. Given the existence of ambiguous expressions, the proponent of the 'type' formulation of the criterion of sameness and difference owes us some non-orthographic explanation of what the relevant way of typing expressions is. But explaining the relevant sense of 'is the same type as' leads – by argument exactly parallel to the one just given – to the same problems as the attempt to specify relation R.

Briefly, being of the same type (in whatever we are told is the relevant sense) must either be sufficient for sameness of sense, or not. Suppose first that it is not. Then, given that every sentence token is of the same type (in the relevant sense) as itself, we can show that every sentence token differs in sense from itself. Let s* be some sentence token. By the right-to-left direction of *Sameness & Difference*, if s* has the same sense as s*, then it must be impossible for there to be an ideal subject who considers some sentence token s′ of the same type as s*, and some token s″ of the same type as s*, and is unsure whether s′ and s″ have the same truth-value. Given our supposition that sameness of type is not sufficient for sameness of sense (and our assumption that every sentence token is of the same type as itself), it follows that s′ and s″ might differ in sense. But then it follows by the left-to-right direction of *Sameness & Difference* that it is possible for some ideal subject to be unsure whether sentence tokens which are, respectively, of the same type as s′ and s″ have the same truth-value – which, given that s′ and s″ are stipulated to be of the same type as s*, entails (given the transitivity of 'is the same type as' under the relevant interpretation) that s* differs in sense from itself. But this is absurd, so our supposition that sameness of type is not sufficient for sameness of sense must be rejected.

Hence, we end up with exactly the same problem. Whether we formulate our criterion in terms of sentence tokens or sentence types, we can get an interpretation of the criterion only if we are given a sufficient condition for sameness of sense of sentence tokens – which is of course part of what we wanted the criterion to provide. This is hardly surprising, as in the present context there seems to be no important difference between specifying a way of grouping sentence tokens into types and specifying a relation between sentence tokens.

A second way of resisting the move to *Sameness & Difference* might be to question the need to introduce relation R in the first place. One might think that the key move in the argument, and the one most open to question, came when I said that when we ask whether an ideal subject could be unsure about whether a pair of sentence tokens have the same truth-value, we're never really asking about an ideal's subject's consideration of *those very sentence tokens* – rather, we are asking about an ideal's subject's consideration of some distinct sentence tokens which stand in some relevant relation R to the sentence tokens we wish to evaluate.

But one might deny this by saying that when we apply principles like these in order to tell whether a pair of expression tokens differ in sense, what we typically do is consider some possible but non-actual scenario in which some perfectly rational subject is considering a pair of sentence tokens which she understands, but is unsure whether they have the same truth-value. But, the objection continues, just as there is no problem in imagining a possible but non-actual scenario in which I exist, there is no problem in imagining a possible but non-actual scenario in which some actual expression token exists. So we can, after all, use ideal subjects in the way envisaged without introducing any relation between sentence tokens at all; all we have to do is consider non-actual scenarios involving the very expression tokens we wish to evaluate.

This is perfectly correct as far as it goes. The problem, though, is that expression tokens – for example, particular inscriptions, or token sound waves – do not have their contents essentially. Hence, if we are allowed to consider, when applying our criterion for sameness and difference of Fregean sense, *any* counterfactual scenario involving the relevant expression token, we will be able to trivially derive the result that every expression tokens differs in sense from itself.

So we need some restriction on the counterfactual scenarios which we are permitted to consider. Then we face a problem already too familiar from the above: either this restriction is sufficient for sameness of sense, or it is not. If it is not, then we will be able (by argument parallel to the above) derive the result that every expression token differs in sense from itself. If it is, then again we reach the conclusion that we can interpret our account of sameness and difference of Fregean sense only if given an independent sufficient condition for sameness of Fregean sense.[7]

I conclude that *Sameness & Difference* does not imply anything about the sameness or difference in sense of anything unless packaged with an independent sufficient condition for sameness of sense. Hence, it cannot, by itself, provide conditions for sameness and difference of Fregean sense.

It is worth emphasizing that one cannot reply to this argument by saying that the Fregean does not intend principles like *Sameness & Difference* to be (in some sense or other) reductive or explanatorily prior to the differences in informativeness that, which the Fregean ultimately wants senses to explain.[8] The problem just raised is not a problem about these principles' lack of explanatory priority; it is a problem with their lack of positive content.

2. Retreat to a condition of difference

A natural thought, at this stage, is that while perhaps *Sameness & Difference* fails to provide conditions for sameness and difference of Fregean sense, we might still preserve the right-to-left direction of this principle, thus giving us at least a sufficient condition for difference of Fregean sense. (This was the second of the responses to the argument of Section 1.) This, after all, might well be enough to give us the wanted result that 'Hesperus' and 'Phosphorus' differ in sense, and hence to validate the informal argument from a Fregean thesis about the individuation of contents to the falsity of the Millian–Russellian view of content.[9]

Let us consider this statement of a sufficient condition for difference in sense:

Difference

$[\![s_1]\!] \neq [\![s_2]\!]$ if $\exists s_1^* \exists s_2^* (R_d(s_1, s_1^*) \& R_d(s_2, s_2^*) \& ?(s_1^*, s_2^*))$

The constraints on the wanted relation 'R_d' here are different than in the case of the relation 'R' in our *Sameness & Difference* principles, because now we are only aiming to give a sufficient condition for difference of sense, not necessary and sufficient conditions. But we can ask the same question about R_d as we asked about R: is R_d sufficient for sameness of Fregean sense, or not?

Again, it seems intuitively clear that it must be. For, as with R, the point of this relation is to tell us which sentence tokens we can look at to determine whether some pair of sentence tokens in which we are interested differs in sense. But it would be bizarre if we could derive the conclusion that s_1 and s_2 differ in sense by finding that a pair of sentence tokens which do not even have the same sense as s_1 and s_2 are ?-related. How could we ever expect to get information about whether s_1 and s_2 differ in same sense by seeing that an ideal subject is unsure whether some pair of sentences which differs in meaning from s_1 and s_2 has the same truth-value?

Moreover as above, we can turn this intuitive worry into an argument. Suppose for reductio that R_d is not sufficient for sameness of sense. Assumptions (i) and (ii) about relation R seem just as plausible when applied to relation R_d. Let A be the class of pairs of sentence tokens which differ in sense from each other.[10] We know that, given our suppositions, every sentence token will be R_d-related to a pair of sentence tokens which themselves differ in sense. Let B be the class of pairs of sentence tokens which are such that some sentence token is R_d-related to each and are elements of A. Now let C be the class of sentence tokens which are ?-related. Given *Difference*, we know that C, like B, will be a subset of A. But what is the relationship between B and C?

The natural thought, surely, is that these sets will overlap. But if *Difference* is true, then we know that B and C must be disjoint. For suppose that there were a pair of sentences in both B and C. We know from the definition of B that there is some sentence token which is R_d-related to each sentence in the pair. But then from the definition of C plus *Difference* it follows that that sentence token differs in sense from itself, which is absurd.

Hence, it would be very convenient for the proponent of *Difference* if B and C were disjoint. But given the definition of B and C, it is very hard to see why this should be true, for any natural candidate for R_d. If every sentence token is R_d-related to a pair of sentence tokens which differs in sense, why shouldn't a sentence token sometimes be R_d-related to a pair of ?-related sentence tokens? The only reasonable answer seems to be: because B is empty. But if B is empty, then R_d must be sufficient for sameness of sense.

So it is hard to see how R_d could fail to be sufficient for sameness of sense. This fact about *Difference* is less damaging than the points made above about *Sameness & Difference*, since *Difference* makes no claim to provide, on its own, a condition for sameness of Fregean sense. So, we have not reached the result that *Difference* cannot do its job without the help of another theory which does exactly that job. But it does mean that we can interpret *Difference* only if we are in prior possession of a criterion for sameness of sense. Are we?

An obvious way to provide such a condition is to consider the reverse direction of our *Sameness & Difference* principles, and try something like

Sameness

$[\![s_1]\!] = [\![s_2]\!]$ if $\neg \exists s_1^* \exists s_2^* (R_s(s_1, s_1^*) \& R_s(s_2, s_2^*) \& ?(s_1^*, s_2^*))$

We argued above that any plausible candidate for R (in the *Sameness & Difference* principles) and R_d (in the case of *Difference*) would have to be sufficient for sameness of Fregean sense. If the same held for R_s, that would be a bad news for *Sameness*, as that would imply that the principle could give a sufficient condition for sameness of sense only with the help of another principle which did exactly that. But we cannot assume that what goes for R and R_d also goes for R_s because the constraints on the latter are different from the constraints on the former two – as it has to make true a sufficient condition for sameness of sense rather than a necessary condition. (For this reason, *Sameness & Difference* is not trivially equivalent to the conjunction of *Difference* and *Sameness*.)

But in fact we can argue, in a similar if not exactly parallel way, that R_s, like its forebears, must also be sufficient for sameness of sense. Suppose that it is not. In that case, the analogues of principles (i) and (ii) discussed in connection with R_d seem just as plausible for R_s. Now select arbitrary sentences s_1 and s_2 which we stipulate to have the same sense. If R_s is not sufficient for sameness of sense and (i) is true, it follows that there will be a pair of expressions $s_1{}^*$ and $s_2{}^*$ which are such that $R_s(s_1, s_1{}^*)$ and $R_s(s_2, s_2{}^*)$, but s_1 differs in sense from $s_1{}^*$ and s_2 differs in sense from $s_2{}^*$. If (ii) is true, it follows that $s_1{}^*$ can $s_2{}^*$ differ in sense from each other. But then if *Sameness* is true, it follows that there will be some ideal subject who understands both and doubts whether they have the same truth-value – and this means that *Sameness* will not deliver the verdict that our initial expressions s_1 and s_2 have the same sense. But nothing was assumed about these expressions other than that they have the same sense; so it follows from our supposition that R_s is not sufficient for sameness of sense that *Sameness* will never succeed in telling us that a pair of sentences have the same sense.

Note that this is not a reductio of the conjunction of *Sameness* with the supposition that R_s is not sufficient for sameness of sense. Quite the contrary; it shows that in that condition *Sameness* is vacuously true, by showing that the condition for sameness of sense which it offers is never satisfied. But a vacuously true condition is no good for our purposes; for, as we saw above, in order to make *Difference* non-vacuous, we need some condition for sameness of sense which sometimes actually tells us that a pair of expression tokens has the same sense.

Of course, we cannot just accept the conclusion that R_s *is* sufficient for sameness of sense, since then R_s would do by itself just what we were hoping that *Sameness* would do with R_s's assistance. So, it looks like *Sameness* is non-vacuously true only if we can, independently, come up with some sufficient condition for sameness of sense. Whether or not we can do this, it is no use to the proponent of *Difference*.

This problem seems a little bit surprising. A standard view on Fregean sense is that, even if we cannot give a perfectly clear account of what senses are, and even if it is not easy to see how to give necessary and sufficient conditions for sameness of sense, we can at least, via something like the conjunction of *Difference* and *Sameness*, provide a clear sufficient condition for difference of sense which is both plausible and will entail that (for example) coreferential names which can give rise to instances of Frege's puzzle differ in sense. But if the foregoing is correct, this is a mistake.

The best move for the defender of *Difference* seems to be to give up on *Sameness*, and try to come up with some other sort of condition on sameness of Fregean sense. But this turns out to be difficult to do.

One idea – which of course is not so far from some of Frege's own uses of the notion of sense – is to give a sufficient condition for sameness of sense in terms of some sort of reportability condition:

Reportability

Token sentence s_1 (as used by A in C) has the same sense as token sentence s_2 (as used by B in C*) if A could use s_2, as he uses it in C, to truly report the claims that B makes with s_1, as she uses it in C*.

This fits nicely with a naive semantics for attitude reports, according to which an ascription ⌜A said that S⌝ is true iff the content of S in the context of the ascription is the proposition which the subject of the ascription said.

Unfortunately, though, *Reportability* faces two sorts of problems.

The first is that it seems to lead to the result that just about any two tokens of a name differ in sense. Remember the example of Peter and 'Paderewski', discussed above. I suggested that given that Peter's use of 'Paderewski is Paderewski' is relevantly like 'Hesperus is Phosphorus' rather than 'Hesperus is Hesperus', any satisfactory Fregean treatment of Frege's puzzle should assign different senses to the two tokens of 'Paderewski.'

Let us divide Peter's uses of 'Paderewski' into pianist-tokenings and statesman-tokenings. Suppose that Paul is an ordinary, unconfused user of 'Paderewski', who knows that Paderewski is both a pianist and a statesman; we can further suppose, if it matters, that he does not know that Peter is confused about the identity of the statesman and the musician. When Peter says, 'Paderewski is my favourite pianist,' it seems that Paul can truly report his speech by saying 'Peter said that Paderewski is his favourite pianist' – and can do so even if he knows nothing about Peter's ignorance, and does not intend to use 'Paderewski' in any special way. Hence, some of Paul's tokenings of 'Paderewski', given *Reportability*, have the same sense as Peter's pianist-tokenings.

Furthermore, when Peter says, 'Paderewski is the very model of a corrupt politician,' Paul can truly report his speech by saying 'Peter said that Paderewski is the very model of a corrupt politician' – and, again, can do so without any special intentions or knowledge of Peter's ignorance. Hence, it seems, some of Paul's tokenings of 'Paderewski', given *Reportability*, also have the same sense as Peter's statesman-tokenings.

But we already know (if the Fregean solution to Frege's puzzle is to be general) that Peter's pianist-tokenings of 'Paderewski' differ in sense from his statesman-tokenings of 'Paderewski,' from which it follows, given the transitivity of identity, that some of Paul's 'Paderewski' tokenings differ in sense from some of his other 'Paderewski' tokenings.

Given that we can come up with Paderewski-type scenarios for virtually any name, it looks like this pattern of argument generalizes to the conclusion that distinct tokenings of a name for a single speaker will almost always differ in sense.

This would certainly be a surprising result. But can the Fregean perhaps simply bite the bullet here, and accept the fact that every expression token differs in sense from every other expression token as a surprising consequence of her theory? Not without undermining the basic argument for Fregeanism. After all, on that view, both 'Hesperus is Hesperus' and 'Hesperus is Phosphorus' would be identity sentences involving names with the same reference but distinct sense – which would leave the intuitive distinction between the sentences unexplained, and Frege's puzzle unsolved.

Fregeans could, of course, simply resist the intuitions about truth-values in the dialogue between Paul and Peter above. But doing this in a principled way would require some account of the conditions under which expression tokens have the same sense – which rules out the attempt to use facts about who can correctly report what to provide such conditions.

The second problem for *Reportability* is that it does not really escape the fundamental problem with *Sameness*. For the condition on sameness of meaning is stated in terms of what B *could* report using a given sentence token. But (to repeat a now-familiar line of reasoning) when we consider what B could report using a given sentence, we're really asking about what B could report using a token of a given sentence type. Then we need to know what the relevant type is – or, equivalently, what relation a sentence token must stand in to the one we want to evaluate. This relation might either be sufficient for sameness of sense, or not. If the latter, we will be able to argue that every sentence token differs in sense from itself. If the former, then *Reportability* will provide a sufficient condition for sameness of sense only with the help of another principle which does exactly that.[11]

We could try instead to give conditions for sameness of sense using the intentions of the speaker:

Intentions

Token sentence s_1 (as used by A in C) has the same sense as token sentence s_2 (as used by B in C*) if A intends in C to use s_1 with the same meaning as B used s_2 with in C*.

The problem, though, is that my intention that my use of a term has the same sense as yours does not guarantee that it will. One way to see this is that I can have multiple intentions in using an expression and that these intentions might conflict – I might, e.g. intend to use e with the same sense as A's use of that expression and with B's, even if, as it turns out, A and B are using the expression with different senses. (Just imagine that I am a committed Millian and intend to use 'Paderewski' with the same sense as all of Peter's tokenings of it.)

To recap: the suggestion was that we get around the problems with our *Sameness & Difference* principles by retreating to a mere sufficient condition for difference in sense. But we found that an understanding of this sufficient condition for difference in sense only entails anything about the sense of particular expressions with the help of a sufficient condition for sameness of sense. That is what we have been trying, and failing, to provide.

In Section 1, I suggested three ways in which the defender of a Fregean criterion of sameness and difference of sense might respond to the argument of that section. The first was to resist the idea that the criterion should be formulated in a way which, like *Sameness & Difference*, requires specification of a relation between expression tokens; the second was to retreat to condition of difference for sense; and the third was to supply a condition for sameness of sense which we might put to use as the value of the schematic letter 'R' in *Sameness & Difference*. In this section, I have been considering the second response. But given that that response, like the third, depends on the specification of a relation between sentence tokens sufficient for sameness of sense, the problems with the above criteria for sameness of sense are also problems for the third line of response to the argument of Section 1.

At this stage, you might have the worry that I have been attacking a straw man. Can't we just assume that our intuitive judgements about sameness of meaning are, by and large, correct, and use these judgements, along with something like *Difference*, to give us the desired result that 'Hesperus' and 'Phosphorus', as we actually use them, differ in sense? Indeed, doesn't our usual practice of evaluating semantic hypotheses *always* proceed via some assumptions about sameness of meaning across tokens? After all, we often evaluate some claim about meaning of an expression by seeing what it entails about various sentences in which that expression occurs – and if this methodology is make any sense at all, it must presuppose that we can tell when two expression tokens have the same content. Surely we are just being obstinate if we will not let the Fregean simply help herself to that.

This line of objection is not implausible. But I think that it is mistaken, for two reasons. First, it is true that we often make use of assumptions about sameness of semantic content across expression tokens when evaluating semantic hypotheses. But that is because the semantic hypotheses in question themselves entail claims about sameness of content across expression tokens. Consider, to take the simplest example, the Millian view that the meaning of a token of 'that' is the object for which the relevant token of 'that' stands. This tells us that, if this Millian view is true, any two tokens of 'that' which stand for the same object must have the same content. Here we are relying on prior judgements about identities of objects to derive claims about sameness of meaning across expression tokens. Parallel remarks apply to any semantic hypothesis which tells us what the semantic content of a given expression is: any such hypothesis will provide us with the resources to make judgements about sameness of meaning across expression tokens.

But of course this is exactly what principles like *Sameness & Difference* or *Difference* do not do: they do not tell us what the meaning of any expression *is*, but instead try to tell us, without doing this, when expressions differ in meaning. So these principles, unlike other semantic hypotheses about the meaning of this or that expression type, simply do not give us the resources to make the relevant judgements about sameness of meaning.

Second, the Fregean is especially badly placed to suggest that we rely on our common sense judgements about sameness of content, for the Fregean is in the business of denying those judgements. Remember the case of Paul and Peter. Imagine these two talking about Paderewski's involvement in politics and then, a few days later, talking about Paderewski's musical abilities. There need be no confusion involved in either of these conversations; they could be, in any intuitive sense, perfect models of communication. By any common sense standard, Paul and Peter's tokenings of 'Paderewski' in these conversations would be standard examples of tokens of name with the same meaning. But the Fregean – at least the Fregean who wants to give a general solution to Frege's puzzle which applies to Peter's use of 'Paderewski is Paderewski' – is committed to denying at least one of these common sense judgements.

The conclusion of this section is parallel to that of the preceding section: like *Sameness & Difference*, *Difference* tells us nothing about difference of sense in the absence of a non-vacuous condition for sameness of sense which we do not know how to provide.[12]

3. Retreat to a weaker sufficient condition

But this conclusion misses an obvious answer to our problem. For of course we *do* know how to provide a sufficient condition for sameness of sense: identity. Haven't we, after all, been assuming throughout that every sentence token has the same sense as itself? Our problems have resulted from our trying to find not just a sufficient condition for sameness of sense, but something like a 'suitably general' condition for sameness of sense, which applies at least sometimes to distinct but synonymous expression tokens.

This gives us a way to repair *Difference*. For if identity is sufficient for sameness of sense, it might seem that we can simply plug in identity as the wanted relation R_d, giving us

$[\![s_1]\!] \neq [\![s_2]\!]$ if $\exists s_1^* \exists s_2^* (s_1 = s_1^* \ \& \ s_2 = s_2^* \ \& \ ?(s_1^*, s_2^*))$

or, more simply,

Restricted Difference

$[\![s_1]\!] \neq [\![s_2]\!]$ if $?(s_1, s_2)$

This principle applies only to sentence tokens which are such that some ideal subject reflectively considers them and is unsure about their truth-value. Just how restrictive this is depends on how demanding our definition of ideal subjects is.

It must be pretty demanding, if any principle like **Restricted Difference** is to hold. Given that principles like **Restricted Difference** are supposed to be not just true of Fregean sense but (in some sense or other) definitive of it, we can safely presume that they must be necessary if true. (It would be very strange if the

Fregean were to say that the world could have been such that an ideal subject's being unsure whether s_1 and s_2 have the same truth-value is consistent with s_1 and s_2 having the same sense.) So we know that

$\Box((x \text{ is ideal } \& \text{ x is unsure whether } s_1 \text{ and } s_2 \text{ have the same truth-value}) \supset [\![s_1]\!] \neq [\![s_2]\!])$

which implies the following statement of the necessary conditions for being an ideal subject in the relevant sense:

$\Box(x \text{ is ideal } \supset \neg (x \text{ is unsure whether } s_1 \text{ and } s_2 \text{ have the same truth-value } \& [\![s_1]\!] = [\![s_2]\!]))$

So whatever else we might think about what it takes for a subject to be ideal, we know that being ideal in the relevant sense is some condition which is inconsistent with a certain sort of mistake: it is metaphysically impossible for an ideal subject to be uncertain as to whether a pair of same-sense sentences have the same truth-value.

Have I ever, even in my best moments, been ideal in this sense? I do not think so. Nor, I think, has anyone. No matter how well we understand a pair of sentences which have the same sense, and no matter how attentive, rational, reflective, etc. we are, it is surely always metaphysically possible that we have all of these properties and yet are not quite sure that those sentences have the same truth-value.

If this is right, then **Restricted Difference** implies nothing about the difference in sense of any two actual sentence tokens – for there are no ideal subjects around to be unsure whether they have the same truth-value and hence make them ?-related.

One might respond that I am taking the reliance on ideal subjects a bit too seriously here. We do not, the objection goes, need to find some noncircular specification of a set of conditions which is such that satisfaction of those conditions is inconsistent with uncertainty in the face of sentences which share a sense. Rather, we can just think of ideal conditions in the following way:

x is ideal with respect to a pair $<s_1, s_2>$ iff ($[\![s_1]\!] = [\![s_2]\!]$ iff (x is sure that s_1 is true iff s_2 is true))

This is of course a condition which (by Fregean lights) I have satisfied with respect to many pairs of sentence tokens at various times. I currently satisfy this condition with respect to the pair of tokens of 'This paper is getting too long' that I have just uttered to myself.

The problem is that if we take this deflationary sort of view of ideal conditions, we empty **Restricted Difference** of any content. For suppose that I propose that the sense of a proper name is the object for which it stands. Surely this Millian thesis should be inconsistent with any criterion of difference for Fregean senses which deserves the name. But it is not inconsistent with **Restricted Difference** plus the above take on ideal conditions. For to show that it is, we would have to find a subject ideal with respect to (say) a pair of tokens of

'Hesperus is Hesperus' and 'Hesperus is Phosphorus' who was unsure whether they have the same truth-value. But suppose a candidate ideal subject, Hammurabi, who is unsure whether these tokens have the same truth-value, is suggested. To see whether this subject really was ideal on the above definition, we'd have to first know that the relevant sentence tokens differ in sense. But that is of course just the result that we wanted **Restricted Difference** to provide.[13]

So we are stuck, it seems, with the result that **Restricted Difference** never directly implies anything about the sense of any actual sentence tokens. The question then arises as to whether, despite this fact, we might still use **Restricted Difference** more indirectly to derive conclusions about the sameness or difference of the sense of any actual sentence tokens. Any attempt to do this would, it seem, have to proceed in two stages: (a) argue that an ideal subject could be unsure whether tokens of 'Hesperus is Hesperus' and 'Hesperus is Phosphorus' have the same truth-value, and (b) argue that on the basis of the fact that these possible tokens differ in sense for an ideal subject, it is reasonable to believe that at least some actual tokens of 'Hesperus is Hesperus' and 'Hesperus is Phosphorus' differ in sense for us, i.e. non-ideal subjects.

One might worry about either step, but step (a) seems to me particularly suspect. The only grip we now have on the notion of an ideal subject is that of a condition which is such that, necessarily, no subject in that condition can be mistaken about whether a pair of sentences with the same sense differs in truth-value. But then, our view about which subjects are ideal will be hostage to our views about sense – rather than (as we wanted) our views about sense being hostage to the facts about what ideal subjects could or would do.

For suppose as above that the Millian advances the thesis that the sense of a name is the object (if any) for which the name stands, and hence (given some standard sort of compositionality principle) holds that tokens of 'Hesperus is Hesperus' and 'Hesperus is Phosphorus' have the same sense. Of course we, non-ideal subjects, can be unsure as to whether these sentences have the same truth-value – but that is neither here nor there. What matters is whether an ideal subject could be similarly unsure. And it is far from clear whether this is possible. For suppose that the Millian's claim is true. Then it just follows from the above necessary condition on ideal conditions that no genuinely ideal subject could be unsure whether tokens of 'Hesperus is Hesperus' and 'Hesperus is Phosphorus' have the same truth-value. And this contradicts claim (a) above.

One might object as follows:

> OK, but this just assumes that the Millian about names is correct. Suppose instead that we hold that the sense of a name is some mode of presentation of a reference. Surely it is possible for a subject to have as complete a grasp of two modes of presentation as is metaphysically possible, and *still* be unsure whether they present the same reference. So, in the end, we can at least be sure that – given **Restricted Difference** – as they are used by ideal subjects, 'Hesperus' and 'Phosphorus' differ in sense. And this surely gives us some reason to believe that they differ in sense out of our non-ideal mouths as well.

But it should be clear that this argument is going in exactly the wrong direction. We wanted to use our test for difference of sense to derive (at least) the result that typical tokens of "Hesperus" and "Phosphorus" differ in sense. What we have now seen is that to derive that result, we have to use it as a premise.[14]

Philosophers often ask whether, or claim that, the meanings of expressions are 'individuated by Frege's criterion of difference'. Our conclusion so far seems to be that this claim is either trivially true or trivially false. If one simply means that one's views about meaning should conform to the criterion, then it is trivially true – a claim that even the most diehard Millian can endorse. If, on the other hand, it means that Frege's criterion of difference tells us what the meanings of expressions are, it is trivially false – because it is consistent with virtually any view of meaning.

This hardly establishes the truth of the Millian–Russellian view of content, but it does show that the Fregean cannot easily accuse the proponent of that view of failing to meet some general constraint on sameness and difference of content.

There are two further consequences of the argument just given which are worth noting. The first is that, if the argument to this point is correct, the Fregean cannot – as is often done – explicate her view via a principle about sameness and/or difference of sense like the ones just considered. It is not that such principles are false, but it is that (if the argument to this point is correct) they lack substantive content. The Fregean has no choice but to directly give us some information about what senses are. This is something which, notoriously, Frege did not do much of, and it is not a very easy thing to do.

But even if this is not easy to do, it need not be impossible. One neo-Fregean theory which is very well placed to meet this explanatory demand is an epistemic two-dimensionalist semantics of the sort explicated and defended in Chalmers (2006). Whatever one might think of epistemic two-dimensionalism, it does not need to be stated using principles of sameness and difference like those discussed above. That is because, like the Millian–Russellian, the epistemic two-dimensionalist tells us straightforwardly what the contents of sentences are.[15]

The second consequence concerns not Fregeanism, but Frege's puzzle. That puzzle, as I set it up above, was to explain the differences between informative and uninformative identities, as exemplified by the stock pair

Hesperus is Hesperus.

Hesperus is Phosphorus.

But now let us ask: what does it mean for two sentences to differ in their 'informativeness', or cognitive value? The very natural answer is to say that this is for those sentences to be such that a fully rational and reflective agent who understood both could yet take different views of their truth-value – such an agent could, for example, know that one is true, but be unsure whether the other one is.

But if we say this, then we have just said that sentences differ in informativeness just in case they satisfy *Difference*. But, as we have seen, it is pretty hard to give a non-vacuous and true interpretation of this principle. Hence, our problems for the above principles of sameness and difference of Fregean sense redound to Frege's puzzle itself.

None of this is to block a Fregean from motivating his position by simply pointing to 'Hesperus is Hesperus' and 'Hesperus is Phosphorus', thumping the table, and saying: 'These sentences just obviously differ in meaning – and something's wrong with any theory which says that they don't!' Personally, I think that this table-thumping argument has more than a little plausibility. But making an intuitive claim about a single pair of sentence tokens (or even several pairs of sentence tokens) is a far cry from presenting a general puzzle about meaning which we can then ask whether various approaches to semantics solve.

One might also try to formulate a version of Frege's puzzle which relied less on differences in 'informativeness' and more on, for example, differences in apparent truth-value of attitude ascriptions which differ only in the substitution or coreferential terms. I think that the present line of scepticism about Frege's puzzle would generalize to those versions – but that conclusion goes beyond what I have argued here.

Acknowledgements

The author thanks for helpful comments on previous versions of this paper to Patricia Blanchette, Ben Caplan, David Hunter, Casey O'Callaghan, and Gurpreet Rattan.

Notes

1. One might think – especially since the problems to be discussed below arise from just this aspect of Frege's criterion – that we should give criteria for sameness and difference of Fregean sense directly in terms of properties of senses, rather than in terms of properties of bearers of senses. But it would be hard to do this without giving an account of what sorts of entities senses are – and if we could do this, we would hardly need an account of sameness and difference of sense of the sort which Frege's criterion aims to provide. I return to Fregean views which do not rely on Frege's criterion in the final section below.
2. See, respectively, Salmon (1986) and Fine (2007).
3. Frege (1979, 197).
4. But see Van Heijenoort (1977) for some scepticism as to whether Frege had an unequivocal view on this topic.
5. For some possible solutions to this sort of problem, see Schellenberg (2012).
6. One might wonder why the modal operator from the previous formulations has disappeared from this one. The reason, as will become clear from what follows, is that sentence tokens have their contents only contingently, so that what we really want to be doing is comparing sentence tokens at worlds and times with each other. See note 7.
7. The fact that sentence tokens do not have their contents essentially is also the explanation for one feature of *Sameness & Difference* which might seem puzzling, and that is the fact that the modal locution used in typical statements of Frege's criterion ('... an ideal subject could do such-and-such') is absent from it. Given that sentence tokens can have different contents in different worlds, we cannot simply

look at all of the possible judgements of ideal subjects about some pair of sentence tokens, on pain of leading to the result that every sentence token differs in sense from itself.

For that reason, when we are talking about subjects' attitudes towards sentence tokens, we should take this as shorthand for attitudes towards sentence tokens in a world and at a time. We can then understand the quantification over sentences tokens in *Sameness & Difference* to be quantification over triples of sentence tokens, worlds and times such that the relevant sentence token exists in that world at that time.

Nor, it is worth noting, would it matter much if we had a view of the metaphysics of expression tokens on which they had their contents essentially. For then our stipulation that we consider the same expression token in different worlds would build in the assumption of sameness of sense, and we could re-raise the dilemma in the text about the conditions under which a given inscription, or sound wave, had the same content as the expression token to be evaluated.

8. Heck and May (2011, 142–143) point out that the view that Frege's criterion is somehow constitutive of sameness and difference of sense is inconsistent with Frege's aim of explaining sameness and difference of sense at the level of sentences in terms of sameness and difference of sense for subsentential expressions.
9. Some Fregeans have been content to rely on a condition for difference of Fregean sense without worrying about a condition for sameness of sense; a prominent example is Evans (1982).
10. As above, more strictly: pairs of triples of a sentence token, time and world.
11. As above, one could object that we might only consider B's possible uses of that very sentence token. But this delays rather than solves the problem. Given that sentence tokens do not have their senses essentially, we will have to provide some restrictions on the relevant class of possible tokenings, which will amount to giving a relation between sentence tokens which will face the dilemma just sketched.
12. One suggestion for avoiding this problem would be to define conditions for sameness of sense, not sentence by sentence, but via requirements for sameness of sense of various types of subsentential expressions. We could then ascend to the sentence level via some appropriate compositionality principle. I do not quite see how this approach would work, since I am not sure how to formulate the conditions for sameness of sense of, for example, two predicates. But it is an approach which is not ruled out by any of the arguments above.
13. Parallel worries arise for the attempt to treat Frege's criterion as part of a 'local holism' involving claims also terms like 'understanding' and 'rational'. The worry is that the ordinary interpretations of these terms are too weak to define Fregean sense, leading to problems like those discussed in connection with Reportability. But if we stipulatively define more demanding interpretations of these terms, we run into the same problems as with the deflationary interpretation of ideal conditions.

Parallel circularity problems also arise for views of ideal subjects as ones who know all the a priori truths. According to the Millian, after all, 'Hesperus is Phosphorus' is a priori (or close enough). One might do better if one could buttress the view of ideal subjects as knowing all the a priori truths with a theory of a prioricity which delivered the result that 'Hesperus is Phosphorus' is not knowable a priori, like that given by epistemic two-dimensionalism. For doubts about the epistemic two-dimensionalist's treatment of the a priori, see Schroeter (2005) and Speaks (2010).
14. One might think that this shows that the Fregean should simply get rid of reference to what a subject who was rational, reflective, etc. would do, and focus on properties of actual subjects. One person who develops an account of Frege's criterion along these lines is Schellenberg (2012). Her account is framed, not in terms of what an ideal

subject would do, but in terms of what our rational commitments with respect to a pair of sentences are. Very roughly, and ignoring some important subtleties, the idea is that sentences differ in sense for a subject if that subject is not rationally committed to taking them to have the same truth-value.

This does avoid the problems to do with ideal subjects, but it seems to me that those problems re-emerge in another form. Consider a pair of subjects, who are, respectively, unsure whether the following pairs of sentences have the same truth-value:

(1a) Hesperus is Phosphorus.
(1b) Hesperus is Hesperus.

(2a) Secretariat is a horse.
(2b) Secretariat is a steed.

In what sense must the second subject violating her rational commitments in a way in which the first subject is not? Neither might be, in any ordinary sense, irrational. It seems to me that to explain the sense in which the second subject must be irrational, even though the first is not, we will have to use (as above) the premise that 'steed' and 'horse' have the same sense, whereas 'Hesperus' and 'Phosphorus' do not. But then we would again be feeding into the account what we wanted to get out of it.

15. Though, perhaps not coincidentally, neo-Fregeans like Chalmers are sometimes sceptical of the idea that we can make clear sense out of the Fregean's distinction between informative and non-informative sentences, and try instead to supply a kind of successor to Fregean senses which can play many, even if not all, of the theoretical roles that senses were supposed to play.

References

Chalmers, David J. 2006. "The Foundations of Two-Dimensional Semantics." In *Two-Dimensional Semantics: Foundations and Applications*, edited by Manuel Garcia-Carpintero and Josep Macia, 55–140. Oxford: Oxford University Press.
Evans, Gareth. 1982. *The Varieties of Reference*. Oxford: Oxford University Press.
Fine, Kit. 2007. *Semantic Relationism*. Oxford: Blackwell.
Frege, G. (1979). *Posthumous Writings*. Translated by P. Long and R. White. Chicago: University of Chicago Press.
Heck, Richard, and Robert May. 2011. "The Composition of Thoughts." *Noûs* 45 (1): 126–166.
Salmon, Nathan U. 1986. *Frege's Puzzle*. Atascadero, CA: Ridgeview.
Schellenberg, Susanna. 2012. "Sameness of Fregean Sense." *Synthese* 189 (1): 163–175.
Schroeter, Laura. 2005. "Considering Empty Worlds as Actual." *Australasian Journal of Philosophy* 83 (3): 331–347.
Speaks, Jeff. 2010. "Epistemic Two-Dimensionalism and the Epistemic Argument." *Australasian Journal of Philosophy* 88 (1): 59–78.
Van Heijenoort, J. 1977. "Frege on Sense Identity." *Journal of Philosophical Logic* 6 (1): 103–108.

CONSTITUENTS AND CONSTITUENCY
The metaphysics of propositional constituency[1]

Lorraine Keller

909 Onondaga Street, Lewiston, NY 14092, United States

In this paper, I criticize Structured Propositionalism, the most widely held theory of the nature of propositions according to which they are structured entities with constituents. I argue that the proponents of Structured Propositionalism have paid insufficient attention to the metaphysical presuppositions of the view – most egregiously, to the notion of propositional constituency. This is somewhat ironic, since the friends of structured propositions tend to argue as if the appeal to constituency gives their view a dialectical advantage. I criticize four different approaches to providing a metaphysics of propositional constituency: set-theoretic, mereological, hylomorphic, and structure-making. Finally, I consider the option of taking constituency in a deflationary, metaphysically 'lightweight' sense. I argue that, though invoking constituency in a lightweight sense may be useful for avoiding the ontological problems that plague the 'heavyweight' conception, it no longer proffers a dialectical advantage to Structured Propositionalism.

[On] the analogy to the part-whole relation: [a proposition] is thereby treated as a complex of some kind and the object belonging to it as a kind of constituent. In many respects this may be in accordance with our insight into the nature of [a proposition], which is as yet still exceedingly defective. However, no one will deny that this analogy is only an initial expedient in our embarrassment and that there would be no grounds for following this analogy rigorously for even part of the way. (Meinong, 1904/1960, 85)[2]

1. Introduction

Nobody wants propositions in their ontology. We believe in propositions because we are convinced that we cannot get by without them: propositions play roles that nothing else could play; we quantify over them using literal speech; they, and only they, make many of our apparently successful theories work.

The most widely held theory of propositions is one according to which they are structured entities with constituents.[3] As Stephen Schiffer puts it, 'Virtually every propositionalist...rejects unstructured propositions' (2003, 18). Jeff King elaborates: '[most propositionalists] assume that an account of propositions on which they are structured entities with constituents and so are individuated more finely than sets of worlds is desirable' (2007, 3).

Structured Propositionalism is the view that a proposition p expressed by a sentence s in a context c is a structured entity that has the semantic values of the meaningful parts of s in c as constituents.[4] Different accounts of the nature of propositional constituents result from differences in the attendant semantics. There are two main camps: Russellianism and Fregeanism.

Both Russellians and Fregeans share a commitment to a compositional semantics that pairs linguistic expressions with entities that are their *meanings* or, to use a more neutral term, *semantic values* (SVs).[5] Sentential SVs are *propositions*; the SVs of sub-sentential expressions, such as names, predicates, logical connectives, etc., are the *constituents* of propositions. Beyond this general agreement, the major divide within SP is over what kind of entities are sub-sentential SVs and, thus, what the constituents of propositions are.

Russellians hold that the constituents of a proposition expressed by an atomic sentence of the form '$F(a_1 \ldots a_n)$' are the contents of (an instance of) 'F' and (instances of) '$a_1 \ldots a_n$'.[6] For example, in the proposition expressed by 'John runs', 'John' denotes John and 'runs' expresses the property of running: the proposition's constituents are the individual, John, and the property of running.

Fregeans hold that the constituents of a proposition expressed by an atomic sentence of the form '$F(a_1 \ldots a_n)$' are the senses expressed by the relevant instances of 'F' and '$a_1 \ldots a_n$' or, alternatively, the modes of presentation of the concept F and the object(s) $a_1 \ldots a_n$. Thus, the proposition expressed by 'John runs' has as constituents the modes-of-presentation of John and of the concept of running (i.e. the senses expressed by the name 'John' and the predicate 'runs').[7]

Contra Meinong, there is plenty of evidence that SPists intend their talk of propositional constituency to be taken at face value. For example, Joseph Almog writes:

> There are nonconceptual, objectual propositional constituents.... [SP] is a metaphysical doctrine about what makes propositions the way they are.... [T]he proposition is thought of as a *construct* "from below". First, we get hold of its constituents. Then, and only then, we combine them in a structured way into a proposition. (1986, 230).

Or take David Braun:

> [A] proposition consists of ... individuals and relations. These items appear within a structure, occupying positions in a scaffolding, or decorating parts of a tree. (1993, 461)

Various virtues have been claimed for Structured Propositionalism: it nicely accounts for semantic compositionality; it explains how propositions manage to stand in logical relations; it individuates propositions finely enough to play the role of objects of belief; it provides a helpful framework for explaining the pragmatics of what is said; and the Russellian variant has proven to be a powerful tool for fleshing out the semantics of direct reference. All of these theoretical virtues seem to grant SP a significant dialectical advantage over its rivals.[8] Indeed, most defenders of SP have focused on its putative theoretical advantages, neglecting to adequately explore its metaphysical presuppositions. As a result, a fundamental problem for the view has not received the attention it deserves: the problem of providing a metaphysics of propositional constituency.

The structured propositionalist owes us an account of what she means when she says that propositions have constituents. For the worry, as Meinong aptly put it, is that there are 'no grounds for following this analogy rigorously'. Though the friends of structured propositions have been tolerably clear about what the constituents of propositions are, they have been frustratingly evasive about the *relation* of constituency itself. Is a proposition related to its constituents as a set is to its members, or a composite object to its parts? Or are propositional constituents "parts" in some other, *non*-mereological sense? If so, does this mean that commitment to SP entails commitment to different fundamental parthood relations? Or is *constituency* supposed to be taken as a theoretical primitive, not explicable in terms of *membership* or *parthood*? If this is the case, how does invoking this notion *explain* anything? In the sequel, I explore these questions and argue that if a satisfactory account of propositional constituency cannot be offered, then, despite all of its professed virtues, SP does not deserve its position of dominance among theories of propositions.

Here is how the paper will proceed: in §1, I situate SP among rival theories of propositions and provide more context for understanding the SPists' claim to dominance. In §2, I examine four different approaches to providing a metaphysics of propositional constituency – set-theoretic, mereological, hylomorphic, and structure-making – as well as the option of taking *constituency* as a theoretical primitive. I conclude that the four approaches all face substantial difficulties, revealing the significant metaphysical costs of SP. Finally, in §3, I distinguish two different senses in which one might wish to invoke the notion of *constituency* in the theory of propositions – a metaphysically "heavyweight" and a metaphysically "lightweight" sense – and point out that there is a harmless way of *talking* about propositions having constituents that lacks the controversial metaphysical presuppositions, but also the purported explanatory potential, of SP.[9] Thus, we can retain a useful way of talking without incurring the costs that attend the SPist's heavyweight conception of constituency.

2. Structured propositions, sets of worlds, and primitive propositions

Recall Jeff King's claim that '[most propositionalists] assume that an account of propositions on which they are ... individuated more finely than sets of worlds is desirable' (*op cit.*). King's remark is instructive, for the most common type of argument in favor of SP is simply the argument that it is better than its main rival, the Possible Worlds View (PW).[10] To have a convenient way to reference this argument in the future, let's call it the 'better than the Possible Worlds View'

(BPW) argument. On PW, a proposition p expressed by a sentence s is the intension of s, a function from possible worlds to truth-values, or, equivalently, the function's characteristic set (the set of worlds at which p is true).

Since, on PW, a proposition is a *set* of worlds, it might seem as if PW, like SP, entails that propositions have constituents: their members. But the notion that a set's members are its constituents (if this is understood in the sense of *parts*) is highly controversial; and in any case most advocates of PW do not talk in this way.[11] Further, even if the "members" of a proposition on PW were its constituents, there would be another crucial difference between PW and SP: the *order* of constituents on PW is irrelevant. Set x = set y iff x and y have the same members. So, on PW, propositions are *unordered* sets – PW propositions would still be *unstructured*, even if their members were taken to be "constituents" or "parts".

SPists tend to assume that their theory deserves prominence of place because it's been convincingly shown to be superior to PW. But even if the BPW argument were successful, this would not entail that we should accept SP, since there is another option on the table: Propositional Primitivism. On Propositional Primitivism (or simply 'Primitivism'), propositions are *sui generis*, fine-grained, *u*nstructured abstract entities.[12] Propositions cannot be reduced to, nor can their nature be explained in terms of, entities from another ontological category. They are not set-theoretic constructions, nor are they composed of objects, properties, or relations (or the modes-of-presentation thereof) – they are theoretical entities the inner nature of which is unanalyzable. Proponents of Primitivism tend to think there is not much one can reasonably say about the inner nature of propositions: propositions are circumscribed by their roles, and the only properties we ought to attribute to propositions are those that are *required* by the roles that they play.

PW has some superficial similarities with Primitivism, for it is also a theory of propositions on which they are abstract, mind- and language-independent entities without structure or constituents. However, there are two important differences: (i) on Primitivism, but not PW, propositions are entities *sui generis*: they are not, and cannot be, "constructed" from or reduced to other types of entities; (ii) on Primitivism, propositions are more fine-grained than they are on PW; Primitivism has no problem accommodating necessarily equivalent propositions that involve reference to different objects and properties (e.g., that $2 + 2 = 4$ and that arithmetic is incomplete). Because propositions are *sui generis*, unstructured entities on Primitivism, this theory has very little to say about their nature – a feature of Primitivism that some proponents consider a virtue, but that structured propositionalists consider a vice.

Many SPists simply do not consider Primitivism as a serious contender. They seem to think that Primitivism is not a viable theory of propositions because it takes their intentional properties as brute, leaving their nature mysterious. For example, Jeff King admits,

> I find the idea of "simple fine grained propositions," fine grained propositions without constituents or parts, mysterious. What would make such a simple proposition be about, say, Paris, as opposed to Santa Monica? In virtue of what

would it have the truth conditions it in fact enjoys? I cannot see that these questions have answers if propositions are held to be simple and fine grained. But it seems to me they should have answers. (2007, 6)

King finds it mysterious how simple propositions acquire their intentional properties and truth-conditions.[13] How does Primitivism account for the difference between, e.g., *Paris is a city* and *Santa Monica is a city*? Simply by saying that the former is about Paris and the latter is about Santa Monica – the former is true iff Paris is a city, while the latter is true iff Santa Monica is a city. But there is no further analysis of what it is for a proposition to be *about* Paris or Santa Monica.

On the other hand, the SPist claims to be able to provide such an analysis. Since her account differs from that of the Primitivist only in that it posits propositional constituents and structure, any explanatory advantage must appeal to the fact that Paris and Santa Monica are *constituents* of the relevant propositions. However, if propositional constituency itself is mysterious, this is no real advantage over Primitivism. If *constituency* cannot be explained in terms of some other relation, such as *membership* or *parthood*, then the SPist is simply adding a primitive relation to the theory of propositions. And it is unclear that there is any reason to take *constituency*, rather than *intentionality*, as primitive ideology. Let us proceed, then, to examine the prospects for fleshing out the notion of propositional constituency.

3. Explaining constituency

In this section, I discuss two basic strategies for explaining propositional *constituency*: (I) taking *constituency* to be *membership* and (II) taking *constituency* to be *parthood*. I'll discuss three different approaches to (II): (i) construing parthood in the classical mereological sense and in two ostensibly promising senses that reject classical mereology: (ii) hylomorphism, and (iii) structure-making. I also briefly consider the option of taking *constituency* as a theoretical primitive.

3.1 Set theory

Consider the set-theoretic approach, according to which a structured proposition such as *Socrates is wise* is (or is modeled by) an ordered pair, or one of its defining sets, with the SVs of 'Socrates' and 'wisdom' as members. In other words, propositional constituency is set-membership. As we discussed above, structured propositions could not be *mere* sets – they would have to be *ordered* sets, since they are individuated, in part, by the order of their constituents. So the proposition *Socrates is wise* might be the ordered pair < wisdom, Socrates >, or – if we take sets as primitive, and define ordered pairs in terms of sets – one of its defining sets {{wisdom}, {wisdom, Socrates}}, or {{{wisdom}, ∅}, {{Socrates}}}, etc.

There are two problems with this view. The first is that the pairing of ordered *n*-tuples and propositions seems arbitrary. For example, is the proposition *Socrates is wise* identical to < wisdom, Socrates > (or one of its defining sets) or < Socrates, wisdom > (or one of *its* defining sets)? It seems as if there's no principled way to choose from among the different candidates.[14]

The second problem is that ordered n-tuples and sets are not plausibly the things we believe and assert.[15] If the SPist replies that she's not *identifying* propositions with, or *reducing* them to, sets, but only using sets as a sort of model to illustrate the sense in which propositions have constituents and structure, then she owes us an account of what structured propositions *are*.

Consider again two of the many different candidates for being the proposition *Socrates is wise*: < wisdom, Socrates > and < Socrates, wisdom > . If the proposition is not identical to, but merely modeled by, one of these pairs, then shouldn't its structure correspond with just one of them? But which one? Any answer seems intolerably arbitrary. And if not – if the relevant pairs don't somehow manifest propositional structure – in what sense are the ordered pairs models of the proposition?

In general, for any given structured proposition p there seem to be too many candidates among ordered n-tuples not merely for *being p*, but also for *modeling p*, and no principled way to choose from among them.[16] This is a version of the so-called "Benacerraf dilemma" for structured propositions. On the one horn is the arbitrary identification of a proposition with just *one* among many ordered n-tuples or sets. On the other horn is deflationism: there are no *real* propositions, but only various abstract structures that can function as propositional surrogates.[17] The prospects for remaining a propositional realist in light of this propositional Benacerraf dilemma look dim; thus, many SPists have abandoned the once-popular set-theoretic approach.[18] Now it is more common to construe propositional constituents as *parts*.

3.2 Mereology

On the mereological approach, a proposition's constituents are its *parts*. Classical Extensional Mereology (CEM), the theory of the part-whole relation devised by Leonard and Goodman, holds that parthood is reflexive and transitive: everything is a part of itself; and if x is a part of y, and y is a part of z, then x is a part of z.[19] Parthood is also anti-symmetric – it is symmetric only in the limiting case where $x = y$. *Proper* parthood is *a*symmetric. Thus, parthood is a partial ordering. But as Achille Varzi points out, 'Not just any partial ordering qualifies as a part-whole relation... and establishing what further principles should be added... is precisely the question a good mereological theory is meant to answer' (Varzi, 2011, Section 3). CEM is the theory that results from extending the theory of parthood beyond the concept of a mere partial ordering.[20]

In CEM, any of the notions of *parthood, proper parthood, overlap, disjointness*, or *sum* can be taken as primitive, and the other notions defined in terms of it. *Overlap* can be defined in terms of *parthood* as follows:

x overlaps $y =_{df}$ there is a z such that z is a part of x and z is a part of y.

If x and y are non-overlapping – i.e. if they have no part in common – then they are disjoint. *Mereological sum* can be defined in terms of *parthood* and *overlap* as follows:

y is a *mereological sum* of the xs $=_{df}$ each of the xs is a part of y & y has no part disjoint from the xs.

On one standard formulation, the three core axioms of CEM are:

(Unrestricted) For any xs, there is at least one sum of the xs.

(Uniqueness) For any xs, there is at most one sum of the xs.

(Transitivity) For any x, y, if x is a part of a part of y, then x is a part of y.[21]

One way of giving a mereological account of structured propositions would be to employ the notion of *parthood* as it appears in CEM. On a mereological account, a proposition's constituents are its *proper parts*: the proper parts of Fregean propositions are senses, while the proper parts of Russellian propositions include objects, properties, relations, and functions. I will first point out the problems faced by this approach to structured propositions; then I will consider potential responses.

First, both Fregean and Russellian propositions obviously violate Uniqueness: on both views, distinct propositions may be composed of the same parts. To take a simple example, *John loves Maggie* and *Maggie loves John* are composed, on Fregeanism, of the same senses (the senses of 'John', 'Maggie' and 'loves') and, on Russellianism, of the same objects (John and Maggie) and relation (*loving*). But by Uniqueness, the senses of 'John', 'Maggie' and 'loves' can compose at most one thing, so there cannot be two distinct propositions with just these proper parts (*mutatis mutandis* for the Russellian variant).[22]

In addition, Russellian (but not Fregean) propositions appear to violate Transitivity.[23] Consider a singular Russellian proposition such as *Socrates is wise*. This proposition has Socrates as a proper part. But now consider one of the cells that composes Socrates – call it 'Carl'.[24] By Transitivity, *Socrates is wise* also has Carl as a proper part: if Carl is a part of Socrates, and Socrates is a part of the proposition, then Carl is a part of the proposition. This result is problematic for a number of reasons.

First, consider the claim that a singular proposition's constituents are the entities that a proposition is *about*. By Transitivity, Carl is a constituent of *Socrates is wise*. But it's absurd to claim that the proposition is about Carl, in any sense of 'about'.

A closely related problem derives from a view shared by both Frege and Russell, which we might call 'the grasping thesis'. According to the grasping thesis, grasping a proposition *requires* grasping all of its parts.[25] This thesis about propositional understanding plays a crucial role in both Frege's and Russell's compositionality arguments for structured propositions. Though these arguments cannot be discussed in detail here, both rely on a premise to the effect that grasping a proposition requires grasping its constituents – the parts must be "recoverable" from the whole.[26]

Now, Carl is not a semantic value of any expression in 'Socrates is wise', but, by Transitivity, Carl is a *constituent* of the proposition *Socrates is wise* – it is a *part* of the semantic value of one of the proposition's constituents. However, it seems absurd to say that a requirement on my grasping *Socrates is wise* is that I grasp Carl – it's extremely plausible that I can grasp this proposition without having any awareness of Carl's existence. Perhaps the grasping thesis ought to be rejected, but this would seem to undermine one of the major arguments for structured propositions.[27]

Third, consider the following highly plausible thesis: propositions have their parts essentially. Though mereological essentialism is highly controversial, *propositional part essentialism* is eminently plausible.[28] Assuming that propositions *are* structured entities with parts, it boggles the mind to consider a structured proposition existing *without* one of its parts existing. In other words, it is difficult to deny the following: if a proposition *p* has an object *o* as a part, then it is not possible that *p* exists and *o* is not part of *p*. But note that the conjunction of propositional part essentialism with Transitivity entails that Carl is essentially a proper part of Socrates.

However, to say that Socrates has any one of his cells essentially is absurd. For consider Socrates and Carl. Surely Socrates could have existed without having Carl as a part; after all, it's highly probable that Socrates *exists* at some times without having Carl (or any part of Carl) as a part. But presumably the existence of Socrates is sufficient for the existence of *Socrates is wise*: i.e., the proposition *at least* exists whenever, and in whatever world, Socrates exists. The result is that *Socrates is wise* exists at worlds/times without having Carl as a part. This result violates propositional part essentialism.

Clearly, this third conflict with Transitivity only arises for certain sorts of contingent-object-dependent propositions – most propositional parts are necessarily existing abstract objects (e.g. properties, relations, functions). If a proposition's *parts* exist in all possible worlds, then there would be no worry about the problematic possibility of the proposition existing without one of its parts. However, if propositional part essentialism is true, and parthood is transitive, then it cannot be the case that Carl is only contingently a part of Socrates.

Given these three problems, it is plausible that propositional constituency cannot be reduced to ordinary parthood.[29] But there are more.

Another worry about applying the mereological approach to Russellianism is skepticism about *transcategorial sums*, where a *transcategorial sum* is an object with parts from different ontological categories (e.g., object and property).[30] Many Russellian propositions contain constituents from different ontological categories; the most egregious examples are singular propositions with material constituents. Skepticism about these hybrid objects is common. Take, e.g., Peter van Inwagen: 'though I think that the color blue and I both exist, I am unable to form a sufficiently general conception of parthood to be able to conceive of an object that has me and a color as parts' (1987, 35).[31]

One problem with transcategorial sums is that it is not clear what category they belong to: does the sum of an abstract object and a concrete particular belong to the category *abstract object* or *concrete particular* (or, more plausibly, neither)? One could reply, however, by arguing that these hybrids might have their own, already recognized, categories. The sum of an abstract object and concrete particular, for example, might belong to the category *fact* or *proposition* (See Varzi, 2006, 111).

There are other mereological problems generated by transcategorial sums, however. Consider the mereological principle Theodore Sider calls 'inheritance of location', according to which 'an object is located wherever any of its parts are located' (2007, 2, 20). According to inheritance of location, the proposition *John runs* is located wherever John is. But since John changes location, the proposition changes location as well. So acceptance of this uncontroversial principle has the absurd consequence that some propositions move.[32]

A final problem for mereological accounts of structured propositions, which does not involve a straightforward violation of one of the axioms of CEM, is the repetition problem.[33] Consider, e.g. the proposition *Roses are red, so something is red*. Does redness appear twice as a constituent of this proposition? It seems as if it must, but it's unclear how *one* part can occupy two different "locations" in a structured entity. It might be objected that properties are typically thought to be repeatable anyway. But the problem is not just that the property is multiply "located" (if an abstract propositional part can be said to have a location – this, of course, is problematic as well), but that the very same property is a *part* twice over of the same entity.

Also, consider the Russellian proposition *John is John*. Is the individual, John, a part twice over of this proposition? This view, which is scarcely intelligible in any case, seems to require commitment to the claim that a material object can be multiply located. Thus, the repetition problem seems like a serious worry, especially for singular Russellian propositions.

Taking stock, then, the following problems beset the mereological approach to structured propositions: (i) they violate Uniqueness, and (ii) have repeating parts. In addition, Russellian propositions (iii) violate Transitivity, and (iv) are vulnerable to skeptical objections to transcategorial sums. There are, however, some ways that the friend of structured propositions could address these problems.

First, it may not seem problematic to deny Uniqueness, according to which any *x*s have at most one sum. This axiom is already rejected by Coincidentalists – those who claim that, e.g., the statue and the lump of clay are distinct objects with exactly the same proper parts. Coincidentalists hold that the most promising solution to the problem of material constitution involves countenancing co-location.

There are two problems with this response. First, simply denying Uniqueness does not *solve* the problem of explaining how it is that some distinct propositions have all of the same parts – it merely blocks the objection that such a scenario is impossible. We are still owed an account of what distinguishes such propositions. The obvious answer would be that they are distinguished in terms of the locations of sub-sentential SVs in their structure. But the idea that there are "locations" in propositional structures is also problematic.

Second, Coincidentalism is itself highly controversial. For this reason alone denying Uniqueness is a significant cost of the mereological approach to propositional constituency for many philosophers.

Similarly, the Russellian could deny Transitivity. This axiom has also been rejected by some philosophers for independent reasons. Some potential counterexamples to Transitivity from the realm of material objects are as follows: (i) John's toe is part of John, and John is part of the team, but John's toe is not part of the team; (ii) the knob is part of the door, and the door is part of the house, but the knob is not part of the house; (iii) the cell is part of the heart, and the mitochondria is part of the cell, but the cell's mitochondria is not part of the heart (cf. Varzi, 2011). One response to these potential counterexamples is that our intuitions supporting the denial of Transitivity in these cases all stem from the limitation of the ordinary language use of 'part'. Strictly speaking, there is nothing absurd about admitting that John's toe *is* part of the team, the knob *is* part of the house, and the cell's mitochondria *is* part of the heart. It is merely awkward to talk in this way.[34]

Unfortunately, a similar response is not available for the Russellian, since it does not help avoid the conclusion that *Socrates is wise* is about Carl, or that grasping *Socrates is wise* requires grasping Carl, or that propositional part essentialism is false. So the denial of Transitivity is still a problem for a mereological account of Russellian propositions.

What about the general objection to transcategorial sums, of which Russellian propositions are an instance? The Russellian might simply reply here by pointing to other widely accepted, apparently transcategorial objects, such as impure sets. Those who believe in impure sets are committed to the existence of abstract objects with material members. Not everyone believes in impure sets, of course, but many philosophers at least talk as if they do. So the Russellian might argue that, insofar as impure sets are ontologically unobjectionable, so are Russellian propositions. Note, however, that this reply is not entirely to the point: impure sets are *not* instances of transcategorial sums, *even* on a mereological conception of sets (as in Lewis, 1991), for on a mereological conception of sets, the *subsets* of a set are its parts.[35] So there is an important dissimilarity between Russellian propositions and impure sets; hence, an appeal to the latter can have only a limited effect in making the former more palatable.

Finally, there is the repetition problem. What sort of response might the structured propositionalist make to this difficulty? The repetition problem was recognized by both Bolzano and Frege, neither of whom offered a satisfactory solution.[36] In fact, this problem led Frege to concede that 'metaphors derived from the corporeal realm fail us' (Frege, 1918–19/1984).

Consider again the proposition *John is John*. On Russellianism, the individual, John, is a part twice over in this proposition. Unless John is thought of as a type, it is difficult to make any sense of how there could be two "instances" (i.e. tokens) of John in a proposition. But it's obviously false that material objects are types, so this is no solution. Even for the Fregean, it is the very same mode-of-presentation of John that is a part, twice over, in the proposition *John is John*, not two tokens of a mode-of-presentation type.

Of course, the friend of structured propositions could simply bite the bullet, claiming that some propositions have "repeating parts" and there is nothing further to be said in the way of explanation. However, if the SPist allows that propositions have repeating parts, it seems that she cannot be using 'part' in the standard mereological sense, but in some other sense, and, therefore, she still owes us an explanation of what she means by 'part'. Furthermore, insofar as the notion of a repeating part is mysterious, SP loses some of its putative advantage over Primitivism.

3.3 Hylomorphism

A third way to explain propositional constituency is to invoke a theory of parthood that rivals Classical Extensional Mereology. One such theory is *hylomorphism*.[37] Hylomorphism, which has its roots in Aristotle, has undergone a contemporary revival.[38] The following discussion will focus on Mark Johnston's version, which he applies specifically to propositions.

On hylomorphism,

> each complex item admits of a real definition, or statement of its essence, in terms of its matter, understood as parts or components, and its form, understood as a principle of unity. When an item's parts are themselves complex, they in turn will have their own principles of unity (forms) and genuine parts (matter), and so on and so forth, either *ad infinitum*, or terminating in indefinables or "simples" (Johnston, 2006, 658).

The term 'matter', as used here, is a translation of Aristotle's *hyle*, which is quite different from the conception we're familiar with from modern physics. On Aristotle's view, even items that are not material objects, such as syllables and geometric shapes, have "matter" in the sense of constituents of which they are composed. Thus, 'the relation between an item and its components or parts is a topic-neutral relation of vast generality, applying wherever the notion of complexity gets a foothold' (2006, 655). It should be noted at the outset that Johnston's hylomorphism departs from CEM by rejecting Unrestricted and Uniqueness. Not every plurality of objects composes something, but only those that have a certain formal arrangement; and, more importantly for our purposes, there may be two distinct objects composed of the same parts due to distinct principles of unity (2006, 672).

Johnston presents a hylomorphic account of propositional constituency as a solution to the problem of the unity of the proposition. A solution to the unity problem requires a principle that explains not only how such disparate items as Socrates and *wisdom* can form a complex whole, but *also* how that whole is non-conventionally a bearer of truth and falsity. For example, the principle should distinguish the proposition *Socrates is wise* from the (putative) mereological sum composed of Socrates and *wisdom* and the ordered pair with those two items as members. For both the sum and the pair, even if they could be *construed* as truth-bearers, would be so only in virtue of some stipulations on our part, not in and of themselves.

Johnston's response to the unity problem incorporates the responses of both Frege and Russell. There are two kinds of propositional constituents, called 'topics' and 'predicables' – this distinction corresponds to Russell's subject-assertion distinction and, roughly, to Frege's concept-object distinction. Like Frege, Johnston holds that predicables are 'unsaturated': a predicable with n argument places must be saturated by n topics, no more and no less, to form a proposition (2006, 684). Like Russell (but unlike Frege), Johnston also holds that *anything* can be the topic of a proposition (2006, 683). The SVs of names, e.g. can only be topics, but the SVs of predicates can be topics or predicables.

Also like Russell, Johnston holds that what unifies the different propositional constituents is the predication relation. This relation can only hold among propositional constituents that fit together; hence, the account of unsaturated predicables and saturated topics that fill their argument places. To avoid making propositions mind-dependent, Johnston claims that 'predictability guarantees predication' (2006, 684). For example, it is sufficient for the existence of *Socrates is wise*, that Socrates and the property of *wisdom* exist, and that the latter is predicable (but not necessarily *predicated*) of the former – propositions are 'objective' predications (2006, 685).

Hylomorphists disagree amongst themselves about whether the principle of unity uniting the parts of an object o is itself a part of o. Johnston holds that an object's principle of unity is *not* a part of the object; hence, he holds that the relation (*predication*) uniting a proposition's constituents is not itself a part of the proposition (2006, 659, 675).

Several problems beset the hylomorphic account of propositional constituency. First, insofar as this approach is committed to propositions having "Russellian" constituents, it still founders on the transitivity of parthood. I take it that, although some hylomorphists may reject Unrestricted and Uniqueness, they are still committed to Transitivity (a principle which is intrinsically plausible anyway). But we saw above why this is problematic for Russellian propositions. The account Johnston fleshes out is broadly Russellian, but it could, of course, be developed along Fregean lines and avoid this problem. However, a Fregean account will still be vulnerable to the repetition problem. *Prima facie*, hylomorphism does not offer any new insight into addressing this problem. Furthermore, insofar as hylomorphism is itself a controversial part-whole theory, appealing to it in an account of propositional constituency should count as a cost of the view that propositions have constituents (even if it counts as a benefit of hylomorphism itself).

Let me elaborate on this last point. There seem to be two options for the propositional hylomorphist: (i) taking hylomorphism to be the correct account of the part-whole relation *tout court*; or (ii) holding that hylomorphism provides the correct account of propositional parthood, while the notion of *part* that applies to material objects obeys CEM. Both options are major deviations from orthodoxy: (i) involves a complete rejection of the standard mereological conception of parthood (codified in CEM); and (ii) is committed to an alternate, *sui generis* notion of *part* in addition to CEM-parthood, and thus involves a proliferation of primitive ideology. Thus, invoking hylomorphism to provide a metaphysics of propositional constituency has substantial costs.

3.4 Structure-making

Kris McDaniel introduces the term 'structure-making' for the type of composition governing states of affairs in D. M. Armstrong's metaphysics (McDaniel, 2009). Given the similarities between propositions and states of affairs, this seems initially like a promising prospect for explaining the composition of structured propositions. *Structure-making* is a *non*-mereological composition relation that builds states-of-affairs out of particulars and/or properties and relations, and structural universals out of simpler universals.[39] On Armstrong's view, states-of-affairs are facts: a state-of-affairs is the instantiation of a property by an object or a property, or a relation by some objects or properties. A structural universal is 'a certain *type* of conjunction of states-of-affairs' (Armstrong, 1993, 432). An example of a state of affairs is *Socrates' being wise;* an example of a structural universal is *being a hydrogen hydroxide molecule*. Since giving a detailed exposition of the structure-making view would deviate from the main thread of this paper, I will narrow my focus to the evidence that applying this approach to propositional constituency faces serious problems.

Following McDaniel, let's call the composition relation involved in structure-making '*s*-composition'. *S*-composition, unlike mereological composition, is restricted. For example, nothing is *s*-composed only from particulars. That is, 'some xs s-compose a y only if at least one of the xs is a property or relation' (McDaniel, 2009, 257). This is a welcome result as far as structured propositions are concerned, since a necessary condition on propositional parts composing a proposition is that at least one should be a property or relation (or mode-of-presentation thereof). However, a mere property or relation cannot, on its own, compose a proposition, but, at most, a gappy proposition or propositional radical (if there are such things).[40]

Like mereological composition, *s*-composition is reflexive, so every state of affairs *s*-composes itself. Apart from this, a necessary and sufficient condition for some xs to *s*-compose a state of affairs is that 'some of the xs s-compose a property or relation R such that the remaining xs s-compose some ys such that the ys instantate R' (2009, 259). Unfortunately, this sort of composition relation cannot be made to work for structured propositions for, as Russell famously noted, it has the unfortunate consequence of ruling out false propositions. If it is false that Desdemona loves Cassio, then Desdemona and Cassio fail to saturate the *loves* relation. But since Othello believes that Desdemona loves Cassio, the proposition had better exist. This problem points to an important sense in which structured propositions are *unlike* Armstrong's states of affairs: propositions need not be true, but Armstrong's states of affairs all obtain – they are facts.

Even if there were prospects for fixing this problem, further difficulties remain. First, structure-making violates Uniqueness. *Prima facie*, the only way for SP to comply with Uniqueness would be to postulate an additional part that encodes the arrangement of a proposition's constituents. But it is difficult to see how a propositional constituent, on its own, could encode the positions of the other constituents, or show what in the proposition is being predicated of what.[41] Plus, this would only push back the question of what unifies propositional constituents – an analogue of the famous "third-man" objection to Platonic forms.

In addition, Armstrong's conception of structural universals suffers from the repetition problem, as Armstrong himself realized.[42] Further, *s*-composition is transitive. Though this perhaps gives structure-making an advantage as a theory of composition, it puts it at a disadvantage for accommodating the most widely held version of SP – as we saw, Russellian propositions violate Transitivity.

One final problem is that structure-making is not intended as a theory of composition for material objects, so commitment to this view involves postulating a plurality of parthood relations.[43] The structure-making approach involves a proliferation of primitive ideology, which is both intrinsically undesirable and threatens to make the notion of constituency explanatorily impotent.

3.5 Taking constituency as primitive

A final option is to construe *constituency* as a *sui generis* relation, i.e., to say that *constituency* is distinct from, and cannot be analyzed in terms of, *parthood*, *membership*, etc. However, this approach, which we might call 'Constituency Primitivism', does not answer the challenge to provide a metaphysics of propositional constituency – *constituency* has not been explained, but is taken as brute. This strategy deprives SP of the dialectical advantage of having fewer primitive predicates than Propositional Primitivism.

Meinong's worry, then, seems to have been justified – for all of the ways that suggest themselves for 'following the analogy [of constituency] rigorously' are beset with difficulties. Attributing parts and structure to propositions brings a whole host of problems not had by merely positing propositions. This makes the need for arguments concluding that propositions *must* be structured entities with constituents more acute. *If we can get by without attributing structure and constituents to propositions, we should.* Such arguments for the indispensability of structured propositions have not been forthcoming.

Instead, the primary way that the friends of structured propositions have argued for their view is with the BPW argument. Now, if structured propositionalists can successfully argue that theirs is the *best* theory of propositions, then, among propositionalists, this should be a convincing argument in favor of SP. But the BPW argument only succeeds in establishing that SP is the best theory of propositions *if* SP and PW are the only serious contenders for theories of propositions. But they are not: Propositional Primitivism is another contender. So the BPW argument does not establish SP as the best available theory of propositions.

4. Conclusion: heavyweight and lightweight senses of constituency

One important reason for invoking *constituency* in the theory of propositions is to account for the inner nature of fine-grained propositions. Again, this is problematic if *constituency* itself is taken as primitive. However, for philosophers who are skeptical of making substantive claims about the inner nature of propositions, constituency primitivism *is* a viable option – i.e. if the notion of constituency is simply a useful heuristic that is *not* meant to bear any explanatory weight, then one can use it in a deflationary, metaphysically "lightweight" sense. In this conclusion, I'll briefly explain why one might want to retain the notion of constituency, even if only in a deflationary sense. Then I will contrast the lightweight and heavyweight senses of constituency, pointing out how the former circumvents the metaphysical difficulties of the latter.

A major reason to invoke the notion of propositional constituency is provided by the enormously popular Millian view of proper names. Millianism is the thesis that names are mere "tags" for their bearers – i.e. the *only* semantic value of a name is the individual (if any) to which it refers.[44] Suppose one is a Millian who holds that the semantic values of sentences are propositions.[45] Invoking propositional constituents is a natural and useful way to distinguish propositions expressed by name-containing sentences from those expressed by otherwise identical sentences containing co-referential rigid descriptions. Consider:

(F) Frege is clever.
(B) The actual author of the *Begriffsschrift* is clever.

Both 'Frege' and 'the actual author of the *Begriffsschrift*' rigidly designate Frege. But a Millian propositionalist needs to explain the difference between the *propositions* expressed by (F) and (B), and it is not at all obvious how to do this, absent an appeal to propositional constituents.[46] For ease of reference, I'll adopt the following convention: if '(S)' names a sentence, then 'P(S)' names the proposition expressed by (S).

Both (F) and (B) contain expressions that pick out Frege in every possible world in which Frege exists. It's a necessary truth that both P(F) and P(B) are true iff *Frege* is clever. Yet, intuitively, the name 'Frege' and the description 'the actual author of the *Begriffsschrift*' do not make the same semantic contribution to P(F) and P(B).[47] 'Frege' is simply a tag for Frege, but 'the actual author of the *Begriffsschrift*' picks out Frege *via* a condition he satisfies (albeit essentially). A straightforward way of recognizing this difference is to say that Frege is a *constituent* of P(F) but not of P(B) – if 'Frege' is a mere tag for Frege, what could the semantic value of 'Frege' be, other than Frege himself?[48]

Similarly, the following sentences

(T) Two is prime.
(E) The even prime is prime.

both contain expressions that rigidly designate the number two, but they are semantically different.[49] One important difference is that (E) is arguably analytic, while (T) is not. Thus, although 'two' and 'the even prime' both pick out the number two in all possible worlds, P(T) and P(E) are different propositions. A straightforward way of recognizing this difference is to say that the number two is a *constituent* of P(T), but not of P(E), even though P(E), like P(T), only exists in worlds in which the number two exists.

Note that this is not an *argument* that there is no way for a Millian propositionalist to account for the difference between the propositions expressed by otherwise identical sentences containing names and co-referential rigid descriptions *except* by appeal to propositional constituency. The point is simply that it is *difficult* to say exactly what the difference is, and invoking *constituency* is a natural and helpful way to do so. But what is the sense of *constituency* being invoked, if it is not that propositional constituents are literally members or parts of propositions?

Constituency is being used in a *heavyweight* sense if it is being invoked as part of an explanation of the "inner nature" of propositions. To say that propositions have constituents in a heavyweight sense is to say that they "contain" sub-sentential SVs as a set "contains" its members or a complex material object its parts – it is to make a claim about their intrinsic properties.

By contrast, *constituency* is being used in a *lightweight* sense if it is being invoked for illustrative purposes to describe the dependence of propositions on, e.g., ordinary objects, for their truth, existence, and identity or individuation. To say that propositions have constituents in this sense is to make a claim about their extrinsic (though essential) properties. Here is one suggestion for fleshing out the lightweight notion of *constituency*:

> (Constituency$_L$) A proposition has *a* as a constituent if (i) its existence depends on the existence of *a* and (ii) it is individuated partly in terms of *a*.[50]

To say that propositions have constituents$_L$ is to say that they are *object-dependent* but does *not* commit one to SP or, perhaps more pointedly, to Russellianism. Singular Russellian propositions are, of course, object-dependent – the Russellian proposition *Socrates is wise* depends on Socrates for its existence and identity. However, a merely object-dependent proposition is not necessarily a *Russellian* proposition – one need not hold that such a proposition has, e.g., Socrates "inside" of it, or that it is "built out of" Socrates and the property of wisdom, or that it has Socrates and wisdom as parts, etc. So, singular Russellian propositions are object-dependent, but the converse is not the case.

How does the notion of constituency$_L$ help distinguish the pairs P(F) and P(B), or P(T) and P(E)? Arguably, P(F) is existentially dependent on Frege, but P

(B) is not. Similarly, P(F) is *individuated* partly in terms of Frege, while P(B) is not (*mutatis mutandis* for P(T) and P(E)). A contrast with PW propositions should help make this clear.

On PW, propositions are individuated by their possible-worlds truth conditions. Thus, P(F) and P(B) are the same proposition: the set of worlds at which Frege is clever. Since 'the actual author of the *Begriffsschrift*' designates the same object across worlds as 'Frege', P(F) and P(B) are true in all of the same worlds. This identification highlights one of the main SPist criticisms of PW – that it does not individuate propositions finely enough.

By contrast, if Frege is a constituent$_L$ of P(F) but not of P(B), these propositions are distinct because Frege himself figures in the individuation conditions of P(F) (but not P(B)). In case it is unclear how P(F) can be individuated partly in terms of Frege without having Frege as a constituent in the heavyweight sense, consider the following analogy.

Assume for the sake of argument that essentiality of origins is true. Now consider the gametes from which Frege was conceived – call them 'gametes z'.[51] Frege has the property of being the product of gametes z essentially and is individuated (in part) in terms of them – i.e. being the product of gametes z distinguishes Frege from every other individual. However, Frege does not have gametes z as *parts* – he merely bears a special relation to them. Similarly, one might hold that P(F) depends for its existence on Frege and is individuated (in part) in terms of him by bearing a special, intimate relation to him, but does not have Frege as a *part*.

In a slightly different context, Jerry Fodor writes about 'the doctrine, familiar at least since Russell, that things that a proposition is about are part of the proposition about them; on this way of putting things, John is part of the proposition that John sneezed' (2009). He seems to advocate taking constituency in a lightweight sense when goes on to say,

> Propositions ... are abstracta, so the question whether their constituents are "inside" or "outside" of them doesn't seriously arise. Indeed, as far as I can see, to say that John is part of the proposition that John sneezed is just to say that whether it's true that John sneezed depends on how things were with John. Sometimes it's useful to talk Russell's way; arguably, doing so helps explain why whether John sneezed doesn't depend on how John is described. But Russell's way of talking about propositions doesn't license claiming that John is part of [the proposition that John sneezed] (or, come to think of it, even that [propositions] have parts) (*op cit.*).[52]

Constituency$_L$ clearly does not inherit the ontological problems of its heavyweight cousin – invoking this notion does not involve commitment to any claims about the "inner nature" of propositions; *a fortiori*, it is compatible with a very cautious, skeptical stance toward such claims about propositions. Thus, constituency$_L$ is compatible with (but of course does not entail) Propositional Primitivism.

Constituency$_L$ lacks the ontological problems but also the purported explanatory potential of its heavyweight cousin. Because constituency$_L$ does not involve any claims about the intrinsic properties of propositions, one who invokes this notion can have no pretensions to giving an account of the inner nature of propositions. However, the prospects of providing such an explanation by invoking *constituency* look dim. For the propositionalist who wants to talk the talk, but is leery of walking the walk, an appeal to constituency$_L$ might seem like an attractive option. Other propositionalists might disdain both the walk and the talk,[53] but they should take comfort at least in seeing the threat posed to them by the explanatory pretensions of Structured Propositionalism evaporate.

Notes

1. Thanks to John Keller, Michael Rea, Jeff Speaks, Marian David, and the editors of this journal for helpful comments on earlier drafts of this paper.
2. I've substituted 'proposition' for 'Objective', the typical translation of Meinong's 'Objectiv' – his favored term for states of affairs and propositions (the objects of thought). Cf. Alvin Plantinga: 'What exactly, or even approximately, *is* this relationship *being a constituent of*? Do we know or even have reason to suspect that propositions *have* constituents' (1983, 164)?
3. Prominent structured propositionalists include Scott Soames, Nathan Salmon, Jeffrey King, Mark Richard, David Braun, Peter Hanks, Kent Bach, and Jason Stanley. Prominent historical structured propositionalists include Bernard Bolzano, Gottlob Frege, Bertrand Russell, and G. E. Moore.
4. I'll drop the reference to context in what follows.
5. Linguists sometimes use the term 'semantic value' to mean *reference*. However, it is often used in a more neutral way to pick out whatever the relevant type(s) of meaning is (are). Here I use it to pick out, at the sentential level, propositions, and at the sub-sentential level, whatever kind of meaning contributes to the propositions expressed.
6. Single quotes function as both corner quotes and mention quotes throughout. Double quotes function as scare quotes.
7. I'm using Frege's terminology here, where concepts are reference-level semantic values associated with predicate expressions. Concepts are *not* semantic-values at the level of sense and, thus, are not constituents of propositions.
8. In Keller, 2012, I evaluate arguments for SP from semantic compositionality, logic, and direct reference theory.
9. Jeff Speaks suggested the helpful labels 'metaphysically heavyweight' and 'metaphysically lightweight': see Speaks (with Jeff King and Scott Soames) (forthcoming).
10. Many structured propositionalists consider the critique in Soames, 1987 to have dealt a deathblow to PW. I will not discuss the details of this well-known argument here, but the gist of it is that sets of worlds are not fine-grained enough to play one of the fundamental propositional roles: objects of belief. If, for example, a necessarily true proposition is the set of all possible worlds, then, given that belief is a dyadic relation between a believer and a proposition, anyone who believes one necessary truth thereby believes *all* necessary truths. Thus, a kindergartener, by virtue of believing that $2 + 2 = 4$, also believes that arithmetic is incomplete. Proponents of PW, of course, have responded to this objection, and it is worth noting that many linguists still accept PW. However, some famous proponents of PW, e.g., Robert Stalnaker and David Chalmers, have made a significant concession to the SPist's criticism by countenancing structured intensions in their account of propositional attitudes. See Stalnaker, 2012 and Chalmers, 2006.
11. Even on David Lewis' famous, but controversial, mereological account of sets, it is their *subsets*, rather than their members, that are parts of a set. See Lewis, 1991. But

see Kit Fine, 2010 for defense of the less common view that takes a set's *members* to be its parts.
12. Proponents of Primitivism include Bealer, 1998, Merricks, 2009, Plantinga, 1974 and van Inwagen, 2004. This view (or something similar) is also referred to as the "primitive-entity theory" (Jubien, 2001), "Magical Ersatzism" (Lewis, 1986), and "Unsound Abstractionism" (van Inwagen, 1986).
13. Soames, 2010 and Jubien, 2001 make similar claims. And see Richard, 1990, 34 for a closely related criticism. Also, see David Lewis' criticism of Magical Ersatzism in Lewis, 1986, 174–191.
14. See Benacerraf, 1965 for the original exposition of this problem as applied to a set-theoretic treatment of numbers, and see Jubien, 2001 and Soames, 2010 for an application of this problem to propositions.
15. See, among many others, Bealer, 1998 and Jubien, 2001. David Lewis was famously unmoved by this objection to his set-theoretic construal of propositions. See Lewis, 1979.
16. This problem is also discussed in Bealer, 1998 and, in somewhat different terms, in Soames, 2010.
17. Cf. Soames, 2010, 91–92.
18. See Braun, 2005 (especially fn. 6), King, 2007, Soames, 2010, and Hanks, 2011.
19. Leonard and Goodman, 1940. Tillman and Fowler, 2012 argue for the claim that propositional constituents *must be* understood as propositional parts (see pp. 528–529), but they also reject CEM.
20. Typically, a principle of strong or weak supplementation (and/or various fusion principles) is added to the three core axioms, though there is disagreement among theorists of CEM about which principle(s) to add. See Paul Hovda, 2009 for discussion. The arguments of this paper only rely on the three core axioms.
21. See, e.g., Lewis, 1991 and Koslicki (Forthcoming).
22. Braun, 1993 seems to think proposition's structure is itself a part. This view provides a way to distinguish the propositions *Maggie loves John* and *John loves Maggie*, but has other problems, which I briefly discuss in §2.4.
23. Frege took note of this problem in an undated letter to Jourdain (see Gabriel et al., 1980: 79). See Gilmore (Forthcoming) for fuller discussion.
24. If you do not like Carl, substitute another part of Socrates.
25. Cf. Gilmore (forthcoming: 6), who calls this the 'acquaintance argument'.
26. Frege presents two brief versions of the compositionality argument, one in "Compound Thoughts" (1923/1984) and one in "Logic in Mathematics" (1914/1979). Russell presents a similar argument in *The Philosophy of Logical Atomism* (1918/1956), but for structured facts, not structured propositions. For detailed discussion of Frege's and Russell's compositionality arguments, see Keller, 2012 and Lorraine Juliano Keller and John A. Keller (Forthcoming).
27. Couldn't the SPist avoid this problem simply by denying that propositions have any constituents other than the semantic values of the parts of the sentences that express them? That move would certainly solve the problem at hand, but at the cost of begging the question. If constituents are supposed to be parts in the mereological sense, then the presumption is that the notion of *parthood* being invoked obeys the axioms of CEM. By those axioms, the proper parts of a proposition include the proper parts of its proper parts, thus Carl is a (proper) part of *Socrates is wise*.
28. It's in general very plausible that, *if* abstract objects have parts, they have them essentially. Given that propositions are abstracta, propositional part essentialism would follow from this more general principle. Gilmore also discusses this 'essentialist' principle in his forthcoming: 7.

29. But see Gilmore (Forthcoming) for a sophisticated attempt to reconcile Russellianism with Transitivity. It would take me too far afield to discuss Gilmore's interesting solution in detail here, but let me just quickly note two potential problems with his approach. Gilmore's solution involves invoking a four-place parthood relation and positing slots at different 'locations' in propositions (see pp. 17–24). Here are a couple of *prima facie* objections. First, construing *parthood* as a four-place relation seems like cheating, and should only be done as a last resort (akin to positing relative identity to "solve" the puzzles about identity). And second, I find the notion of *location* applied to abstract objects obscure. If an object is not extended, in what sense can we speak of different locations in it? Invoking the notion of location seems (to me) not to illuminate the application of 'part-whole' terminology to propositions, but to obfuscate it further. I think this sort of "solution" just points to the depth of the difficulty of applying an idiom designed for material objects to abstracta.
30. See Simons, 2003 and Varzi, 2006.
31. Alvin Plantinga applies this worry specifically to singular Russellian propositions in Plantinga, 1983.
32. It may be objected that because the proposition itself is abstract, *it* has no location. But this objection seems to beg the question. If, in general, objects that have material parts are located where there parts are, what makes propositions the exception?
33. See also Künne, 2008.
34. This is the line that Varzi favors.
35. But see Kit Fine *op cit.* for a defense of the view that the members of a set are its parts. It should be noted that Fine's view is committed to the claim that there are different fundamental *parthood* relations and, thus, is a form of compositional pluralism.
36. Cf. Künne, 2008, 226–230.
37. One might object that hylomorphism is not a theory of parts and wholes, and hence, is not a rival to CEM. One reason for this would be that the notion of *constituent* that is employed in hylomorphism is different than the notion of *part* (not just as it is employed in CEM – of course this is a different notion, otherwise they would not be rival theories – but in its ordinary use). However, as Johnston, 2006 presents the view, hylomorphism is intended to be a rival to CEM (see, in particular, p. 688).
38. For example, Kit Fine, 1999, 2010, Kathrin Koslicki, 2008, and Mark Johnston, 2006.
39. Laws of nature are states-of-affairs with no particulars as constituents. See McDaniel, 2009, 259.
40. To be precise, a proposition cannot have *only a single part* that is a property or relation, but they can be composed of *only* properties and/or relations (e.g. the proposition *Blue is a color*). Gappy propositions and propositional radicals are structured propositions with "missing" constituents. See Braun, 1993 and 2005 and Bach, 2006. On Braun's view, gappy propositions are expressed by sentences containing empty names (e.g., 'Vulcan is a planet' expresses a proposition with an empty place or "gap" where the semantic value of the name 'Vulcan' should be, as modeled by the ordered pair $<\{\}, \text{ is a planet} >$).
41. Cf. Soames, 2010. 28–32 for a closely related point.
42. 'Consider the structural property of *being (just) two electrons*, a property possessed by all two-member collections of electrons. We cannot say that this property involves the same universal, *being an electron*, taken twice over, because a universal is one, not many' (Armstrong, 1978, 69–70).
43. See McDaniel, 2009, 254–255 for fuller discussion of the claim that the structure-making account is a form of compositional pluralism.

44. Note that some philosophers who enthusiastically endorse Millianism have expressed reservations about Direct Reference (DR) Theory (famously, Kripke 1979). Also, DR Theory is, confusingly, commonly presented in (at least) two different ways in the literature, one of which entails SP and the other of which is compatible with the non-existence of propositions. Explaining the different formulations would distract from the main thread of this paper, so I'd rather avoid it here – but see Keller, 2012 for an in-depth discussion.
45. Some Millians are skeptical about propositions (e.g. Kripke 1979 and Wettstein, 2004). Also, some Millians are propositionalists but emphatically *not* Russellians (e.g. van Inwagen, 1986, 2004).
46. One might think that the difference between a name and a co-referential rigid description can be explained by an appeal to *de jure* rigidity, where an expression is *de jure* rigid if its rigidity is due to the rules of the language (Kripke 1972, 21n). However, this will not work for rigid descriptions of the form 'the actual *F*', since the rigidity of this type of description is due to the rules of the language (viz. the semantics of 'actual'); thus they are, like names, *de jure* rigid.
47. Of course, an important semantic difference between (F) and (B), considered as sentence-*types*, is that (B) may express different propositions in different possible contexts, whereas (F) plausibly cannot. If one believes in sentential characters, one might put it this way: holding the *characters* of (F) and (B) fixed, (F) has a stable content across possible contexts, whereas the content of (B) may shift (e.g., consider an utterance of (B) in a world where some obscure German mathematician distinct from Frege writes the *Begriffsschrift*). I'm interested here in how one might account for the difference in the propositions expressed by actual world tokens of (F) and (B). Thanks to the editors of this journal for pointing out the need for more clarity about this issue.
48. As I mentioned above, this is a view that Kripke and some other Millians reject, since they are skeptics about propositions. My remarks in this section are intended *only* for Millian *propositionalists*, not all of whom are friendly towards SP.
49. Though 'the even prime', unlike 'the actual author of the *Begriffsschrift*', is only *de facto* (not *de jure*) rigid.
50. Cf. Schiffer, 2011 and Hofweber, 2005.
51. Cf. Almog, 1986.
52. In this review of Michael Tye's *Consciousness Revisited*, Fodor criticizes Tye's appeal to an analogy with Russellian propositions as part of a defense of his thesis that experiences have parts.
53. Some propositionalists reject SP largely because of their worries about the apparent threat that object-dependent propositions pose to serious actualism. Thus, the ability to accommodate object-dependence will not appeal to such propositionalists. For discussion of this problem, see Plantinga, 1983, 1985, Fine, 1985, David, 2009, and Speaks (Forthcoming).

References

Almog, Joseph. 1986. "Naming Without Necessity." *The Journal of Philosophy* 83 (4): 210–242.

Armstrong, D. M. 1978. *Universals and Scientific Realism*. Volumes I and II Cambridge University Press.
Armstrong, D. M. 1993. "A World of States of Affairs." *Philosophical Perspectives* 7: 429–440.
Bach, Kent. 2006. "The Excluded Middle: Semantic Minimalism Without Minimal Propositions." *Philosophy and Phenomenological Research* 73 (2): 435–442.
Bealer, George. 1998. "Propositions." *Mind* 107 (425): 1–32.
Benacerraf, Paul. 1965. "What Numbers Could Not Be." *Philosophical Review* 74 (1): 47–73.
Bolzano, Bernard. 1837/1973. *Theory of Science*, Edited and introduction by Jan Berg, translated by Burnham Terrell. Dordrecht: D. Reidel Publishing Co.
Braun, David. 1993. "Empty Names." *Nous* 27 (4): 449–469.
Braun, David. 2005. "Empty Names, Fictional Names, Mythical Names." *Nous* 39: 596–631.
Chalmers, David. 2006. "Probability and Propositions.", Online Philosophy Conference, May 2006. http://consc.net/papers/probability.pdf
David, Marian. 2009. "Defending Existentialism?" In *States of Affairs*, edited by Maria Reicher, 1–42. Frankfurt: Ontos Verlag.
Fine, Kit. 1985. "Plantinga on the Reduction of Possibilist Discourse." In *Plantinga*, edited by J. E. Tomberlin, and P. van Inwagen, 145–186. Dordrecht: Reidel.
Fine, Kit. 1999. "Things and Their Parts." In *Directions in Philosophy: Midwest Studies in Philosophy, Volume XXIII*, edited by Peter French, and Howard Wettstein, 61–74. Oxford: Blackwell.
Fine, Kit. 2010. "Towards a Theory of Part." *Journal of Philosophy* 107 (11): 559–589.
Fodor, Jerry. 2009. "It ain't in the head." Review of Michael Tye's Consciousness Revisited, in Times Literary Supplement, October 16, 2009.
Frege, Gottlob. 1892/1952. "On *Sinn* and *Bedeutung*." In *Translations from the Philosophical Writings of Gottlob Frege*, edited by Michael Beaney, translated by Max Black, Blackwell; reprinted in *The Frege Reader*. Malden, MA and Oxford: Blackwell, 1997.
Frege, Gottlob. 1914/1979. "Logic in Mathematics." In *Gottlob Frege: Posthumous Writings*, edited by H. Hermes, F. Kambartel, and F. Kaulbach. Chicago University Press.
Frege, Gottlob. 1918/1956. "The Thought: A Logical Inquiry." Translated by A.M., and Marcelle Quinton, *Mind* 65: 289–311. Reprinted in *Readings in the Philosophy of Language*, edited by Peter Ludlow, 1997. Cambridge, MA: MIT Press.
Frege, Gottlob. 1918–19/1984. "Negation." In *Collected Papers on Mathematics, Logic, and Philosophy*, edited by B. McGuinness, translated by P. Geach, and R.H. Stoothoff. Oxford: Basil Blackwell.
Frege, Gottlob. 1923/1984. "Compound Thoughts." In *Collected Papers on Mathematics, Logic, and Philosophy*, edited by B. McGuinness, translated by P. Geach, and R.H. Stoothoff. Oxford: Basil Blackwell.
Gabriel, G., et al. 1980. *Gottlob Frege: Philosophical and Mathematical Correspondence*. University of Chicago Press.
Gilmore, Cody. Forthcoming. "Parts of Propositions." In *Mereology and Location*, edited by Shieva Kleinschmidt. Oxford University Press.
Hanks, Peter. 2011. "Structured Propositions as Types." *Mind* 120 (477): 11–52.
Hofweber, Thomas. 2005. "Supervenience and Object-Dependent Properties." *Journal of Philosophy* CII (1): 1–28.
Hovda, Paul. 2009. "What is Classical Mereology?" *Journal of Philosophical Logic* 38: 55–82.
Johnston, Mark. 2006. "Hylomorphism." *Journal of Philosophy*, 2006.

Jubien, Michael. 2001. "Propositions and the Objects of Thought." *Philosophical Studies* 104: 47–62.
Keller, Lorraine Juliano. 2012. *Whence Structured Propositions?*, Unpublished Ph.D. Dissertation for the University of Notre Dame.
Keller, Lorraine Juliano (with John A. Keller). Forthcoming. "Compositionality and Structured Propositions." *Thought*.
King, Jeffrey C. 2007. *The Nature and Structure of Content*. Oxford: OUP.
King, Jeffrey C. 2011. "Structured Propositions." In *The Stanford Encyclopedia of Philosophy (Fall 2011 Edition)*, URL=<http://plato.stanford.edu/archives/fall2011/entries/propositions-structured/> edited by Edward N. Zalta.
Koslicki, Kathrin. 2008. *The Structure of Objects*. Oxford University Press.
Koslicki, Kathrin. Forthcoming. "Mereological Sums and Singular Terms." In *Mereology and Location*, edited by Shieva Kleinschmidt. Oxford University Press.
Künne, Wolfgang. 2008. "Constituents of Concepts: Bolzano vs. Frege." In *Versuche über Bolzano (Essays on Bolzano)*. Sankt Augustin: Academia Verlag.
Leonard, H. S., and N. Goodman. 1940. "The Calculus of Individuals and Its Uses." *Journal of Symbolic Logic* 5: 45–55.
Lewis, David. 1979. "Attitudes *De Dicto* and *De Se*." *Philosophical Review* 88 (4): 513–543.
Lewis, David. 1986. "Against Structural Universals." *Australasian Journal of Philosophy* 64 (1): 25–46.
Lewis, David. 1991. *Parts of Classes*. Wiley-Blackwell.
Loux, Michael. 2006. "Aristotle's Constituent Ontology." In *Oxford Studies in Metaphysics, Vol. 2*, edited by Dean W. Zimmerman, 207–250. Oxford: OUP.
McDaniel, Kris. 2004. "Modal Realism with Overlap." *Australasian Journal of Philosophy* 82 (1): 137–152.
McDaniel, Kris. 2009. "Structure-Making." *Australasian Journal of Philosophy* 87 (2): 251–274.
Meinong, Alexius. 1904/1960. "The Theory of Objects." In *Realism and the Background of Phenomenology*, edited by Roderick M. Chisholm. Illinois: Free Press.
Merricks, Trenton. 2009. "Propositional Attitudes?" *Proceedings of the Aristotelian Society* 109: 207–232, url: http://pages.shanti.virginia.edu/merricks/files/2010/05/PropAttitudes.pdf (page numbering from online version).
Plantinga, Alvin. 1974. *The Nature of Necessity*. Oxford: Clarendon Press.
Plantinga, Alvin. 1983. "On Existentialism." *Philosophical Studies* 44: 1–20; reprinted in *Essays in the Metaphysics of Modality*, edited by M. Davidson. Oxford: OUP, 2003.
Plantinga, Alvin. 1985. "Replies to My Colleagues." In *Alvin Plantinga*, edited by J. Tomberlin, and P. van Inwagen, 313–329. Dordrecht: D. Reidel.
Rea, Michael C. 1998. "In Defense of Mereological Universalism." *Philosophy and Phenomenological Research* 58 (2): 347–360.
Richard, Mark. 1990. *Propositional Attitudes: An Essay on Thoughts and How We Ascribe Them*. Cambridge University Press.
Russell, Bertrand. 1903. *The Principles of Mathematics*. Cambridge: Cambridge University Press.
Russell, Bertrand. 1918/1956. "The Philosophy of Logical Atomism." In *Logic and Knowledge: Essays 1901–1950*, edited by Robert Charles Marsh, 175–182. New York: MacMillan Company.
Salmon, Nathan. 1986. *Frege's Puzzle*. Cambridge, MA: MIT Press.
Salmon, N., and S. Soames, eds. 1990. *Propositional Attitudes*. Oxford: OUP.
Schiffer, Stephen. 2003. *The Things We Mean*. Oxford: Clarendon Press.

Schiffer, Stephen. 2011. "Propositions: What Are They Good For?" In *Prospects for Meaning*, edited by R. Schantz. de Gruyter Press, Page numbering from online version: http://philosophy.fas.nyu.edu/docs/IO/1176/SchantzPropositions.pdf

Sider, Theodore. 2007. "Parthood." *Philosophical Review* 116: 51–91, Page numbering from online version: http://www.tedsider.org/papers/parthood.pdf

Sider, Theodore. 2012. *Writing the Book of the World*. Oxford: OUP.

Simons, Peter. 1987. *Parts: A Study in Ontology*. Oxford: Clarendon Press.

Simons, Peter. 2003. "The Universe." *Ratio* 16 (3): 236–250.

Soames, Scott. 1987. "Direct Reference, Propositional Attitudes, and Semantic Content." *Philosophical Topics* 15 (1): 47–87.

Soames, Scott. 2010. "What is Meaning?" Princeton.

Speaks, Jeff. Forthcoming. "On Possibly Nonexistent Propositions." In *Philosophy and Phenomenological Research*.

Speaks, Jeff (with Jeff King and Scott Soames). Forthcoming. *New Thinking About Propositions*. Oxford University Press.

Stalnaker, Robert. 1976. "Propositions." edited by A. P. Martinich. Reprinted in *The Philosophy of Language*. New York and Oxford: OUP.

Stalnaker, Robert. 2012. *Possibilities: Metaphysical Foundations of Modal Semantics*, Princeton.

Tillman, Chris, and Gregory Fowler. 2012. "Propositions and Parthood: The Universe and Anti-symmetry." *Australasian Journal of Philosophy* 90 (3): 525–539.

van Inwagen, Peter. 1986. "Two Concepts of Possible Worlds." In *Midwest Studies in Philosophy* 9; reprinted in *Ontology, Identity, and Modality*, 206–242. Cambridge University Press, 2001.

van Inwagen, Peter. 1987. "When Are Objects Parts?" *Philosophical Perspectives* 1: 21–47.

van Inwagen, Peter. 2004. "A Theory of Properties." In *Oxford Studies in Metaphysics: Volume 1*, edited by Dean W. Zimmerman, 106–138.

Varzi, Achille. 2006. "The Universe Among Other Things." In *Ratio (new series)* XIX: 107–119.

Varzi, Achille. 2011. "Mereology." In *Stanford Encyclopedia of Philosophy (Spring 2011 Edition)*, edited by Edward N. Zalta. URL=<http://plato.stanford.edu/archives/spr2011/entries/mereology/>.

Wettstein, Howard. 2004. *The Magic Prism: An Essay in the Philosophy of Language*. Oxford: OUP.

THEORETICAL ALTERNATIVES TO PROPOSITIONS
Propositions, attitudinal objects, and the distinction between actions and products

Friederike Moltmann

Research Director Centre, Nationale de la Recherche Scientifique (CNRS) Institut d'Histoire et de Philosophie, des Sciences et des Techniques (IHPST), Paris, France

> Propositions as mind-independent abstract objects raise serious problems such as their cognitive accessibility and their ability to carry essential truth conditions, as a number of philosophers have recently pointed out. This paper argues that 'attitudinal objects' or kinds of them should replace propositions as truth bearers and as the (shared) objects of propositional attitudes. Attitudinal objects, entities like judgments, beliefs, and claims, are not states or actions, but rather their (spatio-temporally coincident) products, following the distinction between actions and products introduced by Twardowski (1912). The paper argues that the action–product distinction is not tied to particular terms in a particular language, but is to be understood as the more general distinction between an action and the (abstract or physically realized) artifact that it creates. It thus includes the distinction between the passing of a law and the law itself and an act of artistic creation and the created work of art.

Propositions as mind-independent truth-bearing entities play a central role in contemporary philosophy of language. Ever since Frege (1918/9), it has become an established view that propositions act as the primary truth bearers, the meanings of sentences, and the 'objects' of propositional attitudes. Given their role as objects of propositional attitudes and the meanings of sentences, propositions must be intersubjectively shareable and thus are taken to be mind-independent. Furthermore, propositions as meanings of both independent and embedded sentences are taken to be entities representing content separated from (illocutionary or attitudinal) force.

Propositions in this sense have been subject to a range of recent criticism, though. As mind-independent abstract objects that belong, according to Frege, to a 'third realm', they raise questions of their cognitive accessibility and their causal interaction with agents. Moreover, the way propositions are formally conceived, as sets of circumstances, functions from circumstances to truth values, or structured propositions, and thus formal structures of one sort or another, raises serious difficulties, such as the problem of the truth-directedness and the unity of propositions and the problem of arbitrary identification. Finally, propositions as semantic values of *that*-clauses raise problems for linguistic semantics since *that*-clauses do not appear to act as singular terms referring to propositions. Moreover, quantifiers like *something* that can take the place of *that*-clauses do not appear to range over propositions.

One approach to the conceptual problems for propositions that has recently been pursued by a number of philosophers consists in a return to an act-based, pre-Fregean view of content, in particular by taking predication to be an intentional relation relating an agent to a property and its arguments (Jubien 2001; Hanks 2007a, 2011; Soames 2010, forthcoming; Moltmann 2003a). An important issue that the act-based account raises is the question of what could play the traditional roles of propositions. An answer pursued both by Soames and by Hanks is to identify propositions with types of cognitive acts. There is something fundamentally unsatisfactory about such an identification, however, and that is that cognitive acts do not have the right properties to provide the sort of entity suitable to play the role of propositions. Cognitive acts do not have the right representational, normative, and evaluative properties, and they do not enter similarity relation in the right way. Furthermore, they are not entities suited to play the appropriate role in the semantics of sentences with *that*-clauses or quantifiers in their place.

In this paper, I will argue for a notion of a truth-bearing entity that is distinct both from a proposition and an intentional event, state, or action, and that is the notion of an *attitudinal object* – or the product of a mental or illocutionary event. Attitudinal objects are entities like 'John's belief that S', John's claim that S', 'John's desire that S', or 'John's request that S'. Attitudinal objects, though they belong to a distinct ontological category, share properties both with mental or illocutionary events and with propositions. Like propositions, they are bearers of truth or more generally satisfaction conditions. Moreover, they come close to propositions in that they enter exact similarity relations just in case they share the same content and the same force. But they are as concrete as the corresponding mental or illocutionary event, with which they may share their spatio-temporal location. As such, they do not give rise to the problems that propositions give rise to, such as the problems of cognitive accessibility and truth-directedness. Attitudinal objects are cognitive entities, but they are not cognitive acts, but rather their products.

The notion of an attitudinal object has an important precedent in the work of the Polish philosopher Twardowski (1912), who introduced a general distinction between 'actions' and 'products', with the same aim of conceiving of a cognitively realistic notion of propositional content. The distinction between actions and products includes the distinction between mental actions such as an activity of thinking or an act of judging and the corresponding attitudinal objects, a thought or a judgment, but also that between psychophysical actions such as a screaming or a drawing and their physical products, a scream or a drawing. However, Twardowski left the distinction between an action and its product at an intuitive level, appealing mainly to linguistically reflected intuitions among different nominalizations (gerunds like *thinking, judging*, and *screaming* as standing for actions and various other sorts of nominalizations such as *thought, judgment*, and *scream* as standing for products). Moreover, he left it unclear what role products play in the semantics of attitude reports.

A central aim of this paper is to show that the distinction between actions and products is a philosophically important one, and hardly just a reflection of two sorts of nominalizations. The action–product distinction arguably is the general distinction that obtains between certain types of actions and the abstract or physically realized *artifacts* that the actions create. There are a range of characteristics that distinguish actions and products, and not only actions and products as they would be described by the two sorts of nominalizations. These are the very same sorts of characteristics that distinguish, for example, acts of artistic creation and the resulting objects of art as well as acts of establishing a law and the law itself.

Attitudinal objects as the products of attitudes lead to a view that radically differs from the standard relational view of propositional attitudes. On the standard view, propositional attitudes are relations to propositions. On the present view, attitudes are not relations to a propositional content, but rather are nonrelational (even if perhaps directed toward objects in the world). Propositional attitudes consist in mental acts or states which have products, and it is those products that act as truth bearers, make up shared contents, and play a role in inferences involving quantifiers like *something*. *That*-clauses do not take products as their semantic values, but rather serve to partially characterize products, in one way or another.

The notion of a proposition was to an extent motivated by linguistic intuitions, in particular the linguistic view that attitude reports are relational, *that*-clauses singular terms, and quantifiers like *something* quantifiers ranging only over propositions. The present view is that these intuitions were misguided. What should play the role of propositions instead are attitudinal objects or kinds of them.

1. The motivations for propositions

1.1 The semantic motivations for propositions

A central motivation for positing propositions comes from the apparent semantic structure of natural language sentences, namely simple attitude reports such as (1a):

(1) a. John believes that Mary is happy.

Such attitude reports appear to involve *that*-clauses in referential position, providing an argument for the attitude verb. This is reflected in the most common, *Relational Analysis* of such sentences. According to the Relational Analysis, *that*-clause complements of attitude verbs take a proposition as semantic value and the attitude verb expresses a dyadic relation between agents and propositions, as below:

(1) b. believe(John, [*that Mary is happy*])

Propositions are also generally considered the entities that quantifiers range over and pronouns stand for that occur in the place of a *that*-clause. In English, a restricted class of quantifiers and pronouns can occur in that position, which includes *something, everything*, and *nothing*, the pronoun *that*, and also relative clauses with *what* as in *what Mary believes*. I call these 'special quantifiers'. Propositions as semantic values of such quantifiers or pronouns appear to be needed to account for the validity of the inferences in (2a, b) as well as sentences such (2c) (Schiffer 2003):

(2) a. John thinks that Mary is happy.
John thinks something.
b. Mary believes everything Bill believes.
Bill believes that it is raining.
Mary believes that it is raining.
c. John said that it is raining. What John said is true.

Propositions are taken to be both the meanings of independent sentences and the semantic values of embedded sentences, in particular *that*-clauses..

1.2 Conceptual problems for propositions

There are different conceptions of propositions, as entities that fulfill the above-mentioned roles. The two most prominent conceptions are as sets of circumstances (possible worlds or situations) and as structured propositions, that is, as sequences (or other formal structures), consisting of properties or concepts and objects (and perhaps modes of presentation), or semantic values construed otherwise.[1] The first conception is associated with notorious problems in that it identifies propositions that are necessarily true or necessarily false. The second conception, which is now far more common among philosophers of language, avoids such problems by reflecting (to an extent) in the meaning of the sentence itself the syntactic structure of the sentence as well as the way the truth value of the sentence is compositionally obtained.

A range of problems have been pointed out for both conceptions in the philosophical literature, in particular by Jubien (2003) and more recently Soames (2010). Let me only briefly mention those problems without going into an in-depth discussion. The first problem is the *problem of arbitrary identification* (see also Moore 1999). This problem, familiar from Benacerraf's (1965) discussion of the identification of natural numbers with sets, is that the choice of a formal object to be identified with a proposition is, to an extent, arbitrary. The problem arises for the first as for the second conception of propositions. Given the first conception, nothing in the general conditions propositions that need to fulfill could decide between identifying propositions as sets of circumstances or as functions from circumstances to truth values. Given the second conception, the problem is that, for example, a proposition such as the proposition that John is happy could be represented either as < H, John > or as < John, H > the choice among which appears arbitrary: either pair could fulfill the relevant conditions.

Two further, related problems arise for structured propositions. One of them is the problems of the *truth-directedness* of propositions. That is, why should a mere sequence of entities be true or false? There is nothing inherent in a sequence that would qualify it as a truth bearer. But propositions were meant to be entities that have their truth conditions essentially. The second problem is known as the problem of *the unity of propositions*.[2] This problem arises specifically for the structured-propositions conception of propositions. It is not simply the problem of how an abstract object can have truth conditions at all, but how a proposition as a structured object can have the particular truth conditions it is meant to have, given its constituents and the way they compose the structured object. For example, why should a proposition as a mere sequence of properties and objects have the particular truth conditions that it is meant to have? Why should the relation between H (the property of being happy) and John in the sequence < H, John > be understood in such a way that this structured proposition comes out true in case John is happy? The relation could be understood in many other ways: it could be that the proposition is true just because H and John are different or because John is not H or because John likes H. In fact, it is not clear why the relation between H and John should be understood in any way at all, so as to allow assigning a truth value to the ordered pair.

The problem of the unity of propositions, like the problem of the truth-directedness of propositions, is a problem of the interpretation of a structured proposition. The problem of the unity of propositions specifically is the problem of how to interpret the relation among the propositional constituents in order to obtain the truth conditions of the proposition. It is a problem because a structured proposition simply does not have inherent truth conditions; rather the truth conditions of the structured proposition need to be externally imposed. Whatever external conditions one might impose, the choice of such conditions remains arbitrary.

2. Propositions and cognitive acts: recent approaches

The source of the problem of the truth-directedness of propositions appears that formal objects such as sequences of properties and objects simply cannot be truth-directed without intentionality, without an agent aiming at truth. More recently, a number of philosophers have therefore pursued an approach to the problem of the truth-directedness and the unity of propositions that consists in viewing predication itself as a cognitive act, a relation relating an agent to a property and its arguments (Jubien 2001; Moltmann 2003a, 2013; Hanks 2007; and Soames 2010). On this view, an agent predicating a property of objects is what makes up the 'glue' among the propositional constituents and ensures truth-directedness. An agent is successful predicating an n-place property of n objects just in case the property holds of the objects.

This approach is presented with different options when dealing with the different kinds of propositional attitudes:

[1] Different cognitive acts of predication are distinguished for as many different attitudes as there are – predication in the belief way, predication in the thinking way, predication in the claiming way, etc. On this view, the attitude verb can itself be taken to describe the relevant act of predication, as in Jubien (2001) and Moltmann (2003a, 2013).

[2] Only a single type of cognitive act of predication is posited which corresponds to the most general attitude of 'entertaining' or 'understanding'. With 'entertaining', an agent does not aim at truth, but simply considers the property holding of the objects in question. On this view, it would be natural to take a *that*-clause to stand for a type of act of cognitive predication and the attitude verb to express a dyadic relation between agents and types of acts of cognitive predication of the most general sort (Soames 2010, forthcoming).

[3] Different types of acts of predication of more general sorts are distinguished. Thus, Hanks (2009, 2011), who pursues this view, takes attitude verbs to express relations to different types of cognitive acts of predication depending on the type of embedded clause. Declarative, interrogative, and imperative (infinitival) clause types, on that view, differ in expressing types of acts of predicating in the assertive, interrogative, and imperative way respectively.

There are of course criteria that may weigh in favor of one or the other option, such as tests whether a *that*-clause can be substituted by a term explicitly referring to a cognitive act of one sort of another. The focus in what follows, however, will be on general problems with identifying propositions with cognitive acts.

3. The distinction between actions and products

3.1 Twardowski's distinction between actions and products

There is a serious problem for the act-based approach in general and that is that actions or action types are simply not suited to play the role of propositions, namely as truth bearers and the shared contents of attitudes of different agents. An act or act type simply does not have the right properties, in particular the right representational properties, to play the roles of propositions. However, there is a different sort of mind-dependent entity that can play that role. These are not acts of claiming or states of believing, but rather entities of the sort of 'claims' or 'beliefs'. These are entities that I call 'attitudinal objects'. Claims and beliefs are by nature entities that are true or false; acts of claiming or states of believing are not. Claims and beliefs are not propositions, though. They are cognitive entities, dependent on an agent. They are the products of cognitive acts, not the acts themselves. The notion of a product of an act will go along with a very different logical form of attitude reports than that of the Relational Analysis.

The distinction between acts and states and the corresponding attitudinal objects is part of a more general distinction between 'actions' and 'products' made by Twardowski (1912) in an important article, largely neglected, though, in contemporary analytic philosophy.[3] The distinction between actions and products comprises not just the familiar distinction between an action and its enduring physical product, such as an act of writing and the writing (the written work), an act of drawing and the drawing, and act of folding and the fold. It also comprises a less familiar distinction between a mental action or state and its nonenduring mental product, such as a state of believing and a belief, and an act of claiming and a claim, an act of thinking and a thought, an act of judging and a judgment, a state of desiring and a desire, an act of deciding and a decision, and an act of instructing and an instruction. There are, according to Twardowski, psychological actions and products (an activity of thinking and a thought), physical actions and products (an act of folding and a fold, an activity of walking and a walk, an act of jumping and a jump), as well as psychophysical actions and products (an act of claiming and a claim, an act of screaming and a scream).[4] Thoughts, desires, claims, and judgments are non-enduring products that exist only as long as there is the corresponding mental or illocutionary event. However, thoughts, desires, claims, and judgments can be 'reproduced' by performing actions with similar products.

The difference in truth conditions between actions like a claiming or believing and products like a claim or a belief extends to other representation-related properties than truth. A desire is not true or false, but it can be satisfied or not satisfied. This does not hold for a state of desiring, which intuitively is not something that can be satisfied or not. A command cannot be true, but it can be executed. The same can hardly be said about an act of giving a command, which can hardly be executed. An advice can be followed or not, but to follow someone's activity of advising is something quite different. A decision can be implemented or not, but an act of deciding hardly can.

The notion of a product helps approximate the notion of a propositional content. Crucially, what distinguishes products from actions is that products enter similarity relations strictly on the basis of a shared content. An enduring propositional content, one might say, emerges from the production of actions with exactly similar products.[5] Twardowski's distinction between actions and products remains rather suggestive, though. Twardowski appeals primarily to linguistic intuitions reflected in differences among nominalizations (gerunds like *thinking, judging, screaming* vs nominalizations like *thought, judgment, scream*). While Twardowski appeals to a range of predicates that distinguish between actions and products, he does not give a systematic characterization of the distinction in terms of the types of properties characteristic of actions and products.[6] He moreover says little about how the distinction is to be understood as such, not even whether it is to be understood as an ontological distinction or merely a distinction in the way one and the same object may be viewed. Twardowski's intuitive description of the distinction focuses on different aspects of entities. Thus, nouns describing products are nouns 'that do not bring to force the aspect of action, but bring to force a different aspect, the "phenomenal" or "static" aspect' (Twardowski 1912, §2). Similarly, in the particular case of a shout, as opposed to a shouting, Twardowski says 'in speaking of the shout, we do in fact abstract from the activity of shouting, treating the shout as an acoustic phenomenon' (Twardowski 1912, §3).[7] I myself will consider the distinction an ontological distinction.

There is a potential source of misunderstanding in the way Twardowski draws the distinction between actions and products, and that is his focus on the linguistic properties of two sorts of nominalizations in particular languages. Twardowski makes use of linguistic examples from Polish (in the first version of the paper), from German (in the second version), and from French (in an incomplete third version).[8] The English translation reflects the distinction equally well: terms for actions are translated by gerunds, *thinking, judging, deciding, scream*; terms for products by various sorts of nominalizations such as *thought, judgment, decision, scream*. It is clear, however, that Twardowski took the distinction to be a fundamental philosophical one, not just one reflecting the semantics of particular nouns found in languages such as Polish, German, and French. In fact, Twardowski (1912, §45) took products to make up the general subject matter of the humanities, thus logic, aesthetics, linguistics, law, etc.

The distinction between actions and products is in fact more compelling in cases not directly tied to two sorts of nominalizations. Indeed it appears to be the very same distinction that holds between an artifact and the act of creating it, including that between an abstract artifact in the sense of Thomasson (1999) and the act of its creation. Artifacts, whether or not they have a physical realization, carry representational and normative properties, but not so for the acts of creating them.

The action–product distinction is also the one that holds between a law (a product which may lack a physical realization, thus an abstract artifact) and the act of declaring or passing it by the relevant legislative body. The law should be followed and can be broken, the act of declaring it hardly can. It is the law that is the carrier of normative, behavior-guiding properties, not the act of establishing it.

The action–product distinction is the same as the one that holds between an object of art and the act of creating it. For some types of objects of art, a material realization is in fact inessential (poems, musical compositions).[9] The object of art may carry representational properties; the act of creation certainly does not. The object of art is the target of aesthetic evaluation, not the act of creating it. This even holds for an artistic performance and the act of performing. Evaluative properties when applied to a performance express an artistic evaluation; but when applied to an act of performing they may just as well evaluate circumstances of the act that are irrelevant to the artistic value of the performance, the product of the act, for example the amount of physical effort that the act of performing demands. For a performance to be terrible or interesting means that it is so as an artistic production; but for an action of performing to be terrible or interesting, it may be so because of the circumstances or because of features of the action irrelevant to the artistic production. The difference is obvious also with the distinction between a poem or musical composition and the act of creating it. A poem or musical composition may have a range of aesthetic properties which the act of creating hardly need share. The act has as its aim the poem or composition which may be the bearer of beauty, the act as such isn't. The act may aim at beauty, but it is the product of the act that will be the bearer of beauty, not the act itself.

Products can take various relations to their physical realization. Some products, for example, thoughts, judgments, or desires, are entirely independent of a physical realization. Others, poems and musical compositions, may or may not come with a physical realization. Yet other products may have multiple realizations, for examples bronze statues and books. Such products raise notorious difficulties of individuation and counting since it seems possible to talk about a statue as a material objects and as an object of art at once, and so for a book as a concrete copy and as an information object.

An object of art – like a particular thought, claim, or belief and like any artifact – is mind-dependent. It depends for its identity on an agent and his or her intentions. Whatever its material realization may be, it does not belong entirely to the material world but is partly constituted by the intentionality of the agent, as emphasized by Ingarden (1931).

The distinction between actions and products raises the question of what takes priority, the action or the product. Clearly, the product depends for its existence on the act, and not vice versa. However, there is also a dependence of the act on the product: the identity of intentional acts arguably depends on the intended product. While the intentional act may be performed by performing physical acts, the identity of the intentional act clearly depends on what is intended, the product. The act in fact may also inherit certain properties from the product. Thus, *John painted beautifully* means that John produces beautiful paintings, not that the activity of painting as such is beautiful. *John writes well* implies that the product, the written work, is good, not the act of writing as such. The act may depend for its identity on the product; the product certainly depends for its existence on the act.

3.2 *Properties distinguishing actions and products*

Having established the importance of the action–product distinction as such, we can turn to the types of properties that distinguish actions and products. The focus will be on the action–product distinction in general, by looking at the properties of various types of action–product pairs.

As already said, the action–product distinction is very clear in a range of cases, such as works of art and laws; it is less obvious with attitudinal objects that are mental products or have only an auditory physical realization. Because of the focus in contemporary analytic philosophy on the ontology of material objects, (mental or physical) events, and abstract objects, appeal to ontological intuitions as such may not go very far when trying to identify the properties that distinguish attitudinal objects and the corresponding actions. For that reason, it is helpful to also look more closely at the linguistic terms for products and the readings particular predicates display with them. The action–product distinction, even if not part of standard ontology, is certainly part of the ontology of natural language, the ontology a speaker accepts when using natural language.

As mentioned earlier, in the English translation of Twardowski's article, terms for actions generally are gerunds such as *claiming, believing, thinking, desiring, deciding*, whereas terms for products are generally formed with nominalizations such as *claim, belief, thought, desire, decision*. But, action terms can also be formed with the sortals *act* or *state*, and those terms behave just like simple gerunds with respect to the relevant predicates.

3.2.1 Truth and satisfaction conditions

One important difference between actions and products is that only products have truth conditions or more generally satisfaction conditions. Beliefs, claims, and judgments have truth conditions, but not so for states of believing and acts of claiming or judging. Desires, hopes, and fears may or may not be fulfilled, but not so for states of desiring, hoping, or fearing. The contrasts below illustrate the acceptability and unacceptability (question-marked) of the corresponding truth-related or satisfaction-related predicates:[10]

(4) a. John's belief / claim that that S is true / false.
 b. ?? John's claiming / believing that S is true / false.
 c. ?? John's belief state is true.
 d. ?? John's speech act (of claiming) is true.
(5) a. John's desire to become a king was fulfilled.
 b. John's request to be promoted was fulfilled.
 c. ?? John's desiring / requesting / hoping was fulfilled.
 d. ?? John's state of desiring was fulfilled.
(6) a. John's decision to postpone the meeting was implemented.
 b. John's command that people leave the building was executed.
 c. ?? John's action of deciding was implemented / executed.
 d. ?? John's act of commanding was fulfilled.

It is a common view that belief (as a state) 'aims at truth', just like acts of artistic creation may aim at beauty. However, it is in fact not the act, but the product that is the carrier of truth or beauty. Thus, if 'aiming at' is the relation between an object and the norm or value that it is meant to fulfill, then the more direct aim of a belief state or artistic act is the product, not truth or beauty as such.

Certain types of attitudinal objects carry a normative force in virtue of which they can act as carriers of properties of action-guidance. Thus, an advice, an instruction, or a command can be followed or ignored. Such properties can be considered special cases of satisfaction conditions. The minimal pairs below illustrate the way predicates of action guidance are understood differently with products and with actions:

(7) a. John followed Mary's advice.
    b. John followed Mary's activity of advising.
    c. John complied with the instruction.
    d. John complied with the act of instructing.
(8) a. John ignored the command.
    b. John ignored the act of commanding.

To follow a normative product means to comply with its norm, but to follow the action that created it either means to observe it or to perform an action of the same type. To ignore a normative product means not to comply with its norm, but to ignore an action means not to take notice of it.

Of course, also laws and norms themselves have properties of action-guidance, which the acts of establishing them do not have.

3.2.2 *Correctness conditions*

The truth conditions of certain types of products may be constitutive of the norms that the products themselves are meant to fulfill, that is, they may define their *correctness conditions*. Thus, a belief is correct just in case it is true. For a person's belief to be correct, it need not fulfill conditions of justification or follow any rules or instructions. Predicating correctness of a belief simply means saying that it is true. At least this is how our common-sense notions of correctness and of belief apply (though perhaps not how the way some philosophers may conceive of correctness and of belief). What is important is that the corresponding actions do not share the same correctness conditions, just as they did not share the truth conditions that define the products' correctness. Thus, the correctness of a belief state does not reduce to the truth of what is believed, but rather, if anything, it may be understood as consisting in the fulfillment of other norms, such as instructions to have a particular belief. Truth is not the norm of states of believing, but only of their products, that is, of beliefs.

The same holds for assertions, the products of acts of asserting. An assertion is correct just in case it is true. It need not have followed any other social or justificatory norms. (The way we intuitively understand the correctness of assertions, reflected in the way *correct* applies to products, thus is in conflict with views that take the norm of an assertion to be knowledge, such as Williamson

2000). By contrast, for an act of asserting to be correct, it needs to fulfill whatever the relevant norms are, norms that may vary from context to context. The norm associated with an assertion is always the same: it is truth. By contrast, the norm associated with an act of asserting is entirely context-dependent. In the case of assertions, the discrepancy is particularly striking that holds between the norm associated with the product, which is stable, and the norm associated with the action, which depends entirely on the context.

There are other attitudinal objects besides beliefs and assertions that display the same conditions on correctness. The correctness of a suspicion consists in nothing but the truth of what is suspected. By contrast, an act of suspecting is correct in case it fulfills whatever the contextually relevant norm. An answer is correct just in case it is true (of course, for something to be answer, it needs to address the question in the first place). More generally, attitudinal objects that purport to represent the world have as their condition of correctness just truth, but not so for the acts that produce them, which will have to conform to whatever the relevant contextually given norms are.

The linguistic examples below illustrate this in the understanding of *correct* when applied to terms for products and for actions: with the former *correct* conveys truth; but with the latter it conveys, if anything, conformity with whatever the contextually relevant norms:

(9) a. Mary's belief that S is correct.
  b. (?) Mary's state of believing that S is correct.
(11) a. John's claim that S was correct.
  b. (?) John's act of claiming that S was correct.
(12) a. John's answer was correct.
  b. (?) John's answering was correct.

Correctness conditions for actions are fundamentally different from correctness conditions for content-bearing objects, the products of the actions.[11]

Note that correctness conditions apply in similar ways to other representations than attitudinal objects, for example certain visual representations, that carry representational adequacy conditions rather than truth conditions.

The correctness conditions of truth-directed attitudinal objects may shed light on the connection between truth and the normativity of mental content, in particular of beliefs. Standard accounts relating truth to the normativity of belief try to establish a link between the truth of what is believed to what should be believed, imposing a truth-related norm on belief states (Gibbard 2003; Boghossian 2003). But this gives rise to difficulties. There may be norms for believing in particular contexts that have little to do with truth. Moreover, such an account cannot be generalized, for example to assertions. A speaker may knowingly assert something false as a way of fulfilling a contextual norm (Boghossian 2003). But the correctness of an assertion (a product) requires nothing more than its truth, just like the correctness of a belief. Restricting the normativity of content to products rather than relating it to states and acts promises a way of avoiding the difficulties. Given that a belief is correct just in case it is true, this means that the belief, the product, ought to be true. This does not prevent an agent to fulfill whatever norms by engaging or not engaging in a belief state sustaining the belief. Similarly, an assertion is correct just in case it is true, which means that the assertion, the product, ought to be true. This does not mean that an agent could fulfill some norm by engaging in an act of asserting the opposite. Norms associated with products are independent of the norms that may be associated with actions. Products that purport to represent the world are uniformly associated with one norm, that of truth; but not so for the corresponding actions whose norms may vary and in fact may vary from context to context.

3.2.3 Similarity relations and the involvement of force

Another important difference between actions and their products concerns similarity relations. The way similarity relations apply to products is in fact central to the notion of a product. For two products of the same sort (beliefs, claims, etc.) to be exactly similar means for them to be the same in content.[12] By contrast, for two actions to be exactly similar, they need to fulfill conditions such as having been performed in the very same way. John's thought is the same as (that is, is exactly similar to) Mary's thought just in case the content of John's thought is identical to the content of Mary's thought. By contrast, for John's activity of thinking to be the same as Mary's, this condition is not generally sufficient (and perhaps not even necessary), rather more conditions need to be fulfilled, such as the way John thought being very similar to the way Mary thought. For actions, the manner in which they are performed is essential, but for products the manner in which they are produced is not. Thus, even if John's quick thinking may not be the same as Mary's slow thinking, their resulting thoughts may be the very same. Similarly, John's quick deciding and Mary's hesitant deciding could not possibly be the same, but John's decision may easily be the very same as Mary's. As these descriptions make clear, relations of exact similarity are reflected in the applicability of *is the same as* in English, which expresses qualitative, not numerical identity.[13]

Attitudinal objects come with a particular force unlike propositions. Thus, attitudinal objects can be exactly similar only if they share the same force. This is reflected in the intuition that identity statements such as the following can hardly be true (Moltmann 2003a, 2013):

(13) a. ??? John's thought that it will rain is also his remark that it will rain.
b. ??? John's discovery that it will rain is his hope that it will rain.
c. ??? John's desire to leave is his decision to leave.
d. ??? John's claim that it will rain is his hope that it will rain.

The examples in (13a–d) differ from the one below, which is trivially true:

(14) John's thought that it will rain is John's thought that it will rain.

The involvement of force in an attitudinal object is also responsible for why attitudinal objects differ in what sort of satisfaction or correctness conditions they are associated with. Attitudinal objects not involving a particular force do not naturally have truth or satisfaction conditions. Thoughts in fact are not really entities that intuitively are true or false (which is reflected linguistically in that *John's thought that he can win the race is true* is not generally judged acceptable by ordinary speakers). By contrast, judgments, claims, and beliefs are (thus *John's belief that he can win the race is true* is unproblematic). The involvement of force, we will see, is also reflected in the way attitudinal objects, as opposed to propositions, are evaluated.

The fact that attitudinal objects sharing the same force are similar just in case they are the same in content is crucial for the status of attitudinal objects as the basis for approximating a notion of propositional content. Sharing of a propositional content in fact amounts to exact or close similarity of attitudinal objects with the same force. The understanding of an attitudinal object involves the physical manifestation of the attitudinal object causing the production of a similar attitudinal object (or its simulation).[14]

3.2.4 *Properties of understanding and content-based causation and evaluation*

Actions and products differ in properties relating to the understanding of their associated content. An utterance may be incomprehensible, but not the act of uttering; an act of uttering being incomprehensible means something quite different. Similarly, understanding an answer means something quite different from understanding the act of answering. Only the former relates to the content of the answer, not the latter.

Attitudinal objects may have causal effects, in particular if they are psychophysical products and thus can be perceived. An utterance, a remark, or a scream can be heard. Also here, there is an important difference between actions and products. Unlike in the case of actions, it is the content of the attitudinal object together with its force that has the causal effect. There difference between actions and products again is particularly clear when comparing the way predicates are understood when applying to terms for actions and for products:

(15) a. John's speaking delighted Mary.
   b. John's speech delighted Mary.
(16) a. John's answer caused surprise.
   b. John's giving an answer caused surprise.
(17) a. John's utterance inspired many comments.
   b. John's act of uttering inspired many comments.

Whereas (15a) may be true in a situation in which it is just the manifestation of John's ability to speak that delighted Mary (regardless of its content), (15b) conveys that it is also the content of John's speech (and just its manner) that was the cause of Mary's delight.

Similar examples can be given for laws as opposed to the acts of establishing them, for poems as opposed to the acts of writing them, etc.

Abstract propositions should not have causal effects, given a common understanding of abstract objects. In fact, 'the proposition that S' can hardly cause surprise or inspire comments. A propositional content as a pure proposition cannot be causally efficacious, but only in connection with an attitudinal or illocutionary force and an agent, that is, as part of an attitudinal object.

Related to properties of understanding and content-based causation are properties of content-based evaluation. Attitudinal objects are evaluated with respect to both their content and force, but not so for actions. A thought being interesting is something quite different from the act of thinking being interesting. It is also something different from an abstract proposition being interesting. Similarly, John's thought process may be unusual, without his thought or the corresponding abstract proposition being unusual.

The same sort of distinction is very clear also in the ontology of art. Objects of art are the carriers of the relevant aesthetic or content-related properties, not the acts of their creation.

3.2.5 Part-whole Structure

Another important difference between actions and products concerns part-whole relations. The part structure of attitudinal objects strictly relates to content. A part of a thought, a belief, or a decision is a partial content. By contrast, the part structure of actions is that of events, consisting of temporal parts. Parts of products generally are distinct from parts of actions. Part of John's decision cannot be part of the action of deciding. Part of John's claim cannot be part of the speech act. Part of John's answer cannot be part of John's answering. Clearly, also the parts of a book as an information object are distinct from the parts of the physical copy. The book as a materially realized artifact has in fact two part structures at once, leading to an apparent ambiguity in the notion of part. 'Describing a part of the book' may mean either a part of the information object or a part of the physical object. (There are other artifacts, though, whose parts are the materially realized functional parts. In this case, the part structure is still driven by intention and not just the material itself.)

3.2.6 Relation to time

Actions and products also differ in their relation to time. Philosophical views about events and actions generally take them to have their time of occurrence essentially (most obviously when events are identified with space-time regions or property instantiations in times). But there is a strong intuition that the time of creation is not essential for (non-enduring) products. Actions and products may be spatio-temporally coincident, for example a thought and the act of thinking, a scream and the act of screaming, and a decision and the act of deciding. However, a thought or a scream might naturally have occurred earlier than it did, and a decision could have been made later than it was. It is at least much less natural to say that about a process of thinking, a particular act of screaming, or an act of deciding.[15]

3.3 Kinds of attitudinal objects

The main Fregean argument for propositions being mind-independent was the possibility of propositional contents being shared by different agents. If attitudinal objects take the place of propositions as the truth-bearing objects associated with propositional attitudes, this raises the question of how propositional contents can be shared. The notion of an attitudinal object allows for two answers. First, the sharing of attitudinal objects may consist in the attitudinal objects being exactly similar (though not numerically identical). Second, the sharing of propositional contents may consist in *kinds* of attitudinal objects being shared. Natural language displays not only the first, but also the second option.

Kinds of attitudinal objects naturally form the referents of terms like *the thought that* S, *the claim that* S, or *the belief that* S, allowing for typical kind predicates:[16]

(18) a. The belief that god exists is widespread.
   b. John often encounters the expectation that he should become famous.

The sentence below obviously describes the sharing of a kind of attitudinal object:

(19) John and Mary share the belief that S

Kinds of attitudinal objects are independent of a particular agent, though they still involve a particular attitudinal mode. Kinds of attitudinal objects share representational properties with their instances, again reflected in the applicability of truth- or satisfaction-related predicates:

(20) a. The belief that John won the race is true.
   b. The expectation that John would become famous was not fulfilled.

Kinds of attitudinal objects may seem as problematic as abstract propositions with respect to their cognitive accessibility and representational properties. However, the notion of a kind that is at stake does not face the problems of abstract propositions. Kinds of attitudinal objects are strictly dependent on the particular attitudinal objects that make up their instances. First, kinds of attitudinal objects are strictly based on similarity relations among particular attitudinal objects. The kind of attitudinal object 'the belief that S' has as its instances a maximal class of exactly similar attitudinal objects. Moreover, except for properties measuring the distribution of instances such as 'being widespread', the properties of kinds of attitudinal objects are generally inherited from their instances. 'The belief that S' is true in virtue of all attitudinal objects of the form 'd's belief that S' being true, for some individual d. Furthermore, John has encountered 'the belief that S' just in case he has encountered d's belief that S, for some individual d. Of course, kinds will then inherit not only their representational properties from their instances, but also their cognitive accessibility.[17] Kinds also depend for their existence on instances: the hope that it would rain soon no longer existed at a time t just in case for no individual d, d's hope that it would rain soon existed at t.[18]

I will not go into a discussion of how kinds are to be conceived, whether as entities of their own or as mere pluralities of instances (or possible instances).[19] What is important in the present context is that the instances of a kind of attitudinal object are similar in the sense of sharing content and force and that kinds have content-related properties (including truth or satisfaction conditions) in virtue of their instances having those properties.[20]

4. The semantic role of attitudinal objects in the semantics of attitude reports

Attitudinal objects of the sort of particular beliefs or claims as the products of mental or illocutionary actions match the content of an attitude report as a whole and not just the *that*-clause. They act as the semantic values of nominalizations and not as the semantic values of *that*-clauses. This raises the question what role they play in attitude reports without nominalizations, that is, of the simple sort *John thinks that* S. Twardowski himself does not say anything about the role products play in the semantics of attitude reports. However, there is an obvious role of attitudinal objects to play within Davidsonian event semantics.[21] Given the Davidsonian view that verbs take events as implicit arguments, 'actions' would be the implicit arguments of verbs and attitudinal objects their products. Given that *that*-clauses won't denote propositions acting as arguments of the relation expressed by the verb, their semantic role would either be that of characterizing the event argument of the verb or else that of characterizing the product of the event argument. On the first view, referential NPs might be considered expressing referential act types that characterize referential acts that are part of the event, and the predicate an act of predication, predicating a property of the referents of the referential acts.[22] On the second view, the *that*-clauses would express product types characterizing parts of the event argument, in particular products of referential acts and products of cognitive predication. Clearly *that*-clauses characterize products and not actions: *that*-clauses can specify only content-related features of acts, and not features such as having been done honestly, hesitatingly, etc.

I will leave it open in which way exactly a *that*-clause compositionally specifies a property of products. It is actually quite plausible that the semantics of *that*-clauses exhibits a general flexibility, ranging perhaps from the characterization of 'small' acts composing the product (including referential acts and acts of modification) to acting as a mere measurement of the product, representing its truth conditions (Matthews 2007).[23] The latter would enable the account to apply to implicit attitudes and beliefs of animals and small children. In any case, the logical form of a simple attitude report as in (39a) would be as in (39b):

(39) a. John thought that S.
   b. ∃e(think(e, John) & [*that* S](product(e)))

Special quantifiers such as *something* range over attitudinal objects rather than propositions (Moltmann 2003b, 2013). Thus, sentences with special quantifiers such as (40b) would be analyzed as in (40a):

(40) a. John thought something nice.
   b. ∃e'(think(e, John) & nice(e') & e' = product(e))

Special quantifiers may alternatively range over kinds of products. This requires a function 'product-kind', mapping an event e onto the kind of products exactly similar to the product of e. Quantification over kinds of attitudinal objects is involved in the logical form of (41a) in (41b):

(41) a. John thought what Mary thought.
   b. ∃e e'e''(think(e, John) & e' = product-kind(e) & think(e'', Mary) & e' = product-kind(e''))

This account leaves open how exactly *that*-clauses characterize attitudinal objects and whether there is a unified way or rather different, context-dependent ways in which *that*-clauses do so. In particular, it is neutral regarding the role of predication in the constitution of attitudinal objects. All that is captured is that attitudinal objects play the role of carriers of propositional content, though not as objects of attitudes, but their product.

5. Conclusion

This paper tried to show the importance of the notion of an attitudinal object, within a more general distinction between actions and products. Attitudinal objects are entities that inherently have truth or satisfaction conditions and form natural similarity classes on the basis of a shared content and a shared attitudinal mode. Yet they are as concrete as the corresponding mental events or speech acts, the latter themselves entities unsuited for the roles that propositions were supposed to play.[24] Being cognitive entities with essential truth- or satisfaction conditions, attitudinal objects are able to fulfill the roles of propositions without leading to their conceptual problems. Attitudinal objects share relevant properties with artifacts; in fact they are generally abstract artifacts in the sense of Thomasson (1999). Recognizing attitudinal objects thus goes along with recognizing (abstract) artifacts as belonging to an ontological category of their own, as mind-dependent entities distinct from mental events and abstract objects. The semantic account proposed in this paper was neutral as to the ontological conception of attitudinal objects as abstract artifacts and the conception of their propositional structure. The account may thus share the recent view that a cognitive notion of predication notion drives the composition of attitudinal objects and provides the solution to the conceptual problems for propositions as abstract objects. However, it is not directly tied to that view, but would allow attitudinal objects as cognitive products to in principle be constituted differently.

Attitudinal objects are not the objects of attitudes, but their products. This is reflected in the semantics of attitude reports in that *that*-clauses serve to characterize the product of the implicit action argument of the verb, rather than taking it as their semantic value. Attitudinal objects instead are the semantic values of nominalizing expressions, such as *John's thought that* S, and kinds of attitudinal objects the semantic values of terms of the sort *the thought that* S. Both attitudinal objects and kinds of attitudinal objects form the domain of entities that special or 'nominalizing' quantifiers in sentential position range over.

Acknowledgements

For stimulating discussions on the research of this paper, I would like to thank in particular Paul Boghossian, Kit Fine, Claudia Maienborn, Wioletta Miskiewicz, David Rosenthal, David Velleman, and audiences at the University of Texas at Austin, the Graduate Center at CUNY, the IHPST, the University of Dusseldorf, and the University of Tuebingen. I would also like to thank the editors for comments on an earlier version of this paper.

Notes

1. See, for example, Cresswell (1985), Soames (1987), and King (2007) for structured propositions approaches.
2. See Gaskin (2008) for a recent discussion of the problem, also in its historical context.
3. For a presentation of Twardowski's view in its historical context, see Bobryk (2009), Betti (2010), and Dubucs/Miskiewicz (2010).
4. The category of actions, for Twardowski, includes states, such as belief states. Of course, there are fundamental differences between actions in a narrow sense and states, and the action-product distinction may not apply in the very same way to them. This is an issue, though, that goes beyond the scope of this paper and needs to be pursued on another occasion.
5. A 'shared content' here means a common feature of attitudinal objects, not an entity that attitudinal objects stand in a relation to. Of course, like an enduring propositional content, a shared propositional content might also be viewed as an entity that emerges from the production of attitudinal objects by different agents.
6. More specifically, Twardowski (1912, §22) mentions *define* as a predicate applying to concepts but not the activity of conceiving, *unintelligible* as applying to questions but not the act of posing of a question, *unsolvable* as applying to problems but not to the act of posing a problem, *overlook* as applying to errors but not acts of erring, *unfulfilled* as applying to expectations but not the action of expecting, *implement* as applying to resolutions but not acts of resolving to do something, and *inspiring* as applying to thoughts but to the activity of thinking.
7. The distinction between actions and products that Twardowski draws obviously does not match the distinction that is common in linguistics between event and result nominalizations; result nominalizations are taken to refer to the physical product of an event.

8. The German version 'Funktionen und Gebilde' and the French version 'Actions et Produits' are available on http://www.elv-akt.net/
9. See Thomasson (2004) for discussion.
10. Aune (1967) notes that in English *truly* can act as an adverbial, predicating truth of the described action:

   (i) a. John truly believes that he won the lottery.
       b. John truly asserted that Mary is French.

   Given Davidsonian event semantics, the described action acts as an implicit argument of the attitude verb and the adverbial as a predicate predicated of it. *Truly* thus appears to on a par with *firmly* and *quickly* in (iia) and (iib), which clearly act as predicates of actions:

   (ii) a. John firmly believes that S.
        b. John quickly asserted that S.

   This appears a problem to the generalization that actions do not have truth conditions, but only their products. However, a quick look at other languages indicates that English *truly* is exceptional in conveying truth when applied to actions. German and French do not have adverbial counterparts of *wahr* or *vrai* that act that way. The adverbial counterparts *wahrlich* and *vraiment* mean 'really' rather than 'truly', as in the German and French translations of (ib) below:

   (iii) a. Hans hat wahrlich behauptet, dass Maria Franzoesin ist.
         b. Jean a vraiment dit que Marie est Française.

   Note also that *true* is not felicitous as a noun modifier applying to actions (?? *John's true state of believing*, ??? *that true act of claiming that* S), just as *true* cannot apply to actions in predicate position (4c, d). This means that *truly* as an adverbial has a derivative meaning, sharing its meaning with *accurately*. *Accurate* is the adjective that specifically conveys adequacy of the representational content associated with an action (as well as a product).

11. In English, the adverb *correctly* appears to act as a predicate of belief states and acts of assertion, conveying the truth of what is believed or asserted (and it figures in that way in the literature on the normativity of belief):

   (i) a. John correctly believes that S.
       b. John correctly claims that S.

   However, as for *truly* (Fn 10), there is evidence that the meaning of *correctly* conveying truth is derivative and not an indication of a link between the correctness of a belief state with truth. In other words, *correctly* does not express the same property as the adjective *correct*, as in the examples (9)–(12). For example, in German the adverb *richtig* 'correctly' can only mean something like 'effectively', as in (iia), unlike its adjectival correlate, which like the adjective *correct* in English conveys truth when applied to beliefs as in (iib) and some other form of correctness, if anything, when applied to belief states as in (iic):

   (ii) a. Hans glaubt richtig, dass die Welt enden wird.
           'John effectively believes that the world will end soon'.
        b. Hans' Glaube ist richtig.
           'John's belief is correct.'
        c. (?) Hans' Glaubenszustand ist richtig.
           'John's belief state is correct'.

12. Note that this does not mean that the products stand in a relation to the same object, a propositional content. Propositional content is to be considered a feature of products, not an object products relate to.
13. By contrast, the *is* of identity, which *does* express numerical identity, seems false of distinct attitudinal objects, at least under normal circumstances (let's say in which John's and Mary's thoughts were not coordinated):

    (i) ?? John's thought *is* Mary's thought.

    Note that the predicate *is identical to* is better in that context:

    (ii) John's thought is identical to Mary's thought.

    This indicates that *is identical to* expresses qualitative identity like *is the same as*, not numerical identity.
14. See also Twardowski (1912, §33, §34).
15. The attribution of counterfactual temporal properties appears possible with certain kinds of events. Wars could have taken longer than they did, demonstrations could have taken place at different times than they did, and a death might have occurred earlier than it did. Note, however, that all these cases may involve events as 'products', not as 'actions'. Certainly, *demonstration* and *death* are product nominalizations, contrasting with *demonstrating* and *dying*.
16. Terms for kinds of attitudinal objects are semantically on a par with bare mass nouns and plurals such *gold* or *tigers* when acting as kind terms (Moltmann 2003b, 2013, 4).
17. A kind of attitudinal object can be attributed to a particular agent, as below, in which case the agent is required to be the subject of a particular instance of the kind:

    (i) John had the thought that S.

    The construction *John's thought that* S may also involve reference to a kind rather than a particular attitudinal object, specifying that John 'has' the kind in the sense of (i). This needs to be assumed to make sense of sentences like (ii):

    (ii) John's thought that S had also occurred to Mary.

18. Uninstantiated kind, one might think, would provide a way of accounting for the apparent possibility of content-bearing entities that have never been entertained and will never be entertained, let's say in sentences like *there are things no one will never know*. However, kinds as referents of kind terms like *the belief that* S should better not be allowed to be uninstantiated. That is because of the way *exist* is understood with kind terms: *the belief that S exists* is true just in case there is an instance of the belief that S. Also, compare the choice of conditional and indicative mood below:

    (i) a. John might claim that he has won the race. But that would not be true.
    b. John might claim that he has won the race. ?? But that is not true.

    There is a preference of conditional over indicative mood in the second sentence, which indicates that *that* could not just stand for the kind 'the thought that John has won the race' as an uninstantiated kind.
19. For the view that kinds in that sense are not single entities, but pluralities (as many), see Moltmann (2013).
20. Note that *the entertaining that* S is an action nominalization and thus not as suited for capturing the most general kind of attitudinal product on a nontechnical use. *The thought that* S is a product nominalization, though 'thinking' is often considered a positive attitude of acceptance, not the most general attitude that is neither positive nor negative.

21. An alternative account is the neo-Russellian trope-based account, which I pursued in Moltmann (2013, 4). It relies on the neo-Russellian analysis of attitude reports according to which attitude verbs are multigrade predicates taking as arguments the agent as well as the propositional constituents given by the *that*-clause (see also, Moltmann 2013b). On the account of Moltmann (2013, 4), attitudinal objects are tropes, more precisely, instantiations in an agent of a multigrade attitudinal relation applied to the propositional constituents.
22. *That*-clauses would thus express complex event types as roughly in Hanks (2011). But on the present view, *that*-clauses would be predicated of the event argument, rather than providing an argument of a two-place attitudinal relation.
23. For a similar view about structured propositions, according to which *that*-clauses may specify propositions of different degrees of fine-grainedness see Cresswell (1985).
24. Note that in addition, products may have a material manifestation such as a drawing, something which events cannot have.

References

Aune, B. 1967. "Statements and Propositions." *Nous* 1: 215–229.
Betti, A. 2010. "Kazimierz Twardowski." In *Stanford Encyclopedia of Philosophy*. Online.
Benacerraf, P. 1965. "What Numbers could not be." *Philosophical Review* 74: 47–73.
Bobryk, J. 2009. "The Genesis and History of Twardowski's Theory of Actions and Products." In *The Golden Age of Polish Philosophy. Kazimierz Twardowski's Philosophical Legacy*, edited by S. Lapointe, et al., 33–42. Berlin: Springer.
Boghossian, P. 2003. "The Normativity of Content." *Philosophical Issues* 13: 31–45.
Dubucs, J., and W. Miskiewics. 2009. "Logic, Act and Product." In *Knowledge and Judgment*, edited by G. Primiero, 85–108. Berlin: Springer.
Frege, G. 1918/9. "Thoughts." In *Collected Papers on Mathematics, Logic, and Philosophy*, edited by B. McGuiness, 351–372. Oxford: Blackwell.
Gaskin, R. 2008. *The Unity of Propositions*. Oxford: Oxford UP.
Gibbard, A. 2005. "Truth and Correct Belief." *Philosophical Issues* 15: 338–350.
Hanks, P. W. 2007. "The Content-Force Distinction." *Philosophical Studies* 134: 141–164.
Hanks, P. W. 2011. "Propositions as Types." *Mind* 120: 11–52.
Ingarden, R. 1931. *Das Literarische Kunstwerk. Niemeyer, Halle* [The Literary Work of Art]. Translated by George G. Grabowicz. Evanston, IL: Northwestern University Press.
Jubien, M. 2001. "Propositions and the Objects of Thought." *Philosophical Studies* 104: 47–62.
King, J. 2007. *The Nature and Structure of Content*. Oxford: Oxford UP.
Matthews, R. 2007. *The Measure of Mind. Propositional Attitudes and their Attribution*. Oxford: Oxford UP.
Moltmann, F. 2003a. "Nominalizing Quantifiers." *Journal of Philosophical Logic* 35 (5): 445–481.

Moltmann, F. 2003b. "Propositional Attitudes without Propositions." *Synthese* 135: 70–118.
Moltmann, F. 2013. *Abstract Objects and the Semantics of Natural Language*. Oxford: Oxford UP.
Moore, J. G. 1999. "Propositions, Numbers, and the Problem of Arbitrary Identification." *Synthese* 120: 229–263.
Schiffer, S. 2003. *The Things we Mean*. Oxford: Clarendon Press.
Soames, S. 1987. "Direct Reference, Propositional Attitudes, and Semantic Content." *Philosophical Topics* 15: 47–87.
Soames, S. 2010. *What is Meaning?* Princeton: Princeton UP.
Soames, S. Forthcoming. *Hempel Lectures*.
Thomasson, A. 1999. *Fiction and Metaphysics*. Cambridge: Cambridge UP.
Thomasson, A. 2004. "The Ontology of Art." In *The Blackwell Guide to Aesthetics*, edited by P. Kivy, 78–92. Oxford: Blackwell.
Twardowski, K. 1912. "Actions and Products. Some Remarks on the Borderline of Psychology, Grammar, and Logic." In *Kazimierz Twardowski. On Actions, Products, and Other Topics in the Philosophy*, edited by J. Brandl and J. Wolenski, 1999, 103–132. Amsterdam and Atlanta: Rodopi.
Williamson, T. 2000. *Knowledge and its Limits*. Oxford: Oxford University Press.

THEORETICAL ALTERNATIVES TO PROPOSITIONS
What are Propositions?

Mark Richard

Philosophy Department, Emerson Hall, Harvard University, Cambridge, MA

This paper defends the view that propositions – that is, what are picked about by complement clauses and the range of quantifiers like that in 'Sanna believes all that Matti said' – are states of affairs. States of affairs – and thus propositions – are not, in the primary sense, representational; what is representational and what is true or false in the first instance are mental states and sentence tokens that represent propositions. There is, it is argued, a derivative sense in which propositions are bearers of truth, but truth in *that* sense is a derivative, non-explanatory notion. This view is contrasted with views like the one Scott Soames develops in *What is Meaning?*. It's argued that this view is superior to Soames' in various ways.

1.

When I think there is snow in the street, I represent the world as being a certain way, the way things would be were there snow in the street. It is natural to speak of what is represented as: snow's being in the street; the state of affairs of snow's being in the street; the possible fact or possibility that snow is in the street. What are these things – ways for things to be, states of affairs, possible facts?

Well, ways for things to be are just that – properties that a situation may or may not have. The way the world is when Tibbles is on the mat is the property of being a situation (be it a maximal one like the universe as a whole, or a more minimal one like the one that currently obtains in downtown Lille) which contains Tibbles and the mat and in which the first is related to the second by the relation *resting upon*.

In general, the properties that are states of affairs are ones of there being a sequence O of objects and a sequence P of properties and relations such that the O's instantiate the Ps in way I, I one or another pattern of objects having properties and relations.[1] Ignoring niceties (having to do with permutations of objects and properties within sequences and corresponding permutations of the instantiation relation), two such properties are identical iff they involve exactly the same sequences of objects and properties and pattern of instantiation.

The states of affairs I have in mind are considerably more finely individuated than ways that things might be when they are thought of as sets of possible worlds. The set of worlds in which Hesperus is Phosphorus is the set of worlds in which Twain is Clemens. But the property of being a situation in which <Venus, Venus> and identity are such that the terms in the sequence bear the relation to each other is not the property of being a situation in which <Twain, Twain> and identity are such that the terms in the sequence bear the relation to each other. So what is represented, when one represents that Hesperus is Phosphorus is not what is represented, when one represents that Clemens is Twain.[2] Since there are properties that are not possibly instantiated[3], we don't need to invoke metalinguistic beliefs – as some advocates of possible worlds semantics do – in order to explain how two representational states can represent different things when each represents something impossible. Note that there is no problem, on this way of understanding what a state of affairs is, with the idea that there are many states of affairs that don't obtain. There is such a thing as the way things would be were I six feet tall, even though (alas) I am not.

Suppose we are studying a well regimented language, so that what looks like a term is indeed a term, what looks like a predicate is indeed a predicate. Then it will be easy enough to get from a sentence of the language to the state of affairs that someone who utters the sentence represents as obtaining.[4] In general, a sentence is used to represent a state of affairs which is the property of being a situation such that in it the members of some sequence O of objects instantiate some sequence P of properties in some way I. What objects and properties are constituents of the state of affairs represented by S is determined by what objects and properties are the semantic values of the terms and predicative constituents of the sentence and what pattern of instantiation is systematically determined by S's syntax.

There are, of course, several ways one might spell out this idea, thereby giving a definition of *Sentence S is used (in language L) to represent state of affairs P*. A simple way would be to read the way of instantiating properties and relations associated with a sentence off it more or less directly, using lambda abstraction to form names of ways of instantiating. For example, the sentence

Fa & Gb

represents the referents of *a* and *b* as instantiating the properties expressed by *F* and *G* in this way:

$\lambda x \lambda y \lambda P \lambda Q. [Px \& Qy]$.

Here, the abstract names the way x, y, P, and Q are when x has P and y has Q. A sequence <X,Y> instantiates a sequence <p,q> in this way just in case $\lambda y \lambda x \lambda Q \lambda P [Px \& Qy] (p)(q)(X)(Y)$. The sentence as a whole represents the state of affairs of a situation's being one in which <a, b> instantiates <being F, being G> in way λyλxλQλP[Px & Qy].[5]

Suppose that the language we are studying contains sentential complements, verbs like 'believes', predicates like 'is true' and 'is necessary', and quantifiers like that of 'Mary denied everything I said'. Then we will eventually face the question, How are we to understand the propositional idioms? I say we already have what we need in hand. We should identify the proposition expressed by a sentence S – and thus the semantic value of the complement *that S* – with the state of affairs represented by a use of S. To believe that there is snow in the street is to represent the state of affairs that there is snow in the street, with the representation playing a certain role in one's cognitive economy. A proposition is true in a situation s provided s instantiates it – provided, that is, that it's a way situation s is. Such a proposition is true *simpliciter* provided that the world, the maximal way things are, instantiates it. For the proposition to be necessary is for every maximal possible situation to instantiate it.

Summarizing: Propositions – what are picked out by complement clauses such as 'that there is snow in the street' in 'I think that there is snow in the street' – are states of affairs. States of affairs are certain properties, ones picked out by terms of the form *the property of being a situation in which the objects o1,...,on instantiate the properties p1,..,pj in way I*. These properties are individuated in terms of the objects, properties, and mode of instantiation named in this last sort of expression.

This last suggestion may give pause. Individuating properties in the way just suggested is tantamount to saying that they have a constituent structure. Why should we think that properties have parts or constituents? I say in response: why shouldn't we think of properties in this way? Not only is there a relation of admiring, there is the property of admiring Carrie Brownstein. The property presumably depends on Brownstein (and the relation) for its existence. Such dependence is a mark of (though of course does not entail) mereological relations. Not only are there properties, being a male and being a sibling, there is a property of being a male sibling. It seems quite natural to think of this last property as being 'made up' of the first two, in so far as 'what it is' for an object to have the last property is for the object to have both of those properties. We thus recognize that some properties have other properties (and individuals) as parts. And things with parts are often individuated in terms of such. While I cannot deduce the existence of complex, structured properties from first principles, I don't see any bar to admitting them once we admit the existence of properties to begin with. And they certainly seem a useful addition to our ontology.

My proposal is a proposal about the objects of the propositional attitudes, and not a proposal about the nature of those relations or about their ascription. So I want to sidestep debates about these latter issues. But a comment about the attitudes themselves is in order.

To believe, doubt, imagine, or have some other propositional attitude towards a proposition involves representing it. We distinguish among such attitudes in terms of their typical cognitive roles (it is to this that we appeal to differentiate belief from desire) as well as other non-functional properties of the representation. For example, it is in terms of something like the reliability of the mechanism that generated it that we differentiate knowledge from mere belief.

You probably want to know what it is, for someone or something to represent a proposition *cum* state of affairs. I don't envision a one-size-fits-all account of what it is to represent a state of affairs. If something – you or I or a dog – believes that John threw a ball, it is in a cognitive state that represents John's throwing a ball. Myself, I think it's as close to analytic as it gets, that if one represents John's throwing a ball, one has a representation of John's throwing a ball. So if you or I or the dog believe that John threw a ball, we have a representation of the state of affairs, John's throwing a ball. This representation will typically be tied to behavior in a way that co-ordinates with desire to produce behavior that tends to satisfy the desire when the belief is true.[6] But the ways in which we represent the state of affairs may be very different. You and I are cognitively sophisticated, and we may represent the state of affairs *by* (more or less consciously) ascribing the property of throwing a ball to John. That is one way to represent the state of affairs. The dog is less sophisticated, cognitively. It may be in a perceptual state that is correlated with dispositions to respond in particular ways to throwing activity, a state that also has a component that is associated with something in the dog that is tracking John over time. That is, what represents the state of affairs of John's throwing the ball in the dog is a complex state involving various behavioral dispositions and perceptual states that relate the dog to the objects and properties that are constituents of the state of affairs represented.

Does the dog represent the state of affairs of John's throwing the ball *by* ascribing the property to John? Well, the *upshot* of the dog's being in the belief state is that it could be described as ascribing the property. But while you and I come to have the belief *by* classifying John, one worries that it gets things backwards to describe the dog as having the belief *by* making the classification. I will come back to this below.

2.

Propositions, if they are states of affairs, are what is represented. They are representational in the minimal sense that they are true or false: given that propositions are states of affairs, and states of affairs are the sort of properties I pointed to above, propositional truth is instantiation by the maximal situation, the situation that is all the objects there are instantiating the properties there are in the way that those objects in fact do.

Propositions are states of affairs; states of affairs are properties. Now properties do not, in and of themselves, represent anything. There is nothing about the property of being a situation in which snow is in the street *considered independently of our representational activity* that makes it represent snow's being in the street – or anything else, for that matter. One might think that this is a problem for the suggestion I've made. After all, if the proposition that snow is in the street is representational only in virtue of our cognitive activity, then it is only true or false in virtue of that activity. So the proposition isn't 'inherently' or 'essentially' representational. But then, one might ask, how can it have the sorts of properties that propositions have to have? Propositions, after all, must be plentiful, and have their truth conditions necessarily, and thus independently of us. So all of the following have to be true:

1. For any molecule m, there is a true proposition that m is a molecule.
2. For any molecule m, the proposition that m is a molecule is, of necessity, true iff m is a molecule.
3. Even if we hadn't existed, so long as m was a molecule, it would be true that m was a molecule.

It's hard to see how these things could be so unless propositions exist independently of us and themselves determine what they represent. There are lots of molecules no one will ever think about; let m be one of them. If the representational powers of states of affairs depend on our cognitive activity, how could the state of affairs of m being a molecule represent anything, given that no one has used it representationally or had any other cognitive contact with it? It can't. But if it doesn't represent anything, it's not true or false. So (1) and (2) must be rejected, if propositions are states of affairs. Likewise, if we hadn't existed, the state of affairs that m is a molecule would have had no representational powers at all. So, if propositions are states of affairs, then if we hadn't existed, the proposition that m is a molecule would not have represented anything, and so would not have been true. So (3) isn't true.

The argument that (1) is false if propositions are states of affairs depends on the claim that the only way something can come to be representational – given that it is not 'intrinsically representational' – is by someone's using it to represent something. But why would we want to say *that*? Consider sentences of English. There are – I repeat: *there are* – infinitely many sentences of English. Sentences of English, I take it, are types – they are something like properties of utterances and inscriptions. The sentences of English are determined by the linguistic activity of English speakers. But only finitely many sentences of English will ever be realized. Whatever makes all the unrealized sentences sentences is **not** their actually being used by someone. What makes them sentences is the fact that our behavior and mental states make a certain grammar the grammar of English. Behavior and psychology can invest an infinity of items with linguistic properties without going through them one by one.

Brain and behavior can implicitly invest an infinity of things with syntactic properties. Ditto for semantic properties. Take the sentences of natural language. We make assertions by using sentences to represent states of affairs; such assertions are true (false) as the represented state of affairs obtains (does not). The association of sentences and states of affairs represented is systematic. It is determined *prior* to the use of a sentence what state of affairs its (literal) use represents, and thus under what conditions its use is true or false. This is so even if the sentence was not previously used or entertained.

We consistently and projectibly use our language in a particular way; that use and its consistency and projectibility invests an infinity of sentences with representational properties. Our usage *also* confers an infinity of semantic properties on the states of affairs that are the (potential) *representans* of our sentences.

How so? Well, the primary bearers of truth – that is, the things that are true in the primary sense of 'true' – are representations of states of affairs, things like natural language sentence tokens and (certain) token mental states. Representations are true / false as what they represent obtains / does not obtain. For example, for any state of affairs p, a representation of p – say, a belief in p – is true just if p obtains. It is natural and perfectly harmless to give 'true' a secondary sense that encapsulates this relation. In this secondary sense, it is states of affairs that are true (or false), a state of affairs p being true (false) just in case a representation of this state of affairs – a belief in it, a sentence expressing it – would be true (false) in the primary sense. And this is what our linguistic practices have in fact done. When we speak of representational states, we use complement clauses – things of the form *that S* – to pick out the states of affairs represented, and apply 'true' to them in such a way that, on this (secondary) sense of 'true', something is, of necessity, true iff it obtains iff it is something, the representation of which would be true in the primary sense.[7] One might say that, *relative to our linguistic practices*, states of affairs are 'auto-representational' – that is, they have the watered down property expressed by 'true' in the secondary sense just isolated. And a state of affairs has this property, whether or not anyone has ever used it for representational purposes.

The upshot is this. There is, for any molecule m, such a thing as the state of affairs that m is a molecule. For any state of affairs s, s is (relative to our practices) autorepresentational, and thus is true (in the secondary sense) iff it obtains. So when I use STET, using 'true' in this way, what I say is non-problematically correct.

Suppose some uncognized molecule m to be assigned to 'x' in 'that x is a molecule'. Then relative to our linguistic practices, the clause represents the state of affairs that m is a molecule. Our practice is to represent this state of affairs by referring to it with such a clause; we ascribe it the property of propositional truth (i.e., obtaining) by saying that it is true. Since, relative to our practice, states of affairs autorepresent,

O. (It is true that x is a molecule) iff x is a molecule,

relative to the assignment, is true in any situation. So what (O) says is necessary. (2) is true.

What of (3)? The argument that it's false depends on the claim that if the representational powers of a proposition arise from our use of it to represent, it will lack representational powers if we aren't around to endow it with them. But why should we think this? When I use the sentence *It's true that two is a number*, my utterance correctly characterizes a circumstance w just in case the proposition that I actually express with the sentence (that two is a number) is true at w. The proposition that two is a number is true at w just in case the state of affairs, being a situation in which two instantiates being a number, is itself instantiated at w. That state of affairs is instantiated at every w. Even if we hadn't existed, it would be so instantiated. Likewise, relative to our actual representational practices, the proposition (i.e., state of affairs) that m is a molecule, for any molecule m, is true at world w iff m is a molecule, whether we exist at w or not.

The truth or falsity of (3) turns on the representational properties of things relative to our practices, not on the representational properties those things would have had under circumstances other than the actual one. Even if no thinker had ever existed, the state of affairs that m is a molecule would have represented *relative to our actual practices* m's being a molecule. Representation is *always* representation relative to the practices and behavior (really, behavior within a particular environment) of an individual or a group. When we evaluate a representation like sentences (1) through (3), we must take it relative to one or another practice P of representation. If the sentence makes a modal claim, we hold constant its representational properties as fixed by P. So understood, relative to our practices, (3) is true.

Nothing about (1) through (3) gives us any reason to suppose that propositions are 'inherently' or 'essentially' representational. Neither does the truth of (1) through (3) give us any reason to deny that 'proposition' is just another word for states of affairs.

3.

Scott Soames tells us that the objects of the attitudes are representational. This means, he says, that whatever propositions are, they can't be properties. Of the idea that propositions might be properties of cognitive activities – something like the type of thing one does when one ascribes a property to an object – Soames says it involves an 'absurdity':

> Act types....are either themselves a certain kind of property, or something closely akin to properties. As such, they are not the kinds of things that have truth conditions.[8]

What, then, are propositions, and how are they representational?

On Soames' view, what is representational in the first instance are events like judging, in which a thinker ascribes a property to an object. Propositions – the objects of belief and the other propositional attitudes – inherit their representational properties from the acts of predication that occur in such events. According to Soames, propositions are types of cognitive events in which objects and properties are related via predication and other mental acts: '... the proposition that snow is white is the minimal event type in which an agent predicates whiteness of snow...' (104–105) The representational properties of a proposition are derived from its instances:

> ...the proposition *that o is red* is the minimal event-type in which one predicates *being red* of o. This event-type is representational *because* every instance of it is one in which *an agent* represents o as red. Just as torturing someone is said to be a violent act because events in which one performs it are violent episodes, so a propositional event-type may be said to represent ... what is common to its instances. From this we derive its truth conditions. It is true at w iff *at w* o is as it is represented to be by one who entertains it ....[9]

This view teeters on the brink of incoherence. Aren't event types themselves certain kinds of properties, or something closely akin to properties? How, then, can they have truth conditions, if properties aren't the sort of thing that have truth conditions? [10]

The last citation suggests a way to retreat from the view that no property can have truth conditions: If a property is such that every instance of it has truth conditions / is representational, then the property itself is, too. Thus, Soames' predicational event types are representational. But states of affairs *cum* properties are not like this – an instance of a state of affairs is just objects having properties and standing in relations. While *some* such configurations are representational, most of course are not.

The proposal is that a property P has truth conditions provided P itself has a certain property Q (being necessarily such that all of its instances have truth conditions). The proposal isn't intrinsically implausible. But one wonders why we should think it's the only plausible account of what it is for a property to have truth conditions. I suggested above that to say that a state of affairs s is a bearer of truth or falsity is to say that a belief whose object was s would be true or false. To have a true belief is to represent a state of affairs that obtains. The state of affairs is in a straightforward sense the object of the belief. And a state of affairs can thus be said to be true or false, depending on whether a belief representing it would be true or false – that is, depending on whether it does or does not obtain.[11] It's hard to see why this is any worse of an account, of how propositional objects 'derive' their representational properties, than the account Soames offers.

Soames and I agree that what is representational in the first instance are the cognitive acts of (or events involving) agents that represent. We agree that when we talk about agents' representational acts, we describe them using devices – complement clauses like 'that snow is white' – which we use, in part, to characterize the truth conditions of their representations. And we agree that complement clauses so used are well regimented as singular terms; we call what they name when so regimented propositions. Does all this require that representational states like belief are best understood as relations to objects – propositions – that are in some interesting sense representational?

Of course not. What is true or false in an interesting sense are actual and possible acts or events of representation. Propositions are representational only in the shallow sense that it is easy and useful to project talk of potential beliefs and assertions as true or false onto the propositions – i.e. states of affairs – themselves. These latter are both what is represented in states like belief and what determines the truth conditions of the representation. Once we have projected our talk of true and false belief and assertion onto the things we potentially represent in belief and assertion, we have given ourselves a powerful tool for characterizing beliefs and assertions as correct or otherwise, even in the absence of knowledge of what a belief or assertion says.[12]

What are true or false in the primary sense of 'true' and 'false' are acts of representation. It is useful and harmless to extend truth talk beyond this primary sense. We do extend truth talk in this way. So there is a lame, watered down sense in which the objects of the attitudes are true or false and hence representational. It is hard – well, it is hard for me, at least – to see what the point of insisting that propositions need to be representational in some stronger sense might be.

4.

Soames disagrees. He writes

> It is a truism that a belief...represents the world as being a certain way, and so is capable of being true or false. Ordinarily, what we mean by this is that *what is believed*...represents the world, and so is true or false. Using the familiar name 'proposition' for these things, we may ask "*In virtue of what are propositions representational, and hence bearers of truth conditions?*" This was the key question that Frege and the early Russell weren't able to answer. Nevertheless, the problem is genuine. Surely, beliefs...*are* representational. (63–64)

According to Soames, there *is* something about a proposition in virtue of which it is representational. That something is 'what the agent's cognitive attitude adds to the [objects and properties he is thinking about] to bring it about that the world is represented as being one way rather than another.' (64) What is added, Soames says, is not idiosyncratic: what I 'add' to Desdemona, Casio, and loving to 'produce' the belief that Desdemona loves Casio has to be the same thing as what you add to them to produce the belief. That 'addition' is a particular kind of cognitive activity:

> What unites the elements of a proposition, and gives it representational import, is something that agents do when they bear cognitive relations to it – namely, *predicate* one propositional constituent of the others. (65)

Thus does Soames arrive at the idea that the proposition that grass is green is a 'minimal event type' – the type of thing that occurs when one thinks that grass is green. Since what is 'added' to propositional constituents to produce the proposition is the same across thinkers – predicating greenness of grass – the proposition that grass is green encodes necessary and sufficient conditions for entertaining the thought that grass is green. In general, the proposition that P is to be identified with the sort of cognitive event that occurs when and only when one thinks that P. It is the event that consists of 'the structure and sequence of cognitive acts of predication that are necessary and sufficient for entertaining' P. (106) As Soames sees it, this account has the upshot that propositions have their truth conditions 'intrinsically' and 'essentially' (103) 'because of their intrinsic connection to the inherently representational cognitive events in which agents predicate some things of other things.' (107)

It is hard to take issue with the idea that predicating greenness of grass is necessary and sufficient for thinking that grass is green, since (in unadorned, pre-theoretical English) saying that someone ascribed greenness to grass is just giving two dollar expression to the ten cent idea that she thought that grass is green. [13] But Soames wants the notion of predication to do considerable descriptive and explanatory work. The account of propositions that Soames develops in the most detail is one on which 'every proposition is formed simply by predicating an n-place property of n arguments.' (110) This includes the propositions expressed by negations, conjunctions, disjunctions, and the like. On this model, thinking that squirrel A is running away and squirrel B is standing still involves: ascribing running away to A; ascribing standing still to B; thereby producing tokens of the propositions that A is running away and B is standing still; then ascribing joint truth to the tokens. The conjunctive proposition that A is running away and B is standing still is the event type of performing this series of predications.

As Soames realizes, one might well balk at this proposal. Surely there are cognitively unsophisticated creatures – dogs, cats, and two year old humans, for example – that are able to entertain and believe the conjunctive claim that A is running away and B is standing still although it is not plausible that they are in a position to ascribe anything like *untruth* or *joint truth* to complex event types or other such candidates for propositions. Not only is it not plausible that the dog and the two year old have the concepts of truth, it is not plausible that they have the ability to think about representational acts or events in a way that makes them available for predication.[14] Given the range of things that can have conjunctive beliefs – adults, toddlers, dogs, computers – it's less than clear that there is anything substantive one can say about the psychological particulars of believing that Fa and Gb, beyond saying that it's having a belief that represents the state of affairs of a's being F and b's being G. Of course, much the same sort of worry can be raised about other truth functional beliefs.[15]

Soames suggests that we can get around this kind of objection with a modest increase in the inventory of mental activities that constitute the glue that holds propositions together. In particular, he suggests we might identify conjunctive and other complex propositions with event types that don't involve predicating properties of propositions:

> There are two ways to explain how one can believe [truth functional propositions like conjunctive and disjunctive ones] without predicating truth of anything. One is to make them event-types in which one entertains their constituent propositions, without predicating anything further, distinguishing the two by the different roles

they play in thought. Another way of doing the same thing involves relations R& and RV. Predicating these of *a, redness, b,* and *roundness* represents *a as red and b as round* (and only this), and *a as red or b as round*, respectively. To believe these is to believe *that a is red and b is round* and *that a is red or b is* round. To believe their negations is to believe propositions in which one negates R& and RV. None of these beliefs requires making propositions predication targets. By taking R& and RV to be 2-place relations each argument of which is an n-place property followed by an ordered n-tuple, we can embed propositions formed using them under R& and RV themselves, thereby making truth-functional cognition safe for squirrels and 2-year olds.[16]

Toddler cognition posed a problem because (a) Soames wishes to identify the proposition that P with an event type that encodes (necessary) necessary and sufficient conditions for entertaining the thought that P, but (b) the event types with which he (tentatively) identified complex propositions are not events of which all things that can think the propositions are capable of being agents. The proposal above thus solves the problem only if *either* (1) there is a role R (presumably an inferential role) two propositions may play in thought such that (it is a necessary truth that) something entertains a conjunctive thought that P and Q just in case the propositions that P and that Q play role R in the thing's thought, *or* (2) (it is a necessary truth that) someone entertains a conjunctive thought that P and Q just in case they ascribe a relation like the relation R&.

(2) seems like a non-starter so long as we think of predication – as Soames himself does – as a relation which requires some sort of cognitive acquaintance with the objects of predication. The relation R& is a relation that holds between a property or relation and *an n-tuple* of objects of predication. But as Soames himself observes, objecting to the view that propositions are something like n-tuples of propositional constituents:

> Agents perform ... predications because they have both the properties predicated, and that of which they are predicated, in mind.. ....However... it is not obvious that agents can correctly be said to have ...abstract structures [like n-tuples] in mind in a sense sufficiently robust to make them the targets of the agent's acts of predication. (95–97.)[17]

(1) strikes me as involving a change in Soames' view. Soames' original proposal makes having a propositional attitude a little like talking to one's self: To entertain the proposition that P, one (mentally) identifies P's constituents, and predicates some of them of the others; the proposition that P is the event type of such a stretch of interior monolog. Dispositional facts enter into this picture in distinguishing one attitude towards a proposition from another: to believe p, for example, is 'to be disposed to endorse, accept, or subscribe to the predications needed to entertain p.' (65) But now dispositional mental – presumably inferential – roles associated with mental tokens are being called upon to differentiate (for example) entertaining the thought that P and Q from entertaining the thought that if P, then Q. For what inferential role a mental token has is presumably largely a matter of how the tokener is disposed to manipulate

that token in thought. So the conjunctive and conditional propositions will have to be individuated in terms of the possession of (fairly high level) dispositions.

In and of itself this new direction is not objectionable. But it is less than clear that it will provide an adequate account of truth functional propositions and our attitudes towards them. One can certainly believe or assert a disjunctive or conditional claim even when one's grasp of the inferential role of disjunction or implication is less than sterling. Suppose the proposal, for example, is that to believe the conditional, if p then q, one must be disposed, inter alia, to infer not-p from not-q, and to have mastered conditional proof. This, I can assure you, means that many American college students do not have conditional beliefs.

It is of course true that *one way* one can come to believe a truth functional claim is by having within one's cognitive repertoire a well developed grasp of a particular inferential role combined in a belief making way with the claim's propositional constituents. But that's not the *only* way to believe such a claim. One can also be a marginal member of a linguistic community that has a word that is associated, in cognitively refined members, with a well developed inferential ability corresponding to a truth function. A marginal member will be in a position to *represent* the state of affairs expressed by a conditional sentence, even if her command of what's represented is less than sterling. So here are two ways to believe or entertain conditional claims. Why exactly should we think that these are the *only* ways in which one might have the ability to entertain or believe such a claim? Surely it is reasonable to think that there is a somewhat open-ended family of things that count as the relevant sort of representation: one involves subsumption of (tuples of) propositions under one or another category; another involves having refined inferential dispositions vis à vis the relevant propositions; another involves tokening a sentence that normally has a certain inferential role in one's linguistic community; yet another involves behavioral dispositions triggered by perceptual experience. Indeed, arguably one way for it to be true that x believes that such and so is to (be disposed to) behave in a way that triggers *in an observer* of a certain sort an impulse to co-classify x's states with states of believers whose representations are articulated in certain ways.

One might at this point suggest that truth functional propositions are disjunctive event types: the proposition that A and B, for example, is the sort of thing that happens when either one predicates joint truth of the propositions that A and B, or those propositions play a certain functional role in one's thought, or one accepts a sentence that in one's community plays for many members a certain inferential role, or one ascribes R& to the propositions that A and that B, or . . . . In so far as the disjunction is open ended, the suggestion is not far from the suggestion that (for example) the proposition that A and B is the event type of representing that A and B. This suggestion does not give a particularly illuminating answer to the (sort of) question

> In virtue of what is the proposition that A and B representational, and thus the bearer of truth conditions?

which it was Soames' goal to answer. It is not clear what the motivation for adopting this sort of account of propositions might be, as opposed to the more straightforward account of propositions sketched in the first two sections of this paper.

Kindred points, it seems to me, apply to Soames' views about atomic propositions, ones that represent an n-tuple of individuals as standing in one or another relation. Here is why.

Soames thinks – surely correctly – that representational properties are to be explained in terms of the properties and relations of things that represent. He thinks that the fundamental notion in such an explanation is of a thinker *predicating* a property of an object. But what, exactly, is predication? Soames takes it as a primitive, so we are not going to get a definition. We are told that it is '*what the agent does*' (65) in asserting, conjecturing, and so forth. It is something that occurs in perception (when we see x as an F), in judging that an object is F, and when we understand a sentence that says that x is F.

If Soames' proposal were that the proposition that (say) John is smarter than Louis was the event type of ascribing being smarter than to <John, Louis> **and** that believing this proposition was making the ascription in a certain ('belief making') way, it would obviously be wrong. Surely some of our beliefs are tacit, and do not involve anything plausibly described as ascription. Now, Soames does not hold that having a belief that John is smarter than Louis requires actually predicating the relation of the individuals; to have the belief is 'to be disposed to endorse, accept, or subscribe to' the predication. Soames' idea, I take it, is that the basic representational phenomenon is (what we might call) *explicit predication*; propositions are the kinds of events that occur when this basic representational phenomenon occurs; belief and other attitudes are certain dispositions towards what happens when these events occur.

The problem with this view, as I see it, is that ('basic') representation and attitudes like belief are considerably more variegated than Soames allows. We would, for example, normally say that a teacher who suffered from an implicit bias towards her African American students believed that they were inferior in various ways to other students. Though she might *say* that she believed that African American students were equally intelligent as other students, she does not believe this. The prejudiced teacher is disposed to endorse the ascription of the property of being just as intelligent as the average white student to her African American students, though her behavior makes it obvious that she doesn't believe those students to be as intelligent as the white students. More significantly, it is not at all clear why we should want to say that the teacher ascribes the property of being less intelligent than other students to the African American students simply because her behavior manifests a consistent disposition to treat those students in ways appropriate only if they are less intelligent. There are more ways to believe that a is F than predicating, or being disposed to predicate, F of a.

Of course, there is a (philosopher's) use of 'predicating' on which *b thinks a is F* and *b predicates F of a* are more or less synonymous. But surely it's an odd idea, that predication in the sense of some sort of cognitive *activity* generally enters into representation. Take perceptual belief as an example. Properties and objects are in some sense available to human consciousness in human perception. They are available to animal cognition in animal perception. But I'm not sure it makes much sense to speak *quite generally* of the agent, or something subpersonal, or my dog actively predicating properties of objects in perception. Aspects of perceptual states (quasi-) systematically covary with aspects of what produces them; some of these aspects are subpersonally correlated in such a way that they function over time as a representation of a single covarying object or enduring instantiation of a property. Perceptual states control behavior in a way that makes them systematically responsive to the manifest objects and properties that produce them. Historical and social relations of aspects of the mental make some interpretations of such states more reasonable than others. What makes it true that properties are predicated of objects in perception (or that states of affairs are perceptually represented) is that perceptual states have such a complex of causal, counterfactual, psychological, social properties and relations.[18] Perception is representational because of the sort of complex facts just alluded to. That it involves property ascription is not an *explanation* of its representational properties, but just another way of saying that it is representational.

What is right about Soames' idea, that thinking that such and so is a matter of (being disposed to make a sequence of) predication(s) is that **paradigms** of thinking that such and so are cases in which the explanation of why the thinker thinks that such and so is that (a) the thinker has made or at least is disposed to make various predications, and (b) those predications (or states connected with her dispositions to make them) have a functional role more or less well described by various truisms about when adults make/are disposed to make such predications and how such predications / dispositions typically lead to behavior. Attitudes are **states that are in various ways like such paradigms**. Like them in what way? Well, that depends on various things – for example, our interests in talking about beliefs.[19] But it is a familiar fact about paradigm structures that something may be an F but be very unlike paradigm Fs.

If all this is right, notions of a proposition like Soames' notion - on which the proposition that P is something like 'the' cognitive activity involved in thinking that P - haven't much of an explanatory or descriptive role to play, in either philosophy of mind or semantics. Soames' appeal to the notion of predication is, at the end of the day, explanatorily vacuous. I rather doubt that there is just one, or even a handful, of kinds of cognitive activity that are necessary and sufficient for representing that snow is white; likewise for representing that if snow's not white, then grass isn't green. Certainly there is little point in trying to build into an account of *propositions* – that is, an account of the things picked out by the complement clauses of attitude ascriptions – the presumably disjunctive and probably open ended collection of ways in which one might represent a state of affairs. The job of a proposition is simply to provide a way to classify representational states in terms of what would make them accurate or otherwise.

This is achieved if we say that propositions are states of affairs, and attitudes are various representational relations to them.

We invoke propositions in an account of mind and language as the semantic values of complement clauses. An account of propositions that sees them as states of affairs – ways for things to be, ways individuated in terms of the objects and properties they involve – is adequate for this purpose. There is a deflated sense in which propositions *cum* states of affairs are representational – they are representational simply because they are things that *we call* true or false, and their truth and falsity conditions can be straightforwardly defined to verify instances of the schema *it's true that S iff S*. But there is also a sense of 'representational' in which propositions so conceived aren't representational at all: they are what are represented, actual or possible facts. What's representational in the fundamental sense isn't the object of representational states; it's the relation between (a state of) she who represents and the state of affairs represented. There are no facts about representation, attitudes, or belief that require that propositions be representational in any inflated sense. It is pointless, and potentially obfuscatory, to build representational properties into propositions. [20]

Notes

1. Henceforth, I often use 'property' as a blanket term for properties and relations.
2. One might think of the matter as follows. For a state of affairs to obtain is for various objects to instantiate various properties. (Better: for various objects (and properties) to instantiate various properties (higher order ones, in the case of properties)). The properties that are states of affairs will thus be individuated as finely as the configurations of objects and properties that realize those properties: A state of affairs is the property of **this** configuration of objects and properties obtaining. In general, then, necessarily equivalent states of affairs are distinct.

    Of course the state of affairs that Twain is Twain **is** the state of affairs that Twain is Clemens, just as the Russellian proposition that Twain is Twain is the Russellian proposition that Twain is Clemens. If one – as I am about to – identifies propositions with states of affairs, one will have to explain how the propositional attitude ascriptions 'Mary believes that Twain is Twain' and 'Mary believes that Twain is Clemens' can differ in truth value. I have discussed this issue in considerable detail elsewhere. (Richard, 1990, 2013) Though those discussions don't identify propositions with states of affairs, what is said there about the semantics of attitude ascriptions transfers straightforwardly to the view of propositions taken here.
3. The modality here is metaphysical.
4. I ignore context sensitivity throughout.
5. Alternatively, one might associate ways of instantiating with connectives and such, and give an inductive definition of the state of affairs represented by a sentence. Assuming that we already have a definition of truth for the language we're studying, there's no advantage I can see in doing this.
6. Why do I say 'typically tied to its behavior'? Isn't it *definitional* that beliefs tend to interact with desire to produce the relevant sort of behavior?

    I don't think that this is true, much less definitional. There are various pathologies of belief. (Davies and Coltheart (2000) give a nice discussion of some of them.) What is striking about such pathologies is that in them, states we are inclined to call beliefs and desires do not interact in normal ways. In particular, when someone suffers from such a pathology, their belief (-like) state often does not interact with standing desires to produce behavior. The patient suffering from Cotard syndrome who thinks she is dead and wants the dead to be cremated does not report to a crematorium. (Note that this does not seem to be due to 'lack of integration' of the attitudes in any normal sense of integration.)

I think the idiom of belief is the right one to use in such cases, though I grant that for some such cases it may be indeterminate whether they are cases of belief. But if these cases are cases of belief (or even if it is simply indeterminate whether they are), their existence shows that the attitudes are not to be given crisp definitions on which the claim that something is a belief entails that it realizes a stereotypical *belief + desire → action* functional organization.

I'm indebted here to discussions with Bob Matthews.

7. The counterfactual here is not to be understood in terms of a possible worlds semantics, with the whole true if the consequent is true at the 'closest antecedent worlds'. I don't see this as a problem, at least not one for the proposal I am making about truth. Possible worlds semantic accounts of conditionals are useful heuristics. That doesn't mean they are literally correct.
8. Soames, 2010, 102. Subsequent references to Soames 2010 are indicated parenthetically in the text.
9. Soames, ms. A.
10. Why, you may be wondering, does Soames think it absurd to say that a property can have truth conditions? According to Soames

> ascriptions to propositions of *what can be said of act types*, as well as ascriptions to act types of *what can be said of propositions*, strike us as bizarre or incoherent.
> ... it would be incoherent to say "**the proposition that John is brilliant is what I just did*" or "**What I plan to do* (when I plan to predicate brilliance of John) *is false*". ... it would be absurd to say "*What I believe, and what Gödel proved, is something I just did.*" (101–102, italics in original)

But surely it is exactly as 'absurd' to say 'the proposition that John is brilliant just happened / occurred' or 'What happened in the bathroom at 2 pm was false'; likewise for 'What I believe, and what Gödel proved, is something that happened in the bathroom.' This sort of linguistic evidence doesn't allow us to decide that event types, instead of act types, are propositions.

Soames himself says, of the idea that propositions are events

> Since this is a new way of thinking of propositions ... it may be a bit surprising to be told that they are things that occur. However, I don't see this consequence as incoherent.... the theoretical advantages of thinking of propositions in this way are substantial, and justify this modest extension of our view of them. (103–104)

Fair enough. But exactly the same thing might be said about the idea that propositions are act types. And exactly the same sort of thing ought be said of the idea that propositions are states of affairs.

11. As I observed in note 7, the interpretation of the modal here is somewhat delicate. What's meant, of course, is that a state of affairs P is true iff (were one to have a belief whose content was P, the object of one's belief would actually obtain). More generally, to say that P is true at w is to say that were one to believe P, the content of one's belief would obtain at w.
12. Do not interpret me as here endorsing a minimalist notion of truth, but rather as agreeing with the minimalist's observation that the (propositional) notion of truth has enormous descriptive utility.

13. 'thinking' here is supposed to be a generic mental attitude, one common to entertaining, believing, assuming, doubting, knowing, and so on; in this sense, one thinks that grass is green when (for instance) one thinks that if grass in green, then hay is beige.
14. Soames himself poses such an objection to a 'deflationary' account of propositions that takes them to be nothing more than theoretical posits introduced by the theorist. On such an account, a proposition might be something along the lines of an ordered pair of a property and the right number of constituents; to entertain it is to ascribe the property to the constituents. This means that the proposition that A and B is <the property of being jointly true>, <the proposition that A, the proposition that B>; believing it is ascribing joint truth to the propositions.

    The deflationist's propositions are abstract, set theoretical structures. Soames objects that we don't think about such things when we think, for example, that snow is not crimson, and thus can't be credited with making them objects of predication. As he puts it:

    > ...it is not obvious that agents can correctly be said to have *any* of the theorist's abstract structures [any of those she might identify with propositions within the context of her theory] in mind in a sense sufficiently robust to make them the targets of the agents' acts of predication. (97)

    Soames concludes that a deflationary account of propositions is not in offing: we must adopt a 'realist' account of propositions, on which they are 'parts of the reality being modeled, rather than merely components of the model.' (98)

    What is not obvious, I would say, is why propositions *must* be something that an agent 'has in mind in a robust sense'. Their primary purpose, as I see it, is a classificatory one. My point in this section, as will become clear, is that it is implausible that there is a **single** 'robust' sense in which someone needs to have to have a proposition 'in mind', in order to be correctly said to believe or entertain it.
15. Much the same point applies to (quite complicated) account Soames offers at the end of Soames, 2010 for what is involved in beliefs expressed by sentences involving quantification, structured singular terms (like those involving function symbols), and complex predicates. Thanks to the editors for suggesting that I note this.
16. Soames, ms. B.
17. This is just the objection to the deflationary account of propositions discussed in note 14.

    Soames presumably made the relations R& and RV relations to n-tuples so that he could avoid variations to standard objections to Russell's multiple relation theory of belief. The multiple relation theory, as Russell presented it, requires an infinity of belief relations: the three place relation I bear to you and happiness when I believe that you are happy, the four place relation I bear to you, admiring, and Frege when I believe that you admire Frege, the five place relation ..... This seems objectionable because it leaves us without a single relation to assign to the verb 'believes'. If the number of constituents in p and q controls the relation used to form their conjunction, it's not altogether clear that one could give a finitary theory of propositions that would, for example, assign to each conjunction the correct conjunctive propositions.

    Even if this problem and the one in the text can be evaded, the resulting theory would still be liable to the objections lodged below.
18. Whether it's reasonable (and thus, I would say, correct) to say that something has a belief depends on factors that vary across the situations in which we ascribe (or withhold) ascription of the attitude. I discuss this in Richard 2013.

19. We will, for example, generalize from the paradigm in one way if we are trying to give an account of everyday attitude ascription, perhaps in quite another if we are doing cognitive science.
20. This is a revised version of comments on Soames, 2010 delivered at an APA Author Meets Critics session in December 2011. I'm grateful to Soames for his comments on that version of the paper, as well for comments from David Liebesman, Susanna Siegel, Sebastian Watzl, the participants at a workshop on propositions at the École Normale Superior in April 2012 and the editors of this volume.

References

Davies, M., and Max Coltheart. 2000. "Introduction: Pathologies of Belief." *Mind and Language* 15: 1–46.
Richard, Mark. 1990. *Propositional Attitudes*. Cambridge University Press.
Richard, Mark. 2013. "Introduction: Attitudes and their Ascription." In *Meaning and Context, Volume I: Context and the Attitudes*. Oxford University Press.
Soames, Scott. 2010. *What is Meaning?* Princeton University Press.
Soames, Scott. ms. A., "Why the Traditional Conceptions of Propositions Can't be Correct".
Soames, Scott. ms. B. Response to Critics, APA session on Soames 2010, Washington DC, December 2011.

THEORETICAL ALTERNATIVES TO PROPOSITIONS
Conversational implicature, communicative intentions, and content

Ray Buchanan

University of Texas, Austin

At the core of the Gricean account of conversational implicature is a certain assumption concerning the phenomenon that its proponents hope to explain and predict – namely, that conversational implicatures are, essentially, cases of speaker meaning. Heck (2006), however, has argued that once we appreciate a distinctive kind of indeterminacy characteristic of particularized implicatures, we must reject this assumption. Heck's observation is that there are cases where it is clear a speaker has conversationally implicated something by her utterance, but where there is no particular proposition – other than what the speaker said – that we can plausibly take the speaker to have meant, or intended to communicate. I argue that although Heck's observation is ultimately not in conflict with the core Gricean assumption, it is in tension with the widely held thesis that the things we mean and implicate are propositions. I sketch an alternative account of the things we mean and implicate – one that that accommodates the fact that in many cases of successful communicative exchanges, there is no particular proposition that the speaker intends to communicate.

At the core of the Gricean account of conversational implicature is a certain assumption concerning the phenomenon that its proponents hope to explain and predict in terms of various principles governing cooperative communicative exchanges – namely, that conversational implicatures are, essentially, cases of speaker-meaning. More specifically, according to the Gricean, a speaker implicates *p* only if she means, or intends to communicate, *p* by saying (or making as if to say) something else.[1] Call this *the meaning-intention assumption*.

In 'Reason and Language', Richard Heck offers an important challenge to this assumption. Heck argues that once we appreciate a distinctive kind of indeterminacy characteristic of many, if not most, cases of particularized implicatures, there is pressure to reject the meaning-intention assumption.[2] Roughly put, Heck's observation is that there are cases where it is clear a speaker has conversationally implicated *something* by her utterance, but there is no particular proposition – other than what the speaker said – such that we can plausibly take the speaker to have intended to communicate *it*. Call this *the problem of specificity*.

While Heck's observation is indeed of the utmost importance, he has, I will argue, mischaracterized its significance. The phenomenon to which Heck is calling our attention is not so much a problem for Grice's account of conversational implicature as it is for standard assumptions about the nature of our communicative intentions and the contents thereof. I will argue that we should retain the meaning-intention assumption, but eschew accounts of meaning and communication on which the things we mean, assert, and implicate must be propositions. Rather, a solution to the problem of specificity requires an account of communicative intentions which allows for the possibility that a rational speaker can fully intend to communicate 'something' by her utterance *u* even if there is no particular proposition, or set of propositions, *p* such that she believes that her audience will entertain *it* on the basis of *u*, and other facts regarding the context of utterance. In a sense to be elaborated, in many cases of cooperative communicative exchanges, speakers *endeavor* to communicate many propositions without *outright intending* to communicate any particular one.

Before jumping in I should make a few initial points that will help to streamline the discussion to follow. First, the statement of the meaning-intention assumption appeals to 'what is said'. For the last decade, there has been considerable debate about how best to understand this locution, and with it the division of labor between semantic and pragmatic theorizing. In what follows, I'll follow Grice in assuming that what a speaker *says*, or *asserts*, in an utterance *u* is something she means which is 'closely related to the conventional meaning of the words (the sentence) he has uttered' (Grice 1989, 25). For our purposes, we can leave it vague exactly what such 'closeness' of fit requires, allowing that different theorists might disagree on this issue.

Second, even among those theorists most sympathetic to Grice's account, there has been little consensus on the exact nature and role of the Cooperative Principle and related maxims in the explanation and prediction of conversational implicatures. According to some theorists, Grice's principles must be supplemented with others; according to others, they should be replaced altogether. But even, if we could agree on what the relevant principles are, there are further vexing questions concerning what precise role these principles play in the generation and recovery of conversational implicatures. In what follows, however, we can (happily) ignore these difficult issues concerning the exact nature and role of the Cooperative Principle and related principles in the account of conversational implicature. Our aim is to discuss a certain common conception of the phenomenon that these theorists hope to explain in terms of such principles of cooperative communicative exchanges.

Finally, I will use 'what the speaker meant' and 'what the speaker intended to communicate' interchangeably. Moreover, as my interest is in the nature of our *communicative* intentions, I will limit the discussion to those cases in which a speaker utters what she does with a particular audience A in mind, with the overarching aim of communicating *with* A. With this restriction in mind, we can set aside some important, but separable, issues concerning the meaning-intention assumption, such as whether a speaker can conversationally implicate something in the absence of an intended audience.[3]

1. Preliminaries

If the meaning-intention assumption is correct, in order for a speaker to conversationally implicate p, she must mean, or intend to communicate, p. And while there has been controversy among Griceans regarding how, if at all, we might analyze the latter, it is plausible – and we will take it as given in what follows – that the conditions given in (Meaning) are necessary for *speaker-meaning p*:

> (Meaning) S speaker-meant p by u only if, for some audience A, and some feature Ψ of u, S produced u intending (i) for A to entertain p, and (ii) for A to recognize that S intends (i) at least in part, on the basis of their recognition that S's utterance of u has Ψ.[4]

Think of the Ψ-feature as some aspect of S's production of u such that she expects (a) that her audience will recognize the production to have Ψ, and (b) she intends (a) to figure essentially in A's inferring what she meant. In cases of linguistic communication, this Ψ-feature will (typically) include that S uttered such and such words with certain conventional meanings in a shared language.[5]

The conditions given in (Meaning) should, I hope, be familiar from the work of Grice, Schiffer, and others.[6] While theorists sympathetic to (Meaning) might reasonably disagree on how – and indeed whether – we can add to these conditions so as to provide necessary and sufficient conditions for speaker-meaning, these further issues need not concern us given our current interests.

If the meaning-intention assumption is correct, you implicate one thing *by* saying, or making as if to say, something else. To capture this required indirection, the Gricean will add that in cases of conversational implicature, the relevant feature Ψ will (invariably) include that the speaker has said q, and, perhaps, that she said q in a particular way. Putting this thought together with (Meaning), we arrive at the following (official) statement of the meaning-intention assumption:

> (MIA) S conversationally implicates q in uttering u only if (i) S says (or makes as if to say) p in producing u and, for some audience A, S intends (ii) for A to entertain q and (iii) for A to recognize S's intention (ii), in part, on the basis of A's recognition of (i).

Griceans might go on to add further requirements on conversational implicatures – e.g., requiring that they be cancelable, calculable, etc. – but, for present purposes, we can set aside these further issues.

So far, I have said nothing regarding *what* we mean, or implicate – i.e., the sorts of things that 'p' in (Meaning), and (MIA), ranges over. The standard assumption is that the things we mean are *propositions*; i.e., abstract, representational entities that have truth-conditions absolutely, and without relativization to anything else. This assumption, which we will call 'Content', will be especially important in what follows:

(Content) The things we mean/intend to communicate are propositions.

Given (Content), it follows from (Meaning), and (MIA), that if S meant, or implicated, *something*, there must be some particular proposition that she intends (and, hence, expects) A to entertain, at least in part, on the basis of her utterance. These things that are (putatively) the objects of our meaning-intentions might be taken to be sets of possible worlds, Russellian propositions, or Fregean propositions, but the differences between these views won't concern us.

And as a final bit of background, I want to call attention to a thesis concerning the manner in which our beliefs constrain our intentions which is explicit in Grice's work on meaning and intention, and implicit in much of the literature that followed. This thesis, which I we might call 'the Belief-Intention Constraint' (or 'the B-I Constraint'), is widely held among philosophers working in action theory, though far from uncontroversial:

(The B-I Constraint) S rationally intends to do φ only if S believes that she is going to do φ.[7]

I am inclined to think that the B-I Constraint is a conceptual truth the appreciation of which helps us to understand the fact that one especially efficacious way in which we might give expression to our intention to φ is by (assertorically) uttering 'I am going to φ'.[8] Further, I strongly suspect that the B-I Constraint must be correct if we are to explain certain rational requirements on our intentions, including the fact that it is irrational to have intentions that are jointly inconsistent with our beliefs.[9]

While the B-I Constraint might initially sound quite demanding, it is important to keep in mind the following. First, an agent might (fully) believe that she will φ even though her credence that she will φ is significantly less than 1 (where, for present purposes, we take a credence of 1 as an attitude of certainty). (ii) Secondly, when thinking through potential counterexamples to the B-I Constraint bear in mind the distinction between *intending to φ* and merely *intending to try to φ*. Even in cases in which we know the odds are stacked against our success in φ-ing, we might nevertheless intend to try. Finally – and this will become clearer in Section Three – even if we accept that intentions are governed by belief in the way indicated by the B-I Constraint, we might allow that while there are other intention-*like* states relevant to the explanation of our behavior – including linguistic behavior – that are not constrained by belief in this way.[10] With these qualifications in place, we will, until further notice, take the B-I Constraint as a working hypothesis.

Notice that the B-I Constraint has immediate implications concerning the way in which our meaning-intentions are constrained by what we can (rationally) believe our audiences will 'uptake' in a particular communicative exchange.

In tandem with (Meaning), and (MIA), the B-I Constraint entails that if a speaker (rationally) means/implicates p then she must believe, among other things, that her utterance will put her audience in a position to recognize her intention that he entertain p.

With this bit of background in place, let's now turn to Heck's challenge to the meaning-intention assumption (MIA).

2. The problem of specificity

Heck writes that one of the most notable aspects of the Gricean account is 'the specificity of what is implicated' (Heck 2006, 27). According to the Gricean, when a speaker conversationally implicates something she must 'intend to communicate some *particular* proposition and to expect that [her audience] should be able to work out which particular proposition that is' (ibid.) Heck claims that in cases of conversational implicature this condition often does not obtain.

To illustrate Heck's worry, consider his variant of a familiar example from Grice. Suppose that Smith writes a letter of recommendation for a student, Jones, who is applying to graduate school. Smith's letter reads:

(1) To whom it may concern,
Mr. Jones is punctual, and has excellent penmanship.
Yours sincerely,
Prof. Smith

As Heck points out, Smith presumably does not intend to be, nor will admissions committees understand him as, merely offering some helpful information concerning Jones's handwriting and timeliness. But while it is intuitively clear that Smith is implicating *something* concerning his impression of Jones and his candidacy, it is extremely difficult to specify what that 'something' is. In this case, there are a number of non-equivalent candidates for what the professor intended to communicate that seem equally relevant and informative. For example, did Smith intend to communicate (i) the proposition that Jones is not very bright? Or (ii) that Jones is a poor student? Or (iii) that he has no talent in the area of study for which he is applying? Or (iv) that he is not prepared for graduate school? Or (v) that he should not be admitted to graduate school?... Or, did he mean some conjunction, or disjunction, of these candidates?

Given our discussion of (Meaning), (Content), and the B-I Constraint, the answer is that Smith did not – and, moreover, could not – reasonably intend to communicate any one of these propositions. Heck writes:

> Even if Smith does intend to communicate some such message, I see no reason to suppose that there has to be some *particular* such message he intends to communicate; even if there were, he could not reasonably suppose that his audience could work out which specific message that was. (ibid., 27)

If Smith intended to communicate one of the candidates, for example (iii), then he would have to expect his audience to be able to work out that *it* is what he meant.

It would, however, be unreasonable for Smith to expect any such thing. As a competent, rational speaker Smith will be well aware that the evidence his utterance provides his audience will not put them in a position to recognize that he meant (iii), as opposed to (i), or the conjunction of (iv) and (ii), or what have you.

The problem of specificity is reinforced when we consider the situation from the perspective of Smith's audience. Unlike our other intentions – for example, my intention to have a drink of water – communicative intentions are fulfilled only if they are recognized.[11] In order for my communicative intentions to be satisfied – and for my utterance to be understood – my audience must (minimally) recognize what I meant. That is, if S means p by u, then her audience *must* entertain p in order to understand u. Hence, if Smith meant, say, (i), or any other of the candidates, his audience would have to entertain *it* if they are to understand his utterance. Crucially, however, no one of these candidates plausibly has this feature.

Though Heck doesn't go on to offer any further examples, the phenomenon to which he is calling our attention is ubiquitous. Virtually any example of a particularized implicature could be used to make the same point. Consider, for instance, the example Grice uses to introduce the phenomenon of implicature in 'Logic and Conversation':

> Suppose that A and B are talking about a mutual friend, C, who is now working at a bank. A asks B how C is getting on in his new job, and B replies, *Oh quite well, I think; he likes his colleagues, and he hasn't been to prison yet.* (Grice 1989, 24–25)

While it might be clear that, as Grice puts it, 'whatever B implied, suggested, or meant in this example, is distinct from what B said (i.e., that C had not yet been to prison)', it is unclear exactly what B is intending to communicate.

Summarizing, Heck suggests that we give up the meaning-intention assumption, (MIA), on the grounds that even when it is clear that a speaker is conversationally implicating 'something' distinct from what she says, there is often no particular proposition that we can plausibly take her to be intending to communicate. If we accept (Meaning), (Content), and the B-I Constraint then Heck is indeed correct: (MIA) must go.

3. Heck's diagnosis

Heck speculates that the fundamental problem with the Gricean account is an underlying picture on which, in cases of implicature, 'a speaker manages, without speaking literally, to do just what she might have done if she had spoken literally, that is to communicate a specific proposition' (ibid., 27). Heck takes the problem of specificity to show that this picture is incorrect, and that there is 'a case to be made... that a proper understanding of non-literal speech demands the rejection of the Gricean picture' (ibid., 27). If the worries concerning the specificity of communicative intentions were limited to cases of 'indirect' communicative acts, it would indeed be tempting to follow Heck and blame the problem of specificity on (MIA).

While Heck allows that speakers engaged in acts of implicature *might* have the kinds of communicative intentions the Gricean requires, such intentions are not necessary. Rather:

> The basic notion... is a weak notion of implicature that does not require one to have any communicative intentions regarding what proposition is implicated: these propositions are the ones the audience can conclude the speaker believes on the basis of an inference to the best explanation concerning her specific act of saying what she did; it makes no sense for me to have said that [*q*] specifically, in this context, unless I believe that [*p*]; my saying that [*q*] therefore implicates that [*p*], in this weak sense. (Heck 2006, 28)

The Gricean conception of implicature according to which a speaker must intend to communicate something she does not literally say is, claims Heck, a 'special case' of this more 'fundamental' phenomenon of his favored weaker notion of implicature. (ibid.)[12]

Heck's discussion of these matters is brief, consisting of little more than the foregoing quotes. Unsurprisingly, there are different ways of elaborating both his diagnosis of the worry for the Gricean account of implicature, and his favored account of 'weak' implicature. For present purposes, however, I propose to set aside the issue of whether the Gricean notion of *indirectly meaning* is indeed a special case of Heck's 'weak' notion of implicature in order to focus on (a) whether Heck's diagnosis of where the Gricean has gone wrong is in fact accurate, and (b) why Heck's positive suggestion helps to reinforce the problem of specificity, rather than solve it.

First, the phenomenon that leads to the problem of specificity is *not* limited to examples concerning conversational implicature, or, more generally, non-literal speech. I am not going to argue fully for this claim here, but similar problems arise – though perhaps not quite as dramatically – for what is *said*, or *asserted*, by many kinds of utterances involving context-sensitive constructions. Oftentimes in utterances involving constructions for which theorists have been tempted to postulate hidden-variables, or unarticulated constituents, the speaker's meaning-intentions will exhibit a similar unspecificity, which make it implausible to identify what she asserted with any specific proposition. To illustrate, suppose that before a joint dinner party Smith utters (2) to Jones:

(2) Each dish is almost ready.

Intuitively, Smith might successfully assert 'something' by (2) despite the fact that there are many dishes, in many parts of the world, which are, as he speaks, simply not ready in any relevant sense. The context-invariant meanings of the constituents of (2), and the arrangement thereof, constrain, but will fail to fully determine what Smith asserted in uttering (2). But here, as in cases of conversational implicature, there is a problem of specificity. Did Smith assert that (a) that each dish *for their guests* is almost ready *to be served*, or (b) that each dish *for the dinner party* is ready *to be eaten*, or (c) that each dish *they have been working on all afternoon* is ready *to be put on the table*, or ... Though each of these 'candidate assertions' will (likely) have the same truth-value in the context of utterance, they have different truth-*conditions*, and must (given standard assumptions) be distinct propositions.[13] If the things we assert are propositions that we (minimally) intend for our audiences to entertain, there is a strong case to be made for thinking that Smith didn't specifically assert any of these options. I have made that case in detail elsewhere (Buchanan 2010), and I do not want to rehearse those considerations here. But, for now, note that insofar as the phenomenon of multiple, non-equivalent candidates can arise in cases of 'literal speech' (i.e., can arise for what is asserted/stated), then we have good reason for being suspicious of Heck's diagnosis of what has gone wrong: the phenomenon that leads us to the problem of specificity cannot be adequately addressed by simply rejecting the meaning-intention assumption, which is specific to conversational implicature.

Turning to Heck's positive proposal, it is unclear whether appeal to his 'weaker' notion of implicature actually helps with the problem. In the quote above, Heck characterizes a 'weakly' implicated proposition as one that the speaker's audience infers in the course of rationalizing her having said what she did. This is a proposition we must assume the speaker to believe for 'it to make sense' for her to have said q. To a rough first approximation, the proposal seems to be:

S *weakly-implicates p* by uttering u iff, for some proposition q and some audience A, S said q by u and this fact is only intelligible to A if A takes S to believe p.

This weaker, audience-centered conception of implicature is both cogent and interesting; even the proponent of (MIA) might find considerable use for it in her account of utterance interpretation.[14] But, crucially, this 'weaker' notion of implicature is still too demanding to be of help in resolving the problem of specificity.[15] Again consider the example involving Smith's letter. Imagining yourself to be his audience, ask what propositions you **must** take Smith to believe in order to rationalize his having said that Jones has excellent penmanship, etc. Must you take Smith to believe, say, that Jones is a poor student in order to make sense of his saying what he did? No, obviously not. Even if you set aside the possibility that Smith he is speaking metaphorically, ironically, etc., there remain numerous other propositions that you might take Smith to believe which would equally rationalize his production. Assuming that the things we weakly-implicate are propositions, then Smith has not actually weakly-implicated *anything*. The original problem was understanding how it could be that Smith conversationally implicated 'something' other than what he said in his letter, despite there being no particular proposition that he intended to communicate (or could have so intended). We can now add that there is no particular proposition that he weakly-implicated either; no progress has been made yet. By parity of reasoning, we should conclude that satisfying the conditions for weakly-implicating are no more required for conversationally implicating something, than are the Gricean conditions to which Heck is objecting.

If anything, consideration of Heck's positive suggestion helps to underscore the severity of the problem of specificity. Coupling the critical point in the last paragraph with our discussion in Section Two, we are in a position to make an even more general observation: there are cases in which, intuitively, a speaker has conversationally implicated something other than what she said, but there is no specific proposition that the speaker's audience must take her to believe, or to have meant, in the course of rationalizing her utterance. This more general observation also casts considerable doubt on one of the key tenets of Grice's own theoretical account of the generation and recognition of conversational implicatures. This thesis – which Davis (1998) dubs *Determinacy* – is Grice's claim that a speaker has implicated what her audience must take her to believe, or to have meant, in order to preserve the supposition that she is observing the Cooperative Principle, and related maxims. Insofar as the conditions for Heck's weaker notion of implicature are too demanding, so too is *Determinacy*.

Stepping back, the phenomenon to which Heck has directed our attention indeed calls into question the conjunction of (MIA), (Meaning), (Content), and the B-I Constraint. I am, however, doubtful that (MIA) is the thesis to blame. Heck's observation seems as much a worry for standard Gricean assumptions about the 'specificity' of what we say as it is concerning what we implicate. What this suggests is that the real problem is not – at least in the first instance – the meaning-intention assumption, as such, but rather the standard assumption that the things we mean are propositions, i.e. (Content). Perhaps we should explore a different line of response to the specificity problem – in particular, one that gives up the assumption that the things we mean must be propositions.

4. Indeterminacy and openness

Grice was well aware that conversational implicatures often exhibit a certain kind of indeterminacy. Indeed, he concludes 'Logic and Conversation' with the following remarks on the phenomenon:

> Since to calculate a conversational implicature is to calculate what has to be supposed in order to preserve the supposition that the cooperative principle is being observed, and since there may be various possible specific explanations, the list of which may be open, the conversational implicatum in such cases will be a disjunction of such specific explanations; and if the list is open, the implicatum will have just the kind of indeterminacy that many implicata do in fact seem to possess. (Grice 1989, 39–40)

While Grice does not provide examples of the phenomenon he has in mind, one might suspect that his remarks were intended to deal with, among other things, worries very much like the problem of specificity.

Grice's remarks in this passage are as puzzling as they are suggestive. As Wayne Davis has suggested (1998, 70–73), one serious problem concerns the difficulty of squaring Grice's remarks with his advocacy of the *Determinacy* condition. To say that there are cases of implicature in which there is a genuinely 'open' list of specific explanations of what the speaker meant is simply to *deny* that there is, in fact, *any one thing* the speaker must be so taken to have meant in order to maintain that supposition. Moreover, as *Determinacy* also figures essentially in Grice's sketch of how it is that a speaker's audience will 'work-out' what she implicated, the suggestion in the foregoing quote is equally in tension with Grice's requirement that a conversational implicature must be *calculable*.

But even if we were to give up *Determinacy*, it remains unclear whether Grice's suggestion in the foregoing quote would be of help regarding the problem of specificity. To appreciate the worry I have in mind, first suppose that in our case involving Smith and his letter of recommendation, the following four propositions are the only relevant candidates:

P_1 = *that Jones is not very bright*
P_2 = *that Jones is a poor student*
P_3 = *that Jones has no talent in the area of study for which he is applying*
P_4 = *that Jones is not prepared for graduate school*

Moreover, we can add that taking Smith to have implicated any one of these particular candidates would count as 'a specific explanation' of his speech act consonant with the assumption he is being relevant, informative, etc. Given these restrictions, this would presumably be the sort of case in which Grice would claim that the speaker implicates a 'closed' disjunction – here, the proposition that P_1 v P_2 v P_3 v P_4. But, notice that this suggestion fails for now familiar reasons. If Smith intended to communicate this particular disjunctive proposition he would have to have intended it, and moreover expected his audience to have entertained it, on the basis of his letter (and other mutual knowledge). But Smith did not, and could not have, rationally intended any such thing. How could Smith have expected his audience to get just this disjunctive proposition rather than P_1, or the conjunction of P_2 and P_3, etc.? What could make it the case that the *disjunction* is somehow the 'best' candidate among the other potential options? Merely that it is the logically weakest candidate of the bunch?

Though the relevant disjunctive proposition is indeed the weakest candidate in this scenario, it is still implausible that it is what Smith implicated. Notice that if this disjunctive proposition were what Smith implicated, then his audience would **have** to entertain it, in order to understand him. But, intuitively, this is too demanding.[16] Suppose an admissions committee member reads Smith's letter and entertains both P_2 and P_3 as a result (thinking that Smith might have been trying to convey one, the other, or both). On the current suggestion, we would have to say – implausibly, in my view – that the committee member did not understand Smith.

If the foregoing objection is correct, then it is difficult to see how we might clarify what Grice meant by an 'open' disjunction such that it would be of help. If it is too demanding to require that Smith's audience must entertain P_1 v P_2 v P_3 v P_4 in order to understand his letter, then it is no less demanding to require that she entertain $P_1 \vee P_2 \vee P_3 \vee P_4 \vee \ldots$, regardless of how we might go on to fill in, or, for that matter, leave open, the ellipsis. Given the constraints on speaker-meaning with which we started – (Meaning) and the B-I Constraint – we are in a position to make an even stronger point. Pick any particular candidate you like, including the potentially open disjunction of the candidates: it is *determinately* the case that Smith did not mean it, in the sense of 'speaker-meaning' glossed in (Meaning).

What is at issue is not so much whether cases of conversational implicature sometimes exhibit an interesting kind of 'indeterminacy', or 'openness'; they most certainly do. For now, I am just pointing out that the relevant kind of openness and indeterminacy is not helpfully explained in terms of a speaker having intended to communicate a disjunction – open, or closed. Rather, the relevant notion of openness somehow seems to involve the speaker's communicative intentions exhibiting **indifference** with regard to precisely how her utterance is interpreted from among a range of similar, but non-equivalent, propositions. The key to addressing Heck's problem of specificity is to get clearer on what the relevant phenomenon of openness consists in.

In order to see how we might best proceed, recall that the reason that Smith could not reasonably intend to communicate any particular proposition by his letter – e.g., the proposition that Jones is ill-prepared for graduate work – is that he could not reasonably believe that his audience would be able to work out that he meant that on the basis of his utterance and other facts concerning the context. Ultimately, this consideration turns on the B-I Constraint – namely, that S rationally intends to do φ only if S believes that she is going to do φ. But, crucially, while Smith might not, as it were, **all-out** believe that his audience will uptake that specific proposition to the exclusion of others, he will have certain expectations regarding its uptake that help to differentiate it from, say, the proposition that Jones has an excellent collection of antique pens. Imagining myself in Smith's position, I would be surprised, if not shocked, were my audience to entertain the latter proposition, a bit surprised if they did not entertain the former. While I might have an exceptionally small, non-zero credence that my audience will entertain the latter, that is not, by my lights, a serious interpretive possibility.

Let's say that a speaker has *an expectation of uptake* towards a proposition *p*, just in case she has a non-zero credence that her audience will entertain *p* as a result of her utterance. In a typical case, a speaker will have varying degrees of expectation towards the uptake of many, many propositions. Of course, the speaker's credence towards many of these propositions will be so negligible as to be practically irrelevant to the communicative exchange in which she is engaged. For example, even if Smith has a .003 expectation of uptake with regard to the proposition that Jones has an excellent collection of antique pens, this credence will play virtually no role in his communicative plan, or any further plans he might make contingent on how his audience interprets him. Moreover, even if Smith cannot rule out the possibility that his audience will interpret him in this surprising way, he is most certainly not 'open', in any sense, to be interpreted as such; that his audience will entertain that proposition is not, as it were, a 'live possibility' by his lights.

The notion of an agent treating a possibility as 'live' in one's practical deliberation is a perfectly intuitive phenomenon. Consider an example, due to Richard Holton, from whom I borrow the term (2009, 29–34). Suppose that a tree has fallen on your car and that you're deliberating about how to remove it. You are considering the following options: (a) moving the tree with a crowbar (but you aren't sure if you are strong enough), (b) with a rope (but this seems difficult given the position of the car), or (c) with a chainsaw (though your chainsaw oftentimes doesn't start). Or, should those three methods fail, (d) calling the telephone company which will, for a fee, move the tree with a towing truck. While you might fully believe the disjunctive proposition that you will succeed in removing the tree by method (a), or (b), or (c), or (d), your credence in that disjunction will almost certainly not be 1. After all, you might – perhaps, with a bit of prompting – have a non-zero credence that the tree will be moved by a freak tornado, or by a group of passing weightlifters. But unlike (a)-(d), these further possibilities are not 'live' for you, as they play no role in your deliberation, or your further plans contingent on the outcome of that deliberation.

While we would ultimately like an account of the psychological facts in virtue of which an agent treats a possibility as 'live' in her planning and deliberation, the reality of the notion to which Holton is appealing is not open to serious doubt. Following Holton, let's say that in those cases in which an agent S takes p as a live possibility, but also takes $\sim p$ as a live possibility, that S *partially-believes* that p.[17] The contrast here is, of course, with *all-out* belief which, Holton argues, requires treating p as a live option in your practical deliberation (or at least being disposed to do so), should you make plans contingent on whether p, but not treating $\sim p$ as a live option. In Holton's case, you all-out believe that you will succeed in removing the fallen tree by one of the methods (a)-(d), but you (merely) partially-believe that you will move it by method (a), partially-believe that you will move it by method (b), and so on.[18]

Returning to the issue of how to understand the openness of communicative intentions, here is my initial suggestion:

(Openness) In producing u, S's communicative intentions are *open* just in case for some audience A, and feature Ψ of u, there is a class of propositions α such that (i) for any member of α, p, S partially-believes that A will entertain p, at least in part, as a result of recognizing that $\Psi(u)$, and (ii) S (all-out) believes, and intends, that A will entertain some one, or more, of the members of α at least in part, as a result of recognizing that $\Psi(u)$.

As per our discussion in Section One, in cases of implicature that exhibit openness, this Ψ-feature will include that the speaker said what she did in producing u.

Until this point I have spoken without elaboration of 'candidate' propositions. I will now reserve that label for those propositions in a particular communicative exchange that have both of the features (i) and (ii) in (Openness). In slogan form, we can now say that, in such cases, *a speaker's communicative intentions are open with respect to which one, or more, candidate propositions her hearer entertains as a result of her utterance.*

Likewise, while a speaker does not actually intend to communicate any particular candidate, she will have a kind of intention-*like* attitude towards each of the candidates with respect to which her communicative intentions are open. [19] As it might prove helpful to have a label for this distinctive kind of pro-attitude, we can say that in those cases in which a speaker's communicative intentions are open, she *endeavors to communicate* each candidate without outright intending to communicate any one of them.[20]

Where does this discussion of openness leave us with respect to Heck's problem of specificity? Unfortunately, I suspect that the foregoing discussion has just made the problem of specificity seem all the more puzzling. If it is determinately the case that Smith did not mean any specific proposition, or set of propositions, in our case, *then what did he mean?* Can the claim that Smith meant something by his utterance (and that this utterance was thus meaningful) be preserved in light of the problem of specificity?

After all, one of the reasons we have reached this impasse is the intuition that Smith must have meant 'something' other than what he literally said in his letter. What kind of thing might this something be, if not a proposition? To be told that there is a range of candidate propositions with respect to which Smith's communicative intentions are open, just seems to make the problem worse. How can we possibly accommodate this openness by taking Smith to have meant any one specific thing – proposition, or otherwise?

Perhaps we should consider giving up (Content) and allow that among the things we mean are, as John McDowell (2006) puts it, *unspecific contents*.

5. McDowell on unspecific contents

Heck's 2006 paper is a contribution to a *Festschrift* on the work of John McDowell. Both Heck's contribution and McDowell's response are primarily focused on the much larger issues of how, and to what extent, language use is rational. In his response, however, McDowell briefly addresses Heck's worry regarding the specificity of what is implicated. Unsurprisingly, McDowell agrees that in the case of Smith, it would be 'wrong to specify what is implicated' as any particular proposition, including the ones that we have been calling 'candidates'. What *is* surprising is his positive suggestion that we might take 'what is implicated by the author of the taciturn testimonial, not as any one particular proposition from among those and perhaps other candidates, but as **an unspecific content in the general area indicated by those propositions**' (ibid., 46, bold mine). Elaborating:

> A Gricean implicator can intend that her audience take her to have a belief in a general area rather than a belief individuated by its having some particular proposition as its content, so here... what is implicated can be unspecific. There is

[contra Heck] no obvious connection between communicative intentions, in the Gricean sense, and specificity of content. (ibid., 46–47, bracketed material mine).

McDowell is correct on both fronts. First, what a speaker means, and implicates, **can** be unspecific. And second, insofar as communicative intentions in 'the Gricean sense' are characterized along the lines of (Meaning), the thesis that what we mean is a proposition is an independent assumption that we should, in light of the foregoing discussion, seriously consider giving up.

The crucial question is what might these 'unspecific contents' be such that they could be of help to the problem of specificity.

Elsewhere, I have argued that we must allow that the things we mean, and assert are, at least in some cases, a certain kind of 'unspecific content', which I call a *proposition-type* (Buchanan 2010). Roughly put, proposition-types are *properties of propositions*. While a proposition might, of course, have any number of different properties – for example, the property of being about Sean Hannity, the property of being true only if pigs can speak, and so on – some such properties are of more general interest for the theory of meaning and communication than others. For example, consider the sentence-type displayed in (2):

(2) Each dish is almost ready.

If we think of the context-invariant meaning of a sentence-type as a constraint on what a speaker can assert in uttering it, we might, at some level of linguistic representation, think of the 'standing' meaning of (2) as a the entity represented in (2)*:

(2)* ([each x: Dish(x) & __(x)] (Almost-ready$_w$(x))

Where the gap in (2)* can be thought of as placeholder for a domain restriction on 'each dish'; the subscript on 'almost ready' is a placeholder for a specification of a contextually relevant respect or 'way' in which the objects quantified over are not ready. Metaphysically speaking, (2*) represents a property instantiated by all and only those propositions which can be 'constructed' from it via providing values to these gaps; whereas, the proposition that some dishes *in the most famous restaurant in Brooklyn* are not ready *for the visiting food critic*, is a token of this proposition-type, *the proposition that beets are tasty* is not. These proposition-types (i.e., context-invariant sentence meanings) should be familiar, if perhaps, only by other names.

Notice that among those propositions that are of the type displayed in (2*), there are many other properties that might be of interest in a particular context. In a particular communicative exchange, some propositions of this type will, for example, have the further properties of being of relevant and informative with regard to some or other question under discussion. For example, suppose that I utter (2) to you after a long afternoon of preparing dishes for our party later that night. In this case, presumably the 'constructible' proposition above concerning the restaurant in Brooklyn will not have either of these properties, though the proposition that each dish *we have been preparing* is almost ready *for our guests* might.

So far, none of this should be objectionable to the theorist who accepts both (Meaning) and the thesis that the things we mean must be propositions, (Content). Such a theorist could accept this picture of the meaning of the relevant sentence-type, but just add the further requirement that when a speaker speaks literally – that is, when she asserts something – she must mean/intend to communicate some one, or more, *propositions* which are of the relevant type. But for reasons sketched in Section Two, this further requirement is not plausible.

What *is* plausible is that there are successful communicative exchanges in which the speaker has (intuitively) asserted something, even though there is no specific proposition 'consonant' with the standing meaning of the sentence-type uttered which she could reasonably expect her audience to uptake. Rather, there will be a range of truth-conditionally non-equivalent candidate propositions, no one of which the speaker meant, but any one of which is such that the speaker would be satisfied were her audience to entertain it on the basis of her utterance. In such cases, insofar as there is an 'object' of the speaker's communicative intentions, it is a proposition-type that (i) 'restricts' the standing meaning of the sentence-type uttered in a contextually determined manner and (ii) is consequently instantiated by propositions which are otherwise 'compatible' with the speaker's (potentially vague) preferences and expectations for how her utterance will be understood. On this picture, there need be no proposition that the speaker means, nor is there is any particular proposition that her audience must entertain in order to understand her utterance; rather, the speaker's audience must entertain some one, or more, of the propositions of the intended type – i.e., some one, or more, of the candidates.[21]

Returning to conversational implicature, McDowell writes that a speaker might implicate an 'unspecific content' in 'the general area indicated by' the candidate propositions. I agree, but what kind of thing might an unspecific content be? I tentatively suggest we understand unspecific contents as proposition-types; i.e., properties of propositions. If there is, indeed, any one thing that Smith intended to communicate by his letter, it must be something that is compatible with the openness of his communicative intentions; it must be something compatible with the fact that his audience might fully understand his utterance in any number of equally correct, yet non-equivalent, ways. Proposition-types have some promise for meeting this desideratum.

The suggestion that our meaning-intentions might have unspecific objects as their contents will not be of much help in addressing Heck's problem, unless we can say a bit more regarding the question of how we might determine, and individuate, these unspecific, speaker-meant contents in particular cases. It is precisely at this point that our discussion of openness and candidacy from Section Three pays off. Insofar as Smith meant, or implicated, any one thing, it just is a proposition-type instantiated by all, and only that class of propositions with respect to which Smith's meaning-intentions are open. That is, if the relevant candidates are $P_1, \ldots P_n$, we can simply identify *the* object of Smith's meaning-intentions with the property $\lambda q[q = P_1$ or $q = P_2$ or $\ldots q = P_n]$ allowing (i) that it will likely be vague exactly what the candidates are, and (ii) that the speaker's audience must entertain one or more of the propositions that has that property if they are to understand the speaker's utterance.

More generally, I speculate that in **any** case in which it seems appropriate to appeal to 'unspecific contents' – i.e., cases in which the speaker intuitively means something, despite there being no proposition she can reasonably believe her audience will uptake – it is natural to take the speaker to have meant a property instantiated by all and only the candidate propositions, her utterance being understood only if her audience entertains some one, or more, of those candidates as a result of her utterance.

Unspecific contents, understood along the foregoing lines, should seem considerably less exotic that they might have sounded initially. If the notion of a candidate proposition is cogent, so too are unspecific contents in our sense; the latter can be fully individuated and determined by the former. Moreover, it should be clear that, fundamentally, it is the candidate propositions, and the speaker's cognitive attitudes towards them, that will be doing all of the theoretical work; the role of a proposition-type is merely to serve as *the* thing the speaker meant in cases such the ones we have been considering. If an agent's performing an act of speaker-meaning entails that there is something she meant then we should happily allow that unspecific contents are among the things we mean.[22]

6. Conclusion

In Section One, we began with the four theses: (Meaning), (MIA), (Content), and the B-I Constraint. Heck's problem of specificity shows that the conjunction of these theses is untenable. Heck suggests that we give up (MIA), but, for several reasons – including the fact that the problem seems to arise even in cases of literal speech – this suggestion does not get to the heart of the matter. Following McDowell, I propose that we consider giving up (Content) and try to make sense of the idea that a speaker might mean, and implicate, 'something' even if it is determinately the case that there is no specific proposition that she intends for audience to entertain. Towards that end, I suggested that we might take McDowell's 'unspecific contents' to be proposition-types, allowing that, in some cases, a speaker might intend, and, moreover, reasonably believe, that her audience will come to entertain some one, or more, proposition(s) of that type. On this proposal, we keep (Meaning), (MIA), and the B-I Constraint by giving up (Content).

Heck's problem of specificity calls our attention to an extremely important and ubiquitous feature of our meaning-intentions – namely, their potential for openness. A speaker's meaning-intentions can be open with respect to how exactly she is understood, from amongst a range of non-equivalent options; she can endeavor to communicate many propositions without outright intending to communicate any. I have suggested that this openness might be accommodated in the McDowell-inspired account of unspecific contents. But even if this suggestion should ultimately fail, this much is certain: **any** viable response to the problem of specificity – and for that matter, any plausible theory of meaning and communication – must accommodate the openness of our communicative intentions. Moreover, I am confident that further progress on this front will require us to draw upon insights from action theory, as well as from work in formal epistemology concerning how we should understand degrees of belief together with their relation to belief, intention, and other of our folk psychological attitudes.[23]

Notes

1. For discussion of the role of this assumption in Grice's work on conversational implicature, see Neale (1992), and Davis (1998) and (2007). For skepticism concerning whether Grice in fact held the assumption see Saul (2001) and (2002). Though I disagree with Saul's interpretation of Grice for the reasons given in Davis (2007), I am sympathetic to the case she makes for the utility of a 'normative' notion of implicature that she develops in those papers. See fn. 14.
2. A *particularized implicature* is a case in which a speaker implicates p by saying q, but where normally saying q is not a way of implicating p.
3. For a discussion of such worries, see Davis (1998, 122–124). A central issue in Davis's critical discussion of Grice's account concerns an underlying disagreement regarding the kinds of intentions required for speaker-meaning. Davis argues that Griceans confuse *speaker-meaning* with *intending to communicate* and this confusion has led to undesirable consequences for the Gricean account of conversational implicatures. As against the Gricean, Davis (2003) argues that S meant that p just in case S performed a publicly observable action e with the intention that e be an undisguised indication that S has an occurrent belief that p (see (ibid. 54–56) for some important qualifications). Though I am sympathetic to Davis's suggestion, in Buchanan (2012) I argue that he has failed to provide sufficient conditions for speaker-meaning, and I offer some reasons for thinking that what is needed is an account that is more along the lines of (Meaning) below. See Davis (2013) for a response. This disagreement notwithstanding, even proponents of Davis's account of speaker-meaning will be able to find something of interest in what follows concerning the nature of our *communicative* intentions.
4. The conditions in (Meaning) are inspired by the excellent discussion of the problems and prospects for Grice's original attempts at analyzing speaker-meaning in Neale (1992).
5. Of course, the relevant feature *could* be just about anything, especially in non-linguistic cases. To borrow an example from Schiffer (1982), one agent might growl at another intending to communicate that she is angry, in part, in virtue of the fact that the sound she produced resembles that of an angry dog.
6. See Grice (1957, 1989, 86–117) and Schiffer (1972, 1982). For critical discussions of the conditions in (Meaning) see Sperber and Wilson (1995, Chapter 2), Davis (2003, Chapters 4 and 5), and Schiffer (1987, Chapter 9).
7. Proponents include Grice (1971), Harman (1976), Ross (2009), and Velleman (1989). See Setiya (2009), Section Five, and Holton (2009), Chapter Two for an overview of some of the problems and prospects for the B-I Constraint.

8. A similar point holds for the expression of intentions in action: Q: 'What are you doing?'; A: 'I am reaching for a martini'.
9. The B-I Constraint might also help explain why 'it is rationally impermissible to intend an end while failing to intend what one regards as a necessary means to this end' (Ross 2009, 243). See Ross for an excellent discussion of 'cognitivist' accounts of intentions and practical reason.
10. See the discussion in Section Three of communicative 'endeavorings' inspired by Holton's critical discussion of the B-I Constraint in his (2009). As I understand the thesis to be a conceptual truth regarding *intending*, I take Holton's critical discussion of the B-I Constraint as establishing the need for intention-*like* states not constrained by belief in the way suggested. In what follows, I selectively borrow from Holton's discussion, but I encourage the reader to consult his book for his views on the topics. See footnote 19.
11. See Bach and Harnish (1979) and Bach (2011) for discussion of this point.
12. Sperber and Wilson (1986a, 1986b, 1987, 1995) also use the term 'weak-implicatures', but they mean something different by that expression than does Heck. At the core of their account is the principle that (roughly) the correct interpretation of a speaker's utterance is one that optimizes its relevance, where 'an ostensive stimulus is optimally relevant to an addressee if and only if it has enough contextual effects to be worth his attention and puts him to no unjustified processing effort in accessing them' (Sperber and Wilson 1987, 743). When S's audience 'has to recover [p] in order to satisfy himself that the speaker has observed the principle of relevance', S has 'strongly' implicated p (Sperber and Wilson 1986a, 383). However, 'an utterance ... can be given an interpretation consistent with the principle of relevance on the basis of different ... sets of premises and conclusions has a wide range of weak implicatures' (Sperber and Wilson 1986b, 549). For critical discussion of the relevance-theoretic approach, see Davis (1998, 73–74, and 98–107) from which I borrow the foregoing quotes (ibid. 73). Also see fn. 22.
13. Notice, for example, that (a) could be true, and (c) false, even though in the actual world the dishes for their guest are the dishes they have been working on all afternoon.
14. Cf. Saul's (2001) and (2002) discussion of 'audience-implicature'. In her (2001) and (2002), Saul makes an important case in favor of also allowing for a more normative notion of 'implicature' – roughly put, a speaker implicates p in this normative sense if she has done what is required of her in uttering what she did (i.e., being cooperative, etc.) to make p available to her audience (even if they fail to entertain p).
15. Here I am in agreement with McDowell's discussion of Heck's proposal; see (2006, 46–47).
16. I am assuming that in order for an agent to entertain a disjunction, she must entertain each of the disjuncts.
17. What is the relationship between this practical attitude of partial-belief and the quantitative notion of credence discussed by Bayesians and others? Holton claims that we might 'think of credences as the partial beliefs that an agent would have if they were quite unconstrained by cognitive limitations; or, more plausibly, as the partial beliefs that they do have when their cognitive limitations are irrelevant' [2009, 33–34]. Holton suggests that cases of simple, idealized betting behavior illustrate one kind of circumstance in which such cognitive limitations are 'largely irrelevant' (ibid., 34). Here, Holton has in mind the kind of idealized betting behavior that is sometimes appealed to in trying to illicit an agent's credence function – for example, an agent's responses to question concerning how much she would be willing to pay for chance to win a given prize, if a certain outcome obtains.

18. Like Holton, I am somewhat skeptical that we can analyze or give a reduction of all-out belief in terms of formal, quantitative models of credence [2009, 25–28]. I am not, however, fully convinced that it cannot be done. See Sturgeon [2008], for example, for an encouraging discussion of the 'Lockean thesis' according to which all-out believing that p is analyzed in terms of having a credence in p that exceeds some (contextually determined, and potentially vague) threshold r.
19. Holton (2009) suggests that there are two ways we might understand the notion of a 'partial intention':

> We might say that an agent has a partial intention whenever they merely have a partial belief in its success. Or we might say that it is essential to partial intentions that they be only a proper part of an overall plan, i.e., that they be accompanied by alternative partial intentions to achieve the same end. (ibid., 35)

Holton pursues the latter strategy; we are pursuing the former. I suspect that we will ultimately need both notions in the theory of meaning and communication. In work in progress, I argue that appealing to Holton's favored notion of a partial intention helps us better understand the relationship between a speaker's illocutionary intentions in making an utterance and her overarching perlocutionary plan.

20. I borrow the term 'endeavoring' from Bratman's critical discussion of the 'simple view' according to which doing A intentionally requires intending to do A (Bratman 1987). Bratman offers an example concerning an ambidextrous video game player, S, who is simultaneously playing two games, one with each hand, where the goal of each is to hit on a target on the screen with a missile. The games are linked in such a way that it is impossible to simultaneously hit the targets on screen A and on screen B, and S knows this. If S succeeds in hitting target A, we would say that she did so intentionally; likewise, for B. If the simple view were correct this would entail that S acted with the intention of hitting A, and also with the intention of hitting B. But if one can rationally intend to F & rationally intend to G, only if one can rationally intend to F & G, we should conclude that S rationally intended both to hit A and to hit B. But as she knows it impossible to hit both, she can't rationally intend any such thing. Bratman concludes that S, despite acting intentionally, acted with neither the intention to hit A or the intention to hit B. Though she didn't intend to hit A, and she didn't intend B, she 'endeavored' to hit both.
21. Notice that this suggestion is compatible with the fact that in those cases in which your communicative intentions are open, your audience will likely entertain numerous propositions of the relevant type as a result of your utterance. Moreover, when your audience is appropriately sensitive to the openness of your communicative intentions, he will be sensitive to the fact that there are multiple, non-equivalent ways in which he might correctly interpret your utterance. In this sense, your audience's interpretation of your utterance should (in the relevant cases) also exhibit openness. I am inclined to think that when a speaker produces an utterance with open meaning intentions, her audience *must* be sensitive to the openness if she is to understand the utterance, but I will not argue for that here.
22. The view sketched in this section is inspired (in part) by Sperber and Wilson's seminal (1986a and 1995) account of communicative intentions on which:

> S means a set of propositions {I} by u iff, for some audience A, S produces u intending (i) to make {I} manifest, or more manifest, to A, and (ii) to make (i) mutually manifest to S and A. (ibid., 58 and 61)

where (1) a proposition is 'manifest' to an agent to the extent that she is 'capable at that time of representing it mentally and accepting its representation as true or probably true' (ibid.: 39), and (2) a speaker must have a representation of {I}, but not necessarily each of the members thereof – 'any individuating description will do' (ibid., 58). On this account, we give up both (Content) and (Meaning). While I sympathize with the motivations Sperber and Wilson offer for this account, their proposal is too weak. Suppose, for example, you ask me what there is to do in Budapest, and I throw a guidebook, which I have never read, into your lap. There is a set of propositions – *the ones in the Budapest guidebook* – such that by my production I have knowingly made it (and its members) more representable to you, and more mutually representable to us both. But in what sense, if any, did I mean *the propositions in the guidebook*? Likewise, take some proposition in the book – say, *that the hand of the first king of Hungary is in the Basilica in Pest*. Is that proposition among the things I meant? What is needed, I submit, is that each proposition in the relevant set {I} be a 'candidate' in the sense sketched in Section Four, and that (as such) the speaker must (minimally) endeavor that each such proposition be entertain*ed*, and not merely entertain*able*.

23. Earlier versions of this paper was presented were presented at the University of Barcelona, the University of St. Andrews, the University of Manitoba, and the University of Toronto during 2012–2013. I would like to thank the audiences on those occasions for extremely helpful feedback. In particular, questions from Derek Ball, Jacob Beck, Herman Cappelen, Esa Diaz-Leon, Nate Charlow, Josep Macià, Aidan McGlynn, Francois Recanati, Jennifer Saul, and Chris Tillman were especially helpful in me to get clearer on these issues. I am also deeply indebted to the editors of this volume, David Hunter and Gurpreet Rattan, as well as David Beaver, Josh Dever, Sinan Dogramaci, Hans Kamp, Manuel García-Carpintero, Bryan Pickel, Gary Ostertag, Mark Sainsbury, Neil Sinhababu, David Sosa, and Zsófia Zvolenszky for very helpful discussion. I am especially thankful to both Gary and Zsófia for the extensive comments they gave me on an earlier draft of this paper. All of the normal qualifications and disclaimers are in order. Much of this paper was completed during my stay at the University of Barcelona, funded by the Spanish Ministry of Education, during the 2011–2012 academic year. I would like to thank the members of the LOGOS group in Barcelona for their hospitality and the Ministry for its generous support.

References

Bach, K., and M. Harnish. 1979. *Linguistic Communication and Speech Acts*. Cambridge, MA and London: MIT Press.
Bach, K. 2011. "Meaning and Communication." In *Routledge Companion to the Philosophy of Language*, edited by D. G. Fara and G. Russell. Routledge.
Bratman, M. 1987. *Intention, Plans, and Practical Reason*. Cambridge, MA: Harvard University Press.
Buchanan, R. 2010. "A Puzzle about Meaning and Communication." *Noûs* 44 (2): 340–371.
Buchanan, R. 2012. "Meaning, Expression, and Evidence." *Thought* 1 (2): 152–157.
Davis, W. A. 1998. *Implicature: Intention, Convention, and Principle in the Failure of Gricean Theory*. Cambridge University Press.
Davis, W. A. 2003. *Meaning, Expression, and Thought*. Cambridge University Press.

Davis, W. A. 2013. "Meaning, Expression, and Indication: Reply to Buchanan." *Thought* 2 (1): 62–66.
Davis, W. A. 2007. "How Normative is Implicature?" *Journal of Pragmatics* 39: 1655–1672.
Grice, H. P. 1957. "Meaning." *Philosophical Review* 66: 377–388.
Grice, H. P. 1971. "Intention and Uncertainty." *Proceedings of the British Academy* 5: 263–279.
Grice, H. P. 1989. *Studies in the Way of Words*. Harvard University Press.
Harman, G. 1976. "Practical Reasoning." *The Review of Metaphysics* 29 (3): 431–463, Reprinted in *The Philosophy of Action*, A. Mele (ed.), Oxford University Press, 1997: 149–177.
Heck, R. 2006. "Reason and Language." In *McDowell and his Critics*, edited by C. Macdonald and G. Macdonald, 22–45. Oxford: Blackwell.
Holton, R. 2009. *Willing, Wanting, Waiting*. Oxford University Press.
Holton, R. forthcoming. "Intention as a Model for Belief." In *Rational and Social Agency: Essays on the Philosophy of Michael Bratman*, edited by M. Vargas and G. Yaffe. Oxford University Press.
Neale, S. 1992. "Paul Grice and the Philosophy of Language." *Linguistics and Philosophy* 15: 509–559.
McDowell, J. 2006. "Response to Heck." In *McDowell and his Critics*, edited by C. Macdonald and G. Macdonald, 45–49. Oxford: Blackwell.
Ross, J. 2009. "How to be a Cognitivist about Practical Reason." *Oxford Studies in Metaethics* 4: 243–281.
Saul, J. 2001. "Review of *Implicature: Intention, Convention, and Principle in the Failure of Gricean Theory* by Wayne Davis." *Noûs* 35: 630–641.
Saul, J. 2002. "Speaker Meaning, What is Said, and What is Implicated." *Noûs* 36: 228–248.
Schiffer, S. 1972. *Meaning*. Oxford University Press.
Schiffer, S. 1982. "Intention-Based Semantics." *Notre Dame Journal of Formal Logic* 23 (2): 119–156.
Schiffer, S. 1987. *Remnants of Meaning*. Bradford Books.
Setiya, Kieran. 2011. "Intention." In *The Stanford Encyclopedia of Philosophy (Spring 2011 Edition)*, edited by Edward N. Zalta, <http://plato.stanford.edu/archives/spr2011/entries/intention/>.
Sperber, D., and D. Wilson. 1986a. *Relevance: Communication and Cognition*. 2nd Ed. Oxford: Blackwell.
Sperber, D., and D. Wilson. 1986b. "Loose Talk." *Proceedings of the Aristotelian Society* 86: 153–171, Reprinted in S. Davis (ed.), *Pragmatics: A Reader*, pp. 540–549. Oxford: Oxford University Press. (1991).
Sperber, D., and D. Wilson. 1987. "Précis of *Relevance: Communication and Cognition*." *Behavioral and Brain Sciences* 10: 679–754.
Sperber, D., and D. Wilson. 1995. *Relevance: Communication and Cognition*. 2nd Ed. Oxford: Blackwell.
Sturgeon, S. 2008. "Reason and the Grain of Belief." *Noûs* 42: 139–165.
Velleman, J. D. 1989. *Practical Reflection*. Princeton, NJ: Princeton University Press.

THEORETICAL ALTERNATIVES TO PROPOSITIONS
Propositions and higher-order attitude attributions
Kirk Ludwig

Philosophy Department, Indiana University, Bloomington, IN

An important objection to sententialist theories of attitude reports is that they cannot accommodate the principle that one cannot know that someone believes that p without knowing what it is that he believes. This paper argues that a parallel problem arises for propositionalist accounts that has gone largely unnoticed, and that, furthermore, the usual resources for the propositionalist do not afford an adequate solution. While non-standard solutions are available for the propositionalist, it turns out that there are parallel solutions that are available for the sententialist. Since the difficulties raised seem to show that the mechanism by which sentential complements serve to inform us about attitudes and about sentence meaning does not depend on their referring to propositions, this casts doubt on whether talk of propositions should retain a significant theoretical role in the enterprise of understanding thought, language and communication.

—But suppose the word "beetle" had a use in these people's language? — If so it would not be used as the name of a thing. The thing in the box has no place in the language-game at all; not even as a something: for the box might even be empty. — No, one can 'divide through' by the thing in the box; it cancels out, whatever it is.

§293 *Philosophical Investigations*

1. Introduction

In a tradition that stretches back to Frege and Russell, propositions have been taken to be abstract, structured sentence meanings that represent intrinsically and are the timeless bearers of truth-values. In virtue of this they are supposed to play their various roles in our theories of thought and meaning. They are (said to be) the referents of names ('Verificationism'), and demonstratives ('That's unusual'), the values of variables ('Some mathematical hypotheses may never be proven'), the bearers of modal properties ('That there is a greatest prime is impossible'), the meanings of declarative sentences ('"Snow is white" means that snow is white'), and the objects of assertion, belief, and other attitudes ('I've sometimes believed as many as six impossible things before breakfast'). In this tradition, propositions are explanatorily fundamental. They represent intrinsically. They are that from which everything else that represents inherits its representational powers. They are grasped through a sui generis intellectual faculty. Recent objections have cast doubt on whether anything could play all of the roles traditionally identified for propositions, and especially whether as abstracta they can represent intrinsically (Jubien 2001). Defenders have still sought to retain them for at least many of their traditional roles without having them take up the burden of being explanatorily prior to thought and language (King 2007; Soames 2010; Hanks 2011). When we depose propositions from their traditional central explanatory role, the question arises whether they need to play any explanatory role in our understanding of thought and language. I have argued elsewhere that there is no need to invoke propositions in semantic theory, nor any point in doing so (Ludwig 2002; Lepore and Ludwig 2005; Lepore and Ludwig 2006; Lepore and Ludwig 2011, 2007). There is no need since a compositional semantics can be given without invoking propositions as part of the ontology of the theory. There is no point because a recursive assignment of propositions to sentences on the basis of assignments of their constituents to subsentential expressions does not *in itself* give us any insight into how to interpret of the sentences. We need a mode of referring to or denoting the propositions assigned that codes for sentences of a language we already understand. Once that is recognized, and that propositions are not essential to the recursive machinery required for the effect, they are correctly seen as the fifth wheel of semantics, turning endlessly but contributing only the illusion of progress. I will not repeat these arguments, but turn to what may seem to be the last legitimate role for propositions in semantics, namely, as part of the ontology of everyday language, things we treat our terms as referring to, or denoting, by way of various names or descriptions, and by way of the sentential complements of verbs and operators that create intensional contexts. In this paper, I restrict attention to propositions as the referents or denotations of sentential complements in attitude and indirect discourse reports (henceforth 'attitude reports'). I will advance a skeptical thesis about propositions in this connection. I will not argue that propositions are not the referents of sentential complements in attitude reports, but I will argue that they do not have the advantage, as many have thought, over the view that sentential complements refer not to propositions expressed by sentences encoded in sentential complements, but to those sentences understood relative to the context, that is to say, sententialism about attitude attributions.

The initial brief for propositions being the referents or denotations of sentential complements in these contexts is that we can report what people say and think indifferently in any suitably rich language. Sententialists about attitude reports aim to show that this is not an obstacle to taking the sentential complements to refer to sentences provided that we are sophisticated enough about how we tell the story about the relation between the semantic properties of the complement sentence in the context of use and the state or utterance of the person we are reporting about, and are reasonably sophisticated about the point of translation. I have written about some of these matters in earlier work (Ludwig and Ray 1998). I focus here though on a particularly important objection introduced originally by Stephen Schiffer in his 1987 book *Remnants of Meaning*, and repeated, in more trenchant form, in his 2003 book *The Things We Mean*, which he suggests is insurmountable. The objection focuses on problems that emerge in higher-order attitude attributions (§3). I will call this the Higher-order Attitude Objection. This is an objection to which I think there has been no completely adequate response to date. What I want to do is to show that a parallel puzzle arises for the propositionalist. I think that the usual resources for the propositionalist fall short, for interesting reasons, which have not been generally noticed. In particular, I argue that the usual appeal to something in the ballpark of a Fregean mode of presentation of a proposition must meet two requirements. It must present its object in a way that is constitutively sufficient for grasping its object, and it must be plausible to assign it to sentential complements of attitude reports. I argue that it is implausible that anything satisfies the first requirement and that in any case nothing can simultaneously satisfy both, because anything that satisfies the first must make the appearance of the sentence in the complement inessential to how they work in the language, but it is in fact essential. That is not the end of the story, but once we see what further solutions are available, we can see that analogous solutions are available for the sententialist. The nature of the solution and the parallels for the sententialist help us to see the cash value of talk of propositions. The positive solution for the sententialist shows, in any case, that we do not need propositions to understand how higher-order attitude attributions do the work that they do for us. At the end of the day, propositions seem not to do much explanatory work, even in this more limited role, for a reason that is connected with their dispensability in semantic theory, or so I shall argue.

In §2, I sketch a sententialist account and highlight certain features of it. In §3, I develop the Higher-order Attitude Objection. In §4, I show that it is not resolved by treating propositions as the referents of sentential complements. In §5, I consider mode of presentation responses in the context of a traditional Fregean theory, Jeff King's (2007) neo-Russellian account, which derives the structure of propositions from the LF structures of sentences that express them, and the Hanks-Soames Cognitive Realist approach (Hanks 2011; Soames 2010), which identifies propositions with structured cognitive event types. In §6, I sketch a solution that focuses on the relation of propositions to attitude characterized. In §7, I consider approaches that bite the bullet and offer a pragmatic explanation of the intuitions that give rise to the problem. In §8, I show that the sententialist has responses that parallel those for the propositionalist. In §9, I draw some morals.

2. A sententialist theory

Sententialist theories treat attitude verbs as relating their subjects to sentences.[1] For example, in [1], 'that the earth moves' is treated as designating the contained sentence.[2]

[1]   Galileo believed that the earth moves.

Thus, where 'ϕ' ranges over sentences of English, the general rule is given in [R].

[R]   (∀ϕ)(Ref(⌜that ϕ⌝) = ϕ).

Then [1] is given context relative truth conditions, as in (1a), where 'u' is a variable ranging over speakers, 's' over states, 't' and 't'' over times, and '$t' < t$' means 't' is earlier than t' (henceforth I will suppress the universal quantifiers for 'u' and 't').

[1a]   (∀u)(∀t)('Galileo believed that the earth moves' is true taken as if spoken by u at t iff (∃t': $t' < t$)(∃s)(s is a belief state of Galileo at t' and interpreted relative to u at t that the earth moves indicates-the-content-of s)).

The quantifier over states is motivated independently by the need to handle adverbs such as 'firmly' on analogy with adverbs for event verbs.[3] I abbreviate 's is at t a belief state of x' as 'belief(s, t, x)'. I abbreviate 'is true taken as if spoken by u at t' as 'is true(u, t)'. An attitude report is first-order if its complement sentence is not an attitude report. It is second-order if its complement sentence is first-order, and so on. The relation expressed by 'x interpreted relative to u at t indicates-the-content-of y' in the first-order case requires that x have the same representational content as y. The story is more complicated for higher-order attributions. See (Ludwig 1998, 148–150) for details. I abbreviate 'indicates-the-content-of' as ' ≅ ', and further abbreviate 'interpreted relative to u at t that the earth moves ≅ s' as ' ≅ (s, that the earth moves, u, t)'. [1a] may then be rewritten as [1b].

[1b]   'Galileo believed that the earth moves' is true(u, t) iff (∃t': $t' < t$)(∃s) (belief(s, t', Galileo) and ≅ (s, that the earth moves, u, t)).

The expression 'that the earth moves' refers to a sentence but its semantic function is not exhausted by the fact that it refers to 'the earth moves' as in the case of the classical account of quotation names, for it has a feature quotation names lack. One can understand a quotation name without understanding the expression it names.[4] However, one cannot understand the noun phrase 'that the earth moves' unless one understands 'the earth moves'. For its function in the language depends on auditors understanding the embedded sentence, even though this does not figure in the truth conditions. For example,

'La Terre si muove' in Italian means that the earth moves

is true just in case the complement sentence means the same as 'La Terre si muove', but it fails in its purpose if the auditor fails to understand the complement sentence. Uses of quotation marks to represent dialogue in a novel, or to indicate that one is quoting another's words, function similarly. This ensures that one cannot understand (1) without understanding the complement sentence and so being in a position to know what Galileo believes.

Most objections to sententialism have been answered.[5] I draw attention to one relevant to the discussion below, namely, that sententialist analyses fail the Church-Langford translation test, according to which the translation of the analysans must be the analysis of the translation of the analysandum (Church 1950). The charge is that translation preserves reference, but the analysis of the English sentence, 'Galileo said that the earth moves', for example, refers to an English sentence, while the analysis of the Italian translation, 'Galileo detto che la Terra si muove', refers to an Italian sentence. By now it is well-known that this objection relies on a false assumption, namely, that translation, in the ordinary sense in which it is accepted that 'Galileo detto che la Terra si muove' translates 'Galileo said that the earth moves', invariably preserves the referents of referring terms. Tyler Burge made this point long ago (1978). He observed that in translating sentences such as 'This sentence is false', and in translation of dialogue, the purposes of translation often require translations that do not preserve the referents of referring terms. The case of the translation of dialogue is an especially apt. We use direct rather than indirect speech in reporting dialogue. To report correctly we must report the actual words spoken. Yet in translation we substitute the best translation of the quoted material because the function of the original in its linguistic setting requires understanding the mentioned expressions. In ordinary translation practice preserving that function trumps preservation of reference. The point extends to attitude reports, for if the sententialist is right, conveying the content of an attitude is achieved by way of reference to a particular sentence, understood in context. Preservation of the main function requires a similar reflexive reference to a sentence in the target language, and so a shift of reference.

3. Higher-order attitude attributions and the insurmountable objection

Schiffer's objection to sententialism is that that it fails to secure a principle that any adequate account of attitude reports must underwrite, namely, that one cannot know that someone believes that *p* without knowing what it is that he believes (Schiffer 2003, 47):

> ... while each version of sententialism will have its own unique flaws, there is one they all share, and I doubt that it is surmountable. A theorist who eschews contents in favour of things that merely have content must say that a person will believe one of those things S just in case she is in a belief state that has the same content as S. For example, if believing that the earth moves is standing in the belief relation to the sentence 'the earth moves', then my utterance of 'Galileo believed that the earth moves' will be true just in case Galileo was in a belief state whose content matched that of 'the earth moves'. The problem every sententialist account of propositional attitudes confronts comes to this for the example at hand: no one can know that Galileo believed that the earth moves without knowing *what Galileo believed,* the content of his belief, but one (e.g., a monolingual speaker of Hungarian) can know that Galileo was in a belief state whose content was the same as the content of 'the earth moves' without having any idea of what Galileo believed, of the content of his belief.

We can spell this out in reference to sentences [1]–[4]. We stipulate that Zoltán is a monolingual speaker of Hungarian. We consider a particular time T and speaker Σ to fix contextual parameters.

[1] Galileo believed that the earth moves.
[2] Zoltán knows that Galileo believed that the earth moves.
[3] $(\exists t': t' < T)(\exists s)(\text{belief}(s, t', \text{Galileo})$ and $\cong (s, \text{that the earth moves}, \Sigma, T))$.
[4] Zoltán knows that $(\exists t': t' < T)(\exists s)(\text{belief}(s, t', \text{Galileo})$ and $\cong (s, \text{'the earth moves'}, \Sigma, T))$.

Zoltán is told (in Hungarian) and thereby comes to know that [∗].

[∗] $(\exists t': t' < T)(\exists s)(\text{belief}(s, t', \text{Galileo})$ and $\cong (s, \text{'the earth moves'}, \Sigma, T))$.

Prior to this he has never been told, or otherwise learned, that Galileo believed that the earth moves.

Imagine token utterances of [1]–[4], which we refer to below with these labels, by Σ at T. Let us use the expression 'expresses the same thing as' as holding between two token utterances (or two sentences or a token utterance and a sentence) just in case it would be appropriate to say that they express the same proposition.[6] Then the argument against [3] correctly analyzing of an utterance of [1] goes as follows (to avoid confusion, I use numerals without brackets to refer to premises).

1. If [3] is the analysis of [1], then [4] expresses the same thing as [2].
2. If [4] expresses the same thing as [2], then [2] is true iff [4] is true.
3. [4] is true, though [2] is not.
4. Therefore, by 2 & 3, [4] does not express the same thing as [2].
5. Therefore, by 1 & 4, [3] is not the analysis of [1].

Premise 3 is true because [4] reports the new knowledge that Zoltán acquires when he is told [∗], but it does not seem, intuitively speaking, that learning what [∗] expresses is sufficient for him to learn that Galileo believed that the earth moves, and he has not otherwise learned that.

As it stands, the argument is unsound. On the sententialist analysis, [4] does not express the same thing as [2], and so premise 1 is false. The analysis of [2] is [5]. However, the analysis of [4] is [6].

[5] $(\exists s)(\text{knowledge}(s, T, \text{Zoltán})$ and $\cong (s, \text{that Galileo believed that the earth moves}, \Sigma, T))$.
[6] $(\exists s)(\text{knowledge}(s, T, \text{Zoltán})$ and $\cong (s, \text{that } (\exists t': t' < T)(\exists s)(\text{belief}(s, t, \text{Galileo})$ and $\cong (s, \text{'the earth moves'}, \Sigma, T)), \Sigma, T))$.

Since [7] ≠ [8] (that is, the complements are not the same),

[7] that Galileo believed that the earth moves.
[8] that $(\exists t': t' < T)(\exists s)(\text{belief}(s, t', \text{Galileo})$ and $\cong (s, \text{'the earth moves'}, \Sigma, T))$.

[2] and [4] do not express the same thing, for they refer to different sentences.

Unfortunately, this is only a temporary solace for the sententialist. For if what [7] and [8] refer to (the embedded sentences), taken relative to Σ and T, express the same thing, then [5] is true iff [6] is true, and [6] is true iff [4] is true, and, hence, [2] is true iff [4] is true. The argument then can be repaired as follows.

1. If [3] is the analysis of [1], then [5] is the analysis of [2].
2. If [5] is the analysis of [2], then [2] is true iff [5] is true.
3. What [7] refers to expresses the same thing as what [8] refers to.
4. If what [7] refers to expresses the same thing as what [8] refers to, then [5] is true iff [6] is true.
5. If [3] is the analysis of [1], then [6] is the analysis of [4].
6. If [6] is the analysis of [4], then [4] is true iff [6] is true.
7. Therefore, by 1–6, if [3] is the analysis of [1], [2] is true iff [4] is true.
8. [4] is true though [2] is false.
9. Therefore, by 7 & 8, [3] is not the analysis of [1].

We return to the objection to sententialism in §8. Before we do, I want to ask whether the propositionalist is any better off. I begin with a straightforward account, on which complements of attitude reports are treated as directly inserting the proposition they pick out into the proposition expressed by the embedding sentence, where the problem shows up immediately. Then I turn to what the propositionalist can to say to avoid the difficulty.

4. Direct reference to propositions in higher-order attitude attributions

The propositionalist treats expressions of the form 'that p' as referring to or denoting propositions rather than sentences. For now I assume that 'that p' simply introduces into the proposition expressed by the sentence containing it the proposition expressed by 'p' in use. This is expressed in the follow reference rule.

[R'] $(\forall \phi)(\forall u)(\forall t)(\forall x)(x$ is the proposition expressed by u's use at t of ϕ in ⌜that ϕ⌝ iff Ref(⌜that ϕ⌝, u, t) $= x$).

The relativization to speaker, time and use of the sentence is required to handle context sensitivity. While the referent is given relative to a description, all that is introduced into a proposition containing the term is the proposition it refers to. In this respect, it functions like Kaplan's 'dthat[the F]' (Kaplan 1989). We can then analyze [1] as [1c].

[1c] 'Galileo believed that the earth moves' is true(u, t) iff $(\exists t': t' < t)(\exists s)$ (belief(s, t', Galileo) and $\cong$ (s, Ref(that the earth moves, u, t))).

Since 'that the earth moves' is a referring term, the question arises how it is that someone who is told 'Galileo believed that the earth moves' knows what Galileo believed, for he must not only grasp the proposition that Galileo is being related to but also know that it is that proposition he grasps that Galileo is being related to. The answer is that he understands the sentence used to pick out the proposition. Since the rule determining the referent of the complement goes by way of the embedded sentence, and we understand the sentence in understanding the complement, if we understand 'that the earth moves', then we know what proposition it picks out in a way that guarantees that we both grasp it and know that as grasped it is what 'that the earth moves' picks out. Thus, no one can understand [1] without knowing in the relevant sense what it is that Galileo is said to believe.

Now we develop an argument against the propositionalist parallel to the argument against the sententialist. For simplicity, I assume that 'that the earth moves' is not context sensitive. This allows us to discharge the relativized reference clause in [1c]. First we observe that if [3′] gives the interpretive truth condition for [1], as it does according to [1c], then it would seem that [5′] gives the interpretive truth condition for [2].

[1] Galileo believed that the earth moves.
[2] Zoltán knows that Galileo believed that the earth moves.
[3′] $(\exists t': t' < T)(\exists s)(\text{belief}(s, t', \text{Galileo}) \text{ and } \cong (s, \text{that the earth moves})$
[4′] Zoltán knows that $(\exists t': t' < T)(\exists s)(\text{belief}(s, t', \text{Galileo}) \text{ and } \cong (s, \text{dthat}(\text{the proposition expressed in English by 'the earth moves'})))$.
[5′] Zoltán knows that $(\exists t': t' < T)(\exists s)(\text{belief}(s, t', \text{Galileo}) \text{ and } \cong (s, \text{that the earth moves}))$.
[7′] $(\exists t': t' < T)(\exists s)(\text{belief}(s, t', \text{Galileo}) \text{ and } \cong (s, \text{that the earth moves}))$.
[8′] $(\exists t': t' < T)(\exists s)(\text{belief}(s, t', \text{Galileo}) \text{ and } \cong (s, \text{dthat}(\text{the proposition expressed in English by 'the earth moves'})))$.
[9] That the earth moves = dthat(the proposition expressed in English by 'the earth moves').

[7′] and [8′] are the embedded clauses in [4′] and [5′] respectively. [9] is underwritten by [R′]. Now consider Zoltán again. Zoltán does not know (we want to say) that Galileo believed that the earth moves. Suppose, however, Zoltán is told, in Hungarian, and comes to know on that basis what [8′] expresses. This then gives us [4′]. Since [9] is true, [7′] and [8′] express the same proposition. Thus, [5′] follows from [4′], and [2] from [5′], if [1c] provides the interpretive truth conditions for 'Galileo believed that the earth moves'. However, we agreed that in the circumstances [2] was false. By the same token, then, this propositionalist analysis of attitude reports is incorrect. Let us now lay out the argument in a way that shows the parallel with the argument against the sententialist.

1′. If [3′] is the analysis of [1], then [5′] is the analysis of [2].
2′. If [5′] is the analysis of [2], then [2] is true iff [5′] is true.
3′. [7′] expresses the same thing as [8′].
4′. If [7′] expresses the same thing as [8′], then [4′] is true iff [5′] is true.
5′. Therefore (by 1′–4′), if [3′] is the analysis of [1], [2] is true iff [4′] is true.
6′. [4′] is true though [2] is false.

7'. Therefore (by 5' & 6'), [3'] is not the analysis of [1]. 1'–4' here correspond to 1–4 in the argument at the end of §3, while 5'–7' correspond to 7–9 in that argument. The three basic options for the propositionalist are to reject premise 3', 4' or 6'. We take up each in turn.

5. The modes of presentation response

Rejecting premise 3' requires denying that 'that the earth moves' and 'dthat(the proposition expressed in English by 'the earth moves')' contribute the same to what propositions are expressed by sentences containing them in corresponding argument places, at least in attitude contexts. It is natural to say that the solution lies simply in explaining what more 'that the earth moves' contributes than barely the proposition it designates. This turns out to be less promising than it initially looks. I will consider resources for rejecting 3' available in three sorts of theories of propositions: (a) traditional Fregean theories, (b) neo-Russellian views that treat propositions as a certain sort of abstraction over sentences (King 2007), and (c) views that treat propositions as complex cognitive act types (Soames 2010; Hanks 2011). The Fregean response faces two, I think ultimately insurmountable, difficulties, and there are, I will argue, versions of one or the other or both of these difficulties for each the other views I take up.

(a)   Fregean Theories

First, we consider a Fregean approach on which 'that p' following an attitude verb contributes to the proposition expressed by the containing sentence not the proposition it refers to but *a mode of presentation* of the proposition.

What is the relevant mode of presentation? It is natural to say that it is given by the description 'the proposition expressed by "p" in English' (why else is the sentence there?). This won't do, however, because it would involve Zoltán believing [8''].

[8''] $(\exists t': t' < T)(\exists s)(\text{belief}(s, t', \text{Galileo})$ and $\cong (s$, the proposition expressed by 'the earth moves' in English)).

It is clear that if he does not understand English, this will give him no insight into what Galileo believes in the relevant sense, and the fact that the proposition is in part about the English sentence 'the earth moves' means that the propositionalist is saddled with the problems he charges the sententialist with besides.

The Fregean needs, for every proposition p, (i) a mode of presentation of p grasp of which *guarantees grasp of the proposition,* which (ii) plausibly can be said to be *the sense of expressions of the form 'that p'*. Can anything do the job? I believe that it is doubtful that anything satisfies the first requirement and that even if there were something that did, it could not simultaneously satisfy the second.[7]

Is there a knockdown argument against the claim that there are Fregean modes of presentation of propositions grasp of which suffices for grasping the propositions they present? I do not know that I can give one. But I think we can raise some serious doubts about it. A mode of presentation of an object, on the classical Fregean view, is distinct from its object, if any. It is one way among others of presenting it. In general, having any sort of epistemic attitude toward the object of a mode of presentation (assuming it exists) is not required to have the mode of presentation of it. Grasp of the mode of presentation is one thing. Standing in any relation to its object other than thereby thinking about it (if it exists) is another. Some objects of modes of presentation are themselves graspable: concepts and propositions. But still grasp of a mode of presentation of such an object is logically distinct and independent from grasp of its object. If grasp of the mode of presentation is logically independent of grasp of its object (if any), then it can occur without grasp of what it presents. In this case, one could grasp whatever Fregean proposition is expressed by [1] without knowing in the relevant sense what Galileo believed. What it seems that we need is a mode of presentation that at the same time functions like Russellian acquaintance is supposed to function, so that nothing about the essential nature of the object presented (its representational properties in particular) would remain hidden from the person to whom it is so presented. But Russellian acquaintance, itself not entirely unmysterious, is in any case supposed to be direct and unmediated. That is what distinguishes it from thinking of an object via a mode of presentation. Thus, it seems that the Fregean requires something that has one nature and another incompatible with it.[8]

The Fregean must deny, for at least one class of modes of presentation of objects that are themselves graspable, that one can grasp the mode of presentation without grasping the object that it presents. The grasp of the mode of presentation must be logically dependent on grasp of the object presented, and as presented by that mode of presentation (so that as grasped one knows it as the object of the mode of presentation). One might insist that there are such modes of presentation and that our mistake is to try to think of how the object is presented separately from grasping it. They are, it might be said, primitive, fundamental, unanalyzable, and sui generis. One might insist on this precisely because it is what the Fregean needs and because one is committed to the Fregean view. But at this point, it is a 'we know not what.' We have been told nothing about it except that it is a thing that plays a certain role. So far as that goes, there might be many things that could play that role. If so, which of them do we attach to that-clauses? We have, I submit, no positive idea about what this could be, and so no way of answering whether there would be one or many, or what one is actually attached to sentential complements.[9]

That a theory needs something to play a role that we are hard pressed to make sense of and of which we have no positive idea would provide us with a reason to think it existed only if either (i) there were no other way to understand how we can think about thoughts while entertaining them or (ii) there was no other way to understand how we can understand what thoughts are attributed to others (in the relevant sense) than by an abstract mode of presentation of them that constitutively guaranteed grasp of its object. With respect to (i), however, there is another way: by entertaining a thought and at the same time thinking about it, where entertaining the thought is primary, and thinking about it is a reflexive attitude toward the thought one is already entertaining. The manner by which we think about the thought does not have to secure grasp of its content because thinking it already suffices. So the fact that we can think about thoughts whose contents at the same time we grasp does not show that there is anything that satisfies the needs of the Fregean. With respect to (ii), there is also another way, namely, by using a vehicle for referring to the proposition that incidentally to how it secures its referent ensures that one grasps the referent (as the referent). This is, in fact, the way sentential complements actually seem to function, by using a sentence we understand to draw attention to a proposition, i.e., the one the sentence we understand expresses.[10]

One could, if one liked, call the act of thinking about a thought which one is at the same time thinking and so whose content one thereby grasps a 'mode of presentation' of it. But we might as well say that grasp of a mode of presentation of an instance of walking can suffice for walking because we can define the act of thinking about a walking which one is at the same time engaging in as a special 'mode of presentation' of it. Try attaching this mode of presentation of a walking to an expression by convention. It presents only a single walking and only the walker (its agent) could grasp it, and so it fails the test of intersubjectivity. In any case, it is evident that this tells us nothing interesting about a connection between ways of thinking about things and their occurrence, or, mutatis mutandis, about ways of thinking about things and understanding them.

Turning to the next point, even if there were such a thing as a mode of presentation grasp of which guaranteed grasp of its graspable object, it could not plausibly be thought to be the sense of expressions of the form 'that p'. For if it were, it would make the appearance of 'p' in 'that p' an accident of spelling. The point is not that the Fregean could not choose to assign the relevant mode of presentation to 'p'. The Fregean can choose to assign the relevant mode of presentation to any expression. The point is that, for that very reason, it would not be necessary on the Fregean view. It is dispensable. There could be no objection to replacing 'that the earth moves' with, say, 'Bob', attaching the relevant sense to it by stipulation.[11] However, it is obvious that it is crucial (nondispensable) to the way 'that p' fulfills its function that 'p' appears in it. Moreover, it is crucial that we understand the words that appear there in their usual sense for the complement to inform us in the relevant way about what someone believes (etc.).[12] Contrast 'John accepts Logicism' with 'John accepts that mathematics is reducible to logic'. The mechanism by which the latter directs our attention to the right proposition is as the proposition the sentence expresses (in use), and our understanding the sentence is likewise crucial to our coming to see (in the relevant sense) what John accepts.

It is hardly an accident that we use a sentence (in the context) alike in content to the state we are attributing. From the design standpoint, it is an obvious device to use in specifying attitude contents. The sentence itself, and our understanding of it, then, should play a role in our understanding of what proposition is designated by a complement of the form 'that p', if we take 'that p' to refer to propositions. But the most straightforward way of implementing this in a mode of presentation, as we have seen, leaves us with the problem of higher-order attitude attributions. We want the sentence somehow to play its role as an anchor for reference to a proposition without it or its constituents being thought about. But since the role is one in a mode of presentation, this is impossible.

(b) Propositions as Abstractions over Sentences.

It might be thought that more recent theories of propositions provide additional resources. With this in mind, let's turn to Jeff King's theory of structured propositions (King 2007, ch. 2). King's account is Russellian in spirit. It accepts structured propositions that contain as constituents properties, relations and individuals. However, it rejects the tradition assumption that propositions have their representational properties independently of and prior to language and thought. Instead, King sees propositions as deriving both their structure and representational properties from sentences and their users. In particular, King holds propositions to be a certain species of fact about there being sentences with certain syntactic structures in some actual language whose constituent expressions have certain semantic values in some possible context and whose structures encode in the language semantic information about the relation among the constituents that determines under what conditions the sentences are true. The idea is that two sentences relative to any two languages (ignoring context for now) that are to 'express the same proposition' each suffice to witness the relevant fact, which thereby captures what is common to all sentences that express the same proposition. The structure of a proposition is derived from a common LF structure (logical form) of the sentences that witness it. Such facts are to represent not intrinsically, but in virtue of speakers treating them as representing, thus reversing the traditional direction of explanation. We can call these k-propositions. For our purposes what is important is the idea is that the constituents of [7$'$] and [8$'$], 'that the earth moves' and 'dthat(the proposition expressed by "the earth moves")', respectively, do not contribute the same thing to the propositions expressed by each because 'that the earth moves' is a term with internal structure that itself is relevant to the structure of the proposition expressed by the sentence in which it appears. This makes the appearance of the sentence in the complement crucial to the work it does. This is, in a certain respect, a Fregean move, since it has the effect of distinguishing 'ways of presenting propositions' when they are the subjects of propositions. The question is whether it can secure grasp of the k-proposition picked out and avoid explicit reference to a sentence or to the constituents of sentences.

Both of these are problems, but I will focus on the second, which is particularly salient for an approach like King's. We take 'that the earth moves' as our example. Let 'R' express the relevant syntactic relation between 'the earth' and 'moves' in 'the earth moves'. 'The earth' contributes its semantic value, the earth, to the proposition. The predicate 'moves' contributes the property of moving. We'll ignore tense. Then what 'that the earth moves' refers to is:

[F] the fact that there is a sentence S, containing expressions e_1, e_2, in a language L, such that $R(e_1, e_2)$ in S in L, and in L the semantic value of e_1 is the earth, and the semantic value of e_2 is the property of moving, and $R(e_1, e_2)$ in L encodes the instantiation relation.

We say that $R(e_1, e_2)$ encodes the instantiation relation in L iff a sentence consisting of e_1 and e_2 in R is true in L iff the semantic value of e_1 instantiates the semantic value of e_2. What 'that the earth moves' has to do is to determine R and the semantic values of the expressions it relates. And this is where the trouble lies. For the only way it can do this is by providing a sample sentence with the right structure and words whose semantic values are the right one's in the right place in the structure. Identifying the right syntactic relation obviously must be done in relation to the sentence in the complement itself. In the case of the semantic values of the constituent expressions, one might think that we can construe the expressions as simply referring to their semantic values. This works for 'the earth', which simply contributes the earth. But 'moves' is not a name of a property, like 'Bob'. We know what property is its semantic value because we understand it. One might suggest that we can construe it to mean 'the property of moving' in this context. But the same problem arises here because it is not an accident of spelling that 'moving' appears in this description (cf. note 9). We understand the word, and that the property is to be the property it attributes, but the understanding that enables grasp of the referred to property does not enter into how the property is picked out. Thus, identifying the syntactic relation and the semantic values crucial for identifying the k-proposition requires reference to the sentence itself in the complement and constituents of it, and we are no better off than the sententialist.

(c) Cognitive Realism

Let's consider a second recent approach to propositions, developed independently by Scott Soames (2010) and Peter Hanks (2011). This approach takes propositions to be structured cognitive acts of predication and function application. It is motivated by the thought that our cognitive capacities are the ultimate source of the representational properties of sentences and propositions, which do not have their representational powers independently of their relations to us. In this respect, the approach is similar to King's. But it differs in treating propositions as independent of language. The proposition that Alfred is rich on this view would be the cognitive event type of predicating being rich of Alfred. Soames calls this the Cognitive Realist account (CR). Whatever its other virtues, I do not think that CR introduces anything new with respect to the present issue. The problem lies not with the kind of object one identifies propositions with, but with the mechanism by which the linguistic vehicles we use to pick them out do so. CR too must reject 3′, 4′, or 6′. If it rejects 3′, then it must maintain that 'that the earth moves' does not merely contribute its referent to the proposition expressed by the containing sentence. What it contributes must be something, however, which enables the person who grasps the containing proposition to grasp the proposition it is about.

It might be thought that CR can secure this in a particularly neat way. For someone who grasps [1], repeated here,

[1]   Galileo believed that the earth moves.

will think the thought that the earth moves in doing so – since this is involved in understanding the complement – and so be acquainted with the proposition it refers to. Thus, it may seem that [1] expresses a proposition grasp of which guarantees grasp of the proposition it is about. Then there could not be any sentence that expressed the same proposition understanding of which did not afford grasp of the proposition to which it relates Galileo.

But the sententialist can make a parallel point: whoever understands [1] understands 'the earth moves', and so is in a position to say what it is that Galileo believes. This doesn't solve the problem for the sententialist because grasping the sentence that appears in the complement is incidental to how the complement refers. The rule that determines the referent makes use of properties of the sentential complement, but grasping the embedded sentence is incidental, and plays no role in how the referent is determined. The same goes whatever the referent is, whether a sentence or a proposition of whatever sort. The referent is located in relation to the sentence in the complement, as the sentence itself, or the proposition expressed by it, or a structure of things derived from the structure of the sentence and the meanings and referents of its parts, or the event type the grasp of which is integral to the understanding of the sentence. However this is spelled out, we will be able to talk about the features of the complement that the rule operates on without it conveying understanding of them. What we are seeking is again a mode of presentation of the proposition that guarantees grasp of it. But if the mode of presentation involves a relation to the sentence itself, we are no better off than the sententialist.

Is there not a further move to be made? The totality of the cognitive acts involved in understanding [1] involves grasp of the proposition to which Galileo is related as the proposition to which he is related. Let us identify the proposition expressed by [1] *with that type*. If grasp of a proposition expressed by [1] involves executing the totality of cognitive acts involved in understanding it, then any sentence which expresses that proposition is such that grasp of it involves grasp of the proposition to which Galileo is related as the proposition to which he is related. The trouble is that the *totality* of the cognitive acts involved in understanding [1] includes recognition of the expressions as English expressions with certain meanings. But then the translation of [1] into Hungarian will not on this account express the same proposition, since its understanding will involve recognition of expressions as Hungarian with certain meanings, not English expressions. Suppose that we identify the proposition with the totality of cognitive acts involved in thinking *what [1] expresses* rather than understanding

[1]. But our question was whether what [1] expresses suffices for grasp of the proposition to which it relates Galileo, and if so, how. So this is not a solution. We need to understand how it could express something grasp of which suffices for grasping the proposition it is about and without any essential reliance on reference to complement expressions. We need the same thing that the Fregean needed.

Do we not actually, however, think about what others think in a way that enables us to know in the relevant sense what it is that they think? Isn't this a proof that there are propositional constituents which are about propositions but which pick them out in a way that suffices for grasp of them? Yes, and no, respectively. We can think about what others think and know in the relevant sense what they are thinking, how they see the world, in doing so. But the mechanism is just to entertain the proposition itself while thinking about it as the one that gives the content of someone's thought. This is in fact the mechanism that sentential complements invoke. Using a sentence in a language one understands in the complement forces one to (as we say) entertain the proposition it expresses. But this is incidental to how it picks out the proposition. One's entertaining the proposition plays no role in locating the proposition to think about. What the complement adds to the content of [1] is what it contributes to determining the conditions under which it is true, namely, how it secures a proposition the embedding sentence is about. It is not a condition on referring to or designating a proposition that one entertain it, nor is any way of picking out a proposition *ipso facto* to entertain it.

This suggests a strategy, namely, to refer to a proposition at a time as the (or this) proposition one is thinking then. One succeeds in referring to a proposition only if one is in fact entertaining it. This respects the point that the way we have of presenting it does not itself suffice. But this can't be the right account of how 'that the earth moves' designates the proposition it does. It cannot be that for a speaker u and time t, a use of 'that the earth moves' designates the proposition the speaker is entertaining at t, for this does not constrain it to be the proposition expressed by the use of 'the earth moves' in 'that the earth moves'. But if we incorporate reference to the use of 'the earth moves' by saying that it designates the proposition u is thinking at t which is expressed by 'the earth moves', understood relative to u at t, then appeal to the proposition u is thinking at t is superfluous, and in any case we are no better off than the sententialist. In addition, relativizing it to the speaker guarantees only that the speaker entertains the proposition. But in application to [2], it is Zoltán whose entertaining of the proposition we are concerned with, not the person reporting what he knows.

6. Complicating the relation by which the proposition gives the attitude's content

The next option is to reject premise $4'$. If the propositionalist takes this option, then he must take the context following the attitude verb to involve a condition to the effect that, if the proposition referred to itself involves a proposition x which functions to give the content of an attitude, and x is presented using a term of the form 'that p', then the proposition, in being presented as giving the content of an attitude, is presented to the subject of the embedding attitude sentence in a way that involves his grasp of it. This would require treating 'indicates-the-content-of' as having an additional argument place for the subject, Z, '$\cong (s, x, Z)$' (where, as a reminder, 's' is the variable whose values are belief states and 'x' is the variable whose values are propositions – so we have x indicates-the-content of s relative to Z). However, this must be sensitive to not just the referent (or designatum) of the expression that appears in the place of 'x' but also the expression used to refer, for we want this result when we use a term of the form 'that p'. The position of 'x' is then similar to that of 'Giorgione' in Quine's example, 'Giorgione is so-called because of his size'. It must play a dual role. That is, (i) the term δ that appears in the position of 'x' provides a proposition as an argument for the underlying relation and (ii) δ itself is an argument for another position in the underlying relation to ensure the subject grasps any proposition p referred to by a term τ in δ in thinking of p as providing the content of an attitude, *provided that* τ is a term of a special sort. With this in mind we can explicate '$\cong (s, x, Z)$' as follows where a canonical term is of the form 'that p' ('x' is a schematic letter in the following, not a variable).

$\cong (s, x, Z) =_{df} x$ indicates-the-content-of s and for every y in 'x' such that y refers to a proposition p in an argument place a in 'x', if y is a canonical term for referring to propositions, then Z apprehends p in s in a in a way adequate to grasp p.

'Z apprehends p in s in a' means that Z in s thinks about p in a position corresponding to a in 'x'. We must keep track of 'positions' in the representational state because the same proposition may be thought about in different roles in the same thought. When we require Z to apprehend p in s in a in a way adequate to grasp p, we require Z to think about the proposition in being in that state (in that position) in a way that associates the proposition he thinks about with grasp of it. But this does not require that what it is in virtue of which he thinks about it be *itself* what suffices for grasp of it. A model for this would be entertaining the proposition that the earth moves while thinking of it as what Galileo believed. This would suffice intuitively for the truth of [2]. It would in turn suffice for this for Zoltán to be told what Galileo believed using a translation of [2] into Hungarian. For then he would relate Galileo to a proposition expressed by a sentence which he understands. The sentence used anchors the reference, and since it is understood, Zoltán entertains the proposition he thinks of as what Galileo believed while entertaining it. But Zoltán's being told [8'] would not suffice for this.

7. Biting the bullet

Finally we consider rejecting premise 6'. For this, the propositionalist needs a way of explaining away the inclination to judge that in the circumstances described [4′] is true though [2] is false. The natural way to do this is to argue that the inclination we have to judge that [2] is false involves confusing the literal content of [2] with a standard conversational implicature of it, which is not carried by [4′]. The account might plausibly run as follows. Suppose that [1c] gives the interpretive truth conditions for [1]. The proposition expressed could be believed by someone who does not know, in the relevant sense, what Galileo believed – he does not know how Galileo saw the world. However, we know that anyone who asserts [1] will know what Galileo believed because he uses a term to pick out the proposition that gives the content of Galileo's belief that guarantees, given how its referent is determined, that the speaker does grasp the proposition and that it is the proposition which gives the content of Galileo's belief. When we attribute beliefs to people, we tend standardly to attribute them using sentences that we believe they would use to express them, if this is possible. This is because (a) often what people say is one of our best sources of information about what they believe and (b) using the sentences they would use conveys useful information about them, for how they would express their beliefs often plays a role in our anticipations about what they will do in various circumstances, particularly in response to what others say. This is especially important when different directly referring terms may have different sorts of information associated with them, as in the case of proper names. Given this, in the case of second-order belief attributions, we will standardly implicate that the subject would report his belief using the sentence (or a sentence constructed from it by replacing indexicals to preserve reference across context shifts) which we use in the complement, which, if he speaks our language, will in turn convey the information that he is in a position to know, in the relevant sense, what the content of the person's belief is. Now, in the case of an attribution to someone who does not share the language of the speaker, the implication that he would report it using the sentence the speaker uses (or a relevantly similar sentence in the speaker's language) will be canceled. However, minimally, it will be implicated that he would report it using a sentence which is the best translation of the sentence the speaker uses (appropriate adjustments being made in context sensitive terms), and this will include that he would report it using a sentence in his language in which the term that refers to the proposition plays the same semantic role as the term in the reporter's language. This then will carry the information that the other speaker knows, in the relevant sense, what the content of the person's belief is about which he has a belief. Thus, as this explanation goes, an utterance of [2] carries the information that the speaker knows, in the relevant sense, what Galileo believes, while an utterance of [4′] does not. When we judge that an utterance of [4′] is true in the circumstances while an utterance of [2] is not, we are noting the difference in the truth values of the total content conveyed, including the implicatures, and, in particular, that an utterance of [2] will standardly convey that Zoltán knows, in the relevant sense, what Galileo believes, even though it does not state this as part of its literal content.

8. Parallels for sententialism

The options open to the sententialist in responding to the argument at the end of §3 are to reject premise 3, 4 or 8, repeated here along with [5]–[8]. [13]

3. What [7] refers to expresses the same thing as what [8] refers to.
4. If what [7] refers to expresses the same thing as what [8] refers to, then [5] is true iff [6] is true.
8. [4] is true though [2] is false.
[5] ($\exists s$)(knowledge(s, T, Zoltán) and $\cong$ (s, that Galileo believed that the earth moves, Σ, T)).
[6] ($\exists s$)(knowledge(s, T, Zoltán) and $\cong$ (s, that ($\exists t'$: $t' <$ T)($\exists s$)(belief(s, t', Galileo) and $\cong$ (s, 'the earth moves', Σ, T)), Σ, T)).
[7] that Galileo believed that the earth moves.
[8] that ($\exists t'$: $t' <$ T)($\exists s$)(belief(s, t', Galileo) and $\cong$ (s, 'the earth moves', Σ, T)).

(Reminder: here '$\cong$ (s, x, u, t)' means 'x interpreted relative to u at t indicates-the-content-of s'.) Given how we characterized 'expresses the same thing as', namely, as capturing the idea of two sentences expressing the same proposition without the ontology of propositions, if we take 'that the earth moves' and 'the earth moves' to both be directly referring terms that refer to 'the'⌢'earth'⌢'-moves', then, as long as we allow that the analysis of the logical form of a sentence expresses the same proposition as the analysandum, fixing any contextual parameters needed for determining truth conditions, we must accept that premise 3 is true. It is of course open to the sententialist to hold that 'that the earth moves' does not contribute just its referent. For example, the sententialist could hold that it is a description. This is the parallel to the mode of presentation response for the propositionalist. It is just that it is transparent in this case that it does not help, because the sententialist is overtly committed to the complement clause designating the complement sentence, and so however we understand the term on analysis, it seems that what it expresses could be expressed in Hungarian, but the monolingual speaker who grasps it could fail to see how Galileo saw the world. But if the argument of §4 is correct, the propositionalist is no better off, though the difficulties are easier to overlook. This leaves for consideration premises 4 and 8. The options available to the sententialist in rejecting 4 or 8 parallel those available to the propositionalist in rejecting 4' and 6'.

If we reject 4, we must hold that we cannot intersubstitute in the place of 'x' in '$\cong$ (s, x, u, t)' on the basis of the arguments being alike in what they express, and we must explain this in a way that is connected with why [4] can be true while [2] is false. [2] is judged to be false because Zoltán intuitively does not know what Galileo believes. The difference in the terms used to refer to the sentences that fix the content must somehow be involved in this. We employ a maneuver here analogous to the one we employed for the propositionalist, though with one additional twist. If Zoltán were a speaker of English, we would say that, in asserting [2], we attribute to Zoltán a belief about the content of Galileo's belief to the effect that it is the same in content as 'the earth moves' taken relative to the context. But we also want to ensure that in thinking of the sentence in relation to Galileo's belief he understands it. This suffices for him to know in the relevant sense what Galileo believed. To generalize to the case in which Zoltán is not a speaker of English, we need to invoke a relation between the sentence we use and some sentence of Zoltán's which serves likewise to fix the content of Galileo's belief and which he understands in thinking about it. This will require an additional argument place in ' $\cong (s, x, u, t)$ ' for Zoltán, Z, ' $\cong (s, x, u, t, Z)$ '. Then we can explicate ' $\cong (s, x, u, t, Z)$ ' as follows (with 'x' being as before a schematic letter).

$\cong (s, x, u, t, Z) =_{df} x$ indicates-the-content-of s (relative to u and t) and for every z in 'x' that occupies an argument place a in 'x', if z is a canonical term for referring to sentences, then there is a sentence σ and a term y of Z's such that y refers to σ and $\approx (\text{Ref}(z), \sigma, Z)$ and Z apprehends σ in s in a in a way is adequate to understand σ.

Here ' $\approx (a, b, x)$ ' is true iff a in English translates b relative to x, in the ordinary sense of translation, which allows for reference shifts of various sorts to preserve the function of the original in the translation, as we noted at the end of §2. We understand 'Z apprehends σ in s in a' to mean that Z in s thinks about σ in a position corresponding to a in x. When we require Z to apprehend σ in a way adequate to understand it, we require Z to think about it in being in that state (in that position) in a way that associates the sentence he thinks about with understanding of it. This does not require that the way he picks it out itself suffice for understanding. A model for this is thinking about the sentence 'the earth moves' by way of being presented with the sentence itself which one understands. For Zoltán, being told what Galileo believed using a translation of [2] into Hungarian would suffice. For in that case the way of referring to the sentence that gives the content involves being presented with it and he understands the sentence. Being told [*] in Hungarian, however, does not suffice for this.

The last option is to reject premise 8. This requires giving an explanation of the inclination to judge that [2] is false while [4] is true compatible with rejecting [8]. As in the case of the corresponding move by the propositionalist, it seems that the natural, and perhaps only, way to do this is to argue that we are responding to a false implicature of [2] rather than its literal truth value. Again, there is a natural story to tell on the assumption that [1b] gives a correct account of the truth conditions of [1]. Against a standard background practice of attributing beliefs to others using sentences they would use, or the best translations into our language of sentences they would use, there will be a standard implicature in the case of second-order belief attributions, e.g., of an assertion of [2], that the subject of the attitude knows, in the relevant sense, what Galileo believes. For it will be assumed that he would use a sentence in his language with a complement that functions semantically in the way that 'that the earth moves' does in English and is otherwise a best translation of it, which would suffice for him to understand the sentence that is used to indicate the content of Galileo's attitude. This implicature will be absent in the case of an utterance of [4]. Thus, we judge that what is conveyed by [2] is false in the circumstances though what is conveyed by [4] is true. Yet, on this account, the literal truth of [2] and [4] are the same, and the divergence in judgments arises from our attending to the whole content standardly conveyed and not just to literal content.

9. Conclusion

My goal has been to question the utility of propositions in explaining how attitude attributions do their work by arguing that an important objection to sententialism raises a parallel problem for propositionalist accounts as well. The problem arises from an interplay of views about the indicates-the-content relation and the objects it relates states and utterances to and how they are picked out. The basic problem is that, if attitude reports relate subjects to something that has or is a representational content, it seems someone could know someone was so related without knowing what he believed, wanted, etc. The natural response is to appeal to modes of presentation. But there are two problems with this. First, the mode of presentation has to be a mode grasp of which guarantees grasp of its object, but it is mysterious what mode of presentation of a proposition could guarantee grasp of it. A mode of presentation is wanted that involves *entertaining* the proposition designated. But entertaining and thinking about a proposition are logically distinct and independent acts. The only way around this would appear to be to locate a proposition in part by reference to one's own act of entertaining it. Second, whether or not we can make sense of a mode of presentation of a proposition grasp of which suffices for grasp of its object, any adequate account of the role of sentential complements must recognize that the words used after a complementizer are not there as an accident of spelling. They are used to locate what we relate the person's attitude to in giving its content, and our understanding of the words in the sentence is evidently central to their function as well. The upshot is that a 'linguistic mode of presentation' that uses or codes for a sentence we understand is essential to the work that sentential complements do for us in conveying what others think. This leaves us with two responses to the Higher-order Attitude Objection: make truth conditions of attitude attributions employing sentential complements sensitive to the form of the expression used, or bite the bullet and accept one can know the proposition expressed by an attitude report with a sentential complement without knowing what it is that the person to whom the attitude is attributed believes, etc., and argue that the inclination to judge otherwise is to be explained as a response to a conversational implicature. The propositionalist can avail himself of either response. However, both of these options are also open to the sententialist. In light of this and the fact that understanding the sentence in the complement is the mechanism by which attitude sentences illuminate for us how others see the world, the idea that sentential complements refer to propositions seems to contribute nothing to our understanding of the work that language does. It might still be maintained that, even if a sententialist account is adequate to the work actually carried out by such attitude attributions, everyday language still is committed to sentential complements designating one or another style of proposition. But even if that were so, that would not suffice to give talk of propositions a role in explaining how we communicate about each other's attitudes. For were there no such things, but only talk about them, no essential function of language would be disturbed. This is connected in a straightforward way with the inutility of propositions in the theory of meaning, for the same problem arises in attributions of knowledge of meaning: what it is for someone to know what an expression means cannot be captured just by relating him to a proposition that relates an expression to any object as such. In this case too there is an essential reliance on understanding a sentence that is to indicate the content of the sentence whose meaning is being given. I suggest that this casts doubt on whether talk of propositions should retain a significant theoretical role in the enterprise of understanding thought, language and communication.

Notes

1. I draw on the account in (Ludwig 1998). I assume attitude reports are relational, but this is also a presupposition of the puzzle that I want to explore.
2. For convenience I focus on 'that'-clauses. With some more circumlocution the discussion can be extended to other sentential complements which encode sentences without exhibiting them fully in surface structure.
3. See (Schein 2012; Ludwig 2010) for overviews.
4. This point has been urged also by (Burge 1978; Higginbotham 1991, 2006; Seymour 1992).
5. See (Ludwig 1998) for a list with replies; for a different approach, see (Higginbotham 2006).
6. I have in mind the equivalence relation among utterances that propositionalists have in mind when they are willing to say that the utterances express the same propositions. This does not signal or presuppose commitment to propositions.
7. Cf. Kripke 2013, 258–261. Kripke says it must be 'revelatory,' showing what the referent is, but the cash value in this case is that grasp of the mode of presentation must suffice for grasp of what it presents.
8. Perhaps it is *exactly* acquaintance that provides what the Fregean needs. Here is a suggestion by Kripke:

   > My suggestion ... is that Frege, like Russell, has a doctrine of direct acquaintance. Every time we determine a referent, we are introspectively acquainted with how the referent is determined, and that is the corresponding sense. And our introspective acquaintance with this sense gives us a way of determining it, and of referring to it, and this is the indirect sense. (Kripke 2011, 271)

   The idea is that if we think that p, which on Frege's view refers to a truth value, we are acquainted with how we determine it. This 'how we determine it' is to be identified with a mode of presentation of the truth value, i.e., the thought expressed by 'p', i.e., its sense. Being acquainted with how we determine the truth value of the thought that p 'gives us a way of determining it' in turn, which is a mode of presentation of the thought (proposition) itself.

   It is not quite clear how we are to think about acquaintance giving us a way of determining what we are acquainted with. I think the idea is that acquaintance

247

itself is a kind of thinking about an object, and so something of the sort that plays the right role. I will assume this is the intent. Then either acquaintance with the proposition is mediated by a mode of presentation or it is not. Suppose it is mediated by a mode of presentation (and put aside the worry that this undercuts the idea that it is acquaintance that is involved). Then the mode of presentation must be sufficient for grasp of its object or it will fail to meet the needs of the Fregean. But if the relevant notion of acquaintance involves a mode of presentation that must be sufficient for the grasp of its object, appealing to it does not explain how a mode of presentation could be sufficient to grasp a thought, but instead presupposes it. Calling it *acquaintance* doesn't help. Suppose then that it is not. Then, even if it suffices for grasp of the proposition, it does not in fact provide a *sense* that suffices for grasp of its object, for its object is not thought about via a mode of presentation at all. One could say: but can't we say that the sense is given by the phrase (relativized to speaker and time) 'the sense that I am now acquainted with'? Even so: grasp of *that* does not suffice for grasp of the thought one is acquainted with: acquaintance (whatever that is) is what does the trick. (For I could grasp the sense of that expression in someone's mouth without grasping the thought it refers to.) So we have still not found any *account* of a mode of presentation grasp of which suffices for grasp of its object.

Why can't one just say: acquaintance suffices for grasp and is a mode of presentation! The foregoing argument just assumes that if a mode of presentation is involved, it must be something independent of acquaintance because indirect, but we should instead extend our notion of a mode of presentation to cover any way of thinking about an object, even thinking about an object directly. Then if there is a way of thinking about an object (acquaintance) that suffices for grasp of it, we have got what the Fregean, or, at any rate, the propositionalist needs. However, acquaintance is not suitable as a sense to be assigned to an expression in a public language. Obviously, assigning the relation (as a type) to an expression is no help, for to understand 'x is acquainted with y' is not ipso facto to be acquainted with y. And token relations of acquaintance between subjects and objects aren't suitable at all. One might give a rule: the sense of 'that p' as uttered by x at t is the token acquaintance relation obtaining between x at t and that p. But what would it be to 'grasp that sense' (if it is to suffice to grasp its object) except to stand in the relation? But then only x could in principle grasp the sense, and his interlocutors would be at a loss. The situation is not improved if one selects any other pair $<y, t>$. In addition, to come to stand in the relation, one would have to independently figure out what proposition was being referred to and how to grasp it. Appeal to acquaintance in this way does not engage with any mechanism the public language could use to put one in touch with the right objects.

9. In chapter 8 of (Peacocke 2008), Peacocke offers what might be thought to be a way of satisfying the requirement in the idea of a canonical concept of a concept F (can (F)). The idea is that there are ways of referring to concepts that uniquely fix them, namely, by way of their individuative application conditions (The Leverage Account). The general idea is expressed in (*).

(*) For an arbitrary concept C to fall under can(F) is for the fundamental condition for something to fall under C to be the same as the fundamental condition for something to fall under the concept F. (291)

Here we imagine for particular cases that 'the fundamental condition for something to fall under the concept F' to be replaced by a statement of the condition. For example, if 'F' = 'red', then: For an arbitrary concept C to fall under can(red) is for the fundamental condition for something to fall under C to be being red. To put it another way, can(red) = the concept of being a concept the fundamental condition for falling under which is being red. Here the concept of red is deployed in the specification of the condition, and so in deploying the concept can(red) one deploys the concept of red, as in deploying the concept of a red ball one deploys the concept of red, though in the former unlike the latter the concept applies to the concept of red as well. The purpose of this is to describe a way of generating a hierarchy of concepts of concepts by starting with grasp of a first order concept, and tacit knowledge of (*). There is one more thing that we need to add to the story, for what we want is that one thinks about a concept, grasps it, and thinks about it as the one grasped. What is needed for this is that one know that if condition F is the fundamental condition for falling under a concept C, then 'F' expresses C, or the concept one deploys in thinking of the condition F is the concept C. Note that the total effect this is to prompt one to deploy the concept of red and to think of the concept that one there deploys. We are in effect given instructions of the following sort: think of the concept the deployment of which is required in thinking of the condition of being red. This is a clever idea. Does it supply what the Fregean needs?

What is the semantics for 'the condition of being red', for this gives us the sense attached to it. How more specifically does 'being red' pick out the right property or condition? It picks out the property attributed or the condition specified by 'red' in English. But we don't want that to be part of the specification of the concept can(red), because it would make it in part metalinguistic. Moreover, it is clear that using 'red' here as a way of specifying the condition or property is crucial for ensuring that the concept of red is deployed in deploying can(red). Here is a solution: We can say instead that 'being red' refers to that property an object is fundamentally required to have in order to fall under the concept red. Then we avoid the appeal to any metalinguistic element! But now we have another problem. We are now using in the specification of can(red) a term that refers to the concept red (and that is what can(red) is supposed to enable us to do). How does 'the concept red' pick out the concept red? We could say that it picks out the concept that 'red' expresses. But this gets a metalinguistic element back into the content. So we could say that it picks out that concept the fundamental condition for falling under which is being red. But this reintroduces the problem we started with. We could appeal to a mode of presentation of the concept red that suffices for its grasp and attach that to 'the concept red'. But that was what the proposal was supposed to supply us with. The fundamental problem has not actually been avoided, but like the bump under the rug, it has been relocated. Perhaps there are other moves to be made here, but perhaps we do not need to make them. At least, that is what I will suggest in sections 6 and 7 (for the propositionalist) and in section 8 (for the sententialist). We can of course think about a thought that we are entertaining, and we do so by understanding the complement of an attitude report while understanding that it is to refer to what we thereby grasp or understand. In higher-order attitude reports, we need to say that when attributed using that-clauses for content positions, the person to whom we are attributing them grasps what it is that they refer to, or something equivalent, in thinking about them. (There is something similar to this in Peacocke's own suggestion about the semantics of higher-order attributions (see 307).) More details below.

10. In his 'Postscript to "Belief *De Re*"' (Burge 2007, 65–81), Tyler Burge says that a thought about a thought, e.g., the thought that snow is white is true, specifies the thought 'in the that-clause way,' where this is *de re* and 'the *de re* reference feeds directly off immediate understanding of representational contents, the *res*' (70). Of this case, he says that 'the representational thought contents that carry out the *de re* reference are completely conceptualized' and so 'there is a striking relation to a *re*

that goes beyond merely conceiving of it or forming a concept that represents it' (70). Burge goes on to say: 'That-clause forms of representation in thought are individual concepts. They are complex structure- and content-specifying concepts when they name whole representational thought contents. ... Mastery of such an individual concept, of either sort, requires comprehending the representational content that the individual concept names' (70–71). There is, however, something not completely conceptual about the relation to the thought content because it involves 'comprehending the *re*, not merely conceiving of it' (71), and it is for this reason that Burge says that it is a *de re* and not a *de dicto* thought. And, he says, 'This form of *de re* representation is possible only for *res* that are themselves representational contents' (71). Thus, the account appears to hold that there is a mode of presentation (or way of conceiving) of an object that has representational content, namely, a thought content, that suffices for its grasp. Does this help us to understand how a way of conceiving or presenting a thought content could suffice for grasp of it? It does not. It merely describes the idea that we have been trying to make sense of: a way of presenting a proposition that suffices for grasp of it, that is, a mode of presentation of a proposition p grasp of which suffices for the grasp of p (an individual concept whose mastery requires comprehending the content it names). This does not respond to the independence argument, and it does not engage with the fact the mechanism by which that-clauses secure their referents go through our understanding the sentences that appear in them. One could, as I have noted, insist that since the theory requires such individual concepts, they exist, but this is an *ad hoc* defense of the theory, and as there is an alternative account, we should feel no pressure to adopt it.

11. It might be objected that 'that p' is syntactically complex while 'Bob' is not. But, first, we can assign a complex sense to a simple expression, and, second, we could, in any case, introduce a complex expression whose components are not the words in that appear in 'p'.

12. Davidson remarked, 'If we could recover our pre-Fregean semantic innocence, I think it would seem to us plainly incredible that the words "The Earth moves", uttered after the words "Galileo said that", mean anything different ... than is their wont when they come in other environments' (Davidson, 2001, 108). I think this is right, but I think we can say something stronger: if we did not understand those words in their usual sense, what Galileo said would remain opaque to us.

13. Higginbotham (2006, 110–112) offers a response on behalf of the sententialist to Schiffer's objection. If I understand it correctly, it is that the relevant matching-in-content relation the sententialist needs can be construed so that 'that Galileo believed that the earth moves' does not stand in it to, in Higginbotham's phrase, its target truth conditions, as given by the analysis. This would amount, I believe, to rejecting premise 4 in the argument. Perhaps the suggestion I make in the text is a version of what Higginbotham has in mind, for it likewise rejects premise 4. However, it works by treating the position of the complement as sensitive not only to the referent but also the term used to refer to it, and Higginbotham's suggestion appears to be that it is the relation between the referents alone that does the work. Higginbotham does not elaborate, however, and it remains unclear to me how he intends the relation and the relata to be understood so that the right result is obtained.

References

Burge, Tyler. 1978. "Self-Reference and Translation." In *Meaning and Translation*, edited by Guenthner and Guenthner-Reutter, 137–156. London: Duckworth.
Burge, Tyler. 2007. "Postscript to '*Belief De Re*'." In *Foundations of Mind: Philosophical Essays*. Oxford: Oxford University Press.
Church, Alonzo. 1950. "On Carnap's Analysis of Statements of Assertion and Belief." *Analysis* 10: 97–99.
Hanks, Peter. 2011. "Structured Propositions as Types." *Mind* 120: 11–53.
Higginbotham, James. 1991. "Belief and Logical Form." *Mind and Language* 6 (4): 344–369.
Higginbotham, James. 2006. "Sententialism: The Thesis that Complement Clauses Refer to Themselves." *Philosophical Issues: Philosophy of Language* 16: 101–119.
Jubien, Michael. 2001. "Propositions and the Objects of Thought." *Philosophical Studies* 104 (1): 47–62.
Kaplan, David. 1989. "Demonstratives: An Essay on the Semantics, Logic, Metaphysics, and Epistemology of Demonstratives." In *Themes From Kaplan*. Oxford: Oxford University Press.
King, Jeffrey C. 2007. *The Nature and Structure of Content*. Oxford: Oxford University Press.
Kripke, Saul A. 2011. "Frege's Theory of Sense and Reference: Some Exegetical Notes." In *Philosophical Troubles: Collected Papers*. New York: Oxford University Press.
Lepore, E., and K. Ludwig. 2006. "Ontology in the theory of meaning." *International Journal of Philosophical Studies* 14 (3): 325–335.
Lepore, Ernest, and Kirk Ludwig. 2005. *Donald Davidson: Meaning, Truth, Language, and Reality*. Oxford: Oxford University Press.
Lepore, Ernest, and Kirk Ludwig. 2007. *Donald Davidson: Truth-theoretic Semantics*. New York: Oxford University Press.
Lepore, Ernest, and Kirk Ludwig. 2011. "Truth and Meaning Redux." *Philosophical Studies* 154: 251–277.
Ludwig, Kirk. 2002. "What is the Role of a Truth Theory in a Meaning Theory?" In *Meaning and Truth: Investigations in Philosophical Semantics*, edited by D. Shier, J. K. Campbell and M. O'Rourke. New York: Seven Bridges Press.
Ludwig, Kirk. 2010. "Adverbs of Action." In *Blackwell Companion to the Philosophy of Action*, edited by T. O'Connor and C. Sandis. Oxford: Wiley-Blackwell.
Ludwig, Kirk, and Greg Ray. 1998. "Semantics for Opaque Contexts." In *Philosophical Perspectives: Language, Mind, and Ontology*, edited by J. Tomberlin. Cambridge: Blackwell.
Peacocke, Christopher. 2008. *Truly Understood*. Oxford: Oxford University Press.
Schein, Barry. 2012. "Event Semantics." In *The Routledge Companion to Philosophy of Language*, edited by Delia Graff Fara and Gillian Russell, 280–294. New York: Routledge.
Schiffer, Stephen. 1987. *Remnants of Meaning*. Cambridge: MIT Press.
Schiffer, Stephen R. 2003. *The Things We Mean*. Oxford: Clarendon.
Seymour, Michel. 1992. "A Sentential Theory of Propositional Attitudes." *Journal of Philosophy* 89 (4): 181–201.
Soames, Scott. 2010. *What Is Meaning?* Princeton, N.J. Princeton University Press.

MODAL METAPHYSICS
Unnecessary existents
Joshua Spencer

Department of Philosophy, University of Wisconsin-Milwaukee, Milwaukee, WI

Timothy Williamson has argued for the radical conclusion that everything necessarily exists. In this paper, I assume that the conclusion of Williamson's argument is more incredible than the denial of his premises. Under the assumption that Williamson is mistaken, I argue for the claim that there are some structured propositions which have constituents that might not have existed. If those constituents had not existed, then the propositions would have had an unfilled role; they would have been gappy. This gappy propositions view allows for a plausible response to Williamson's argument. Additionally, a slight variant of the gappy propositions view allows for plausible defense of Linguistic Ersatzism from the problem of contingent non-existents (also known as the problem of aliens).

1. Introduction

Let's begin by looking at an argument recently defended by Timothy Williamson (2002). It consists of three premises. Letting o be an arbitrarily chosen object, it may be formulated as follows:

(1) Necessarily, if o does not exist, then the proposition that o does not exist is true.
(2) Necessarily, if the proposition that o does not exist is true, then the proposition that o does not exist exists.
(3) Necessarily, if the proposition that o does not exist exists, then o exists.

It follows from (1)–(3) that necessarily, if o does not exist, then o exists. Hence, if it were possible for o to not exist, then it would possibly both exist and not exist. Clearly that's not possible. So, it must be that necessarily, o exists. Moreover, since o was simply an arbitrarily chosen object, we can generalize and conclude that everything necessarily exists.

Each premise is intuitively plausible and seemingly innocuous. But, the conclusion is clearly incredible. In this essay, I assume that the conclusion is false and develop a novel response to the argument.[1] First, I present the Russellian theory of propositions along with an amendment to that theory according to which there are gappy propositions. Second, I argue for an unusual extension of that theory of propositions under the assumption that there are contingent existents and show how a defender of this unusual theory might respond to Williamson's argument. Third, I consider and respond to an objection to this version of Russellianism. Finally, I show how the theory may be employed to defend the Linguistic Ersatzist from the problem of aliens, or contingent non-existents.[2]

2. Russellianism

The Russellian theory of propositions consists of a package of metaphysical theses and a package of semantic theses. Among the metaphysical theses of Russellianism are the following

i. There are propositions.
ii. Propositions have as constituents various entities like individuals, properties, relations, propositional operators and quantifiers.
iii. Any constituent of a proposition plays a particular role in that proposition.

If there are propositions, as thesis (i) claims, then presumably there is a proposition that Barack loves Michelle. That proposition, in accordance with (ii), contains as constituents the individuals Barack and Michelle along with the loving relation. Moreover, in accordance with (iii), Barack plays the lover role in the proposition whereas Michelle plays the beloved role.

The semantic package of Russellianism includes the following theses:

iv. Declarative sentences express (in a context) propositions.
v. The semantic contents of proper names are the things to which those names refer, the semantic contents of other words are properties, relations, propositional operators, quantifiers and other propositional constituents.
vi. Which propositions are expressed by declarative sentences (in a context) depends on the semantic contents of their meaningful components along with their grammatical structure.[3]

Consider the sentence 'Barack loves Michelle'. In accordance with (iv), that sentence expresses a proposition, namely the proposition that Barack loves Michelle. Moreover, in accordance with (v), the semantic contents of the meaningful components of that sentence include Barack, Michelle and the loving relation. And, in accordance with (vi), that sentence expresses the proposition it does, as opposed to another, at least partly because of the semantic contents of its meaningful components and its grammatical structure.

For example, the sentence 'Barack loves Michelle' expresses the proposition that Barack loves Michelle instead of the proposition that Neil Armstrong walked on the Moon at least partly because the former proposition contains as constituents the semantic contents of each of the meaningful words in the sentence whereas the latter proposition does not; the sentence 'Barack loves Michelle' expresses the proposition that Barack loves Michelle rather than the proposition that Barack loves both Michelle and cookies at least partly because the former proposition contains as constituents *only* the semantic contents of its meaningful components whereas the latter proposition contains more; finally, the sentence 'Barack loves Michelle' expresses the proposition that Barack loves Michelle rather than the proposition that Michelle loves Barack at least partly because there is an appropriate correspondence between the roles played by the meaningful components of the sentence and the roles played by their semantic contents in the former proposition but not in the latter.[4]

One serious problem that faces Russellianism is the problem of non-referring names or empty names. What proposition, if any, is expressed by the sentence 'Willow is a character from *Buffy the Vampire Slayer*' given that 'Willow' fails to refer and hence has no semantic content? On the view I favor, if the name 'Willow' really fails to refer, then the sentence in question expresses a gappy proposition.[5] That is, it expresses a proposition that has a role which fails to be filled by anything. In particular, if 'Willow' fails to refer, then the sentence 'Willow is a character from *Buffy the Vampire Slayer*' expresses a proposition that has a subject role that fails to be filled. Although gappy propositions have traditionally been used to deal with the problem of empty names, I will use them to solve the problems of contingent existence and contingent non-existence.

3. On the contingency of existence

It's generally accepted that propositions have their constituents essentially; or, at the very least, that for any proposition, p, and any constituent of that proposition, c, it's necessary that if p exists, then p has c as a constituent. But, if some things contingently exist, as I have assumed, then those generally accepted claims must be false. Although it may be a bit too quick for this context, here is an argument for that conclusion. Let P be some proposition about a contingently existing thing; let's say that P is the proposition that Barack Obama is tall. It seems that propositions generally, and hence P in particular, are necessary existents. But, since P is a necessary existent and Obama is contingent, it follows that possibly P exists and Obama does not. It's certainly impossible, though, for P to have a non-existent entity as a constituent. So, although P has Obama as a constituent, it is not necessary that if P exists, it has Obama as a constituent. Hence, it is not the case that for any proposition, p, and any constituent of that proposition, c, it's necessary that if p exists, then p has c as a constituent. Hence, propositions don't have their constituents essentially.

One might plausibly respond to that quick argument by claiming that propositions with contingent existents as constituents are themselves contingent existents. Hence, the premise, in the above argument, that propositions are necessary existents is false. That's fine. Here's a second, stronger argument against the views in question. Suppose that propositions have their constituents essentially and, hence, that for any proposition, p, and any constituent of that proposition, c, it's necessary that if p exists, then p has c as a constituent. Let P be a *true* proposition that has as a constituent something that contingently exists; again, P can be the proposition that Barack Obama is tall. Given our supposition that propositions have their constituents essentially, P would not have existed if Obama had not existed. But, P cannot have any properties if it doesn't exist. In particular, P cannot be possibly true if P does not exist. So, P would not have even been possibly true if Obama had not existed. Since, Obama only contingently exists, it follows that P is possibly not possibly true. But, P is true and it cannot be that P is true and possibly not possibly true.[6] So, our suppositions are mistaken: for some proposition, p, and some constituent of that proposition, c, it's possible that p exists and does not have c as a constituent; propositions do not have their constituents essentially.

But, if some propositions, such as the proposition that Obama is tall, do not have their constituents essentially, then those propositions are possibly gappy. For, if Obama had not existed, then the proposition that Obama is tall would have had no one playing the subject role.[7] So, from the assumption that Williamson is mistaken and there are some contingent existents, along with a few plausible premises, we have arrived at the conclusion that possibly, there are some contingently gappy propositions. But, it should be clear, now, that premise (3) of Williamson's argument is false. Premise (3), recall, says of an arbitrary object, o, that necessarily, if the proposition that o does not exist exists, then o exist. But, since propositions that contain contingent existents as constituents might have existed (as gappy propositions) without those constituents also existing, it's clear that (3) is mistaken.

4. Identity of propositions

One surprising consequence of this view is that some distinct propositions are possibly structurally indistinguishable from one another, where we understand structural indistinguishability as follows:

> p is *structurally indistinguishable* from q iff (i) p and q are both propositions with exactly the same roles to be filled, (ii) for any c, c is a constituent of p iff c is a constituent of q and for any role, R, c plays R in p iff c plays R in q.

It's possible, for example, for neither Obama nor Romney to ever have existed. The propositions that Obama is tall and that Romney is tall would have both been gappy if neither of them had ever existed; they both would have failed to have anything playing the subject role. But, if those propositions would have both been gappy if neither Obama nor Romney had existed, then they would have been structurally indistinguishable from one another. After all, the only thing that makes them actually structurally distinguishable is the fact that one has Obama as a constituent and the other has Romney as a constituent. If that distinguishing fact were taken away, then those propositions would be structurally indistinguishable.

But, the fact that some propositions are possibly structurally indistinguishable from one another highlights a potentially powerful objection to the view I am advocating. It seems that, for any p and q, necessarily, the fact that p is structurally indistinguishable from q grounds the fact that p is identical to q. But, it's also plausible that if one fact grounds another, then it's necessary that the first fact obtains only if the second fact obtains. It seems to follow that, for any p and q, necessarily, if p is structurally indistinguishable from q, then p is identical to q. But, if the gappy propositions view I'm advocating is true, then the propositions that Obama is tall and that Romney is tall are possibly structurally indistinguishable from one another. So, since structural indistinguishability entails identity, if the view I'm advocating is true, then those propositions are possibly identical to one another. But, since, those propositions are actually distinct from one another; they can't be possibly identical to one another. So, the objection goes, the view in question must be mistaken.

Although this is a potentially powerful objection, I do think there is a plausible response. I deny that, for any p and q, necessarily, the fact that p is structurally indistinguishable from q grounds that p is identical to q. Of course, one might legitimately wonder what does ground the identity of propositions if not structural indistinguishability. My preferred view is that nothing grounds the identity of propositions; those identity facts are brute facts. This doesn't mean, of course, that there aren't informative conditions under which those identity facts obtain. One might, for example, adopt the following identity conditions:

> For any propositions p and q, necessarily, p is identical to q iff p and q would be structurally indistinguishable were they both non-gappy.

These conditions, though, do not allow for the possibility of certain distinct yet structurally indistinguishable propositions that are necessarily gappy. Suppose that merely fictional characters can't even possibly exist and consider the propositions that Buffy kills vampires and that Holmes kills vampires.[8] These propositions seem distinct. After all, the former is true according to the television series *Buffy the Vampire Slayer* whereas the latter is not. But, given that Buffy and Holmes can't even possibly exist, those two propositions are necessarily gappy. According to the standard semantics, counterfactuals with impossible antecedents are vacuously true. So, those two propositions would be structurally indistinguishable were they non-gappy even though they seem to be distinct.

Perhaps, instead, we could adopt the following restricted identity conditions:

> For any propositions p and q, if p and q are possibly non-gappy, then necessarily, p is identical to q iff p and q would be structurally indistinguishable were they both non-gappy.

Given these restricted identity conditions, if p and q are non-gappy and structurally indistinguishable, then they must be identical. Some people might think, though, that if there can be structurally indistinguishable gappy propositions, then there can be structurally indistinguishable *non*-gappy propositions as well. The following merely necessary condition of identity allows for such a possibility:

> For any propositions p and q, necessarily, if p is identical to q, then p and q would be structurally indistinguishable were they both non-gappy.

The truth of this necessary condition can be explained in one of two plausible ways. First, one might claim that for any propositions p and q, the fact that p is identical to q grounds the fact that p and q would be structurally indistinguishable were they both non-gappy. Given that grounding connections imply necessary connections, the above necessary condition of identity immediately follows. Alternatively, one might claim that for any p and q, the fact that p and q would be structurally distinguishable were they both non-gappy grounds the fact that p is distinct from q. Again, given that grounding connections imply necessary connections, it follows that necessarily, if p and q would be structurally distinguishable were they both non-gappy, then p and q are distinct. The above necessary condition of identity immediately follows by simple modal logic. Although both explanations are plausible, the first explanation is preferable to the second primarily because it seems that identity facts generally ground indistinguishability facts (both actual and counterfactual). Moreover, it seems that non-modal facts ground modal facts rather than the other way around. Both of these intuitive claims support the first explanation over the second.

5. On the contingency of non-existence

According to one version of Linguistic Ersatzism, a possible world is merely a set or conjunction of maximally metaphysically consistent propositions. The propositions are maximal in the sense that for any proposition p, either p or not-p is entailed by those propositions; they are consistent in the sense that no metaphysically impossible proposition is entailed by those propositions. A proposition is true according to a possible world iff it is entailed by the conjuncts or members of that world.

One famous objection to Linguistic Ersatzism stems from the problem of contingent non-existents (a.k.a. the problem of aliens). Roughly, the objection is as follows. Possibly, there are some properties or individuals that don't actually exist. So, it seems that there must be a world according to which those properties or individuals exist. But, if Linguistic Ersatzism is true, then there is such a world only if there is a sentence or proposition, which is true according to that world, about those actually non-existent properties or individuals. But, no sentence or proposition is about a non-existent property or individual. So, the objection goes, Linguistic Ersatzism is false.[9,10]

I argued above, though, that there are propositions which are actually non-gappy yet possibly gappy. My argument was based on the possibility that certain actually existing things could have failed to exist. Similarly, if certain possibly existing things fail to actually exist, as the objector to Linguistic Ersatzism assumes, then there are also actually gappy yet possibly non-gappy propositions. But, if there are such propositions, then some versions of Linguistic Ersatzism are immune to the objection. Suppose, for example, that possible worlds are maximally metaphysically consistent conjunctions of propositions. Then, some such conjunctions will entail propositions that are actually gappy yet possibly non-gappy. If one of those conjunctions had been true, then the gappy propositions entailed by that conjunction would have been non-gappy; if those conjunctions had been true, then the gappy propositions entailed by them would have been about some things (even though they aren't actually about any things).[11] Those conjunctions are possible worlds according to which there are some properties or individuals that don't actually exist.

The problem of contingent non-existents is often bolstered by certain embedded modal claims. For example, although I don't actually have an older sister, I certainly could have had one. Moreover, I could have had an older sister who was not a doctor, but might have been one. But, these embedded modal claims are not a problem for the gappy propositions version of Linguistic Ersatzism. Consider two gappy propositions which we might *represent* as follows:

R1: <____$_n$, being an older sister of Joshua>
R2: <____$_n$, is a doctor>

Each of R1 and R2 contains a blank space because each represents a proposition that contains a gap in the subject position. Note that I have added subscripts to the blanks in these representations. I have added subscripts because there may be, and on my view are, many propositions that are structurally indistinguishable from the proposition represented by R1 and many propositions that are structurally indistinguishable from the proposition represented by R2. The blanks in these two representations are subscripted with the same number because necessarily, if either one of the proposition represented had been non-gappy, then the other would have been non-gappy as well and contained the same constituent in the subject position as the first. But, now suppose that there are two worlds, one of which entails the proposition represented by R1 and not the one represented by R2 whereas the other entails the proposition represented by R2. The first world is a world according to which I have an older sister who is not a doctor and the second world is a world according to which that older sister is a doctor. Hence, given that the first world is accessible from the actual world and the second is accessible from the first, I could have had an older sister who was not a doctor, but might have been one. So it seems that the strengthened problem of contingent non-existents is not a problem for this version of Linguistic Ersatzism.

6. Conclusion

The views introduced here are not without problems. For example, one might wonder what it is in virtue of which two distinct propositions that are gappy in their subject positions would have contained the same constituent in those subject positions had they been non-gappy. One might wonder what it is in virtue of which one gappy proposition is essentially gappy whereas another is not. And one might wonder what it is in virtue of which a sentence expresses a particular gappy proposition given that there are other propositions that are structurally indistinguishable from the one that sentence in fact expresses. Clearly there are many problems that one must face if one is to defend the views introduced in this paper. But, since the views introduced in this paper provide a solution to two difficult problems in modal metaphysics, the problem of contingent existents and the problem of contingent non-existents, it seems worthwhile to investigate them further and attempt to find solutions to these problems.[12]

Notes

1. There have been several responses to this style of argument, some of which predate Williamson's paper and others of which postdate it. Plantinga (1983) believes that a proposition can exist without the thing of which it's about existing. A defender of Plantinga's view may reject premise (3). Prior (1977), Fine (1985) and Adams (1981) believe that there are two senses of 'true' in modal contexts. A defender of Fine and Adams may claim that premises (1) and (2) equivocate. Rumfitt (2003) and Efird (2009) believe that there are some true necessities that are not necessarily true. A defender of this view may reject premise (1). Among those who accept the conclusion of the argument, though not necessarily on the basis of the argument, are (of course), Williamson (1990), (1998), (2000), (2002), (2013) and also Linsky and Zalta (1994), (1996).
2. The views advanced here may also be employed to solve certain problems faced by the presentists, in particular, the problems of temporary existents and temporary non-existents. The gappy propositions solution to certain similar presentists problems is considered and rejected by Markosian (2004). However, Markosian's objections to the gappy propositions solution does not apply to the view I advance here.
3. In the remainder of this essay, I will ignore the 'in a context' qualification. This is merely done to conveniently simplify our discussion. This simplification should not significantly impact the main points that I wish to make.
4. A fuller story must be told about how declarative sentences express particular propositions. Unfortunately that story will have to wait for another time. I will note, though, that some of the augmentations I'm going to make to the metaphysical package will throw a wrench into the standard story about how declarative sentences express particular propositions.
5. This view is introduced by Kaplan (1989) and defended by Braun (1993) and Salmon (1998).
6. The claim that P is true but possibly not possibly true is practically a rejection of the modal system B, which includes as theorems any instance of $\Phi \rightarrow \Box\Diamond\Phi$. I say 'practically' because some may not accept as equivalent the claim that P is possibly not possibly true and the claim that possibly, it's not possible that P. But, I *do* accept that equivalence and believe that the plausibility of B provides further support for my argument. Especially given that B is one of the weakest normal systems of modal logic; metaphysical possibility should verify the axioms of B.
7. One might claim that someone else might have played the subject role in the proposition that Obama is tall if Obama had not existed. But, there is no particular individual that it could have been. Suppose, for example, that Romney would have

filled the subject role in the proposition that Obama is tall if Obama had not existed. Then if Obama had not existed, then the proposition that Obama is tall would have been the proposition that Romney is tall. But, since it's possible both that Romney is tall and that Obama doesn't exist, then it looks like the proposition that Obama is tall could have been true even if Obama had not existed! That's clearly absurd. What if something that couldn't have been tall would have filled the subject role of the proposition that Obama is tall if Obama had not existed. What if, for example, Larry the electron would have filled the subject role? Then, if Obama had not existed, then proposition that Obama is tall would have been the proposition that Larry is tall. But, the proposition that Larry is tall would have been necessarily false if Obama had not existed whereas the proposition that Obama is tall would have been merely contingently false if Obama had not existed. So, the proposition that Obama is tall couldn't have been the proposition that Larry is tall and, so, Larry could not have played the subject role in the proposition that Obama is tall if Obama had not existed.

8. The thesis that fictional characters can't possibly exist can be defended using argument similar to those advanced by Kripke in (1980) and (2013). The view that fictional characters can't possibly exist, however, is not defended by Kripke.
9. This problem of contingent non-existents was first raised by McMichael (1983). Lewis (1986) presents the problem as one aimed at Linguistic Ersatzism and broadens the problem to include alien properties. Hazen (1996) and Nolan (2002) both extensively discuss the problem of contingent non-existents.
10. Solutions to this problem which do not involve rejecting the claim that there are contingent non-existents have been advanced by Heller (1998), Nolan (2002), and Sider (2002).
11. I am assuming that for any proposition p, p is about x only if x is a constituent of p. Alternatively, one might have thoughts that p is about x only if had p been non-gappy, then x would have been a constituent.
12. Thanks to Ben Caplan, Sam Cowling and Chris Tillman for discussing these issues with me.

References

Adams, Robert Merrihew. 1981. "Actualism and Thisness." *Synthese* 49: 3–41.
Braun, David. 1993. "Empty Names." *Noûs* 27: 449–469.
Efird, David. 2009. "Is Timothy Williamson a Necessary Existent?" In *Modality: Metaphysics, Logic, and Epistemology*, edited by Bob Hale, and Aviv Hoffman. Oxford: Oxford University Press.
Fine, Kit. 1985. "Plantinga on the Reduction of Possibilist Discourse." In *Alvin Plantinga*, edited by J. Tomberlin, and P. van Inwagen, 145–186. Dordrecht: D. Reidel.
Hazen, Allen. 1996. "Actualism Again." *Philosophical Studies* 84: 155–181.
Heller, Mark. 1998. "Property Counterparts in ErsatzWorlds." *Journal of Philosophy* 95: 293–316.
Kaplan, David. 1989. "Demonstratives." In *Themes from Kaplan*, edited by J. Almog, J. Perry, and H. Wettstein. New York: Oxford University Press.
Kripke, Saul. 1980. *Naming and Necessity*. Cambridge, MA: Harvard University Press.

Kripke, Saul. 2013. *Reference and Existence: The John Locke Lectures*. Oxford: Oxford University Press.
Lewis, David. 1986. *On the Plurality of Worlds*. Oxford: Basil Blackwell.
Linsky, Bernard, and Edward N. Zalta. 1994. "In Defense of the Simplest Quantified Modal Logic." In *Philosophical Perspectives 8: Logic and Language*, edited by J. Tomberlin, 431–458. Atascadero: Ridgeview.
Linsky, Bernard, and Edward N. Zalta. 1996. "In Defense of the Contingently Concrete." *Philosophical Studies* 84: 283–294.
Markosian, Ned. 2004. "A Defense of Presentism." In *Oxford Studies in Metaphysics*, Vol. 1, 47–82. Oxford: Oxford University Press.
McMichael, Alan. 1983. "A Problem for Actualism about PossibleWorlds." *Philosophical Review* 92: 49–66.
Nolan, Daniel. 2002. *Topics in the Philosophy of Possible Worlds*. New York: Routledge.
Plantinga, Alvin. 1983. "On Existentialism." *Philosophical Studies* 44: 1–20.
Prior, A. N., and Kit Fine. 1977. *Worlds, Times and Selves*. Amherst: University of Massachusetts Press.
Rumfitt, Ian. 2003. "Contingent Existents." *Philosophy* 78: 461–481.
Salmon, Nathan. 1998. "Nonexistence." *Noûs* 32: 277–319.
Sider, Theodore. 2002. "The Ersatze Pluriverse." *Journal of Philosophy* 99: 279–315.
Williamson, Timothy. 1990. "Necessary Identity and Necessary Existence." In *Wittgenstein—Towards a Re-evaluation: Proceedings of the 14th International Wittgenstein Symposium*, vol. I, edited by R. Haller, and J. Brandl. Vienna: Holder - Pichler - Tempsky.
Williamson, Timothy. 1998. "Bare Possibilia." *Erkenntnis* 48: 257–273.
Williamson, Timothy. 2000. "Existence and Contingency." *Proceedings of the Aristotelian Society* 100: 117–139.
Williamson, Timothy. 2002. "Necessary Existents." In *Logic, Thought, and Language*, edited by A. O'Hear. Cambridge: Cambridge University Press.
Williamson, Timothy. 2013. *Modal Logic as Metaphysics*. Oxford: Oxford University Press.

MODAL METAPHYSICS
Contingently existing propositions

Michael Nelson

Department of Philosophy, University of California, Riverside, USA

> I argue that propositions are contingent existents. Some propositions that in fact exist might not have existed and there might have been propositions that are distinct from every actually existing proposition. This is because some propositions are singular propositions, which are propositions containing ordinary objects as constituents, and so are ontologically dependent on the existence of those objects; had those objects not existed, then the singular propositions would not have existed. I provide both a philosophical and technical understanding of the contingent status of propositions.

Propositions are the bearers of truth value, the contents of sentences in context, and the contents of attitudes like belief, desire, intention, and wish. (Although we say things like 'I want to go to the movies' or 'I intend to stay home and work', where the attitude verb takes an infinitive phrase that does not seem to designate a proposition, I subscribe to the Quinean view that the true form of such sentences are better represented as 'I want that I go to the movies' and 'I intend that I stay home and work' and hence are indeed propositional attitudes, although I won't argue for the position here.) My focus here is with a further role propositions play: Propositions are the bearers of alethic modal properties. Some sentences have an air of contingency, like the sentence 'Barack Obama is the 44th US president', while others, in some sense, couldn't been false, like the sentence 'If Barack Obama exists, then he is human'. It is tempting to say that this is so in virtue of the fact that the first expresses a proposition contingently true while the second expresses a proposition that is necessarily true. The modal profile of a sentence, then, is a function of the modal profile of the proposition it expresses.

I argue that we should conceive of propositions as contingently existing objects and that this mandates abandoning straightforward combinations of standard quantificational and propositional modal logics. In particular, I argue that we should reject the unrestricted Rule of Necessitation, the principle that the necessitation of any theorem of our system is also a theorem of our system (i.e., the principle that, if Φ is a theorem of S, then $\Box\Phi$ is a theorem of S). Instead, I argue, we should accept that there are contingent logical truths. I claim that the theorems of standard quantificational logic are indeed logically true, but some of them express contingently true propositions.

The problems I shall focus on arise from the fact that ordinary objects seem to be contingent existents. Many of Obama's features, like being president of the US, are contingent, in the sense that there are possibilities in which he lacks those features. Furthermore, his very existence seems contingent. Had Obama's parents never met, which is certainly a possibility, or had the particular ovum and sperm that formed the zygote from which Obama actually developed never combined, then Obama would not have been – nothing that would have existed would have been Obama. But it seems that there nonetheless would have been truths about Obama; indeed, that Obama does not exist seems to be a truth about these Obama-less possibilities.

Let **w** be a possibility in which Obama's mother never conceives a child. Intuitively, **w** is a possibility in which Obama does not exist, supposing a plausible form of origin essentialism. So, the proposition [NOT[Obama exists]] is true with respect to **w**. But this seems to conflict with the view that that proposition is a singular proposition and singular propositions are object-dependent. A proposition is made up of constituent parts and so would not exist were its constituent parts not to exist. An object-dependent proposition has an object as a constituent and so would not exist were that object to not exist. So, a possibility in which Obama does not exist is a possibility in which the singular negative existential [NOT[Obama exists]] does not exist. If a proposition does not exist in a possibility, however, then it is hardly true in that possibility; it is no way in that possibility, as it does not exist.

There seems, then, a deep conflict between the theses that singular propositions are bearers of alethic modal properties and that there are possibilities in which the ordinary objects those propositions are about do not exist. I think that both theses are true and so I aim to resolve that conflict.

Object Dependency

The argument for the conflict presented above turns on the incompatibility between the following three theses. (I follow (Plantinga 1983), although he presents his argument as an argument for the negation of (1). There is a similar argument for the negation of (3) in (Williamson 2002).)

(1) The proposition [NOT[Obama exists]] is ontologically dependent on Obama.
(2) For any proposition **p** and possibility **w**, if **p** is true of **w**, then **p** would have existed had **w** been actual.
(3) There are possibilities in which Obama does not exist and so with respect to which the proposition [NOT[Obama exists]] is true.

Each principle is individually plausible. There are a host of familiar arguments for (1) and the thesis of direct reference about ordinary proper names, pronouns, indexicals, and demonstratives that supports it. I shall not review them here. One way to support (2) is as follows. A proposition **p** is true of a possibility **w** just in case, had **w** been actual, then **p** would have been true. But being true is a way of being and so requires that there *be* something that is true. This strongly suggests that propositions are necessary existents, as any proposition can be evaluated for truth and falsity with respect to any possibility and so exists in all possibilities. (3) rests on the intuitions described above regarding the contingency of Obama's existence.

While individually plausible, these principles are mutually inconsistent. Suppose that, in accordance with (3), [NOT[Obama exists]] is true of a possibility **w**. Then, by (2), were **w** actual, [NOT[Obama exists]] would have existed and, by (1), Obama would have existed (as, necessarily, (if [NOT[Obama exists]] exists, then Obama exists)). But if Obama exists in **w**, then [NOT[Obama exists]] is false of **w** and **w** isn't a possibility in which Obama does not exist, which contradicts our initial assumption.

At least one of (1)–(3) is false. But which? Plantinga rejects (1) and Williamson (and Linsky and Zalta, in (Linsky and Zalta 1994), before him) rejects (3). On Plantinga's view, a so-called singular proposition is really a proposition with an individual essence of an object as a constituent, where **o**'s individual essence is a property such that: (i) necessarily, if **o** exists, then **o** instantiates it and (ii) necessarily, if it is instantiated, then only **o** instantiates it. Obama's individual essence – call it P – can exist, Plantinga argues, uninstantiated. The proposition that Obama does not exist, then, is really the proposition [NOT[P is instantiated]], which necessarily exists, existing even in possibilities in which Obama does not. Given Plantinga's conception of so-called singular propositions, then, (2) and (3) are consistent and (1) is false. There are possibilities in which Obama does not exist and the proposition [NOT[P is instantiated]] is true of those possibilities. That proposition would still exist even if one of those Obama-less possibilities were actual, as P is not dependent upon Obama. On Williamson's view, by contrast, necessarily everything necessarily exists – everything that could exist actually does exist and everything that exists necessarily exists. This is a fairly immediate consequence of the simplest quantified modal logic (QML), as I shall show below, and there is much to be said in favor of the simplest QML. Ordinary objects like Obama are necessary existents but only contingently concrete. A possibility in which Obama is nonconcrete seems to ordinary intuition like a possibility in which Obama does not exist. Ordinary intuition systematically conflates, then, Obama's possible nonconcreteness and his nonbeing, mistaking (or misdescribing) possibilities in which he is nonconcrete with possibilities in which he does not exist. So, (1) and (2) are both true and (3) is false, where the intuitions that support (3) are explained in terms of there being possibilities in which Obama is nonconcrete.

While both (1) and (3) are open to dispute, I believe that they are true. And while neither Plantinga's view nor the contingent concretist's view is open to decisive refutation, both are deeply problematic. A commonality between them is the thesis that every proposition exists in every possible world. This is true on

Plantinga's view because propositions, or at least propositions expressed by natural languages and entertained by minds like ours, are object independent; it is true on the contingent concretist's view because nothing, including object dependent propositions and the objects that they are dependent upon, is a genuine contingent existent. By contrast, I think that it is better to embrace the idea that some propositions – in particular, atomic singular propositions and any proposition built there from – are contingent existents and reject (2). Such a view is not novel, having its origins in the work of Arthur Prior (Prior 1957), with different versions developed in (Adams 1981), (Deutsch 1990, 1994), (Fine 1977, 1978, 1981, 1985), (Fitch 1996), (Menzel 1991), and (Stalnaker 2012), among others. I hope to provide a deeper philosophical understanding of the notion of a proposition's being true at a possibility when it would not exist were that possibility actual. This notion is crucial for any adequate account of the alethic properties of contingently existing propositions. My primary novel contribution, however, is the development of a contingentist QML in the context of a classical theory of quantification. I argue that a proponent of the view that some propositions exist contingently must embrace a contingentist classical quantification QML, as the alternatives lead to either the Plantingian or Williamsonian views.

Quantified Modal Logic

Let's approach our problem from another angle. $\exists y(y=x)$ is a theorem of standard quantificational logic (SQL). (The formula's validity derives from the fact that every standard model has a nonempty domain and every object is identical to something – namely, itself. Some are uncomfortable counting an open sentence as a theorem, as open sentences do not have truth values in interpretations simpliciter but only in an interpretation under an assignment of values to variables. We can instead consider $\exists y(y=a)$. Any interpretation of that sentence must include an assignment of an object from the domain of that interpretation to the individual constant a and so there is something – namely, that object – that is identical to that value. So $\exists y(y=a)$ is true in any standard interpretation. The argument to follow works just as well for this closed sentence as it does for the original open sentence.) T is the weakest propositional modal logic adequate for alethic modality (the weaker system K, which is like T but without the Truth Axiom below, is clearly too weak). T extends propositional logic with a modal operator $\Box$ and includes the following rule and two axiom schemas.

RN: If Φ is a theorem of MPL, then $\Box \Phi$ is a theorem of MPL
Distribution Axiom: $\Box(\Phi \rightarrow \Psi) \rightarrow (\Box\Phi \rightarrow \Box\Psi)$
Truth Axiom: $\Box\Phi \rightarrow \Phi$

Suppose that we simply combine the resources of SQL with T. Call the result the simplest QML. By RN and our earlier observation that $\exists y(y=x)$ is a theorem of SQL, $\Box\exists y(y=x)$ is a theorem of SQML. By Universal Generalization and another application of RN, $\Box\forall x\Box\exists y(y=x)$ is also a theorem of SQML. But, assuming that 'x exists' is regimented as $\exists y(y=x)$, this says that necessarily everything necessarily exists.

There are three alternatives, which are related, I argue, to the three alternatives to the earlier version of our problem. First, we can accept the result that $\Box\forall x\Box\exists y(y=x)$ is logically true and accept a fixed domain semantics for modal discourse. One benefit of this alternative is that we avoid the need to complicate our logic. A downside is that we must explain the intuition that existence is a contingent property in an indirect manner, construing it in terms of the contingency of concreteness or some other contingent, nonuniversal property that we plausibly conflate with existence, generating the illusion of contingent existents. This first option clearly overlaps with the contingent nonconcreteness theory considered above.

The other two alternatives are similar in that they involve complicating our logic in order to avoid the result that $\Box\forall x\Box\exists y(y=x)$ is a theorem of a QML adequate for ordinary objects. The options differ over what aspect of the logic they complicate.

The first, and more common, version rejects SQL in favor of a free logic. In a free logic, there are interpretations with empty domains and that do not assign values to individual constants occurring in the sentences being interpreted. The upshot is that $\exists y(y=x)$ and $\exists y(y=a)$ are not theorems of FQL. Consider a natural deduction proof theory for SQL with introduction and elimination rules for the quantifier $\exists$. Simple modifications of those rules result in a proof theory sound and complete with respect to the model theory for a free logic described above. Where the standard introduction rule allows the transition from any instance of $\Phi\alpha$ to a corresponding instance of $\exists x\Phi x$, where x does not occur in Φ, at least one occurrence of α is replaced by x and all else remains the same, the free logic rule allows a transition from any instance of $\Phi\alpha$ and $\exists x(x=\alpha)$ to corresponding instance of $\exists x\Phi x$. This small adjustment is sufficient to block the derivation of the unwanted results described above. (I'll show this in greater detail below.) The final response to the argument is based on a rejection of RN and an insistence that some logical truths, and in particular logical truths like $\exists y(y=x)$ and $\exists y(y=a)$, are contingent. So, a proponent of FL rejects the first step of the above outlined derivation of $\Box\forall x\Box\exists y(y=x)$, as $\exists y(y=x)$ and $\exists y(y=a)$ are not counted as theorems, while a proponent of the last view rejects the second step, which relies on RN.

I do not claim that there are strict equivalences between the two sets of solutions to the two puzzles I have presented. But there are natural alliances. There are obvious similarities between the first solutions to each of the puzzles, as both turn crucially on the claim that there is a fixed domain across all possibilities while what is concrete varies. One may accept the first solution to one of our problems and another solution to the other, but such a position is hard to justify; why struggle to cling to genuine contingent existents in one context, say, combining quantification and modal logics, when one has already rejected it in another, say, accounting for the alethic properties of propositions? There are less obvious but more important connections between the other two pairs of solutions. I claim that a free logic solution to our second problem is best aligned with a rejection of object dependent propositions as the contents of sentences like $\exists y(y=a)$ and so with a rejection of (1) in our first puzzle, while a solution to our second problem involving a rejection of RN is best aligned with the third solution to our first puzzle and so with a rejection of (2) in that puzzle. I don't claim that the proponent of the second solution to our second problem must accept Plantinga's positive account about the propositions expressed by sentences like 'Obama exists' and the theory of object independent individual essences that account presupposes. That is one alternative to the direct reference thesis of object dependent propositions. My claim instead is that the proponent of the free logic solution to the problem of necessary existence must embrace some alternative; she is in no position to combine her account of our second problem with a theory of direct reference. Here's why.

There is a propositional version of our second problem. A proponent of the free logic solution to the original version of that puzzle must deny that there are object dependent singular propositions in order to solve that version of the puzzle. This is because any of the other solutions on offer undermine, I argue, her own solution to the original puzzle, as they threaten to supplant that solution with a more general solution that accounts for both our original and a related propositional version of our second puzzle, thereby undercutting the payoff of rejecting SQL in favor of a free logic. I argue for this contention in the following four paragraphs.

Recall that our second problem arises because there are sentences that are logical truths of SQL that appear contingent and the free logician promises to account for this by denying that those sentences are in fact logical truths. The notion of logical truth, in the sense of being true in every interpretation, does not apply to propositions, as only sentences are interpreted and so only sentences are true in interpretations. But some propositions have an analogous feature of being true in virtue of their form and general metaphysical truths. Propositions expressed by logically true sentences plausibly have this feature, as do propositions expressed by analytically true sentences. If the free logician is correct, the sentence 'Obama exists' is neither logically nor analytically true. But suppose that it expresses a singular proposition containing Obama himself as a constituent. Then that proposition is true in virtue of its form and the general metaphysical fact that absolutely everything exists. (I return to the latter below.) For reasons paralleling the support for the Rule of Necessitation, it seems that such propositions are also necessarily true. But then the proposition that Obama exists is necessarily true, which is a similar, albeit weaker, problematic result as that found in our second puzzle. Notice that the resources of free logic are of no help in solving this version of the problem. We can grant that there are interpretations in which an individual constant (and so a proper name in natural language) does not have a value, in which case 'Obama exists' (or its translation in the language of QL) is not a logical truth. The most recent argument for the claim that Obama necessarily exists does not rest on claims about what sentences are logically true but instead claims about the proposition expressed by those sentences. So, the solution the proponent of free logic offers to the original puzzle does not apply to the propositional variant; she must develop an alternative solution and that solution must not undermine her solution to the original problem.

There are, I think, four ways to solve the propositional version of this problem. The first is to deny that sentences like 'Obama exists' express singular propositions, the second is to accept that Obama necessarily exists and explain the intuitions to the contrary in terms of the contingency of some other property, like concreteness, the third is to accept that there are propositions true in virtue of their form and general metaphysical truths that are nonetheless contingent, and the fourth is to reject that absolutely everything exists. I claim that the first is the only solution available to a proponent of the free logic solution to our second problem. This is because all the other solutions undermine the free logician's favored solution to our second problem.

If we pursue the second strategy for the propositional version of our problem, it is unmotivated to claim that there are instances of $\exists y(y=\alpha)$ that are not logically true in order to avoid counting $\Box\forall x\Box\exists y(y=x)$ as a theorem, as one has already accepted a metaphysics of necessary existents. The strategy of explaining our intuitions of the contingency of existence in other terms cannot be contained to just the propositional version of the puzzle.

The third strategy involves cleaving apart the notion of truth in virtue of form from the notion of necessity. The proposition expressed by 'Obama exists' is such that its very existence suffices for and guarantees its truth, but it is nonetheless only contingently true. It is unprincipled to then deny the analogous status to the sentence 'Obama exists', which we regiment in the language of QL as $\exists y(y=o)$, letting o translate 'Obama'. But the proponent of the free logic solution to our second problem denies that sentences of this form are ever logically true. If one has already accepted that there are contingently true propositions whose mere form and general metaphysical truths guarantee their truth, it is hard to see why one would resist the suggestion that there are also logically true sentences that are only contingently true.

The final solution I suggested above involves adopting a Meinongian metaphysics according to which there are entities that do not exist. On this account, there are singular propositions with o as a constituent, even though o does not exist. While there is an object o, o's existence is a further matter. Existence, then, cannot be captured with quantifiers, as $\exists y(y=x)$, and must instead be expressed with a primitive predicate $E!x$, where $\exists x\neg E!x$ is consistent. As with the two solutions considered above, the Meinongian solution extends to the original second puzzle and supplants the free logician's favored account. The Meinongian should accept that $\Box\forall x\Box\exists y(y=x)$ is logically true even though it is not necessary that everything necessarily exists, as existence is distinct from being. It is unprincipled, then, to accept a Meinongian solution to the propositional version of the problem and a free logic solution to the original version, as the latter is motivated by the thought contingent existence requires varying domains, which the Meinongian rejects.

It follows, then, that a proponent of the free logic response to our second problem should reject the claim that the natural language correlates of instances of $\exists y(y=\alpha)$, sentences like 'Obama exists', express singular propositions. For only then can they have a solution to the proposition version of that problem that does not undermine the cogency of their favored solution to the original problem.

With our problems described and landscape of views sketched, in the remainder of this essay I develop a version of the view according to which the Rule of Necessitation is false and there are contingent logical truths. I begin by presenting a logic adequate for modal discourse about contingent existents. I then return to the more philosophical issues connected to making sense of a contingently existing proposition's being true at possibilities in which it does not exist.

Classical QL and Contingent Beings

The semantics of our logic is familiar, being a standard version of a varying domain possible worlds model theory, but the proof theory is distinctive. So in what follows I focus more on the latter, although I begin with a brief description of the former. Our vocabulary consists of an infinite stock of n-ary predicate-letters, for each positive integer n,

$$F_1, G_1, H_1, F'_1, G'_1, H'_1, \ldots$$

$$F_2, G_2, H_2, F'_2, G'_2, H'_2, \ldots$$

$$\vdots \quad \vdots$$

an infinite stock of individual constants

$$a, b, c, d, a', b', c', d', \ldots$$

an infinite stock of variables

$$x, y, z, x', y', z', \ldots$$

the two-place logical predicate $=$, and the operators $\rightarrow$, $\neg$, and $\square$ and quantifier $\exists$. (We can introduce the other truth functional connectives ($\leftrightarrow$, $\wedge$, $\vee$, the universal quantifier $\forall$ and possibility operator $\diamond$ as defined symbols in the standard ways. Later we will extend the language with an actuality operator $\mathcal{A}$, which is not definable in terms of the material of the simpler language.) The grammar is familiar, although we will require all occurrences of quantifiers to bind variables in their scope.

An interpretation of a set of sentences in our language begins with a set W of possible worlds and a distinguished actual world w^* from that set. Because our system will validate all instances of the T axiom above and all instances of the characteristic S5 axiom $\diamond \phi \rightarrow \square \diamond \phi$, which requires that, for any interpretation I, every world of W_I is accessible from any other, we don't include accessibility relations in the characterization of an interpretation, stipulating that the accessibility relation is always reflexive and Euclidean and so an equivalence relation. The members of W serve as indices against which we relativize semantic values. So it is useful to first describe how the nonmodal vocabulary is regularly interpreted and then show how those values are relativized to possible worlds in our system.

We specify a nonempty domain D, an assignment function from an individual constant, for each individual constant occurring in the sentences being interpreted, to exactly one object from D, and an assignment function from an n-place predicate-letter, for each predicate-letter in the sentences being interpreted, to a set of n-tuples from the members of D, where the set can be empty. One of the sources of difficulty in combining a propositional modal logic with quantificational logic is the lack of mandate about how to relativize these three assignments to worlds. Each world w in W needs a domain D_w. But can members of different domains overlap? For each w and w' in W, must $D_w = D_{w'}$? There is latitude and different choices lead to profoundly different results. Because we are constructing a noncounterpart-theoretic, contingentist theory, we will allow overlap between the world domains of a model and allow for shrinking domains, so that members of D_{w^*} need not be in D_w, for all w in W, and growing domains, so that a member in D_w, for some w in W, need not be in D_{w^*}. Consider the following simple interpretation.

Interpretation I_1 : $W = \{w^*, w_1\}$; $D_{w^*} = \{1, 2\}$, $D_{w1} = \{2, 3\}$.

2 is a necessary existent; 1 is an actually existing, contingent existent; 3 is a merely possible existent – an alien. We want our model theory to include interpretations like I_1 and so to allow for all three kinds of objects.

We now know how domains are relativized to possible world indices. We turn to the other two components of classical interpretations. An individual constant is rigid and so has the same value with respect to all possible worlds in an interpretation. So, we do not need to relativize the assignment function for individual constants to possible worlds. An assignment of extensions to predicate-letters, however, is world-indexed. So, for each n-place predicate-letter Φ^n in the sentences being interpreted (except for the logical predicate $=$, which is stipulated to always have the set of all identity pairs as its extension) and possible world w in W_I, we assign a set of n-tuples of objects from D_w, where the set may be empty; that set is Φ^n's extension relative to w. So, for each predicate letter Φ^n in the sentences under interpretation, $V^I(\Phi^n, w) = \Delta$, where Δ is a set (possibly empty) of n-tuples of objects from D_w. I shall adopt a simple treatment of the logical predicate $=$, where the extension of $=$ at w, for any world w in W, is the set of all identity pairs on the union of $D_{w'}$, for all w' in W.[1]

Our basic truth predicate is relativistic, in the sense that a sentence is true or false in an interpretation at a world. (We can say that a sentence is true or false in an interpretation I just in case it is true at w^*, which is the closest we get to a monadic truth predicate.) Our atomic sentences are of the form $\Phi^n(\alpha_1 \ldots \alpha_n)$.

We define truth for an atomic sentence in terms of a sequence of objects satisfying a condition. An n-tuple $<o_1, \ldots, o_n>$ satisfies $\Phi^n(x_1 \ldots x_n)$ in I at w under an assignment of o_1 to $x_1, \ldots,$ and on to x_n just in case $<o_1, \ldots, o_n>$ is a member of $V^I(\Phi^n, w)$ (i.e., $<o_1, \ldots, o_n>$ is in the extension of Φ^n in I at w). So, the atomic sentence $\Phi^n(\alpha_1 \ldots \alpha_n)$ is true in I at w just in case $V^I(\alpha_1) = o_1, \ldots V^I(\alpha_n) = o_n$ and $<o_1, \ldots, o_n>$ is a member of $V^I(\Phi^n, w)$. We define truth and satisfaction for sentences containing truth-functional connectives in the familiar way. (For example, $\phi \to \psi$ is true in I at w just in case either ϕ is false in I at w or ψ is true in I at w; $\neg \phi x$ is true of o in I at w just in case o does not satisfy ϕx in I at w under an assignment of o to x; etc.) $\Box \phi$ is true in I at w just in case ϕ is true in I at w', for all w' in D_I; an object o satisfies the condition $\Box \Phi x$ in I at w just in case o satisfies the condition Φx in I at w', for all w' in D_I, under an assignment of o to x. $\exists y \Phi y$ is true in I at w just in case, for some object o in D_w, o satisfies Φy in I at w; an object o' satisfies the condition $\exists y \Phi xy$ in I at w just in case, for some object o in D_w, the pair $<o', o>$ satisfies Φxy in I at w under an assignment of o' to x and o to y. We say that a sentence is logically true just in case it is true in every interpretation and so, for each interpretation I, the sentence is true in I at w^*.[2]

I said earlier that our semantics is a standard varying domains QML. What is distinctive is our proof theory, which is a natural deduction system consisting of the following inference rules. Call the system CC-QML, for Classical Contingentist QML.

hyp
$i. \phi$ hyp

=I
$i. \alpha = \alpha$ =I

=E
$i. \alpha = \beta$ *justification*
$j. \Phi \alpha$ *justification*
$k. \Phi \beta$ =E:i,j

→I
$i. \phi$ [temp hyp]
$\vdots$ $\vdots$
$j. \psi$ *justification*
$k. \phi \to \psi$ →I:i,j

→E
$i. \phi \to \psi$ *justification*
$j. \phi$ *justification*
$k. \psi$ →E:i,j

∃I
$i. \Phi \alpha$ *justification*
$j. \exists x \Phi x$ ∃I:i

□I
$i. \underline{\Box}$
$j. \phi$ *justification*
$k. \Box \phi$ □I:i,j

□E
$i. \Box \phi$ *justification*
$j. \underline{\Box}$
$k. \phi$ □E:i

T
$i. \Box \phi$ *justification*
$j. \phi$ T:i

S5
$i. \neg \Box \neg \phi$ *justification*
$j. \Box \neg \Box \neg \phi$ S5:i

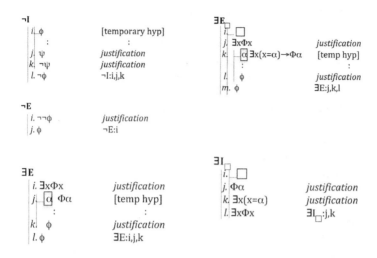

Many of these rules are familiar. (I illustrate the use of the rule in the sample derivations in the appendix.) They use the Fitch format for subproofs, which allow the introduction of temporary premises that are discharged as the rule is used. The ∃E rules involve assuming an arbitrary instance Φα of the existential generalization ∃xΦx cited on the top line. There are various ways to characterize arbitrariness in proof-theoretic terms. All require that the singular term α not occur in the formula φ justified by the use of ∃E. But there are two ways of characterizing the further demand. On the stringent version, we also require that α not occur in any formula on any line above the line at which the arbitrary instance is assumed. On the permissive version, we instead further require that α not occur in the ultimate dependency of any line above the line at which the arbitrary instance is assumed. (In the appendix I offer reasons for preferring the stringent conception.)

The box-subproof environment, employed in □I and □E, is less familiar. It is based on the system presented in (Garson 2006). A box-subproof does not mark an environment tainted by a temporary assumption to be discharged, as the subproofs in the previously mentioned rules do. Instead, it marks an environment in which 'only necessary truths' occur. We characterize this in proof-theoretical terms as follows. A line earlier in the derivation, above the introduction of the box-subproof on line i, cannot be cited in support of a line inside that subproof except by the □E rule. This ensures that every line brought into a box-subproof is necessary, conditional on the truth of the earlier lines in the proof. As our inference rules preserve necessary truth, anything that we can derive from something brought into a box-subproof using those rules will also be necessary, with the exception of ∃I and ∃E, the use of which are banned inside the box-subproof environment and replaced with the weaker, free logic quantifier rules ∃I□ and ∃E□. (∃E□ is actually stronger than its classical correlate ∃E. But we need the stronger version to derive desired results when we only have the weaker $\exists I_\Box$; for example, if we only had $\exists E$, we couldn't derive $\exists xFx$ from $\exists x\neg\neg Fx$ inside a box-subproof, which would be bad indeed. And it is simpler to just require that both classical quantifier rules are banned inside box-subproofs, even though $\exists E$ does not cause problems.) $\Box I$ allows us to write immediately outside a box-subproof environment the necessitation of any formula occurring inside that box-subproof. Finally, when a box-subproof environment is embedded inside another box-subproof environment, a use of $\Box I$ and $\Box E$ can only reach across one of those subproofs.

One version of a QML based on a free quantificational logic is the above system without the classical quantifier rules just like $\exists I$ and $\exists E$ are banned altogether and $\exists I_\Box$ and $\exists E_\Box$ are the sole quantifier rules. The simplest QML is like the above proof theory, but $\exists I$ and $\exists E$ are allowed to operate inside box-subproofs and so $\exists I_\Box$ and $\exists E_\Box$ are eliminated as unnecessary. CC-QML can thus be seen as a compromise between the two extremes. Unlike with a free QML, all of the classical validities are provable in CC-QML. And the payoff to banning the use of classical quantification rules inside a box-subproof is that it blocks derivations of $\Box\forall x\Box\exists y(y=x)$. Recall the derivation sketched earlier, which is valid in the simplest QML. It will be helpful to make use of the following derived rules governing the defined universal quantifier $\forall$ in transforming that derivation to a natural deduction system.

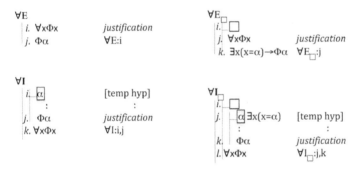

Consider then the following derivation of $\Box\forall x\Box\exists y(y=x)$.

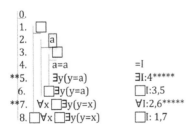

While this derivation is without fault in the simplest QML, where the classical quantifier rules function without restrictions, in CC-QML it fails at lines 5 and 7, because of the uses of ∃I and ∀I inside box-subproofs, which are banned. (The derivation fails for the same reason in a free QML.)

We cannot simply replace the uses of the classical rules with the box-subproof quantifier rules, as can be seen by the following attempt.

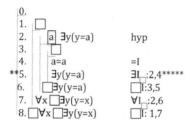

The use of ∃I$_\square$ on line 5 is illegitimate, because it reaches across a box-subproof on line 3; all of the lines cited by the rule must occur within the same box-subproof as the line being justified. So, one thing in favor of CC-QML is that $\square\forall x \square\exists y(y=x)$ is neither a theorem of the proof theory nor valid in the model theory.

Growing Domains and the Logic of Actuality

Earlier I distinguished interpretations with shrinking domains and interpretations with growing domains, which correspond to the two sides of our intuitions concerning the contingency of existence. The domain of a possible world shrinks relative to the actual domain when there is an object in the actual domain that is not a member of that possible domain. Obama's possible nonexistence is an instance, which we can model as follows.

Interpretation I_2 : $W = \{w^*, w_1\}$; $D_{w^*} = \{1, 2\}$, $D_{w1} = \{2\}$; $V(\text{'Obama'}) = 1$.

The domain of a possible world grows relative to the actual domain when there is an object in that possible domain that is not a member of the actual domain. My possible brother, where nothing that actually exists could have been my brother, is an instance, which we can model with the following interpretation.

Interpretation I_3 : $W = \{w^*, w_1\}$; $D_{w^*} = \{1\}$, $D_{w1} = \{1, 2\}$;

$V(\text{'m'}) = 1$; $V(\text{'}x\text{ is a brother of }y\text{'}, w^*) = \emptyset$;

$V(\text{'}x\text{ is a brother of }y\text{'}, w_1) = <1, 2>$.

In this section I discuss the problems aliens and growing domains present for theories of contingent existents. I address both the technical problems of regimenting these intuitions and the metaphysical problems of entities like 2 in I_3, which threaten to conflict with the plausible thesis of actualism, according to which absolutely everything, including entities employed in our model theories, is actual. I begin with the technical problems and then turn to the more philosophical problems.

We want to make sense of the idea that there could have been things that do not actually exist. For reasons familiar from the literature (see (Crossley and Humberstone 1977)), regimenting this sentence requires an actuality operator $\mathcal{A}$, which grammatically is a sentential operator with the following truth definition: $\mathcal{A}\phi$ is true in I at w just in case ϕ is true in I at w^*. So, the truth value of $\mathcal{A}\phi$ at any world in an interpretation is a function of the truth value of ϕ at the distinguished world of the interpretation. We can now regiment the sentence that there could have been something that does not actually exist as $\exists x \neg \mathcal{A} \exists y(y=x)$. That sentence is true in an interpretation I only if there is a world w in W_I such that there is an object **o** in D_w where **o** is not in D_{w^*}; that is, the sentence is true only in interpretations with growing domains. We can see that I_3 above is an example of this.

We begin by extending our earlier system with three additional rules of inference for the operator $\mathcal{A}$.

$\mathcal{A}$E			$\mathcal{A}$I	
i. $\mathcal{A}\phi$	*justification*		i. ϕ	*justification*
j. ϕ	$\mathcal{A}$E:i		j. $\mathcal{A}\phi$	$\mathcal{A}$I:i

$\Box\mathcal{A}$

i. $\mathcal{A}\phi$	*justification*
j. $\Box\mathcal{A}\phi$	$\Box\mathcal{A}$:i

$\Box\mathcal{A}$ may raise eyebrows, but it is in fact beyond dispute. The truth value of $\mathcal{A}\phi$ in an interpretation at any world of the interpretation is determined by the truth value of ϕ at the distinguished world of the interpretation, which does not vary within the interpretation. So, the truth value of $\mathcal{A}\phi$ at any world does not vary across worlds of the interpretation. But the other two rules are more complex and cause problems when added to a modal logic and allowed to operate without restriction in box-subproof environments.

$\mathcal{A}$E and $\mathcal{A}$I are justified by our adoption of the real-world conception of validity (see note 2 above), which guarantees that any instance of $\mathcal{A}\phi \leftrightarrow \phi$ is logically true, but, in cases in which ϕ is contingent, $\Box(\mathcal{A}\phi \leftrightarrow \phi)$ is false. So, the logic of actuality gives rise to contingent logical truths, assuming we cling to the real-world conception of validity. Recall that a sentence is logically true when it is true in every interpretation, where a sentence is true in an interpretation just in case it is true in the interpretation at the distinguished world w^* of the interpretation. Because the truth value of $\mathcal{A}\phi$ at any world in an interpretation is determined by the truth value of ϕ at the distinguished world w^* of the interpretation, when we evaluate $\mathcal{A}\phi$ and ϕ at w^*, they are guaranteed to have the same truth value. But, again, if ϕ is contingent, there is a world w in W_I such that $\mathcal{A}\phi$ has that same truth value at w – recall, the truth value of $\mathcal{A}\phi$ in an interpretation does not vary from world to world of the interpretation – but ϕ has the opposite truth value at w and so $\mathcal{A}\phi \leftrightarrow \phi$ is false at w.

Because all instances of $\mathcal{A}\phi \leftrightarrow \phi$ are logically true but some are contingent, we need to take care of the interaction between $\mathcal{A}$ and $\square$. In particular, for our system, we restrict $\mathcal{A}E$ and $\mathcal{A}I$ from being used inside box-subproofs, much as we did above for the quantifier rules. Begin with $\mathcal{A}E$. The transition from $\mathcal{A}\phi$ to ϕ is legitimate if the world of index is w^* both before and after the transition. But the box-subproof environment corresponds to a shift of the world index and we can't assume that, just because $\mathcal{A}\phi$ is true at w, in which case ϕ is true at w^*, ϕ is also true at w, for any arbitrary world w. Indeed, allowing such a transition would amount to a modal collapse, allowing us to infer $\square\phi$ from ϕ, as can be seen by the following derivation.

```
  1. Fa              hyp
  2. 𝒜Fa             𝒜I:1
  3. □𝒜Fa            □𝒜:2
  4.  □
  5.   𝒜Fa           □E:3
**6.   Fa            𝒜E:5*****
  7. □Fa             □I:4,6
```

This is a very unhappy result for a modal logic. The use of $\mathcal{A}E$ on line 6, inside the box-subproof, seems the only step to fault. So, the use of $\mathcal{A}E$ inside box-subproof environments must be banned.

While an unrestricted version of $\mathcal{A}I$ is also invalid inside box-subproof environments, we need to propose a restricted version of $\mathcal{A}I$ to function inside box-subproof environments in order for our logic to be complete. (I discuss the reasons for this in deeper detail in the appendix.) The simplest way to see this is to realize that $\square Fa \to \square \mathcal{A}Fa$ is a logical truth,[3] but to derive it in our system, we must have some rule that allows us to add $\mathcal{A}$-operators inside box-subproofs. I propose, then, the following weaker rule, $\mathcal{A}I_\square$, that governs the introduction of $\mathcal{A}$-operators inside box-subproofs. (Like the classical quantifier rules, both $\mathcal{A}I$ and $\mathcal{A}E$ are banned inside box-subproof, and only the following weaker rule can be used. $\square\mathcal{A}$ can be used in any environment.)

$\mathcal{A}I_\square$
```
  i.  □
  j.   □φ            justification
  k.  𝒜φ             𝒜I_□:j
```

I illustrate this rule in the text by showing how it can be used to derive $\Box Fa \rightarrow \Box \mathcal{A}Fa$. (I give further uses of the rule in the appendix.) The derivation makes use of the characteristic S4 axiom, which allows a transition from $\Box \phi$ to $\Box\Box \phi$, as a derived rule. A derivation of this derived rule is provided in the appendix.

```
0.
1.  □Fa                 hyp
2.  □□Fa                derived rule S4:1
3.  □
4.    □Fa               □E:2
5.    𝒜Fa               𝒜I_□:3
6.  □𝒜Fa                □I:3,5
7.  □Fa→□𝒜Fa            →I:1,6
```

Call the combination of CC-QML and the above logic of actuality CC-A-QML.

CC-A-QML is a promising quantified modal logic for genuinely contingent existents. I know of no other like it in the literature.

Aliens

In the previous section I claimed that $\Diamond \exists x \neg \mathcal{A} \exists y(y=x)$ is an adequate regimentation using the resources of CC-A-QML of the claim that there could have been something that does not exist and showed that it seems to be true in all and only interpretations with growing domains. The following is an example.

Interpretation I_4 : $W = \{w^*, w_1\}$; $D_{w^*} = \{1\}$, $D_{w1} = \{1, 2\}$

While I_4 is fine as a 'play' model of the truth of $\Diamond \exists x \neg \mathcal{A} \exists y(y=x)$, as we simply leave some of what there really is out of the domain of w^* to use only in the domain of a nonactual world like w_1, it is problematic to think that the intended interpretation of the language of CC-A-QML makes our sentence true in a similar fashion. That is because I_4 seems to carry a commitment to merely possible objects, in violation of the dictates of the thesis of actualism, according to which absolutely everything is actual. If I_4 is the intended interpretation of our modal talk, then w^* is the actual world and so everything in w^* consists of absolutely everything there is simpliciter. In the intended interpretation, the domain of the actual world is all there is; reality does not include a reserve of 'extras' to populate alien worlds. But our modal models are surely constructed only out of what there is. So, reality simply doesn't contain anything that corresponds to 2 in the intended interpretation. How then can we account for the truth of $\Diamond \exists x \neg \mathcal{A} \exists y(y=x)$ in the intended interpretation?

The intended interpretation does not look like I_4. What we want, then, is an account of the truth of $\Diamond \exists x \neg \mathcal{A} \exists y(y=x)$ compatible with the thesis of actualism and so an account of its truth that does not require an interpretation like I_4. We know how to regiment, formalize, and model growing domains, but, given the truth of the thesis of actualism, the intended interpretation is not a growing domain interpretation, as absolutely everything in that interpretation, including the entities that model the merely possible domains, actually exists. How, then, can we make sense of the truth of $\Diamond \exists x \neg \mathcal{A} \exists y(y=x)$?

Consider a standard account of the truth of an existential quantified proposition like the proposition [Something is a book]. That proposition is true in virtue of a witness of that proposition, a corresponding singular proposition of the form [o is a book], being true. Where no corresponding singular proposition is true, the existential proposition is not true. And a possibility proposition is true just in case the embedded proposition is a member of a maximal consistent set of propositions. For example, the proposition [It is possible that George is sitting] is true in virtue of the fact that the proposition [George is sitting] is a member of a maximal consistent set of propositions. ([It is possible that George is a banana] is false, then, because [George is a banana] is not a member of any maximal consistent set of propositions. The notion of consistency here is clearly not a narrow notion, as the proposition [George is not a human] is not inconsistent in the same sense that [George is human and not human] is.) Apply these two points to the proposition [It is possible that there is something distinct from every actually existing object]. If the proposition is true, then the embedded existential quantified proposition [There is something distinct from every actually existing object] is a member of a maximal consistent set of propositions. If the set of propositions is maximal, then, it seems plausible to insist, there is a singular proposition of the form [o is distinct from every actually existing object] that is the grounds of truth of the existential proposition. This is problematic as actualism entails that everything actually exists and so, where o is an actually existing object, the proposition [o is distinct from every actually existing object] is not a member of any consistent set, as o is itself in the domain of the quantifier. In that case, there is no singular proposition to be a member of a maximal consistent set of propositions that grounds the possible truth of the proposition [There is something distinct from every actually existing object]. But then it is hard to see how the original proposition [It is possible that there is something distinct from every actually existing object] is true. That, then, is the problem.

The solution begins with an observation made in Adams (1981) that an existential quantified proposition can be true at a world even though there is no corresponding singular proposition true at that world that is an instance of the first. The proposition [There is something distinct from every actually existing object], then, is a member of a maximal consistent set of propositions even though there is no corresponding singular proposition that is a member of that set. The set is maximal because, for every *actually existing* proposition p, either p or its negation is a member of the set. Had a possible world corresponding to the set itself been actual, then there would have been a corresponding singular proposition and it would have been true; but as things in fact are, there is no such proposition to be true or false or to be a member of any sets. So, the maximality of the set of propositions does not require that it include a singular instance of the quantificational proposition [There is something distinct from every actually existing object]. The plausible connection between quantificational and singular propositions claimed in the previous paragraph holds for truth at the actual world, but it breaks apart for truth at merely possible worlds, at least insofar as we accept both the thesis of actualism and the possibility of aliens. Adams insight is that this is just what we should expect.

Singular propositions are constructed out of actually existing objects. Every object in the domain of the actual world satisfies the condition $\mathcal{A}\exists y(y=x)$. And if an object satisfies the condition $\mathcal{A}\exists y(y=x)$, then it necessarily satisfies that condition. For that reason, no singular proposition of the form [o is distinct from every actually existing object] could have been true. (Proof: If a singular proposition about o exists, then o exists in the domain of the actual world and so necessarily satisfies $\mathcal{A}\exists y(y=x)$. In that case, the proposition [o is distinct from every actually existing object] couldn't have been true. Contradiction.) So, while there are maximal consistent sets that include the proposition [There is something distinct from every actually existing object], they do not contain a singular instance of that proposition of the form [o is distinct from every actually existing object].

Return now to the language of CC-A-QML. It is tempting to think that there are interpretations, like I_{2+} below, in which $\Box \mathcal{A}\exists y(y=a)$ is false and so interpretations in which corresponding singular instances of our sentence $\Diamond \exists x \neg \mathcal{A}\exists y(y=x)$ (i.e., sentences of the form $\Diamond \neg \mathcal{A}\exists y(y=\alpha)$) are true.

Interpretation I_{4+} : $W = \{w^*, w_1\}$; $\{D_{w^*} = \{1\}, D_{w1} = \{1,2\}\}$, $a = 2$.

I_{4+} is just like I_4, except it assigns a merely possible object 2 as value to the individual constant a. But that is problematic. Notice that $\mathcal{A}\exists y(y=a)$ and $\exists y (y=a)$ are also false in I_{4+}, as nothing in D_{w^*} is identical to the value of a. As the quantificational base of CC-A-QML is classical, every instance of $\exists y(y=\alpha)$ is logical true. In that case, I_{4+} is not in the class of interpretations for CC-A-QML. We exclude it on the grounds that each individual constant is assigned an object *from the domain of the distinguished world*, while I_{4+} involves assigning an object not in D_{w^*} as the value of a. (I_4 is still among the interpretations of CC-A-QML. While the domains of the possible worlds are the same between I_4 and I_{4+}, the former does not assign a merely possible object as value to an individual constant, which is what I am claiming is problematic about I_{4+}.) The requirement is plausible if we think that merely possible individuals cannot be named. In that case, there is no countermodel to $\Box \mathcal{A}\exists y(y=a)$. Its truth does not enforce domain constancy, only requiring that, for any possible world w, $\mathcal{A}\exists y(y=a)$ is true in w, in which case $\exists y(y=a)$ is true in w^*, and so is consistent with the truth of $\Diamond \exists x \neg \mathcal{A}\exists y(y=x)$. But we then get the following result: While there are interpretations, like I_4, in which $\Diamond \exists x \neg \mathcal{A}\exists y(y=x)$ is true, there are no interpretations in which a corresponding singular instance of $\Diamond \neg \mathcal{A}\exists y(y=\alpha)$ is true. While I don't claim that this is a desirable result, I do claim, first, that a proponent of contingentism who subscribes to SQL as the appropriate quantificational base for QML is committed to it and, second, that it is tolerable. The cost, however, is that we deny ourselves of a purely extensional account of quantification when we prefix modal operators in front.

Here is a derivation of $\Box \mathcal{A}\exists y(y=a)$ in CC-A-QML.

0.		
1. $a=a$		=I
2. $\exists y(y=a)$		$\exists$I:1
3. $\mathcal{A}\exists y(y=a)$		$\mathcal{A}$I:2
4. $\Box \mathcal{A}\exists y(y=a)$		$\Box \mathcal{A}$:3

So, $\Box \mathcal{A}\exists y(y=a)$ is a theorem of CC-A-QML. $\forall x \Box \mathcal{A}\exists y(y=x)$ is also a theorem and logically true. However, its necessitation, $\Box \forall x \Box \mathcal{A}\exists y(y=x)$, is not. The last sentence is false in any interpretation with growing domains and so is false in I_4. (Proof: $\Box \forall x \Box \mathcal{A}\exists y(y=x)$ is false in I_4 because there is a world in W_{I4} (namely, w_1) such that $\forall x \Box \mathcal{A}\exists y(y=x)$ is false at w_1; $\forall x \Box \mathcal{A}\exists y(y=x)$ is false at w_1 because there is an object in D_{w1} (2) that does not satisfy $\Box \mathcal{A}\exists y(y=x)$, as 2 is not identical to anything in D_{w^*}.)

Consider now the following failed derivation of $\Box \forall x \Box \mathcal{A}\exists y(y=x)$.

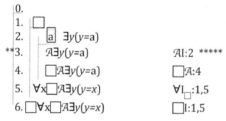

The derivation fails on line 3 because $\mathcal{A}$I cannot be used in a box-subproof. $\mathcal{A}$I$_\Box$ cannot be used in its place, as that would require that we first derive $\Box \exists y(y=a)$. The failure of this derivation, of course, does not establish that $\Box \forall x \Box \mathcal{A}\exists y(y=x)$ is not a theorem of CC-A-QML. But it illustrates how straightforward derivations of the result are blocked in our system.

In summary, the model theory for CC-A-QML includes 'play' models like I_4 but not I_{4+}, as we require that all individual constants have values from the domain of the distinguished world w^*. In that case, $\Diamond \exists x \neg \mathcal{A}\exists y(y=x)$ is satisfiable, even though no corresponding singular instance $\Diamond \exists x \neg \mathcal{A}\exists y(y=a)$ is satisfiable, as $\Box \mathcal{A}\exists y(y=a)$ is a logical truth.

Conclusion

The thesis that natural language sentences express singular propositions faces a puzzle. If those propositions are singular with respect to ordinary objects like tables, trees, people, and planets, then they are ontologically dependent upon those entities as they contain those entities as constituents. But those entities exist only contingently. In that case, propositions are not necessary existents. Some singular propositions that in fact exist might not have existed and other singular propositions might have existed instead or in addition.

The first of these consequences, that ordinary objects that in fact exist might not have existed, is problematic because the singular negative existential proposition [o does not exist], where o is a contingent being, is intuitively true with respect to a possibility in which o does not exist, even though that proposition would not exist were that possibility actual. Many have found plausible the idea that a proposition is true relative to a possibility just in case it would have been true had that possibility been actual, in which case such singular propositions are either not, in fact, object dependent or are not possibly true. Let's adopt the view that nonactual possible worlds are characterized by a maximal and consistent sets of actually existing propositions. The singular proposition [o does not exist] would not exist were an o-less world actual. But as things in fact are, it does exist and is a member of the set of propositions that characterize that o-less world, as that set is maximal and consistent with respect to all actually existing propositions. In that case, however, the proposition is true at that world. We characterize possibilities from the perspective of the actual world, using all and only the resources available there, not from the perspective of how things would have been were the possibility being characterized actual. Our first problem, then, is solved.

The first aspect of our puzzle offers support for the argument at the start of this essay that the existence of singular propositions is inconsistent with the modal facts by seeming to be inconsistent with principle (2), which I have argued we should reject. But it is the second aspect of our puzzle that proves most troubling. And that aspect arises quite naturally from the first, as it would be hard to maintain that, while some things that do exist might not have existed, nothing could exist that is distinct from everything that actually exists. I have argued that the second aspect also has a solution that is consistent with the thesis of direct reference and neither bloats our ontology, by requiring us to accept mere possibilia or any other strange kind of entity, nor carries a commitment to a class of necessary existents, only some of which are concrete (or, on a cousin, Meinongian view, existent) in the actual world and others that are concrete (or existents) in nonactual worlds. Truth at a nonactual world is from the perspective of the actual world. From that perspective, a possibility in which there is something distinct from every actually existing object can only be characterized either entirely generally or in relation to actually existing objects. So, while there is a possible world at which the proposition [There is something distinct from every actually existing object] is true, there is no possible world at which a singular proposition [o is distinct from every actually existing object is true], although there would have been had one of those possibilities been actual (and the actuality operator in the proposition is still indexed to the actual actual world!). We abandon, then, the idea that all quantified propositions owe their truth to atomic proposition when we characterize truth at a nonactual world; some quantified propositions are true at a world even though there is no witness singular proposition true at that world that grounds the former. I believe that this is a small price to pay compared to the costs of the alternatives.

While many have argued that singular propositions are poor candidates as the objects of the attitudes and what a competent speaker of a language grasps when she understands an utterance of a sentence, there are also those who argue that singular propositions are implausible as the fundamental objects of alethic properties, as they would not exist were the entities they are dependent upon not to exist and so they are never necessarily true or possibly false because the object they concern might not have existed. In this essay I have defended singular proposition from that second threat by sketching an account of possibility that fits with object dependent singular propositions being the fundamental objects of alethic properties.

Notes

1. In interpretations with varying domains, this choice carries the consequence that objects are in the extension of a predicate at a world where it does not exist, which seems problematic. The upside of this decision is that it does not require complications to the proof theory, which is why I adopt it here. A more semantically and metaphysically satisfying alternative is to assign, for each world w in W, the set of all identity pairs on D_w as the extension of $=$ relative to w, thus allowing the extension of identity to varying across worlds. This alternative requires a more complicated proof theory, which is why I opt for the first, simpler semantics for identity for the purposes of this essay. I show how to modify the identity rules for a sound and complete proof theory for a semantics in which the extension of $=$ relative to w is the set of all identity pairs on D_w in my 'Things that might not have been'.
2. This is to adopt a real-world, as opposed to a general, conception of validity, where a sentence Φ is a general validity just in case, for every interpretation I and every world w in W_I, Φ is true at w in I. There are sentences that are real-world validities that are not general validities, like the sentence $\mathcal{A}Fa \rightarrow Fa$, which I discuss later in the text. While the choice between the two conceptions is contentious, see (Zalta 1988) and (Nelson and Zalta 2012) for a defense.
3. Proof. Suppose, for purposes of reductio, that $\Box Fa \rightarrow \Box \mathcal{A}Fa$ is false in some interpretation I. Then, by the semantics of $\rightarrow$, 1. $\Box Fa$ is true in I and 2. $\Box \mathcal{A}Fa$ is false in I. 1. $\Box Fa$ is true in I just in case, for all worlds w in W_I, Fa is true at w, in which case, where o is the value of a in I, o is in the extension of F at w. 2. $\Box \mathcal{A}Fa$ is false in I just in case, for some world w' in W_I, $\mathcal{A}Fa$ is false at w', in which case Fa is false at w*, in which case o is not in the extension of F at w*. But w* is a world in W_I and so, because what is true of w in 1 is true of every world in W_I, what is true of w in 1 is also true of w*. So, by 1, o is in the extension of F at w*. But then o is both in and not in the extension of F at w*, which is a contradiction. So, there is no interpretation I in which $\Box Fa \rightarrow \Box \mathcal{A}Fa$ is false.

References

Adams, R. 1981. "Actualism and Thisness." *Synthese* 49: 3–41.
Crossley, J., and I. Humberstone. 1977. "The Logic of 'Actually'." *Reports on Mathematical Logic* 8: 11–29.
Deutsch, H. 1990. "Contingency and Modal Logic." *Philosophical Studies* 60: 89–102.
Deutsch, H. 1994. "Logic for Contingent Beings." *Journal of Philosophical Research* 19: 273–329.
Fine, K. 1977. "Prior on the Construction of Possible Worlds and Instants." In *Worlds, Times and Selves*, edited by A. Prior, and K. Fine, 116–161. Amherst: University of Masssachusetts Press.
Fine, K. 1978. "Model Theory for Modal Logics: Part I — The De Re/De Dicto Distinction." *Journal of Philosophical Logic* 7: 125–156.
Fine, K. 1981. "Model Theory for Modal Logic — Part III: Existence and Predication." *Journal of Philosophical Logic* 10: 293–307.
Fine, K. 1985. "Plantinga on the Reduction of Possibilist Discourse." In *Profiles: Alvin Plantinga*, edited by J. Tomberlin, and P. van Inwagen, 145–186. Dordrecht: D. Reidel.
Fitch, G. 1996. "In Defense of Aristotelian Actualism." *Philosophical Perspectives* 10: 53–71.
Garson, J. 2006. *Modal Logic for Philosophers*. Cambridge: Cambridge University Press.
Linsky, B., and E. Zalta. 1994. "In Defense of the Simplest Quantified Modal Logic." *Philosophical Perspectives* 8: 431–458.
Menzel, C. 1991. "The True Modal Logic." *Journal of Philosophical Logic* 20: 331–374.
Nelson, M., and E. Zalta. 2012. "A Defense of Contingent Logical Truths." *Philosophical Studies* 157: 153–162.
Plantinga, A. 1983. "On Existentialism." *Philosophical Studies* 44: 1–20.
Prior, A. 1957. *Time and Modality*. Oxford: Clarendon.
Stalnaker, R. 2012. *Mere Possibilities*. Princeton: Princeton University Press.
Williamson, T. 2002. "Necessary Exitents." In *Logic, Thought, and Language*, edited by A. O'Hear, 233–251. Cambridge: Cambridge University Press.
Zalta, E. 1988. "Logical and Analytic Truths that are Not Necessary." *Journal of Philosophy* 85: 57–74.

Appendix: Two Sample Derivations in CC-QML

-- Derive Fa from ¬□¬□Fa

1. ¬□¬□Fa	hyp	
2. ¬□Fa	hyp [for ¬I]	
3. □¬¬Fa	hyp [for ¬I]	
4. □		
5. ¬¬Fa	□E:3	
6. Fa	¬E:5	
7. □Fa	□I:4,6	
8. ¬□¬¬Fa	¬I:3,2,7	
9. □¬□¬¬Fa	S5:8	
10. □		
11. ¬□¬¬Fa	□E:9	
12. □Fa	hyp [for ¬I]	
13. □		
14. Fa	□E:12	
15. ¬Fa	hyp [for ¬I]	
16. ¬¬Fa	¬I:15,14,15	
17. □¬¬Fa	□I:13,16	
18. ¬□Fa	¬I:12,11,17	
19. □¬□Fa	□I:10,18	
20. ¬¬□Fa	¬I:2,19,1	
21. □Fa	¬E:20	
22. Fa	T:21	

NEW ESSAYS ON THE NATURE OF PROPOSITIONS

-- Derive □□Fa from □Fa (i.e., derive an instance of the characteristic S4 axiom).

1.	□Fa	hyp
2.	□¬□Fa	hyp [for ¬I]
3.	¬□Fa	T:2
4.	¬□¬□Fa	¬I:2,1,3
5.	□¬□¬□Fa	S5:4
6.	□	
7.	¬□¬□Fa	□E:5
8.	¬□Fa	hyp [for ¬I]
9.	□¬¬Fa	hyp [for ¬I]
10.	□	
11.	¬¬Fa	□E:9
12.	Fa	¬E:11
13.	□Fa	□I:10,12
14.	¬□¬¬Fa	¬I:9,8,13
15.	□¬□¬¬Fa	S5:14
16.	□	
17.	¬□¬¬Fa	□E:15
18.	□Fa	hyp [for ¬I]
19.	□	
20.	Fa	□E:18
21.	¬Fa	hyp [for ¬I]
22.	¬¬Fa	¬I:21,20,21
23.	□¬¬Fa	□I:19,22
24.	¬□Fa	¬I:18,17,23
25.	□¬□Fa	□I:16,24
26.	¬¬□Fa	¬I:8,25,7
27.	□Fa	¬E:26
28.	□□Fa	□I:6,27

285

Appendix: The Interaction of Modality, Quantification, and Actuality

In the body of this essay I proposed a logic of actuality in which the introduction and elimination rules for the actuality operator 𝓐, reproduced below, are banned inside box-subproof environments.

𝓐E
| *i.* 𝓐φ | *justification* |
| *j.* φ | 𝓐E:*i* |

𝓐I
| *i.* φ | *justification* |
| *j.* 𝓐 φ | 𝓐I:*i* |

I then offered the following inference rule as a restricted introduction rule valid inside box-subproof environments.

𝓐I$_\Box$
i. □
j. □φ   *justification*
k. 𝓐φ   𝓐I$_\Box$:*j*

We can help motivate these complications by seeing that the following three sentences are not logically true, as there are interpretations in our model theory in which they are false, and so should not be counted as theorems of our proof theory, as they are in a system in which the original introduction and elimination rules apply without restriction.

(A1) □(Fa → 𝓐Fa)/ □(𝓐Fa → Fa)
(A2) □∀x∃y(y=x) → □∀x𝓐∃y(y=x)
(A3) ∀x□∃y(y=x) → □∀x𝓐∃y(y=x)

Countermodel to A1a: $W = \{w^*, w_1\}$; ($D_{w^*} = \{1\}$; $D_{w1} = \{1\}$); $(V(F,w^*) = \{\emptyset\}$; $V(F,w_1) = \{1\})$. There is a world in W – namely, w_1 – such that (Fa → 𝓐Fa) is false at w_1. And (Fa → 𝓐Fa) is false at w_1 because Fa is true at w_1, as 1 is in the extension of F at w_1, and 𝓐Fa is false at w_1, as 1 is not in the extension of F at w^*. Countermodel to A1b: $W = \{w^*, w_1\}$; ($D_{w^*} = \{1\}$; $D_{w1} = \{1\}$); $(V(F, w^*) = \{1\}$; $V(F, w_1) = \{\emptyset\})$.

A2 and A3 have a common consequent and so I begin with a word about that. □∀x𝓐∃y(y=x) can be seen to be a contrary of our earlier sentence ◇∃x¬𝓐∃y(y=x). So, if the truth of the first guarantees growing domains, the second sentence is true only in interpretations I in which the domain of any possible world in W$_I$ is a subset of the domain of the distinguished world w^*. (We ignore accessibility relations as we are assuming the validity of S5.)

Turn now to A2. A2's antecedent is a logical truth. So, a countermodel to A2 will be any interpretation with growing domains. Recall our earlier interpretation I$_4$, reproduced below.

$$I_4 : W = \{w^*, w_1\}; D_{w^*} = \{1\}, D_{w1} = \{1, 2\}.$$

The antecedent of A2 is true in this interpretation as, for each possible world w in W, everything in the domain of w is identical to something in that domain – namely, with itself. The consequent of A2, however, is false, as there is a world in W – namely, w_1 – such that there is something in the domain of that world – namely, 2 – that is not identical to anything in the domain of the distinguished world w^*.

It turns out the same interpretation is a countermodel to A3. We have already shown that the consequent of A3 is false in the above interpretation. It remains to be shown, then, that its antecedent is true. Unlike the consequent of A2, $\forall x \Box \exists y(y=x)$ is not logically true. $\forall x \Box \exists y(y=x)$ forces domain constancy, but only by banning what we above called shrinking domains. $\forall x \Box \exists y(y=x)$ is true in an interpretation I only if the domain of the distinguished world w^* of I is a subset of the domain of every world w in W_I. As 1 is the only object in the D_{w^*} and 1 is in the domain of every possible world in W_I, as it is a member of D_{w1}, $\forall x \Box \exists y(y=x)$ is true in the above interpretation. Indeed, that sentence is true in any interpretation with growing but not shrinking domains. So, A3 is false in I_4.

But the following two sentences are logically true.

(B1) $\Box Fa \rightarrow \Box \mathcal{A}Fa$
(B2) $\Box \forall x \Box \exists y(y=x) \rightarrow \Box \forall x \mathcal{A} \exists y(y=x)$

It is easy to see that B1 is logically true. Suppose that there were an interpretation I such that $\Box Fa \rightarrow \Box \mathcal{A}Fa$ is false in I at w^*. Then, by the truth definition for $\rightarrow$, $\Box Fa$ is true in I at w^* and $\Box \mathcal{A}Fa$ is false in I at w^*. $\Box Fa$ is true in I at w^* only if, for every world w in W_I, Fa is true in w. (Recall that ours is an S5 system, so we do not need to concern ourselves with accessibility relations.) But w^* is a world in W_I and so Fa is true in w^*. But then $\mathcal{A}Fa$ is true in I at any world w in W_I. So, $\Box \mathcal{A}Fa$ is true in I at w^*. Contradiction. So there is no interpretation in which $\Box Fa \rightarrow \Box \mathcal{A}Fa$ is false.

Consider now B2. B2 is similar to A3 except the consequent of B2 contains an outermost $\Box$. $\Box \forall x \Box \exists y(y=x)$ is true in an interpretation I just in case, for every possible world w in W_I, for every o in D_w, o satisfies $\Box \exists y(y=x)$, in which case, for every world w' in W_I, there is some object o' in $D_{w'}$ such that o is identical to o', in which case o is in the domain of w', for all w' in W_I. But then, for all w and w' in W_I, $D_w = D_{w'}$. In that case, however, $\Box \forall x \mathcal{A} \exists y(y=x)$ is true in I. We saw above that $\Box \forall x \mathcal{A} \exists y(y=x)$ is false only in interpretations with growing domains and we have just established that I has a fixed domain. So, the consequent of B2 is true in I so B2 is true in I. So, B2 is true in all interpretations.

This result rests on the fact that we have limited ourselves to only S5 interpretations. The following is a countermodel to B2. I_{not-B}: $W = \{w^*, w_1\}$; $\{D_{w^*} = \{1\}, D_{w1} = \{1,2\}\}$; $R = \{<w^*,w^*>, <w^*,w_1>, <w_1,w_1>\}$, where R is the accessibility relation on W. This is an S4 but not B, and so not S5, interpretation, as the R relation is reflexive and transitive but not symmetric, as w_1 is accessible from w^* but w^* is not accessible from w_1. $\Box \forall x \Box \exists y(y=x)$ is true is true in I_{not-B} because $\forall x \Box \exists y(y=x)$ is true at every world in $W_{I_{not-B}}$ accessible from w^*. There are two such worlds to consider: i) w^* and ii) w_1. i) $\forall x \Box \exists y (y=x)$ is true at w^* because everything in D_{w^*} – namely, 1 – satisfies $\Box \exists y(y=x)$. 1 satisfies $\Box \exists y(y=x)$ because, for every world in $W_{I_{not-B}}$ accessible from w^*, namely, w^* and w_1, there is something, namely, 1, identical to 1. ii) $\forall x \Box \exists y(y=x)$ is true at w_1 because everything in D_{w1} – namely, 1 and 2 – satisfies $\Box \exists y(y=x)$. 1 satisfies $\Box \exists y(y=x)$ at w_1 because, for every world in $W_{I_{not-B}}$ accessible from w_1, namely, w_1, there is something, namely, 1, identical to 1; 2 satisfies $\Box \exists y(y=x)$ at w_1 because, for every world in $W_{I_{not-B}}$ accessible from w_1, namely, w_1, there is something, namely, 2, identical to 2. So, because w_1 is accessible from w^* but w^* is not accessible from w_1, $\forall x \Box \exists y(y=x)$ at w_1 even though 2 is in the domain of w_1 but not w^*.

$\Box \forall x \mathcal{A} \exists y(y=x)$ is false in I_{not-B} because $\forall x \mathcal{A} \exists y(y=x)$ is false at a world, namely, w_1, accessible from w^*. $\forall x \mathcal{A} \exists y(y=x)$ is false at w_1 because there is an object in D_{w1}, namely, 2, that does not satisfy $\mathcal{A} \exists y(y=x)$ at w_1. 2 does not satisfy $\mathcal{A} \exists y(y=x)$ at w_1 because 2 does not satisfy $\exists y(y=x)$ at w^*. So, $\Box \forall x \Box \exists y(y=x)$ is true in I_{not-B} and $\Box \forall x \mathcal{A} \exists y(y=x)$ is false in I_{not-B}. So, B2 is false in I_{not-B}.

As I argued above, B2 is true in every S5-interpretation. We have seen that it is not true in every S4- and weaker-interpretation. I think that the fact that B2 is logically true only if the accessibility relation is at least symmetric speaks in favor of a logic at least as strong as

B as being the correct logic for modal discourse, as the truth of B2's antecedent seems to force a fixed domain, which it does not do in these weaker logics.

Let's turn from the considerations of the logical statuses of A1-A3 and B1-B2 to our main topic of stating inference rules for the interaction of □ and 𝒜. We demand that our proof theory be sound and would prefer it also be complete. The first requires that A1-A3 not be provable in our system and the second that B1-B2 are provable. Suppose that the rule original introduction and elimination rules are allowed to function without any restrictions at all. Then our system would license the following faulty derivation of A1.

We have seen that there are countermodels to □(Fa → 𝒜Fa), so we do not want it as a theorem of our proof theory. This suggests that AI should be banned inside a box-subproof environment, as step 3 is clearly at fault. Similar consideration can be raised against 𝒜E using A1b, □(𝒜Fa → Fa).

The following derivation of the common consequent of A2, A3, and B2 shows that A2 and A3 are provable if we allow 𝒜I to function inside a box-subproof environment.

0.		
1.	□	
2.	⌐a⌐∃y(y=a)	hyp
**3.	𝒜∃y(y=a)	𝒜I:2*****
4.	∀x𝒜∃y(y=x)	∀I_□:3,6
5.	□∀x𝒜∃y(y=x)	□I:2,7

We have already seen that □∀x𝒜∃y(y=x) is not logically true and so we must find fault with this derivation. I suggest that step 3 is the problem.

If we allow only 𝒜I_□ to function inside a box-subproof environment, banning 𝒜I and 𝒜E, then the above derivation is blocked, as well as the following faulty derivation of A3.

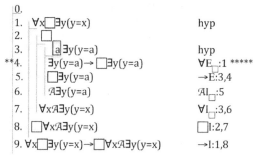

The application of ∀E_□ on line 4 is illegitimate, as it reaches across the box-subproof on line 2. The formula on line 1 is not a modal formula and so there is no way to use it inside a box-subproof. One might attempt to first use ∀E outside the box-subproof, as follows.

288

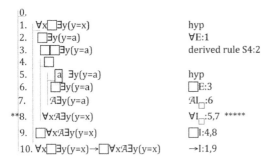

This second derivation fails because the instance of the universal generalization derived on line 7 is not arbitrary, as the individual constant a occurs above the start of the subproof of line 5 in lines 2 and 3. The failure of these derivations does not, of course, establish that the results are not theorems of our system; instead, they are meant to illustrate the way in which our restricted rule blocks straightforward attempts to derive them.

Consider now the following derivation of B2, which we want to be a theorem of our system.

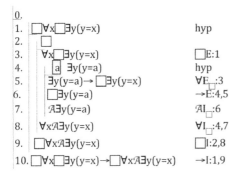

The key difference between this derivation and the failed derivations of A3 is that the antecedent is modal and so the universal generalization can be brought inside the box-subproof.

Finally, banning $\mathcal{A}I$ in box-subproof environments blocks natural attempts to derive A2, as follows.

|0.|
|1. □|
2.	∃y(y=a)	hyp
**3.	$\mathcal{A}$∃y(y=a)	$\mathcal{A}I$:2 ****
4. ∃y(y=a)→ $\mathcal{A}$∃y(y=a)	→I:2,3
5. □(∃y(y=a)→ $\mathcal{A}$∃y(y=a))	□I:1,4

The use of $\mathcal{A}I$ inside the box-subproof on line 3 is illegitimate. Because the formula on line 2 is not modal and there is no way to derive the modalization of that formula from the resources available, there is no way to use $\mathcal{A}I_\square$ in its place. This suggests that A2 cannot be derived in our system.

289

Index

aboutness 86, 90
abstract objects 1–2, 150, 165–6, 169, 174, 183
accessibility of propositions 1, 84, 165–6, 180–1, 270
act/object or act/content distinction 48–52
act/product distinction 48–51, 166–7, 170–82
act-theoretic approach 4–16, 20–41; interpretation 7–16; predication 4–6, 10–16; structured propositions 4–7; traditional views of propositions 4–16; truth-conditions 6, 7–9, 12–16; unity of the proposition 4–16
action theory 209, 222
acts, states, or event types 69–70
actuality, logic of 274–81, 286–9
actually existing propositions 257, 270, 274–5, 278–9, 281
Adams, Robert Merrihew 278–9
agents: Agent-Based Representation Extension 68–70; Agent-Based Universal Extension 68–9; beliefs 171; claims 171; cognitive theory 23–7, 29, 31–6, 41; conversational implicature 217; live possibilities 217; predication 54; Relevant Agent-Based Representational Extension 70; type view of propositions 62–3
alethic modal properties 262–3, 265, 282
aliens: contingent existence 274–5, 277–80; contingent non-existents (problem of aliens) 252–4, 257–8
Almog, Joseph 142
animals 182, 201
anti-realist approach 45–6
arbitrariness 93, 272, 276; contingent existence 252, 255; extensions 37–8;

identification, problem of 168–9; sameness and difference, conditions for 125, 130; set theory 145–6; unity of the proposition 7–8, 10–11, 14
Aristotle 151
Armstrong, DM 153–4
art, works of: artistic creation and created work of arts, distinction between 167, 172–3, 174, 179; token/type distinction 52–4
assenting 29, 31
assertions: belief 244–5; candidate assertions 213, 217–18, 220; category errors 46; cognitive theory 26, 29, 31; correctness conditions 175–7; event types 23; noun-phrases 48–52; objects 228; practical norms 51–2; predication 170; representation 196, 200 ; sentientialism 110; states of affairs 192–3; structured propositions 10; subject-assertion distinction 152; truth-conditions 44–57; truth-values 213; type view of propositions 49, 63–4
assertoric propositions 30
assignment 34, 39–40, 270, 279
atomic propositions 24, 200, 281–2
attitude *see* attitudinal objects; higher-order attitude attributions
attitudinal objects 3, 165–83: action-products distinction 166–7, 170–82; beliefs 166, 170–1, 174–8, 181; claims 166, 170–1, 174, 178; intention 166, 173, 169–70; judgments 166–7, 171–4, 178; kinds of attitudinal objects 180–1; nominalizations 167, 171–2, 174, 181, 183; ontology 166, 172, 174, 179, 182–3; products 166–7, 170–83; Relational Analysis 167–8, 171; replacement of

291

INDEX

propositions as truth-bearers 165–83; semantics 166–8, 181–2; sentences 165, 168; states of affairs 188, 190–1; *that*-clauses 166, 167–8, 170, 181–3; truth-bearers, replacement of propositions as 165–83; truth-conditions 50, 169, 171, 174–5, 180–2; understanding 170, 178–9; unity of the proposition 166, 169 *see also* higher-order attitude attributions
Austin, John L 46–7

Bach, Kent 103, 108
Bar-Hillel, Yehoshua 47–8
belief: action-products distinction 170–1, 174, 178, 181; all-out beliefs 216–17; attitudinal objects as replacements 170–1, 174–8, 181; Belief-Intention (B-I) Constraint 209–11, 214–17, 221–2; classical Quantificational Logic (QL) 269–73; cognitive theory 21, 27, 29, 38; communicational unarticulated constituents 114; contingent beliefs 269–73; conversational implicature 209–11, 214–17, 221–2; correctness conditions 175–7; epistemology 38, 222; intention 21, 27; not-normal interpretations 38; objects 152; perceptual belief 201; predication 29; puzzle of belief 31; representation 194–6, 200; second-order belief attributions 243, 245; semantics 31; state of believing and a belief, distinction between 171, 174; states of affairs 191, 194–6, 200–1; truth-conditions 49, 171, 174–5; type view of propositions 49
Benacerraf, Paul 6, 15, 77–9, 83–5, 91, 93–5, 146, 168
Benacerraf problem/dilemma 77–9, 83–5, 91, 93, 95, 146
Bolzano, Bernard 150
box-subproof environment 272–6, 280
Braun, David 142–3
brute facts 62–3, 66, 70–1, 256
Burge, Tyler 231

Caplan, Ben 83, 85
Cappelen, Herman 113
category errors 46–7
causal effects 178–9
Chalmers, David J 137
Chomsky, Noam 80, 103, 115
Church-Langford translation test 231

claims: act of claiming and claims, distinction between 171, 174; action-products distinction 170–1, 174, 178; attitudinal objects as replacements 170–1, 174, 178; functional claims 199; truth-conditions 171, 174, 199
Classical Contingentist QML (CC-QML) 271, 273–4, 277–80, 284–5
Classical Extensional Mereology (CEM) 145, 146–53
classical Quantificational Logic (QL) 269–73
classical theory of quantification 265, 271, 273–4
co-extensional terms 27–9, 35–6
cognitive accessibility of propositions 165–6, 181
cognitive acts: act-theoretic approach 4–5; attitudinal objects as replacements 169–70; cognitive realism 239–41; complex cognitive act types 234; declarative, interrogative, and imperative clause types 170; entertaining 170; predication 201; states of affairs 192, 194–7, 201; truth-conditions 196–7; understanding 170
cognitive realism 239–41
cognitive theory of propositions 20–41, 43
Coincidentalism 149–50
Collins, John 86, 102, 115–16
communication: cooperative exchanges 206–7, 219–20; Determinism (DET) 104; intentions 206–8, 211–12, 217–22; linguistic communications, theories of 117; pragmatics 103–4; successful communication, what makes 1–2; unarticulated constituents 104–8, 113
complex phrases 80, 88–90
complex propositions 24, 89, 197
compositional semantics 30, 82, 116, 142, 228
compositionality principle 121, 136
conceptual-intentional systems 82, 94
conjunctive propositions 24, 148, 197–9, 215, 257–8
constituents of propositions 2, 3; articulation of constituents 102–3; objects, properties and relations 120; senses 3, 21, 143, 145, 147, 155–8; singular propositions 98, 263–4, 268, 278–82; structure of propositions 78; Structured Propositionalism (SP),

INDEX

criticism of 141–58; sub-propositional constituents (SPC) 89; unarticulated propositions 99, 104–8, 112–13; words as constituents 98, 102

content: act/object or act/content distinction 48–52; action-products distinction 178–9; assertoric contents 30; attitudinal objects as replacements 165, 178–9; causation and evaluation 178–9; complicating relations 241–2; Content-Force Distinction 63; conversational implicature 209–10, 218–21; definition 209; higher-order attitude attributions 241–6; illocutionary or attitudinal force, separates from 165; metaphysics 106; Millenian-Russellian views of content 120–1, 133, 136–7; proper names 253; sentences 267; structure of propositions 77; syntax-based account 77–8, 80, 83, 85, 88–95; unspecific contents 212–14

context: conversational implicature 208, 219; higher-order attitude attributions 233–4, 241–2, 244–5; hyperintensionality 36, 39; look-for contexts 27–33; truth-conditions 230, 244; utterances 207, 212, 219

contingent a priori, problem of 31–2

contingent beliefs 269–73

contingent existence 252–5, 262–89

contingent non-existents (problem of aliens) 252–4, 257–9

conversational implicature 206–22; Gricean account 206–14, 218–19; higher-order attitude attributions 243–6; intention 206–22; meaning-intention assumption (MIA) 206–14, 220–2; openness 214–18, 220–2; specificity, problem of 207, 210–14, 218–19, 221–2; weak implicature 212–14

cooperation 206–7, 214, 219–20

co-referential rigid descriptions 155–6

correctness conditions 175–7, 178, 182

co-substitutional terms 27–9

cultural differences 34

Davidson, Donald 181
Davis, Wayne A 214–15
de dicto propositions 26–7
de re propositions 27
de se propositions 26–7, 37
declarative clause types 170

declarative sentences 227–8, 253–4, 256

deflationary sense of taking constituency 143, 155

denoting concepts, theory of 22

derived nominals 51

desire 166, 171, 173, 174, 177, 191, 262

determinacy condition 214–16

Determinism (DET) 99, 101, 104–16

dialectical advantage 141, 143, 154

difference see sameness and difference

disjunctive propositions 24, 197, 199, 201, 214–17

Distinct Combination, Distinct Propositions (DCDP) 87, 117

drawing and the drawing, distinction between 171

embedded propositions 26, 278

empiricism: cognitive theory 32–4, 41; identification of sentence structure with propositional structure 104, 107; language comprehension 33; language production 33; logical form (LF) 102; premise, doing without the empirical 109–15; unarticulated constituents 104, 107

empty names, puzzle of 31–2, 254

English/English case 88, 90, 92–3

entertaining 241–2: beliefs 210, 216–17; cognitive acts 25, 170, 196–8; contingent concretists 265; de se propositions 27; disjunctive propositions 215; embedded sentences 36; existence of propositions 2; intention 217–18, 220–1; logicism 26; representation 69–70, 236–7, 246; speaker meaning 208–9; specificity, problem of 207, 211, 213; states of affairs 199; traditional view of propositions 45, 241–2; truth-conditions 1

epistemology: abstract objects 2; beliefs 38, 222; cognitive theory 25, 32, 39; conversational implicature 222; modes of presentation response 236; semantics 36, 127, 137; unarticulated constituents 106

equipollence criterion of sameness and difference 122

essentialism 26–7, 148, 150, 157, 263

event types 61–71; cognitive realism 229; cognitive theory 23, 26; disjunctive

293

INDEX

event types 199; intention 41; location 113; predication 28, 195–8, 239; representation 200, 240; semantics 40; structured propositions 10
existence: actually existing propositions 257, 270, 274–5, 278–9, 281; contingent existence 253–5, 262–89; contingent non-existence (problem of aliens) 252–4, 257–8; non-existence 252–9
existential quantifiers 28, 278–9
explanatory chores 1–3
expressions 233, 235, 237–42, 246–7; ambiguity 126; cognitive theory 25; communicational unarticulated constituents 104–8, 113; conversational implicature 209; definition 103; Determinism (DET) 108, 112–13, 116; *explicature* 103; extensions 34–5; hyperintensional expressions 36–7; implicature 103; instantiation 190, 197; intuition 33; predication 11; psychological notion 103; sameness and difference, criterion for 124–8, 130, 132–4, 137; semantics 34, 121, 142, 147–8, 155–6, 183, 230–2, 238–42; technical sense 99, 101, 103–4
extensions 34–7; Agent-Based Universal Extension 68–9; assignments 34, 39–40, 270; hyperintension 37; model 67–71; possible-worlds account 23; problems with model 64–7; Relevant Agent-Based Representational Extension 70; representations 23, 70; structured extensions 35

facts: brute facts 62–3, 66, 70–1, 256; clarification of 79–83; components of a fact 79–80; Identity (ID) 100–1; instantiation relation 79–82, 91–2; natural-language sentences, about 76–7, 79–80, 95; representational properties 80, 91–2; states of affairs 153; structure 77, 91–2; syntax-based account 76–7, 79–83, 91–2, 95; truth-conditions 80
Fodor, Jerry 157
Forbes, Graeme 27–8, 32
force, involvement of 177–8
free logic solution 266–9, 272–3
Frege, Gottlob: attitudinal objects 180; beliefs 196; classical view 236; cognitive theory 25; content 166; expressions 101; grasping thesis 147; higher-order attitude attributions 227, 229, 235–8, 241; individuation 120–38, 156–7; intention 209; modes of presentation 235–6; predication 22; sameness and difference, criterion of 120–38; senses 3, 147; structured propositions 21, 142, 156–7; traditional view of propositions 44–5, 235–8, 241; truth-bearers 165; Uniqueness, violation of 147; unity of the proposition 152

gappy propositions 253–9
gerundive nominals 50–1
Gödel case 33
Goodman, Nelson 146
grain-size problem: Distinct Combination, Distinct Propositions (DCDP) 87; GRAIN 86, 90; MIRROR claim 77, 79, 88–93; possible-worlds account 77–8; Same Syntax, Same Structure (SSSS) 87–8; syntax-based account 77–9, 85–93, 95
grasping 1–2, 25, 80, 91–2, 147–8, 150, 228–9, 233–46
Grice, Herbert Paul 1–2, 206–14, 218–19

Hanks, Peter 6, 10–12, 61–7, 166, 170, 229, 239
Harman, Gilbert 102
Hawthorne, John 102
heavyweight senses of constituency 143, 155–8
Heck, Richard G 101, 206–7, 210–22
Heim, Irene Roswitha 102–3
hidden assumptions 27–32
hierarchical structure of syntax 88–9, 92–3
higher-order attitude attributions 227–47; attitude reports 230–4, 246; context 230, 233–4, 241–2, 244–5; conversational implicature 243–6; direct reference to propositions 233–41; Fregean traditional theories 235–8, 241; insurmountable objection 231–3; k-propositions 238–9; LF (logical form) 229, 238, 244; modes of presentation response 235–41, 246; representation 228, 239–41; semantics 228–30, 238–9, 243; sentences 229–31, 234–41, 243–7; sententialism 229–41, 244–7; truth-values 227, 243, 245
Holton, Richard 217

294

INDEX

hylomorphism 143, 145, 151–3
hyperintensionality 25–9, 31–2, 36–41

ideal language 21
ideal subjects 122–4, 127, 129–30, 134–6
identification: arbitrary identification, problem of 166, 168–9; attitudinal objects as replacements 168–9; Benacerraf problem 78; facts, identification of propositions with 76–7, 92, 95; *n*-tuples 146; Structured Propositionalism (SP), criticism of 157
identification of sentence structure with propositional structure 98–117; Determinism (DET) 99, 101, 104–16; expression, technical sense of 99, 101, 103–4; refutation of theory 98–117; Same Syntax, Same Structure (SSSS) 115–17; sentences 98–9, 101–3; structured propositions 98–117; unarticulated constituents 99, 104–15
identity 99–101, 115–16; brute facts 256; conditions 107–8, 256; definition 100–1; Determinism (DET) 116; Identity (ID) 99–101, 107–8; non-existence 255–7; syntax-based account 86, 88, 92, 95; trivial, uninformative identities and non-trivial, potentially informative identities, difference between 121, 123, 137–8
illocutionary events 165–6, 179, 181
imperative clause types 170
implicature *see* conversational implicature
indeterminacy 22, 206–7, 214–18
indexicals: demonstratives 37–8; essential indexical, problem of the 26–7; hyperintensionality 37–8; lexical items 81; object dependency 263–4; representation 81; semantics 121
indirectly meaning, Gricean notion of 212
individuation of propositions 120–38; collapse views 116–17; compositionality principle 121; conditions for sameness and difference of Fregean sense 122–38; coreferential singular terms, substitution of 120–1; difference and sameness 120–38; epistemic two-dimensional semantics 137; Fregeans 120–38, 156–7; interpretation 121–4, 126, 138; Millenian-Russellian views of content 120–1, 133, 136–7; nature of propositions 120; possible worlds account 156–7; Same Syntax, Same Structure (SSSS) 116–17; sameness and difference 120–38; sense 122–8; speech acts 45–6; states of affairs 189–90, 202; Structured Propositionalism (SP), criticism of 142, 156–7; syntax-based account 86, 90; thought acts 45–6; trivial, uninformative identities and non-trivial, potentially informative identities, difference between 121, 123, 137–8; truth-conditions 45–6, 57; truth-values 120–1, 134–7
informativeness: contingent a priori 31–2, 36, 39; identity facts 256; negative results 50; sameness and difference 121, 123, 128, 137–8; specificity, problem of 210; speech acts 215; syntax-based account 94–5; trivial, uninformative identities and non-trivial, potentially informative identities, difference between 121, 123, 137–8; unspecific contents 210
Ingarden, Roman 173
inheritance: attitudinal objects 180–1; cognitive acts 24; extensions 68–9; intention 173; location 149; model 62–8, 71; predication 194–5; Propositional Semantic Inheritance 66; representation 228; semantics 65–6; syntax-based account 79, 93; tokens 46, 54–7, 62–7, 71, 81; truth-conditions 46, 54–5, 57, 62–7, 71, 82; Universal Inheritance 68
inner nature of propositions 144, 156–8
instantiation: contingently existing propositions 264; conversational implicature 219, 221; facts 79–82, 91–2; higher-order attitude attributions 239; states of affairs 188–91, 194–5; syntax-based account 79–85, 89–92, 94
instrumentalism 45
intensions 24–9, 31–2, 34–41, 144, 228
  see also hyperintensionality
intention: action-products distinction 173; agents 32; beliefs 21, 27, 209, 217–18; communicative intentions 206–8, 211–12, 217–22; communicational unarticulated constituents 114; conceptual-intentional systems 82, 94; conversational implicature 206–22; intentionality, problem of 20–9, 31–2, 41; judgments 21, 27; meaning-intention assumption (MIA)

295

INDEX

206–14, 220–2; multiple intentions 132; outright intention 207; predication 22–3; representation 20–5; senses 21; sentences 21–2, 132–3; speakers 132–4; Structured Propositionalism (SP), criticism of 145; truth-directness 169–70
interrogative clause types 170
intrinsic properties of propositions 157–8
intuition: action-products distinction 174, 177; attitudinal objects as replacements 167, 174, 177, 179; belief contexts 33; contingently existing propositions 264, 274–7; conversational implicature 217–18, 221; higher-order attitude attributions 229, 244; introspection 33; linguistic theories 33–4, 36–7; metalinguistic intuitions 33; non-existence 252–3, 257; primary 33–4, 37; reportability 132; sameness and difference, criterion for 123–4, 128–9, 133–4, 138; secondary 33; sentences 36; syntax-based account 86; time, relation to 179; Transitivity, violation of 150

Johnston, Mark 151–2
Jubien, Michael 168, 170
judgments: action-products distinction 166–7, 171–4, 178; attitudinal objects as replacements 166–7, 171–4, 178; category errors 46; cognitive theory 21, 27, 29; intention 21, 27; judging and judgments, distinction between 174; predication 29; truth-conditions 45–52, 174; type view of propositions 49, 63

k-propositions 238–9
Kaplan, David 7, 29, 102, 233
King, Jeffrey C 2–3, 6–7: Determinism (DET) 104, 106, 110, 115; Distinct Combination, Distinct Propositions (DCDP) 87, 117; higher-order attitude attributions 229, 238; instantiation 15; propositional relations 100–1; Same Syntax, Same Structure (SSSS) 87–8, 115–17; sentential relations 100–1; Structured Propositionalism (SP), criticism of 141–5; syntax-based account 76–95; tokens 47, 50; unity of the proposition 10
Kratzer, Angelika 102–3
Kripke, Saul 30, 33, 123

language: comprehension 33; conventional meanings on a shared language 208; cross-language variations 87–8; English/English case 88, 90, 92–3; ideal language 21; independent of language, propositions as 1; linguistic theories 33–7, 104, 110–15, 117; production 33 see also natural language; semantics; translation
law itself and passing of a law, distinction between 167, 172, 174, 179
Le Verrier, Urbain 31, 40
Leonard, Henry S 146
Lepore, Ernie 102, 113
lexical items 79–94, 100, 108
Lewis, David 27
lightweight senses of constituency 143, 155–8
Linguistic Ersatzism, defence of 253, 257–8
linguistic theories 33–7, 104, 110–15, 117
literal speech 141, 211–13, 221
live possibilities 217
logical form (LF): attitude reports 171, 182; location 111, 113; representation 80, 238; semantics 102–3; sentences 229, 244; unarticulated constituents 107
logical relations 142
logical truths 263, 266–7, 269, 274–7, 280
logicism 26, 30–1, 237
look-for contexts 27–33

McDaniel, Kris 153
McDowell, John 218–22
MacFarlane, John 47, 50
McGlone, Michael 62–3
Martí, Luisa 107
May, Robert 101
meaning-intention assumption (MIA) 206–14, 220–2
Meinong, Alexius 142–3, 154, 268
membership, taking constituency to be 145
mental states 2, 45, 62, 192, 199
mereology: anti-symmetric, parthood is 146; Classical Extensional Mereology (CEM) 145, 146–53; Coincidentalism 149–50; mereological sum 146–7; repetition problem 149, 150–2, 154; states of affairs 190; Structured Propositionalism (SP), criticism of 143, 145, 146–53; transcategorical sums 148–9, 150; Transitivity, violation of

INDEX

147–8, 149–50; Uniqueness, violation of 147, 149–50
Merge operation 80
messy shopper example 26–7
metaphysics: abstract objects 2; communicational unarticulated constituents 105–6, 112–13; content, of 106; contingently existing propositions 268, 275; deflationary, metaphysically lightweight sense of taking constituency 143, 155; non-existence 253, 257–9; Structured Propositionalism (SP), criticism of 141–58; syntax-based account 76–7; truth 268
Mill, John Stuart: content of 120–1, 133, 136–7; proper names, notion of 28–34, 41, 155–6
mind-independent, propositions as 1, 165–6, 180
MIRROR claim 77, 79, 88–93
modality: interaction of modality 286–9; properties of propositions 30, 34, 262–3, 265, 282; quantification, interaction of 286–9; sentences 262
modes of presentation 22, 120–1, 136, 235–8, 240, 244, 246–50
Moltmann, Friederike 170
motivations for propositions 21, 86, 93–4, 113, 167–70

names: empty names, puzzle of 31–2, 254; Millian notion of proper names 28–34, 41, 155–6; non-referring names, problem of 254; quotation names 230; Russellian account 33–4
natural language: action-products distinction 174; attitudinal objects, kinds of 180; contingently existing propositions 265, 269, 280; Determinism (DET) 106; facts about natural language 76–7, 79–80, 95; logical form (LF) 102; motivations for propositions 167; proper names 267; sentences 76–7, 79–80, 95, 192–3; unarticulated constituents 106, 109–11
naturalism 25, 63, 71
necessity 1, 101, 198; contingently existing propositions 262–4, 267–9, 272–3, 280; necessary and sufficient conditions 126, 128, 153, 196, 198, 201; Rule of Necessitation (RN) 262–3, 267,

269; sameness and difference, criterion for 126, 130
neo-Russellian accounts 33–4, 78, 186, 228, 235–6
nominalizations 167, 171–2, 174, 181, 183
non-existence 252–9; contingent existence 253–5; contingent non-existents (problem of aliens) 252–4, 257–8; declarative sentences 253–4, 256; gappy propositions 253–9; identity of propositions 255–7; intuition 252–3, 257; Linguistic Ersatzism, defence of 253, 257–8; metaphysics 253, 257–9; non-referring names or empty names, problem of 254; Russellianism 252, 263–4; semantics 253–4, 256; sentences 257–9; structural indistinguishability 255–8; structured propositions 252–9
non-referring names or empty names, problem of 254
noun phrases 48–52
n-tuples 20, 22–3; contingently existing propositions 270–1; hyperintensionality 37; Identity (ID) 100; models of propositions 41; objects 20–1; predication 198, 200; properties 20–1; sentences 35, 78–9; set-theoretic approach 145–6; traditional view of propositions 20–1

objects: abstract objects 1–2, 150, 165–6, 169, 174, 183; act/object or act/content distinction 48–52; belief 142; concept-object distinction 152; constituents, propositions as objects with 98; content, views of 120; contingent existence 3; dependency 55–6, 263, 280–1; lightweight senses of constituency 156; material properties of material objects 52–3; *n*-tuples 20–1; object-directed, propositions as 2, 263–5; properties 23–4, 32; sequence O of objects 188; speech acts 2 *see also* attitudinal objects
ontology 78–80, 141, 144; action-products distinction 172, 174, 179; artistic creation and created work of arts, distinction between 179; attitudinal objects as replacements 166, 172, 174, 179, 182–3; constituency 157; dependence 263, 280–1; everyday language 228; fact-structure and content-structure, distinction between

297

INDEX

92; impure sets 150; language, of 110; *n*-tuples 78; object dependency 263, 280–1; semantics 228; sentences 244; states of affairs 190; syntax-based account 79; transcategorical sums 148
openness 214–18, 220–2
optimists 62–3, 72
origin essentialism 263

paradigms 33, 48, 64, 201
part-whole structure 179 *see also* mereology
perception 23, 33, 41, 191, 199–201
Perry, John 26–7, 104–7, 112
philosophy of language 98–9, 104, 106, 117
Plantinga, Alvin 264–5, 267
Platonic forms 154
play model 277
possible worlds account 37, 77–8, 148, 154–5, 168; contingently existing propositions 269–70, 274; individuation 156–7; mereology 143–4, 156–7; unordered sets 144
pragmatics 103–4, 142, 207
predication: act-theoretic approach 4–6, 10–16; assenting 29; bare predication 29; beliefs 29; cognitive acts 201; cognitive theory 23–35, 40–1, 43; conjunctive and disjunctive propositions 24; definition 46; evaluative property 54; hyperintensionality 31–2, 43; intention 22–3; interpretation 25; judgments 29; material objects and acts of predication, analogy between 54; *n*-tuples 198, 200; order 11–12, 14; paradigms of thinking 201; representation 24–5, 63; states of affairs 189–90, 194–201; tokens 46, 54–5; traditional view of propositions 5; truth-conditions 45–57, 194–8; type view of propositions 45–6, 55, 63
primitive propositions 143–6, 151, 153, 157
Principles of Mathematics. Russell, Bertrand 22
Prior, Arthur 265
products: act/product distinction 48–51; attitudinal objects as replacements 166–7, 170–83; psychophysical products 178
proof theory 271–4
proper names, Millenian notion of 28–34, 41, 155–6

properties: action-products distinction 173–80; content, views of 120; extrinsic properties 156; modal properties of propositions 30, 34, 262–3, 265, 282; models 28, 41; *n*-tuples 20–1; objects 23–4, 32; sequence P of properties 188
psychology: expression, notion of 103; psychophysical actions 166–7, 178; psychophysical products 178; speakers 111–12
proto-propositions 83–4

quantification: Classical Contingentist QML (CC-QML) 271, 273–4, 277–80, 284–5; classical Quantificational Logic (QL) and contingent beliefs 269–73; classical theory of quantification 265, 271, 273–4; contingently existing propositions 286–9; modality, interaction of 286–9; quantified modal logic (QML) 264–9, 271–4, 277–82, 284–5; standard quantificational logic (SQL) 265–7, 279–80
Quine, Willard Van Orman 242, 262
quotation names 230

rational speakers 207, 211, 218
real-world conception of validity 275
Recanti, François 103, 105–7
Relational Analysis 167–8, 171
relational view of propositional attitudes 167
relations-that-relate 45
relativized reference clause 233–4
relevance theorists 103
repetition problem 149, 150–2, 154
reportability 131–4
representation 2, 180; act-theoretic approach 4–5; agents 32–3, 68–70; assertions 196, 200; belief 194–6, 200; cognitive realism 239–41; cognitive theory 23–5, 32–3; complex propositions 24; conversational implicature 209; facts 80, 91–2; higher-order attitude attributions 228; identical, representations which are 26–7; indexicals 81; intention 20–5; logical form (LF) 80; *Merge* operation 80; non-representational properties 70; object, property of an 23–4; predication 24–5, 63; semantics 62; SHANE 89; states of affairs 188–97, 201–2;

298

INDEX

STREET 89; Structured Propositions 63; syntax-based account 76, 78, 80–1, 89–92; truth-conditions 26, 44–5; truth-functional operations 24; type view of propositions 62–4, 67–71; unity of the proposition 76
Rule of Necessitation (RN) 262–3, 267, 269
Russell, Bertrand 1, 25, 44–5, 78–9; act-theoretic approach 10, 12, 14–16; beliefs as representational 196; content, notion of 120–1, 133, 136–7; conversational implicature 209; denoting concepts 22; grasping thesis 147; higher-order attitude attributions 227, 235, 238; hyperintension 38–9; lightweight senses of constituency 156; mereology 147–50; *n*-ary relation 4; neo-Russellian accounts 33–4, 78, 186, 228, 235–6; non-existence 252, 263–4; *n*-tuples 22–3; predication 21, 30; *Principles of Mathematics* 22; relations actually relating 8; repetition problem 150–2; satisfaction conditions 5; semantics 7, 147–8; Structured Propositionalism (SP), criticism of 142, 147–50, 152–4; transcategorical sums 148–9, 150; Transitivity, violation of 147–50; Uniqueness, violation of 147; unity of the proposition 6, 152

Salmon, Nathan 7, 78
Same Syntax, Same Structure (SSSS) 87–8, 115–17
sameness and difference: expressions 124–8, 130, 132–4, 137; Frege's criterion of sameness and difference 120–38; individuation 120–38; pairs of sentences expressing same or different propositions 120–38; restricted difference 134–8; retreat to a condition of difference 128–34; right-to-left direction 125, 127–8; senses 121–8, 130–2, 135–7; sentence tokens or types 122–38; sufficient condition of difference 128–9, 130–3; sufficient condition of sameness 129–34; trivial, uninformative identities and non-trivial, potentially informative identities, difference between 121, 123, 137–8; truth-values 120–2, 127, 132, 134–7; weaker sufficient condition, retreat to 134–8

satisfaction conditions 5–6, 174–5, 178, 180, 271
Schiffer, Stephen 141–2, 208, 229, 231
search verbs 27–8
self-ascription theory 27
semantic values: attitudinal objects as replacements 166–8; communicational unarticulated constituents 105–6, 108–9; compositional semantic values 30; Constituency Primitivism 154; contingently existing propositions 270; deflationary, metaphysically lightweight sense of taking constituency 143, 155; explaining constituency 145–55; heavyweight senses of constituency 143, 155–8; higher-order attitude attributions 238–9; lexical items 108; lightweight senses of constituency 143, 155–8; membership, taking constituency to be 145; mereology 148–9; metaphysics 141–58; Millenian view of proper names 155; parthood, taking constituency to be 145; primitive, taking constituency as 143, 154–5; Same Syntax, Same Structure (SSSS) 116; sententialism 142; special quantifiers 168; states of affairs 189, 202; Structured Propositionalism (SP), criticism of 142–3, 145–55; syntax-based account 76–95; *that*-clauses 166; tokens 65; truth-conditions 109; unity of the proposition 152
semantics: belief 31; co-extensional terms 35–6; cognitive significance, puzzle of 31; cognitive theory 25–6, 28, 30–41; communication 104; compositional semantics 30, 82, 116, 142, 228; contingent a priori, problem of 31–2; contingently existing propositions 266, 270–1; direct reference 143; epistemology 137; extensions 24, 39–40, 67; formal semantics 102–3; higher-order attitude attributions 228–30, 238–9, 243; intentions, propositions modelled as 34–6; motivations 167–8; noncompositional assetoric contents 30; non-existence 253–4, 256; normal interpretations 34–5; ontology 228; pragmatics 207; proper names, contents of 253; Propositional Semantic Inheritance 66; puzzles 30–2; quotation names 230;

INDEX

representation 62; structured extensions of sentences 35–6; *that*-clauses 181–2; truth-conditions 45, 55; truth-values 356; two-dimensional semantics 127; type view of propositions 61–6, 71 *see also* semantic values

Sennet, Adam 105–6

senses: constituency 3, 21, 143, 145, 147, 155–8; heavyweight senses of constituency 143, 155–8; intention 21; lightweight senses of constituency 143, 155–8; modes of presentation 142; predication 48, 50; sameness and difference, criterion of 121–8, 130–2, 135–7; tokens 131–2

sentences 2, 265–71: abstractions over sentences, propositions as 235, 238–9; atomic sentences 270–1; attitudinal objects as replacements 165; cognitive realism 239–41; cognitive theory 21–2, 25, 37; complement sentences 230; contents 267; contingently existing propositions 262, 265–71, 275, 279; declarative sentences 227–8, 253–4, 256; Determinism (DET) 99, 101–2, 104–15; embedded sentences 168, 230; extensions 37; higher-order attitude attributions 229–31, 234–9, 243–7; identification of sentence structure with propositional structure 98–117; Identity (ID) 101; intention 21–2, 132–3; interpretation 265; intuitions 36; logical form (LF) 102–3, 229, 238; meaning 98, 101–3, 165; modal profiles 262; natural language 76–7, 79–80, 95, 192–3; non-existence 257–9; *n*-tuples 35, 78–9; non-indexical sentences 37; pairs of sentences expressing same or different propositions 120–38; relevance theorists 103; sameness of structure, definition of 100–1; satisfaction 271; states of affairs 188–93; structured extensions 35–6; structured propositions 98–117; tokens 25, 122–38, 188; trees, structure of sentences as 99–100; truth 271; type view of propositions 49; words as constituents, sentences as complexes with 98, 102 *see also* sententialism; syntax-based account of propositions

sententialism: context 234; higher-order attitude attributions 229–41, 244–7; Identity (ID) 100; insurmountable objection 231–3; parallels for sententialism 244–6; quotation marks 230; semantic-values 142; subsential expressions 142, 238; translations 231; truth-conditions 230

sequences: act-theoretic approach 4, 6, 12, 16; O of objects 188; P of properties 188; structured propositions 4; unity of the proposition 7–9

set-theoretic approach 143, 145–6

sets of worlds 143–5

SHANE 89

Sider, Theodore 149

similarity relations 171, 177–8

singular propositions 2–3, 4, 147–8, 156, 263–8, 278–82

Soames, Scott 2–3, 168, 194–201; act-theoretic approach 5–7, 10, 20–31, 34, 39–41; cognitive acts 166, 194–5; Determinism (DET) 109; higher-order attitude attributions 229, 239; predication 194–201; representation 5, 194, 196, 200–1; structured propositions 78; type view of propositions 61–71

speaker-meaning, cases of 206, 208, 216, 220–2

specificity, problem of 207, 210–14, 218–19, 221–2

speech acts 2, 45–57, 63, 179, 215

Stainton, Robert J 110

standard quantificational logic (SQL) 265–7, 279–80

Stanley, Jason 102–3

statements 46–52

states as tokens 61–71

states of affairs, propositions as 3, 188–202; atomic propositions 200; beliefs 191, 194–6, 200–1; cognitive acts 192, 194–7, 201; conditional propositions 199; conjunctive propositions 199; facts 153; individuation 189–90, 202; instantiation relation 188–91, 194–5; predication 189–90, 194–201; propositional attitudes 188, 190–1; representational, propositions as 188–97, 201–2; *s*-composition 153–4; semantic-values 189, 202; sentences 188–93; structure-making approach 153; truth-bearers 193; truth-conditions 192, 195–9

Strawson, Peter F 46–7

STREET 89

structured hyperintensions 39–40

INDEX

Structured Propositionalism (SP), criticism of 141–58; constituents 141–58; deflationary, metaphysically lightweight sense of taking constituency 143, 155; dialectical advantage 143; direct reference, semantics of 143; explaining constituency 145–55; Fregeans 142, 147, 156–7; heavyweight senses of constituency 143, 155–8; hylomorphism 143, 145, 151–3; individuation 142, 156–7; inner nature of propositions 156–8; intrinsic properties of propositions 157–8; lightweight senses of constituency 143, 155–8; membership, taking constituency to be 145; mereology 143, 145, 146–54; metaphysics of propositional constituency 141–58; Millian view of proper names 155–6; parthood 145, 146–7; Possible Worlds View (PW) 143–4, 154–7; primitive propositions 143–6, 151, 153–5, 157; primitive, taking constituency as 154–5; Russellianism 142, 147–50, 152–4, 156; semantic compositionality 142; semantic-values (SVs) 142–3, 145, 147–8, 152, 155; set-theoretic approach 143, 145–6; sets of worlds 143–5; structure-making approach 143, 145, 153–4; sub-sentential SVs 142; theoretical primitive, constituency as 143, 145; truth-conditions 145; truth-values 144

structure of propositions 24, 77, 100, 229

structured propositions: act-theoretic approach 4–7; attitudinal objects as replacements 168–9; cognitive theory 21–2; constituents 78; higher-order attitude attributions 238; ideal language 21; identification of sentence structure with propositional structure 98–117; indistinguishability 255–8; interpretation 169; meaning, structure as key ingredient of 99; non-existence 252–9; object-directed, propositions as 2; representation 63; sentences, mirroring 21; sequences 4; syntax-based account 77–9, 87–8, 90–4; truth-values 21–2 *see also* Structured Propositionalism (SP), criticism of

sub-propositional constituents (SPC) 89

substitution 25–30, 33, 40–1, 51, 120–1, 138, 170, 231, 244

supplicate propositions 62–71

syntax-based account of propositions 76–95; aboutness 90; Benacerraf problem 77, 79, 83–5, 91, 93, 95; complex phrases 88–90; content of propositions 77–8, 80, 83, 85, 88–95; cross-language variations 87–8; English/English case 88, 90, 92–3; facts 76–7, 79–83, 91–2, 95; grain-size problem 77–9, 85–93, 95; hierarchical structure of syntax 88–9, 92–3; identity of propositions 86, 88, 92, 95; instantiation relation 79–85, 89–92, 94; King's syntax-based account 76–95; lexical items 79–94; natural-language sentences, facts about 76–7, 79–80, 95; representation 76, 78, 80–1, 89–92; semantics 76–95; structure of propositions 77–9, 87–8, 90–4; syntactic structures 77, 79–80, 86–93; truth-conditions 77–8, 80, 82–5, 86–8, 90–1, 94; truth-evaluation 82, 89–90, 93; unity of the proposition 76–9, 94–5

that-clauses: attitudinal objects as replacements 166, 167–8, 170, 181–3; Determinism (DET) 104; higher-order attitude attributions 236; predication 56; semantics 166, 181–2; truth-conditions 181–2

Thomasson, Amie 172, 182

thought acts 45–6

Tillman, Chris 83, 85

time, relation to 179–80

tokens: acts 61–71; agents 68; art, works of 52–4; events 61–71; extension model 67; inheritance of truth-conditions from tokens 46, 54–7, 62–7, 71, 81; predication 46, 54–5; semantics 65; sentences 25, 122–38, 188; states 61–71; token/type distinction 48–54; truth-conditions 46, 54–5, 57, 62–7, 71; type view of propositions 54, 61–71

traditional view of propositions 1, 4–16; act-theoretic approach 4–16; attitudinal objects as replacements 166; cognitive theory 20–1, 27, 29, 32–4; entertaining 45, 241–2; Fregean theories 44–5, 235–8, 241; higher-order attitude attributions 228, 235; linguistic theories

301

34; *n*-tuples 20–1; predication 5; truth-conditions 44–7, 57; unity of the proposition 44–5
transcategorical sums 148–9, 150
Transitivity, violation of 147–8, 149–50
translation 86, 229, 231, 240–3, 245; Church-Langford translation test 231; higher-order attitude attributions 245; syntax-based account 86
trivial, uninformative identities and non-trivial, potentially informative identities, difference between 121, 123, 137–8
truth: bearers 165, 167, 169–70, 180, 188, 193; contingently existing propositions 262–3, 266–8, 271–2, 275–8, 281–2; directness 166, 169–70; evaluation 82, 89–90, 93; instructions 89–90; logical truths 263, 266–7, 269, 274–7, 280; metaphysics 268; necessity 101, 272; nonactual world 281–2; play model 277; primary bearers of truth, propositions as 44–57; syntax-based account 82, 89–90, 93; theoretical roles of propositions 1 *see also* truth-conditions; truth-values
truth-conditions 44–57: abstract objects 1; action-products distinction 171, 174–5, 182; adverbial modification 47–8; anti-realist approach 45–6; assertions 45–52; assignment 12–14; attitudinal objects 50, 169, 171, 174–5, 180–2; beliefs 49, 171, 174–5; category errors 46; characterizing 45, 57; claims 171, 174, 199; classification of acts 45–6, 56–7; cognitive acts 196–7; context 244; conversational implicature 209; functional claims 199; higher-order attitude attributions 234, 244; individuation 45–6, 57; inheritance 46, 54–5, 57, 62–7, 71, 82; interpretation 234; intrinsic truth-conditions 83–5; linguistic communication 109; judgments 45–52, 174; language-independent, propositions as 1; mind-independent, propositions as 1, 165–6; necessary and sufficient conditions 198; possible worlds account 77–8; predication 45–57, 194–8; primary bearers of truth, propositions as 44–57; propositional attitudes 50; representational properties of propositions 26, 44–5; object dependent reference type 55–6; semantic reference types 55–6; semantic-values 109; sentences 45, 49, 55, 271; source of truth-conditions 45; speech acts 45–57; states of affairs 192, 195–9; statements 46–50, 52; Structured Propositionalism (SP), criticism of 145; syntax-based account 77–8, 80, 82–5, 86–8, 90–1, 94; *that*-clauses 181–2; thought acts 45–6; tokens 48–55, 57, 62–7, 71; traditional view of propositions 44–7, 57; truth-values 57; type view of propositions 45–6, 49–57, 62–71; unity of the proposition 7–9, 13, 44–5; *what-is-said* 103
truth-values: attitudinal objects as replacements 166, 169; cognitive theory 27–8, 31, 35–6, 38; communicational unarticulated constituents 105; contingently existing propositions 275–6; higher-order attitude attributions 227, 243, 245; hyperintensionality 26; reportability 132; sameness and difference, criterion of 120–2, 127, 132, 134–7; semantics 35–6; sentences, mirroring 21; Structured Propositionalism (SP), criticism of 144; structured propositions 21–2; truth-conditions 57; type view of propositions 64
Twardowski, Kazimierz 166–7, 170–4, 181
type view of propositions 3, 61–71: acts, states, or event types 69–70; agents 62–3; assertions 49, 63–4; beliefs 49; conversational implicature 219–20; extension model 67–71; inheritance of truth-conditions from tokens 62–7, 71; judgments 49, 63; optimists 62–3, 72; predication 45–6, 55, 52–7, 63; representational properties 62–4, 67–71; semantics 61–6, 71; sentences 49; statements (acts) 49–50; sub-types 66; super-types 57; supplicate propositions 62–71; tokens 48–54, 61–71; truth-conditions 45–6, 49–57, 62–71; truth-values 64 *see also* event types

unarticulated constituents 99, 104–15
understanding: act/product distinction 170, 178–9; higher-order attitude attributions 228, 230–1, 234, 237, 239–40, 245–7; individuation of propositions 122–3;

INDEX

Structured Propositionalism (SP), criticism of 147
Uniqueness, violation of 147, 149–51, 154
unity of the proposition: act-theoretic approach 4–16; attitudinal objects as replacements 166, 169; generic unity 8; hylomorphism 151–2; interpretation 7–16; particular unity 8; representation 4–5, 76; satisfaction conditions 5–6; sequences 7–9; structurally determined unity problem 6, 8–10; syntax-based account 76–9, 94–5: traditional view of propositions 44–5; truth-conditions 7–9, 13, 44–5

Universal Generalization 265–6
unordered sets 144
Unrestricted, rejection of 151
utterance-pairs 86

values *see* truth-values
Varzi, Achille 146
von Neumann, John 6

what-is-said 7, 103, 142, 207, 212
Williamson, Timothy 175–6, 252–3, 264–5
Wollheim, Richard 52–3
writing and the writing, distinction between 171

Zermelo, Ernst 6